The Awkward Embrace

The Awkward Embrace

ONE-PARTY DOMINATION AND DEMOCRACY

Edited by

Hermann Giliomee and Charles Simkins

harwood academic publishers
Australia • Canada • China • France • Germany
India • Japan • Luxembourg • Malaysia
The Netherlands • Russia • Singapore • Switzerland

Amsteldijk 166
1st Floor
1079 LH Amsterdam
The Netherlands

British Library Cataloguing in Publication Data

The awkward embrace : one-party domination and democracy
   1. Totalitarianism – Case Studies   2. Democracy –
   Cross-cultural studies
   I. Giliomee, Hermann, 1938 –   II. Simkins, C.E.W. (Charles Edward Wickens)
   321.9

   ISBN: 90-5702-374-1 (softcover)

TABLE OF CONTENTS

FOREWORD

When I began organizing the project that led to *Uncommon Democracies: The One-Party Dominant Regimes*, I and my colleagues chose to focus our research on one-party dominance within the advanced industrial democracies. Unlike the situation in the less industrialized countries of the world, long-term one-party rule was comparatively rare in the narrower universe we explored. And within that universe democracy had real meaning: civil liberties were deeply entrenched, the media was relatively free, opposition was both real and legitimate, electoral contestation had genuine consequences. Meaningful transfers of national power had taken place in all of our cases and could be practically envisioned in the near future; one-party dominance was by no means simply a veil for autocracy.

Those conditions seemed to us far less prevalent throughout the rest of the world. True, one-party regimes were in ample supply, and most of them claimed to be 'democratic'. Yet, one-party regimes that had come to power through free elections and/or that had yielded power as a result of the ballot box were all but impossible to find. Far more pervasive were regimes built around an inherent skepticism toward power sharing. More common among dominant parties and their leaders was the conviction that only through their own continuance in power would the national interest, as they chose to define it, be served. In short, most shared the sentiments of Thomas Carlyle toward democracy: "I do not believe in the collective wisdom of individual ignorance."

The Awkward Embrace proves that our original bifurcation of one-party dominance into a small number of 'true' democracies and the much larger number of hollow parodies was wrong. As Giliomee and his colleagues demonstrate, single-party rule within the industrializing countries covers a broad spectrum. Some are indeed merely facades for predatory rent-seekers but many others are ruled by single parties which allow for a host of individual and group freedoms and provide meaningful contests for power among office holders.

This book examines the broad range of one-party rule within what the authors call "semi-developed countries". The individual chapters focus in depth on four intriguing cases—Mexico, Taiwan, Malaysia and South Africa—that themselves offer an extensive array of diversities. The geographical locations and regional problems of all four are quite different; Taiwan and

THE AWKWARD EMBRACE   ix

Malaysia are far richer and more economically egalitarian than South Africa or Mexico; quite different types of ethnic and racial divisions run deeply through three of the four, and even in Mexico, relations between mestizos and Indians are far from harmonious. Furthermore, the political agendas of the dominant parties have been quite different: Taiwan's KMT for most of its history pursued an ideological war with neighboring China; more recently that has given way to economic competition and the possible embrace of Taiwanese independence. Malaysia's UNMO has pursued ethnic harmonization through economic growth. Mexico's PRI has long been a party of pork and patronage. South Africa's National Party was a vehicle for minority white control over a black majority, while the more recently dominant African National Congress has at least initially pursued racial integration and national economic development. The truncheon, the machete and the machine gun have far more often been the tools of rule in some of these countries than in others. Once the supplementary cases are added, the range of political experiences covered by the book becomes even wider.

The end of the Cold War, the transformation of Eastern Europe, and the sweeping expansion of trade and foreign direct investment have collectively unleashed a wave of democratization in numerous countries of the world. This book makes an important contribution to grappling with the complexities of that democratization by its attention to the possible role of one-party rule as a vehicle for enhanced political openness.

Thus, a central question driving each of the authors, despite their specific cases, is that of democratization: to what extent are current examples of one-party rule providing vehicles for the long-term transition to democracy? As various of the chapters point out, examples abound of single parties that indeed are working to marginalize political extremes, fuse ethnic differences, and create a more pervasive consensus around compromise solutions to national problems. In such instances, genuine democratization is often being advanced by the dominant party, wittingly or not, despite the emergence of serious competition that might ultimately topple it from its controlling perch. In other instances, however, such transformations are undoubtedly much more remote. In those cases, single-party rule is unquestionably more of an impediment to democratization than its champion.

Writing about the contemporary world always carries with it the risk that sudden events will overtake the analysis. Certainly this study is no exception with its specific hints at how each dominant party is or is not advancing democratization. What emerges from the book collectively is a picture of the many ways in which the same institutional container, namely a dominant single party, has the potential to hold quite different contents, depending on numerous other conditions within the political system in which it is created. The varying roles of the different dominant parties examined are quite sweepingly broad.

This study is unusual in that it finds a middle ground among contesting approaches to democratization. Seymour Martin Lipset's now famous analysis of the relationship between economic development and the onset of democratic practices was advanced in 1959 and has subsequently generated a massive amount of research. His finding of a strong linear relationship between GNP and democracy has most typically been interpreted to imply that as nation-states reach some particular level of economic development, social structures become more complex and the country can no longer be run through simple dictatorship or authoritarianism. Hence, domestic pressures reach irresistible levels and increased democratization emerges as a by-product of economic development. From such a perspective, one-party dominance would become far less likely and greater democratization far more probable with any nation's economic success.

Yet this is a far from universally accepted proposition. Importantly, as Dankwart Rustow reminded us as early as 1970, the transition to democracy involves an explicitly political process more complex than anything implied by notions of democracy as the foreordained derivative of economic improvement. Rustow's argument is that democratic institutions come into being following "a hot family feud" and "a prolonged and *inconclusive* struggle" at which point angry and exhausted elites conclude that their interests are better served by democratic compromise than by continued battle. A subsequent wave of studies has demonstrated the importance of this perspective in recent transformations, primarily in Latin America and Southern Europe. These strongly suggest that even if high levels of economic performance tend to stabilize democracies, there is far less evidence that they actually generate democratic institutions.

This book shows the value of sensitivity to both perspectives. Democratic institutions are far more than the simple by-products of economics. Indeed, democracy is more often the outcome of actions by a Machiavelli than a Madison, of a Robespierre rather than a Rousseau. Still, no matter how messy the creative process that gives rise to democracy, economic conditions can surely shape the willingness of political elites to enter into, or to reject, any democratic pact. Without a doubt, the bigger the national economic pie the easier it is to make politically-driven side payments that can minimize otherwise contentious problems.

Perhaps most significantly, an increasing body of literature suggests that even if economics is not a precondition for democratization, once a nation-state reaches a level of per capita income of about $5000 and it is democratic, there is almost no likelihood that it will revert to authoritarianism. In this sense, the studies in this book provide an opportunity to examine what may well prove to be the cutting edge of a sweeping new wave of democratization as once-dominant parties begin to lose sway. Many of the countries in this study seem poised for transitions to democracy, and all, except for South Africa, are at relatively high levels of per capita income. As several of the studies make clear, once the leaders of dominant parties decide that their own legitimacy demands an adherence to democratic forms, they have sown the seeds for their possible demise.

At the same time, dominant parties are by no means resourceless in the political contests that follow. In the euphoric embrace of democracy's potential, it is easy to delude ourselves into believing that the only impediment to toppling one-party rule is that party's unwillingness to permit genuine contestation. Yet, even when the rules are democratized, most dominant parties will retain tremendous resources by which to reinforce their own control.

Thus, to draw a post-publication lesson from the cases examined in *Uncommon Democracies*, the once-formidable Christian Democracy in Italy virtually disappeared in the face of the combination of the Cold War's end and the exposure of the intense corruption that had prevailed under the DC. Aha, we conclude, the logical demise of one-party dominance. But almost simultaneously in Japan, the apparent end to Liberal Democratic Party control in 1993 proved extremely short-lived.

Committed democrats will undoubtedly pick up this book expecting examples of how one-party rule will prove transitional toward enhanced democracy. More cynical skeptics will surely expect to find ample evidence for precisely the opposite. The real world seems to offer far more complicated and variegated experiences. It is in its capacity to capture such variations, and to challenge both presuppositions, that this book holds perhaps its greatest promise.

LIST OF CONTRIBUTORS

Heribert Adam is Professor of Sociology at Simon Fraser University, Vancouver, Canada.

Yun-Han Chu is Professor of Political Science at National Taiwan University in Taipei and has published widely on democratization and the East Asian political economy.

Ruth Berins Collier is Professor of Political Science at the University of California, Berkeley, USA.

Maria Lorena Cook is Assistant Professor at the New York State School of Industrial and Labor Relations at Cornell University, Ithaca, USA.

Donal B. Cruise O'Brien is Professor at the School of Oriental and African Studies, London, UK. He has published several books and articles on West Africa.

Pierre du Toit is Associate Professor of Political Science at the University of Stellenbosch, South Africa.

Steven Friedman is Director of the Centre for Policy Studies, Johannesburg, South Africa.

Hermann Giliomee is Professor of Political Studies at the University of Cape Town, South Africa and former President of the South African Institute of Race Relations.

James V. Jesudason is a senior lecturer in the Department of Sociology at the National University of Singapore.

Robert R. Kaufman is Professor of Political Science at Rutgers University, New Brunswick, USA.

Shelley Rigger is Assistant Professor of Political Science at Davidson College, North Carolina, USA.

Lawrence Schlemmer is a previous Vice-President of the Human Sciences Research Council, South Africa.

Charles Simkins is Helen Suzman Professor of Political Economy at the University of Witwatersrand, Johannesburg, South Africa.

Recently the focus in democratic studies has shifted from analysing the dynamics of transitions to a deeper understanding of the problems of consolidation and state-building, the performance of democratic institutions and the sustainability of party competition. This makes an emphasis on industrialising middle-income countries a rewarding exercise. Here we have countries that have begun to move away from a situation of severe inequalities, unfree labour and gross violations of human rights to one where the middle class has broadened, labour has become better organised and education more universal. The democratic plant is nevertheless rather frail and democracies may get diminished to a mere facade. The range stretching from liberal democracy to pseudo-democracy is most clearly illuminated in Latin America where the tension between formal political equality and vast socio-economic inequalities has produced institutional distortions and great popular disenchantment with political parties.

A focus on dominant party rule in industrialising countries presents in magnified form many of the challenges and problems of new regimes whether they be democratic or semi-democratic. In particular, a dominant party brings with it mixed blessings. A ruling party with a large and seemingly permanent majority can offer much-needed political stability and predictability in economic policy. If it is inclusive in its recruitment, representative of a large section of society and pluralist in its functioning it can impart a great degree of legitimacy to a new regime. But the strengths also contain the seeds of weakness. The unique democratic remedy of peacefully 'dismissing the government' in practice is not available. By making the power and coherence of the dominant party the chief condition of national survival the party blurs the distinction between the ruling party and the state. This in turn can open the door to large-scale corruption and the suppression of dissent. Genuine democratic competition largely falls by the wayside.

Dominant party rule has long figured prominently in classifications of party systems and forms of democratic rule. This volume deals with dominant party rule not as a subtype of democracy but as a particular political configuration within a framework in which at least some democratic rules or practices have to be observed. Seven years ago a well-conceptualised study was published under the editorship of T.J. Pempel with the suggestive title *Uncommon Democracies*.[1] It concentrated on dominant party rule in the industrialised societies of

---

[1] T.J. Pempel, ed. *Uncommon Democracies* (Ithaca: Cornell University Press, 1990).

dof
dominance

Japan, Italy, Israel and Sweden and the impact of domination on democracy in these countries. Pempel established the following criteria for such rule: electoral dominance for an uninterrupted and prolonged period, dominance in the formation of governments, and dominance in determining the public agenda. The latter is particularly important: If the dominant party succeeds in formulating a successful historic project—"a series of interrelated and mutually supportive public policies that give particular shape to the national political agenda"[2]—a "virtuous cycle of dominance" develops. A party's political supremacy and its successful execution of the historic project generate even more dominance. This volume accepts Pempel's definition of dominant party rule and extends the investigation to dominant party rule in semi-industrialised countries.

Our emphasis is on four of the five most prominent dominant parties of the past four decades: the Institutional Revolutionary Party (PRI) in Mexico, the United Malays National Organisation (UMNO) in Malaysia, the Kuomintang (KMT) in Taiwan and the African National Congress (ANC) in South Africa. The Congress Party of India (or Indian National Party of India) could have been added, but this party's dominance of the political system since the split of 1969 has declined considerably, and India remains a poor country. Moreover, it has already been extensively studied as a dominant party, particularly in the illuminating work of Morris-Jones.[3] Our selection of parties gives us two which operate in deeply divided societies (South Africa and Malaysia) and two in societies with relatively mild ethnic divisions (Taiwan and Mexico). In two societies (South Africa and Mexico) the corporatist triangle of government, labour and business supplements dominant party rule while in the two others this triangle is much less evident or absent. The choice allows us to demonstrate some important points. As Pempel observes in the foreword to this book, there exists no simple dichotomy between a few 'true' democracies and the rest which are labelled sham or pseudo-democracies. The parties discussed in this volume comprise a large variety. One (the ANC) has had a major role in crafting the country's democratic constitution; another (KMT) has progressively extended the range of democratic liberties, while yet another (UMNO) has reduced the quality of democracy in Malaysia to a point where it can be labelled as at best a semi-democracy. The degree of internal pluralism also varies considerably.

---

2 Pempel, "Introduction", *Uncommon Democracies*, p. 1.
3 W.H. Morris-Jones, "Dominance and Dissent: The inter-relations in the Indian party system", *Government and Opposition*, 1 (1966), pp. 451–66; "The Indian Congress Party: A Dilemma of Dominance", *Modern Asian Studies*, 1, 2 (1967), pp. 109–132; *The Government and Politics of India* (London: Hutchinson, 1964).

awkward embrace [handwritten margin note]

We describe the dominant party's embrace of democracy in semi-industrialised countries as awkward. Domination has not led to continuous mass
repression or the aggrandisement of power by an unaccountable elite, but
there is a greater unwillingness to disperse power, a readier inclination to
delegitimise opponents, and a more widespread abuse of state patronage than
in systems where there is a periodic changeover of government. There are
major reasons why a real prospect of alternation is important for the consolidation of democracy. True protection for the citizens of a liberal democracy
lies less in the separation of powers or a Bill of Rights than in the actual use of
elections to change bad and corrupt governments. Thus what James Madison
called "dependence on the people" is essential for the proper functioning of
democracy.[4] By avoiding rejection at the polls, and retaliation by an alternative future majority, chosen politicians act in some rough way as agents of the
electorate.

While the definition of democracy in terms of a procedural minimum
(competitive elections, universal franchise, the absence of massive fraud and
the effective exercise of civil liberties) is generally accepted, it is much more
difficult to define a democratic regime.[5] In one of the most comprehensive
recent comparative studies Przeworski and Limongi insist on alternation in
office before classifying a regime as democratic. There is a good case for considering a regime as not democratic if "tenure in office ended up in the
establishment of a non-party or one-party rule". The study accordingly classi-
fies Malaysia, Taiwan and Mexico between 1981 and 1990 as dictatorships.[6]
As editors we use in our contributions to this volume a less rigorous categorisation than that cited above. We make the following distinctions:

(a) Authoritarian dominant party system with some pluralist/democratic fea-
    tures but clearly not liberal democratic and unable to sustain or tolerate a
    competitive party system:
    Mexico until 1994
    Taiwan until 1987
    Singapore
    Malaysia (some would classify it as liberal democratic until 1969)
    Some of the states on the border of South Africa (not Botswana and
    perhaps not yet Namibia, but certainly the others)

---

4   W. Riker, *Liberalism against Populism* (San Francisco: Freeman, 1982).
5   David Collier and Steven Levitsky, "Democracy with Adjectives", *World Politics*, 49 (1997),
    pp. 430–51.
6   Adam Przeworski and Fernando Limongi, "Modernization: Theories and Facts", *World Politics*,
    49 (1997), pp. 155–83.

(b) A democratic system with a dominant party playing according to some liberal democratic rules, but still well short of the alternation in power:
   post-1987 Taiwan
   South Africa 1994 to present
   arguably post-1994 Mexico

This volume takes particular interest in three remarkable developments in the recent history of democratisation. The first is the tortuous process in Mexico where the PRI is attempting to establish untainted democratic institutions and generally accepted rules for competition. The second is the remarkable rejuvenation of the KMT from an authoritarian dominant party (or what Sartori calls a hegemonic party[7]) to the leading party in a competitive party system functioning in what is increasingly becoming a liberal democracy.

The other development (and one which receives special attention in this volume) is the coming to power in South Africa of the ANC in a racially inclusive democracy. It won the 1994 founding election by outstripping its nearest rival by 40 percentage points, winning more than 80 per cent of the vote of blacks (but only two to three per cent of whites), and 62 per cent of the overall vote. On the basis of this 'ethnic census' type of election the general tendency is to predict prolonged ANC dominant party rule. But dominance is not guaranteed. Unlike the other dominant parties the ANC assumed power after orthodox liberal ideas came to dominate the international economic order. Punishment of regimes which deviate substantially from economic dogma likewise take the form of a falling currency or declining fixed investment. Consequently the ANC faces sharp constraints on its ability to tax and spend, which in turn is putting tremendous strain upon the party in its efforts to maintain coherence.

The other open question concerns the survival of a liberal democracy in South Africa. The post-apartheid settlement that was negotiated in South Africa between 1990 and 1996 amounted to a *Rechtsstaat* based on progressive human rights, the rule of law, the supremacy of the constitution, and a Constitutional Court as guardian of the constitution. Yet this constitution has to operate within a political system based on the Westminster tradition of winner-takes-all. It has not taken long for an acute tension to develop between the sovereignty of the constitution and the 'sovereignty' claimed by a party with an overwhelming majority. At the ANC Conference held at the

---

7   Giovanni Sartori, *Parties and Party Systems* (Cambridge: Cambridge University Press, 1976), see particularly Chapters 6 and 7.

end of 1997 President Nelson Mandela read a paper drawn up by the leadership of the party in which the white opposition parties were accused of having decided "against the pursuit of the national agenda" and being inspired by the fallacious assumption that their only obligation was to discredit the ruling party so that they may gain power. The speech also attacked the liberal press and some Non-Governmental Organisations as anti-democratic forces. (*Cape Times*, 23 December 1997). An article by a leading party ideologue in the movement's mouthpiece which was distributed at the conference branded some liberal NGOs and opposition parties as "reactionary" and "counter-revolutionary" (*Mayibuye*, November/December 1997).

In May 1998 the ANC's secretary general, Kgalema Motlanthe declared that the party is campaigning for a two-thirds majority in the 1999 election which would enable it to form a government "unfettered by constraints". Among the independent institutions the ANC would review were the Judicial Service Commission, which advises the President on the appointment of judges, the auditor general and the Reserve Bank (*Sunday Times*, 3 May 1998). After some court rulings which displeased the ANC the provincial leadership of the party in the KwaZulu-Natal decided to launch a programme of mass action to "rid the courts, the attorney general and the police of their apartheid past" (*Die Burger*, 15 June 1998). If the ANC were to give concrete effect to such sentiments South Africa would be transformed from a fledgling liberal democracy to a mass illiberal democracy. To an important extent South Africa would travel in the opposite direction to that of Taiwan over the past ten years. This volume hopes to make a contribution to the understanding of the political system evolving in South Africa by situating the ANC in the context of dominant parties in other industrialising countries.

The volume also attempts to describe the process which led to the rise of party dominance and both the decay and persistence of party domination under democratic or semi-democratic rules in the countries studied. The first section, written by the editors, looks at the process of democratic consolidation from a comparative perspective. They do so by taking into account both a functional approach stressing socio-economic prerequisites, on the one hand, and, on the other, a process-driven approach emphasising the crucial role of political elites, contingent choice and bargaining.

In the chapters on Mexico, Kaufman describes how a dominant party can remain in power despite stumbling from one crisis to another. Collier shows how difficult globalism has made it for the PRI as a labour-based dominant party to retain its dominance while shifting from import substitution to export-led growth. The theme of Cook's chapter is the durability of the alliance between the party leadership and its corporate labour leg despite the enormous strains in their relationship.

Malaysia, which is described in Jesudason's chapter, falls in a quite different category. Contrary to Duverger's assumption that dominant parties over time inevitably decay[8], UMNO shows no signs of that after four decades in power. At the same time the regime shows no signs of progressing in the direction of a fully fledged liberal democracy and doing away with the controlled electoral process. Despite high economic growth, the middle class, dependent on state power and patronage, does not insist on the broadening of democracy.

The chapters by Chu and Rigger sketch how the KMT's authoritarian domination of Taiwan was steadily transformed into a much more pluralistic and accountable system. Nevertheless they also reveal how the vested interests of the dominant party and non-democratic practices make full democratisation difficult.

In the chapters on Southern Africa, Du Toit's contribution demonstrates vividly the brittleness of democracy in countries with stagnant or falling per capita incomes. This weakness is compounded when a country is also divided by deep ethnic rifts. South Africa is much more advanced than its northern neighbours with a well-developed corporate structure, but apart from the class and ethnic cleavages in the black population South Africa also has racial divide between whites and blacks. Friedman's chapter analyses the difficulties the ANC faces in attempting to establish a virtuous cycle of dominance. The form of corporatism discussed by Adam indicates how much the new dominant party is trying to win at least the acquiescence of big business. Schlemmer's analysis points to the ANC's sheer electoral dominance which could lead the party to ride roughshod over the minorities whose support is necessary for economic growth. Cruise O'Brien's contribution is a useful reminder that particularly in rural parts of Africa democracy may not have much to do with liberal values and multi-party competition.

The editors wish to thank the following colleagues and friends who made critical comments and helpful suggestions: Sean Archer, Ruth Collier, Larry Diamond, Donald Horowitz, Robert Kaufman, Ian Shapiro and Lawrence Schlemmer. They express gratitude to the South African Institute of Race Relations and the Institute for Multi-Party Democracy which were co-hosts for the conference held in November 1996 at Waenhuiskrans, South Africa on which the book is based. Cheerfully sceptical of political analysts and academics, Sean Jacobs was an efficient research assistant and conference

---

8   Maurice Duverger, *Political Parties* (London: Methuen, 1959), p. 312.

secretary. A special word of thanks is due to the Embassy of the Republic of China in Pretoria, the Chairman's Fund of Anglo American Corporation and De Beers, Standard Bank and Old Mutual who sponsored the conference without setting any demands with respect to the participants the organisers wanted to invite and the interpretations offered in this volume.

Chapter 1

THE DOMINANT PARTY REGIMES OF SOUTH AFRICA, MEXICO, TAIWAN AND MALAYSIA: A COMPARATIVE ASSESSMENT

HERMANN GILIOMEE AND CHARLES SIMKINS

INTRODUCTION

This chapter traces the rise and persistence of party domination in four semi-industrialised countries, namely Mexico, Taiwan, Malaysia and South Africa, with a side look at Singapore. It takes into account three major differences with the history of dominant parties in advanced industrialised countries like those in Sweden, Japan and Italy. Dominant parties in advanced countries went through a cycle of domination, beginning with the inauguration of dominant party rule, passing through a consolidation phase and ending with its first-time defeat. By contrast, this study deals with an unfinished history. The PRI in Mexico appears to many to be coming to the end of its prolonged dominance, which creates a major crisis for the party; the KMT in Taiwan is surviving quite well the shift to a competitive party system and a liberal democracy; UMNO in Malaysia presides over what seems to be a durable semi-democracy which is less pluralistic than the system of three decades ago; and the ANC in its term of what in all likelihood will be a fairly lengthy period of dominance.

Secondly, the societies of Sweden, Japan and Italy are all ethnically homogeneous, which facilitates democratic competition about socio-economic issues rather than social identity. By contrast ethnicity is of great importance in Malaysia and South Africa, and plays some role in Mexico and Taiwan. Thirdly, in the dominant party regimes of advanced industrialised countries general respect for political liberties was much more deeply rooted than in our cases. As Pempel remarks in *Uncommon Democracies: The One-Party Dominant Regimes*, politics was conducted in a context of free electoral competition, relatively open information systems, respect for civil liberties and the right of political association.[1] In the cases we shall discuss politics is a much rougher game, partly because of the founding history of the different regimes and partly because of the fact that large numbers of the electorate have been trapped in abject poverty.

---

1 T.J. Pempel, "Introduction", T.J. Pempel ed., *Uncommon Democracies: The One-party Dominant Regimes* (Ithaca: Cornell University Press, (1990), p. 1.

The following is a preview of the argument developed in this chapter. There is a major difference among democracies between a one-party dominant form of regime, which we shall describe below, and a liberal democracy. A liberal democratic regime can be defined as one in which the executive power is constrained, minority groups express their interests effectively, party competition is strong and electoral outcomes are uncertain with an alternation of ruling party constituting a real prospect. As a result rights are effectively protected and enjoyed, and corruption is kept within bounds.[2] Dominant party regimes in developing countries lack these features in significant ways.

Dominant parties are rare occurrences in either advanced industrialised or industrialising countries. All the major parties discussed in this chapter have wielded power in exceptional circumstances. They all come out of a background of revolution (or counter-revolution in the case of Taiwan), decolonisation and liberation. All of them quickly discovered that their efforts to pursue their historic mission as a ruling party ran up against their lack of autonomy with respect to the prevailing capitalist system and class structure. Their political survival is to a large degree due to the fact that even prior to the founding election they had staked a strong claim to represent the new nation (or regime or dominant racial/ethnic group) with its particular historic project, and had managed to occupy a strategic position of power. From this position it could dictate or exploit the electoral system and adopt a successful form of political mobilisation, both of which were perpetuated long after the first election.

There are two possibilities for a shift of this system towards a liberal democracy with a competitive party system. The one is represented by Taiwan where broad-based social and economic development has occurred in the absence of any strong corporatist structures. This confirms the Lipset model of democratic consolidation with its emphasis on an expanded middle class. The other is represented by Mexico. Dominant party rule rested on a corporatist consensus born out of the trade-offs of business and organised labour under an economic regime of import-substitution. The major blow to this corporatist consensus as a result of global economic forces could lead to a split in the party and its eclipse as a dominant party. In countries like South Africa, Malaysia or Singapore the forces of globalisation cause major tensions within the party but the chances of a split are greatly reduced by the ethnic or racial "cement" which holds the dominant party together. In these

---

2   Larry Diamond, "Is the Third Wave over?" *Journal of Democracy*, 7, 2 (1996), pp. 23–24.

situations a middle class which has risen as a result of ruling party patronage does not play any significant role in broadening and strengthening democracy. It may in fact stifle such a development.

THE FOUNDING

The dominant parties in our four main cases were not born or revitalised in some crisis of political mobilisation, but in a much greater trauma. As R.W. Johnson remarked at the conference on which this book is based, all four dominant parties came to power in the wake of a nightmare—in South Africa's case apartheid, in Malaysia's case colonial rule, foreign occupation and a war of insurgency, in Mexico's case prolonged revolutionary turmoil, and in Taiwan's case the continuing struggle against the communist regime in Beijing. In two cases (Malaysia and South Africa) it involved the liberation of an indigenous people from social and economic subordination to another people. In all four cases the dominant party provided the platform for the society's transition from authoritarian rule to democracy (or in the cases of Mexico and Malaysia a semi-democracy). From an early stage politics revolved around the identity of the regime and more particularly the dominant party's claim that its rule was necessary for both social progress and democracy.

A pioneering article by Arian and Barnes on the dominant party as a neglected model of democratic stability makes two claims: (a) the dominant party is a much better stabilising mechanism than fragmented parties and (b) a dominant party which combines its rule with political competition and a large measure of civil liberties can serve quite well as a necessary platform for a durable democratic system. We can endorse and elaborate the first proposition by pointing to the stabilising role our dominant parties played in the inauguration of a democracy or semi-democracy. This is particularly true of South Africa and Taiwan where, in the last half of the 1980s, the National Party (NP) and the ANC and the KMT took their respective countries away from authoritarian one-party dominance to an inclusive democracy. In a fragmented party system with a huge prize at stake the competition might well have been so fierce as to derail the democratisation process.

The second proposition can be accepted given its important qualifying conditions, but the example of the dominant parties in countries north of South Africa shows that, with the exception of that of Botswana, civil liberties and competition are constantly under pressure. As Du Toit argues, it cannot simply be assumed that dominant parties brought to power through elections will be benign bridge builders facilitating the development of a competitive liberal democratic regime. In poor countries the trend is for the dominant party to establish what the chapter calls bridgeheads to an authoritarian order with a hegemonic party system. The dangers are compounded if the country is deeply divided along ethnic lines. As Horowitz has pointed out, in ethnic politics inclusion in the ruling coalition determines the distribution of goods, the prestige of the various ethnic groups and the identity of the state as belonging more to one ethnic group than another. It can clearly be seen in the case of Zambia whose democratic election in 1991 was hailed as a great success. However, just as in the case of the independence election 25 years earlier, a dominant party in the form of a broad multi-ethnic coalition took power. A repetition of the previous cycle saw the leaders of ethnic groups in the coalition peeling away as they lost struggles for power. To end the haemorrhage, Frederick Chiluba outlawed the opposition and kept power in the hands of a minority, just as Kenneth Kaunda had done in the 1970s and 1980s.[3]

While the dominant party profoundly shapes the political system and society, it is itself also transformed by social forces that at critical junctures compel it to make choices about ways in which to perpetuate its rule. The most important decision is that of moving purposefully away from an exclusionary to an inclusionary party, thus paving the way for a multi-party democratic system. The history of the KMT in Taiwan and the NP in South Africa demonstrates how and why parties become transformed. Both came to power in the period 1945–48 with the KMT overwhelmingly based on the mainlander *emigres*, who formed about 15 per cent of the population. In South Africa, the NP initially was almost exclusively based on the Afrikaner ethnic group who formed between 50 and 60 per cent of the white group, which in turn contained about 20 per cent of the population. As a result of a steadily growing level of economic development the mainlander–islander bifurcation in Taiwan weakened as did the Afrikaner–English one in South Africa. By the mid-1960s the KMT had to decide whether to suppress the moderate demands of the prosperous islander middle class or assimilate it in growing numbers into the party and government.

Huntington suggested that the maintenance of an exclusionary one-party system depends on three variables: whether it would be tolerated by the international community, the unity of the dominant elite and its ability to repress excluded social forces.[4] In Taiwan it was above all the last of these factors

---

3 Donald Horowitz, "Democracy in Divided Societies", *Journal of Democracy*, 4, 4 (1993), pp. 25–27.

4 Samuel P. Huntington, "Social and Institutional Dynamic of One-Party Systems", Samuel Huntington and Clement H. Moore eds, *Authoritarian Politics in Modern Society: The Dynamics of Established One-Party Systems* (New York: Basic Books, 1970), p. 21.

which swung the decision against undiluted single-party rule and full-scale oppression. The islanders dominated the private sector and its suppression could not occur without fatally damaging the economy and with that the main goal of the KMT—that of re-establishing itself on the Chinese mainland. Moreover the leadership did not want to reverse the process of indigenisation of the KMT which had started at an early stage. The controlled electoral competition on the local level brought growing numbers of islanders into the KMT. The proportion of such members rose from 14 per cent in 1950 to 67 per cent in 1980. The KMT was transformed from an elite to a mass party. By 1983, just before the democratic opening, one-fifth of the electorate were members of the KMT.

As the chapter by Chu makes clear, the process of slow liberalisation was facilitated by the export-oriented industrialisation strategy pursued since the early 1960s. Small and medium-sized businesses predominated in the economy, which also attracted most of the labour force. Relatively free from undue pressure by either big business or trade unions, the dominant party could successfully pursue a strategy of high growth together with redistribution. At the start of the 1980s the income gap between the top and lowest quintile of households in Taiwan was the smallest of all the developing countries in the world. Taiwan is indeed one of the best demonstrations of the connection Seymour Martin Lipset established between democracy and economic development. It experienced the emergence of an independent, assertive middle class and intellectuals demanding democracy together with the rise of social movements and the spread of literacy and Western culture. In terms of the socio-economic requisites, the polity at the start of the 1980s was clearly within the economic zone in which the transition to democracy usually occurs.

In both Taiwan and South Africa determined leadership at the helm of a dominant party was crucial in the democratic transition. In both cases it occurred in the context of the perceived need to break through the mounting diplomatic isolation in which undemocratic one-party dominance and repression had landed the regime. In both cases the initiative came from a member of a younger generation of leaders keen to explore new ways of securing the future of their respective parties and countries. During the 1980s the KMT leadership skilfully used state institutions and its control over the mass-media to bring about a carefully controlled democratic opening.[5] The party leadership started allowing the rank and file to elect the overwhelming

---

5   Stephen Haggard and Robert Kaufman, *The Political Economy of Democratic Transitions* (Princeton: Princeton University Press, 1995), pp. 294–95.

majority of delegates democratically. Higher centralised power was further diluted by allowing competition in the election for members of the powerful Central Committee.[6]

In South Africa the NP also arrived at a critical juncture in the mid-1960s. Dominating the all-white democratic system, it had to decide whether to move in the direction of single-party rule to maintain apartheid in undiluted form or to liberalise both the economy and the political system. In 1965 B.J. Vorster, who would become Prime Minister the following year, suggested that South Africa could become a one-party state.[7] In 1966 the party captured three-quarters of the parliamentary seats and for the first time attracted considerable numbers of English voters. Nevertheless the party was, and would remain until the 1970s, a movement that was dedicated primarily to Afrikaner survival, using apartheid to secure this goal. By the 1960s, Afrikaners formed close to 60 per cent of the white electorate and dominated the senior levels of the central state bureaucracy and the security forces. Nevertheless, as in Taiwan's case, the cost of subjecting important social forces to single-party rule was much too great with English-speakers controlling more than 90 per cent of the companies listed on the Johannesburg Stock Exchange. Moreover, English-speakers could look back to a history of more than a hundred years of enjoying the vote along with Afrikaners. Alienating important sectors of the English-speaking community would weaken the economy and damage the state's ability to counter the rising resistance to white minority rule. Both apartheid and exclusive dominant party rule could only be maintained if the NP was prepared to arrest the steady shift from an economy primarily based on agriculture and mining to one based on manufacturing.

The NP's long-term decline as dominant party to a position where it today has no formal power and enjoys the support of considerably less than 20 per cent of the electorate lies in its inability to become inclusive as successfully as the KMT has done. It nevertheless scored some successes. As it embarked on the reform of some of the apartheid structures in the 1970s and 1980s it managed to draw a growing share of white English-speakers' votes. More than half of them would vote for the party in the first inclusive election of 1994. In this election it also managed to capture the vote of 60 per cent of the coloured and Indian communities despite the fact that it opened its ranks

---

6   See the essays in Tun-jen Cheng and Stephen Haggard, ed. *Political Change in Taiwan* (Boulder: Lynne Riener, 1992), particularly those by the editors and by Ping-lung Jiang and Weng-cheng Wu, and Constant S. Meany.

7   Leonard Thompson, *Politics in the Republic of South Africa* (Boston: Little, Brown, 1966), p. 151.

only in 1992 to people who are not white. The reason was that the Tricameral Parliament, introduced in 1984, had brought the coloured and Indian communities into the political system and had conferred considerable benefits upon them in the fields of education, housing and pensions. The NP was much less successful in attracting blacks who had suffered in greater measure from oppression. As late as 1992 opinion polls still gave the party the support of 20 per cent of blacks, but this all but evaporated in the next two years. Black supporters had believed that the NP as dominant party would carry over an important part of its power into the new regime. However, once the ANC had secured the principle of majority rule and had managed to establish itself on the ground as the new dominant force, the NP's black support wavered and collapsed.[8]

When the apartheid regime in the late 1980s came round to accepting black inclusion, the prospects for a stable democratic system in terms of Lipset's economic requisites looked bleak. By the mid-1980s the black middle class was still extremely small. Less than 1 per cent of employed black people were owners and managers, and only 5 per cent of blacks had an annual income of above R16,000 (US$ 5,000) in 1985. This figure has since risen considerably, but it is unlikely that the black middle class presently stands at more than 10 per cent of this population group, who forms close to three-quarters of the country's population. South Africa's shift to an inclusive democracy occurred not because of socio-economic ripeness but as a response to two great pressures. There was first the steady decline of the ratio of whites in the demographic composition of the country—from 20 per cent in 1960 to 15 per cent in the mid-1980s and a projected 11 per cent by 2005.

The second pressure was the crisis of domestic capitalism, greatly exacerbated by international sanctions and popular resistance. Lack of investor confidence saw Gross Fixed Investment plummeting from 26 per cent of GDP in 1983 to 16 per cent in 1991. At this rate it was impossible for South Africa to grow since a 14 per cent rate of gross investment is needed simply to replace the capital stock which had worn out.[9] Organised business now began to clamour for a new political order. It was less interested in a competitive liberal

---

8   This is dealt with in some detail in Hermann Giliomee, "Surrender without Defeat: Afrikaners and the South African 'Miracle'", *Daedalus*, 126, 2 (1997), pp. 113–146.

9   For an extended discussion of the prospects for a democracy in South Africa see Hermann Giliomee, *Liberal and Populist democracy in South Africa: Challenges, New Threats to Liberalism* (Johannesburg: SA Institute of Race Relations, 1996), pp. 4–5, and the editors' conclusion of Hermann Giliomee and Lawrence Schlemmer, eds., *The Bold Experiment: South Africa's New Democracy* (Johannesburg: Southern Books, 1994), pp. 168–202.

democratic system than in bringing into the political system a mass-based dominant party that could serve as a black counterpart of the NP. The hope was that the dominant white and the dominant black party would jointly manage the transition to a new regime that would restore political stability and capitalist profitability. By the late 1980s the ANC began to look like the only party capable of fulfilling the role as NP partner.

The transition in South Africa required both the NP and ANC leadership to be in full control of their respective followings and (in the NP case) safe from electoral defeat. The NP faced charges of selling out by the white right-wing in Parliament while a partially free press made it difficult to manipulate public opinion effectively. President F.W. de Klerk and a handful of advisers made all the strategic decisions on their own with the party's parliamentary caucus and congresses dutifully ratifying everything. The endorsement of the negotiation process by the white electorate in 1992 was acquired by way of posing an innocuous-sounding (and in retrospect misleading) question in a referendum. The party did not face an extra-parliamentary revolt. Over many decades white business, white labour and the white bureaucracy had become so dependent on the NP as dominant party that they had abandoned the capacity to organise independently for political purposes. Under NP guidance the white minority ceded power permanently to blacks in return for qualified constitutional protection of its property and the maintenance of a market-oriented economy.

It is unlikely that a stable democracy would have been established in South Africa if black politics had been fragmented to the point where there was no dominant grouping. After it was proscribed in 1960 the ANC disappeared into virtual political obscurity until the late 1970s. During the 1980s it managed to establish control over virtually the entire black electorate, except rural Zulu-speakers and a small Zulu ethnic professional elite. This was due to a combination of factors—a history of more than 80 years of championing black rights, its favoured status in the international community, the almost mythical aura of Nelson Mandela and other imprisoned leaders, its ability to use violence for various purposes, its alliance with the independent trade union movement, and, as we shall see, the use of the closed list Proportional Representation electoral system. Above all there was the highly visible wealth of whites living in their exclusive residential areas which spurred black mobilisation to seek redress. The ANC's control of a unified black bloc and its launching of "rolling mass action" during the negotiations enabled it to secure its core demand of simple majority rule or what Mandela has called an "ordinary democracy". What might well have happened had the ANC faced stiffer black competition across the country can be gauged by looking to the bloody political competition between it and Chief Buthelezi's Inkatha movement in KwaZulu-Natal. It caused the death of at least 12,000 people since the early 1980s.

In the 1994 election there was no real uncertainty about the outcome. Polls predicted consistently that the ANC would win by a margin of 40 percentage points over the runner-up. Whites were nevertheless assured of their main party being represented in cabinet and taking up one deputy presidency. Indeed it was the lack of democratic uncertainty which guaranteed success. Interference with the political transition by the security forces stopped a few months before the election when the writing was clearly on the wall. The NP condoned the semi-chaotic way in which the election was conducted in some areas of major voter concentration because it was perceived as making only a marginal difference. (At most it would have gained another seat or two in the cabinet in a Government of National Unity.) It is unlikely that the result would have been accepted had the contest been a closely-run thing.[10]

In Mexico dominant party rule was also introduced in the historical context of vast socio-economic inequalities and in response to a populist challenge. The existing turmoil created a great need among political elites to end the deadly internecine struggles among them. Rather than revolutionary social transformation they sought generally accepted rules about political conduct and succession to high office. Again the existence of a single dominant party was vital. The revolutionary party, first called the Party of the National Revolution, and after 1946 the Institutional Revolutionary Party (PRI), became the platform on which the new state was created. In the political system the crucial feature was the President and the institutionalisation of presidential succession every six years with the rule of no re-election firmly applied. Presidential succession went hand in hand with a considerable change-over of personnel in the executive, legislature and civil service. (By 1970 it was estimated that a person who under one president had reached national office had a chance of only 1 in 3 of holding a comparable position under another president.) This created the hope among non-elites that under a new president things would improve both nationally and as far as personal career paths were concerned. The dominant party always covered a broad policy spectrum; hence support for it has long meant an endorsement of this system of conflict regulation rather than of any particular policies. PRI supporters accepted that goals had to be pursued within a controlled framework

---

10   The definitive study is that by R.W. Johnson and Lawrence Schlemmer, eds., *Launching Democracy in South Africa: The First Open Election, April 1994* (New Haven: Yale University Press, 1996).

that included much bargaining, highly elite decision-making and manipulated and rigged elections.[11]

In the aftermath of the revolution the party incorporated into its body four corporate sectors—labour, peasants, the military and the popular sector (an amorphous mixture of state employees, teachers, students, women's organisations and professionals). Political activity was confined to the party while each corporate sector supposedly enjoyed autonomy in its own sphere of economic activity. In effect, the leadership of various sectors from the outset exerted authoritarian control over their members while the state controlled the four sectors through their incorporation into the dominant party. Party committees on the local, state and national level co-ordinated the four sectors.[12] The party has never developed sufficient internal pluralism to allow a party convention to decide on the party's candidate for the presidential election. It has remained a closed and oligarchic process with the incumbent president ultimately choosing his successor.

In the case of Malaysia a dominant party did not underpin the process of inaugurating a democracy to the same extent as in the other three cases. It was Britain, the colonial power, that held the ring for the transition to democracy. This is the main reason why the dominant party took so long to consolidate its power and embark on its national project.

Malaysia proves Horowitz's rule that in an environment of ethnic conflict there is room for only one multi-ethnic party or alliance.[13] Here the formation of such an alliance was facilitated by the fact that while Malays formed the majority in the country the Chinese dominated the towns and the cities. Also important was the fact that in the run-up to independence local elections preceded the founding national election. The Malayan Chinese Association and UMNO became the principal partners in the Alliance after successfully contesting the local elections. The partnership then went on to win a large victory in the first national election.

The extent of income disparities on the eve of independence in 1957 was only slightly less than that in South Africa by the mid-1980s. Only a quarter of the Chinese urban and rural households could be considered poor (M$ 150 or less) against three-quarters of the Malay rural households. While about a quarter of the Chinese households in the urban and rural households

---

11 Dan A. Cothran, *Political Stability and Democracy in Mexico: The "Perfect Dictatorship"?* (Westport: Praeger, 1994), pp. 21–34.

12 Nora Hamilton, *The Limits of State Autonomy: Post-Revolutionary Mexico* (Princeton: Princeton University Press, 1982), pp. 241–44.

13 Donald Horowitz, *Ethnic Groups in Conflict* (Berkeley: University of California Press, 1985), p. 410.

had an income of M$ 300 or more, only 3 per cent of the rural Malay house-holds did.[14] Nevertheless the Malay, Chinese and Indian parties making up the Alliance (the emerging dominant party) needed a compromise which they could sell to their respective constituencies to enable them to pool their votes. The result was the "Bargain" of 1957. This endorsed Malay political domination and a special, privileged position for Malay citizens in return for Malay acceptance of the free-enterprise system and the continuation of Chinese economic power.

If we put our selected dominant parties along a spectrum the NP in apartheid South Africa appears at the exclusivist extreme. Its rejection of black membership until two years before the founding election of 1994 has virtually ruled out its chance of becoming an alternative government in post-apartheid South Africa. On the other end is the inclusivist KMT which after the first decade has successfully attracted members across ethnic and class lines, thus paving the way for the democratic opening in the 1980s. Also inclusionary with a universal orientation is the PRI. Historically it had a formal commitment to organised labour and the other "revolutionary" sectors. In actual fact it retained their support in exchange for very little. Keeping on a good footing with business, it attracted considerable support from this sector. As an inclusive party it long had a considerable capacity to stabilise society despite deep class cleavages. Somewhere in the middle of the spectrum are UMNO and the ANC. UMNO remained an ethnic party but its alliance with Chinese parties and its commitment to retaining a broadly based cabinet have helped to address the problem of representivity in government.

It was only in the 1980s that the ANC started to incorporate non-blacks into the organisation itself (as distinct from absorbing non-Africans into the South African Communist Party with which it formed an alliance). At present it welcomes electoral support across the spectrum and on its party list minorities are overrepresented. At the same time the leadership makes it clear that black political unity and black interests are of overriding concern. Since 1996 the NP as the second largest party, with majority support in the white, coloured and Indian communities, has not been represented in the cabinet. This poses a problem for the development of democracy that may become more acute over time. The more inclusive a dominant party is in its recruitment and in decision-making on various levels of government the better the prospects for a democracy that extends further than mere majoritarianism. Democratic consolidation also depends on how well the dominant party keeps the

---

14 Karl von Vorys, *Democracy without Consensus: Communalism and Political Stability in Malaysia* (Princeton: Princeton University Press, 1975), p. 226.

foundational bargain, which regulates the electoral process, citizenship, the protection of private property, and the scope of redistribution.

CONSOLIDATING DOMINANCE

To assess the consolidation of dominance we have to look at (a) the electoral process, (b) the position of the dominant party in the party system, (c) the dominant party's ability to pursue a historic project that changes the national agenda and secures it a long-lasting support base, and (d) the strategic place of the opposition, as well as consociational and corporatist elements in the system.

It is in the consolidation phase that the difference between the dominant party and the competitive systems becomes increasingly distinct. Dominant parties, particularly if they are liberation or revolutionary movements, tend first to become identified with and then synonymous with the regime they established. For a competitive democratic system to come about it is necessary for a dominant party to break up into a variety of organisations which represent the different interests and conflicts of a real country rather than of an idealised "oppressed nation".[15] In a competitive system the main fight is rarely about sub-national ethnic or racial identities or about the effects of a revolutionary conflict. Competitive politics takes place because there is a substantial floating vote which makes the prospect of a changeover in government a real one and which prompts major interest groups to consider transferring its support between parties. Contenders vie for power on the basis of their respective economic and social policies.

In a dominant party system, by contrast, there is a hardening of the line between the dominant party, which claims to be the regime, and the opposition. Major shifts in economic policy are not the result of competition within the electoral arena or between contending social groups in civil society, for instance between organised labour and business. It is the dominant party elite, subject to pressure from its support base, that readjusts policy. It does so after assessing the contending forces in own ranks and taking into account domestic and external pressures. As Friedman in his chapter on the ANC remarks, social groups pressing their interests succeed only if they manage to link up with factions within the dominant party. Because the dominant party in all four of our cases acts as a catch-all party transcending class divisions, the opposition, almost against its will, is compelled to exaggerate exclusive

---

15 Marina Ottoway, "Liberation Movements and Transition to Democracy: The case of the ANC", *The Journal of Modern African Studies*, 29, 1 (1992), p. 82.

cultural characteristics, which plays into the hands of the dominant party's attempt to delegitimise it.[16]

(a) The Electoral Process

The decision about the electoral system at the inauguration of a democracy is of lasting importance because such a system changes only slowly and marginally. It largely shapes the kind of ruling alliance (or absence of it), the nature of the dominant party's control over its representatives, the extent of its hold over society and the type of opposition that will emerge.

The first point to notice is the repeated overwhelming majorities won by the dominant party in our four cases despite the variety in electoral systems used. Dominant parties that come to power in an advanced industrialised society cannot hope to secure on a regular basis the same sweeping victories. Pempel concludes that a variant of proportional representation was essential to dominance because it fostered multi-partyism and allowed a party that attracted 35 per cent of the vote to dominate coalitions.[17] In all our four cases the dominant party succeeded in getting much more than 50 per cent support in national elections. In the Malaysian case alliance politics makes it possible for the ruling party to win an absolute majority in a plurality system of single-member constituencies. In South Africa PR managed to give more than 60 per cent of the seats to the largest party (which it is not normally supposed to do) as well as securing minorities' representation in Parliament, which is its great benefit.

The choice of an electoral system can facilitate national integration or at least constrain secessionist tendencies. Had a plurality system been used in South Africa in 1994, politics might have taken a very different course. An academic simulation of the 1994 election under the plurality formula found that the ANC would have secured 71 per cent of the seats, compared to the 62 per cent it actually got.[18] Under this system the ANC would have captured virtually all the seats, except those in rural KwaZulu, in the eastern half of the country. But it would have won very few in the western half. The NP would have taken more than three-quarters of the seats in the Western Cape province—the heartland of the Afrikaners and coloured people. With the ANC government depending for 94 per cent of its support on blacks and the

---

16 James V. Jesudason, "The syncretic state and the structuring of oppositional politics in Malaysia", G. Rodan ed., *Political Opposition in Industrialising Asia* (London: Routledge, 1995), pp. 128–160.

17 T.J. Pempel, "Conclusion" *Uncommon Democracies*, p. 336.

18 Andrew Reynolds, "Re-Running the 1994 South African and Malawian Parliamentary Elections under Alternative Electoral Formulae", unpublished paper, 1995.

NP for 86 per cent on whites and coloureds, pressures for a secessionist movement in the Western Cape would have been formidable.

The third point ties up with the distinction Horowitz makes between coalitions of commitment and coalitions of convenience.[19] Both kinds are a response to the need for a larger base than the dominant party initially can provide on its own. Coalitions of convenience are usually opportunistically cobbled together after an election and tend to fall apart soon. Coalitions of commitment by contrast are much more durable. They are arrangements in which the parties had agreed on amicable ethnic relations at an early stage and in which they actually profit electorally as a result of their co-operation. In Malaysia the cross-ethnic Alliance was established *before* the founding election was contested under the plurality system. With UMNO's Malay support coming from the rural areas and that of the MCA from urban Chinese, the two parties clearly stood to do better as a team. UMNO depended for funding on the Chinese merchants in the MCA, who in turn relied on a strong Malay party to protect their business interests. Their Alliance (soon afterwards joined by the Malayan Indian Congress) pooled their votes for candidates, who were judiciously selected with the ethnic composition of each seat in mind. In the 1955 elections the Alliance managed to win 81 per cent of the vote and 51 out of the 52 contested seats. Some form of alliance existed in all subsequent elections. Compared to South Africa where there are few curbs on free speech and where virtually all sensitive political issues are racialised, Malaysia preserves the ruling coalition by keeping the debate on ethnically sensitive issues within narrow bounds. A PR system would probably have produced fragmented ethnic parties and politicised the divisive issues to such an extent that a democracy would have been difficult to sustain.

Once firmly established in power, the Alliance could write the rules to its own liking. It did so to such an extent that the system has become generally known as only a "semi-democracy" or even stronger as a "quasi-democracy". Over the past 40 years the Electoral Commission has left unchecked practices such as gross gerrymandering of electoral districts, hurried campaign periods, bans on open-air opposition rallies and the government's uninhibited use for electoral gain of media outlets, state facilities and on-the-spot development grants. The system can be considered more a "control" than a consociational model. Indeed Dr Mahatir bin Mohamad has been trying to develop an anti-liberal ideology, attacking Western countries for democratic

---

19 Horowitz, *Ethnic Groups in Conflict*, p. 328.

extremism, but it is difficult for such ideas to gain much currency as long as the collusive business–political links of his regime lead people to think that such rhetoric is merely self-serving.

In South Africa's case much of the debate in the 1980s over an alternative to apartheid focused on the need for a broad-based, multi-racial government resting on a multi-party coalition of commitment. Lijphart, the most prominent academic proponent of consociationalism, based his advocacy of this form of democracy on the assumption that black ethnic divisions would almost certainly lead to a break-up of the black majority segment. In his view consociationalism or power-sharing would work because coalitions would be necessary in the absence of a single party able to command at least half of the seats.[20] All this came to nothing when the ANC won 62 per cent of the seats. There had been no pre-election pact in 1994 between the ANC and NP and the ruling coalition turned out to be very fragile. The NP withdrew from the Government of National Unity (GNU) in 1996 despite the fact that the constitution provided for a coalition of five years. Consociationalism has all but disappeared from the public agenda.

The collapse of the GNU has polarised politics. By its nature the PR system (and least of all the closed list system used in South Africa) provides only limited incentive for racial moderation. Each party has to solidify its primary voting base by claiming that it is the only viable party to vote for, and that all other parties are mistaken in their policies or simply sinister.[21] Only once this has been done does it try to aggregate its votes by appealing to other groups in society. This is achieved by the expedient of putting up multi-ethnic candidate lists and articulating an ideology of inclusiveness that is usually not much more than vaguely reassuring. But the multi-ethnic lists may only create a dangerous illusion of representation, one that obfuscates a discussion of the real issues. In the case of the ANC (and this is true also of the NP) most of its white, coloured and Indian candidates would have great trouble winning a seat in their respective ethnic communities under the first-past-the-post plurality system. A considerable proportion of minority group ANC members of parliament are or were members of the SA Communist Party and hold opinions about redistribution which are in direct conflict with the interests of their communities. Once in power a racially based dominant party is under great temptation to dismiss all opposition criticism as racially inspired. Party

---

20 Arend Lijphart, *Power-sharing in South Africa* (Berkeley: Institute of International Studies, 1985), pp. 119–123.

21 Andrew Reynolds, *Voting for a New South Africa* (Cape Town: Maskew Miller Longman, 1993), p. 45.

representatives who do not belong to the majority racial bloc will not speak up to challenge this interpretation.

In South Africa the closed PR list electoral formula under which the 1994 election was fought greatly contributed to the ANC's success in managing its constituency. Indeed it suited the ANC so well that it would have had to invent it if it did not exist. It is not as if intra-black ethnic differences were insignificant. Throughout the years of segregation and apartheid the divisions of the black population, comprising about 10 sizeable ethnic groups, greatly assisted whites to retain power. Nevertheless blacks share a common history of subjugation and humiliation and the material experience of living in great poverty (about three-quarters of blacks live below the poverty datum line and many who are now above it have only recently escaped). The closed list PR formula has made it possible for the ANC in 1994 to mobilise blacks as a compact majority (except for traditional Zulu voters) behind the party. It is vital to note that the judicious balancing of the different black ethnic elites on the ANC closed list happened *before* the first election.

In its 1994 election platform the ANC gave a considerably greater role to the state in economic life than the NP or IFP but for the rest the election platforms of the main parties differed little. This, together with the racially mixed party lists, may suggest that race as a factor has become sufficiently sublimated to allow for a competitive system based on class interests rather than identity politics. In the 1994 election campaign the ANC and the NP carefully projected a non-racial image when appearing on national platforms. Nonetheless the primary racial identification in each case was transmitted through a host of symbolic messages, the racial composition of the leadership corps, the different ways in which leaders referred to the "people", and the flavour of the political meetings or rallies.

The brutal history of apartheid together with the racial mould of the electoral process has led to historically white parties being unable to campaign in the black townships because of violence and intimidation. The Independent Electoral Commission reported during the 1994 election campaign that as many as 13 million voters (approximately two-thirds of the total) "live in areas where the right to campaign is abridged". A respected analyst of black politics wrote in the aftermath of the election: "Ideological loyalties are absolute and concepts of political choice and tolerance are at best weakly sanctioned by local leaders. Popular party adherence is mainly determined by territorial occupation."[22] This situation has not improved after the first

---

22 Tom Lodge, "Election of a Special Kind", *Southern African Review of Books*, March/April 1994, p. 4; SA Institute of Race Relations, *Watchdog on the election*, no. 9, (1994).

election of 1994. In his contribution to this volume Schlemmer reports on a 1996 study which found that just under half of the black population felt that it is difficult to live in their neighbourhoods if their political views differ from those around them. There is no evidence that these practices are encouraged by the ANC national leadership. At the same time, however, the muscular mobilisation and rituals of black solidarity serve to boost the leadership's power and the party's support.

With different ethnic concentrations in different provinces, a limited measure of federalism allows the ANC to bestow patronage and accommodate ethnicity as a safe form of sub-national identification. Strict formulae for central government transfers to provincial governments prevent charges of ethno-regional favouritism from gaining credence. The ANC has forestalled criticism of a black bias by drawing up its party list in such a way that 30 per cent of those elected to Parliament come from the coloured, Indian and white communities despite the fact that these communities contributed only six per cent to the overall ANC vote. The commitment to dismantle the preponderance of white economic power has made the dominant party, like its counterpart in Malaysia, almost invincible over the short to medium term.

Buoyed by pre-election polls and its success in the 1994 election, the ANC demanded the biggest say in cabinet for the largest party. The NP, by contrast, had anticipated for itself a strategic role in the GNU on the basis of its number claim to be the gatekeeper to three important sectors—the white bureaucracy, the security agencies and the big business community. Yet with polls showing a huge ANC lead and with the NP steadily retreating in the political negotiations before 1994, these sectors reassessed their situation. Business, the personnel of the security agencies and white bureaucrats all made their own deals with the new regime.[23] The NP was further weakened once it had become clear that its presence in the cabinet did not secure any new fixed investment. The absorption of ANC operatives into the officer echelon of the Army has virtually ruled out the possibility of a coup by the military which is still largely white-led. Marginalised, the NP walked out of the cabinet in 1996.

Given these conditions, the only possibility of a competitive party system lies in a realignment, after a faction of the dominant party's parliamentary caucus, particularly one close to the trade unions, has revolted against the leadership. The constitution, however, enables a party's leadership to expel from Parliament any member who challenges it or crosses the floor. The

---

23 Steven Friedman, "Yesterday's Past" unpublished paper, 1995, Centre for Policy Studies, Johannesburg.

closed list, together with the anti-defection clause, gives the ANC leadership a degree of control over party representatives almost unmatched in any form of democratic politics.[24] (If the Mexican-style form of presidentialism can be labelled "the perfect dictatorship" the South African system must be close to an equivalent for an established leadership of a parliamentary system.)

Since 1994 electoral competition has continued in highly publicised disputes in Parliament, where the traditional Westminster style of adversarial politics quickly got the upper hand. Electorally the ANC has everything to gain by branding the NP as a chauvinistic white party. Nelson Mandela has often claimed that the NP has little chance of making headway since blacks consider criticism of the government as evidence of the NP being against blacks.[25]

In Taiwan the KMT from the outset used an element of controlled popular participation to bolster its legitimacy as an emigre regime. It introduced a limited form of home rule in 1950 by which natives could elect representatives up to the provincial level and for quasi-state organisations. As Rigger's chapter demonstrates, the use of the Single Non-Transferable Vote (SNTV) electoral system profoundly shaped the nature of dominant party control. Under this unusual system voters select a single candidate to represent them in multi-member districts. Effective control at the local level largely determines the shape of national politics. The electoral districts for all elections except those for the two highest executive offices follow the boundaries of the municipalities. To win the maximum number of seats the KMT in the authoritarian period rarely used massive fraud or coercion but stimulated fierce competition between local factions. Factions were almost all KMT-aligned and candidates ran as nominees of the dominant party. Rigger's chapter describes how vote brokers, called *tiau-a-ka*, used promises of civil service jobs and public construction projects to solicit votes. As an enormously wealthy organisation the KMT could also deploy party funds on a large scale to buy votes. In this way dominance tended to beget more dominance.

Once democratic reform deepened, however, factional competition under KMT auspices became a double-edged sword. The lifting of all the bans on

---

24 There has been criticism of the NP's "myopia" in holding out for power-sharing instead of demanding electoral rules and mechanisms that offered a chance of breaking up the ANC as a liberation movement: see Ian Shapiro, *Democracy's Place* (Ithaca: Cornell University Press, 1996), pp. 210–19. This ignores the fact that when the NP leadership negotiated an interim constitution it needed the PR closed list system to assure its caucus that all members interested in prolonging their career would be almost certain of retaining their seats. Without that De Klerk would almost certainly have faced a caucus revolt that would have stopped the transition in its tracks. When the final constitution was negotiated in 1995–96 the ANC had enough power to insist on the perpetuation of the PR closed list.

25 See De Klerk's comments on this in *Cape Times*, 27 May 1997.

privately sponsored political meetings together with the rise of free media made it impossible to control the flow of information. Factions became more difficult to control and party discipline much harder to maintain. Heavy involvement of criminal gangs in factions and vote-buying has become a national embarrassment. But the KMT's troubles on the local level were offset by victories in elections for executive offices, particularly that of Lee-Teng-hui for President, where issues like national identity and security predominate. As Chu's chapter points out, the KMT has managed to present itself as a born-again party. Through a skilful combination of flexibility and rigidity, the KMT builds up its electoral strength in much the same way as dominant parties in advanced industrial societies. It has also introduced electoral reform by reducing the SNTV system to 78 per cent of the seats with the rest elected by the list PR system.

The dominant party that came into power in Mexico in 1929 enjoyed a long-lasting revolutionary legitimacy which made it less important for it to get electoral endorsement than the KMT. Nevertheless the revolutionary elite's democratic commitment was strong enough to make it hold elections on all levels of government. The party has always had a significant social base on which it could rely for support without any undue pressure. However, the party's goal was not a mere majority but dominance through the ballot box. It used all means, both fair and foul, to ensure overwhelming victories. As the chapter by Rigger explains, Mexico's method of election by a plurality enables a dominant party to use a variety of ways of getting itself re-elected. Where possible the PRI has used its corporatist ties to make sure that the votes of the workers, peasants and popular sectors are delivered. In poor communities where these ties are weak, it deploys a local party boss to use both the carrot of patronage and the stick of intimidation and even murder to ensure that his community or region remains loyal to the dominant party. In more recent times the party, using state funds, has massively outspent its rivals during campaigns.

Fraud at the ballot box was added to the mix, which more often than not produced results that were scarcely credible. In 1958 the PRI presidential candidate won 90 per cent of the vote, and before the electoral reform of 1963 the opposition share of seats in the Chamber of Deputies was only 3 per cent. The electoral laws were changed several times subsequently but until recently the PRI designed and wrote these laws to suit its own needs.[26] Elections had to meet the fundamental objective of maintaining a

---

26 The Mexican system at present has 33 first-past-the-post plurality constituencies and 200 PR list
    seats.

minimum amount of organisational space for partisan opposition so that it does not disappear or conduct political activities outside of the institutions. Indeed the entire spirit and letter of the legislation was to control, standardise, regulate and channel the participation of political parties without diluting PRI dominance too much.[27] Only the most recent electoral reforms begin to meet the criteria a liberal democracy sets for fair and free elections. In the most recent Mexican elections the PRI lost for the first time control of the lower house.

(b) The Identity of the Dominant Party and the Hegemonic Project
An essay on the dominant parties of Sweden and Japan makes the point that to understand the dominant party's behaviour one must look beyond its electoral strength or its ideology to focus its particular position within the party system.[28] Dominance in industrialised democracies rests on a majority coalition of socio-economic blocs. By contrast, dominance in the industrialising countries described in this volume rests on the claim to predominant power of a national liberation or revolutionary movement and its pursuit of liberation goals. It goes hand in hand with the demand for extensive state intervention.

To retain dominance, a combination of dynamism and flexibility is needed, particularly for ethnically based parties. When supporters rise into middle class positions or when workers get frustrated with orthodox liberal economics, the party must make it attractive enough for them to retain their original political identification rather than turn to political action focusing solely on class interests or narrow racial or religious sectionalism. Furthermore it must be flexible enough to keep strategic outsiders such as the Chinese in Malaysia and the whites in South Africa participating in the system. As Joel Netshitenzhe, a leading ANC thinker, formulated it: While the principle of black leadership and the right racial balance was non-negotiable, an outcome had to be avoided "where a perception of dominance can take root".[29] The party must reshape the identity of the nation in such a way that outsiders also can recognise a place for themselves in it.

The dominant parties in Malaysia and South Africa illustrate various aspects of the attempt to reconcile the dominant party's mission to achieve

---

27 Cesar Cansino, "Mexico: The Challenge of Democracy", *Government and Opposition*, (1995), pp. 71–72.

28 Ellis S. Kraus and Jon Pierre, "The Decline of Dominant Parties: Parliamentary Politics in Sweden and Japan", *Uncommon Democracies*, p. 227.

29 Joel Netshitenzhe, *City Press*, 1 June 1997, editorial page.

liberation for the ethnic or racial group on which it is based with the need for national integration. In Malaysia the Alliance initially comprised mainly a coalition of Malay and Chinese elites that recognised the political and symbolic paramountcy of Malays and the safeguading of Chinese citizenship and business interests. During the 1960s the government followed a *laissez faire* policy which enabled Chinese business and foreign companies to prosper. By the end of the 1960s the system was showing signs of serious strain. Some Chinese attacked Malay political paramountcy and nascent policies of affirmative action while Malays pointed to the failure of UMNO to promote access of Malays to business opportunities from which they were still largely excluded. By the end of the 1960s Malays and state agencies acting on their behalf had only two per cent of the total share ownership of manufacturing, 1.4 per cent in commerce and 2.4 per cent in mining. Foreigners owned more than 60 per cent of all the corporate equity capital invested in Malaysia, with the Chinese holding three-fifths of the remaining domestically owned corporate investment. There was a growing fear that Malay economic weakness would create a situation where the Chinese would use their great economic power to attack the political predominance of the Malays and destroy any hope of their economic and social advance.[30]

In 1969 the Bargain on which the Alliance was based became unstuck. Poorer Malays defected in large numbers from the Alliance to a radical flank party, the Parti Islam SeMalaysia. In the 43 constituencies where there were straight fights between UMNO and PAS, the latter drew more votes. The proportion of non-Malays voting for the Alliance also dropped compared to the previous election. The stability of the entire political system seemed to be imperilled. Widespread rioting was followed by the temporary suspension of democracy. In 1971 the government announced the New Economic Policy as the basis of a new national project of Malay economic empowerment. The government abandoned any pretence of being neutral by massively intervening on behalf of Malays. It imposed preferential policies in university admission and employment in the civil service and the financial and manufacturing sectors. With respect to the latter it acquired the discretionary power to coerce the larger enterprises to use Malay distributors for a minimum of 30 per cent of turnover, and to train Malay employees in sufficient numbers for their companies to reflect the population composition up to the managerial level. A crucial concomitant was that international capital failed to support the protests of Chinese business. By the end of the decade the dominant

---

30 James V. Jesudason, *Ethnicity and the Economy: The State, Chinese Business and Multi-nationals in Malaysia* (Singapore: Oxford University Press, 1989), pp. 44–45, 66–67, 192–94.

party had created the conditions for a rapid growth of the Malay middle class in both the private sector and state bureaucracy.[31]

All the main parties committed themselves to the NEP. In subsequent elections UMNO, now in an alliance with a broader range of parties, called Barisan Nasional, managed to win at least four-fifths of the seats. Zakaria comments on the events of 1969 that the most interesting aspect was the "unstated notion that losing an election means virtually total political defeat...[and] the end of the primary rights of the Malays".[32] Subsequently attaining at least a two-thirds majority has acquired major symbolic significance. Having the power to change the constitution affirmed the political paramountcy of the Malays in the country. Such dominance is also a firm base for implementing a high-profile programme to better the lives of the dominant party's constituency.

Commenting on this, Horowitz remarks that status discontents arise when groups do not receive the recognition they feel they deserve. More is at stake than simply a matter of an ethnic elite not getting the jobs they want. For the group as a whole it is a question of how they fare in the struggle for group worth.[33] An ethnic party that fails to deliver on this is sure to face trouble at the polls. But parties that mobilise an ethnic or racial group do not achieve success by single-mindedly playing on the issue of identity. They offer a package deal designed both to celebrate the distinctive identity and status of a group and to promote its material interests. This means that they must be able to shed shrinking old bases of support. In their place they must create dynamic new ones and attract fresh allies from across the ethnic divide. To do so successfully they have to reformulate the dominant party's organisation and ideology.

During the 1960s UMNO was still predominantly a party with a rural base in which teachers and local officials played a major role. Depending on the Chinese merchants for funds and on the MCA for Chinese votes they gave this party the vital portfolios of Finance, and Commerce and Industry. The MCA influence steadily declined as UMNO created a Malay urban middle class. The main instrument for this was the NEP which forced Chinese and foreign companies to grant shares at a discount to Malays and to employ them in managerial positions. Malays advancing in the industrial and commercial sectors and the civil service now became the party's main bases

---

31 James V. Jesudason, *Ethnicity and the Economy: The State, Chinese Business and Multi-nationals in Malaysia* (Singapore: Oxford University Press, 1989), pp. 128–163.

32 Zakaria Haji Ahmad, "Malaysia: Quasi democracy in a Divided Society"; Larry Diamond, Juan Linz and Seymour Martin Lipset, eds., *Democracy in Developing Countries* (Boulder: Lynne Riener, 1989), p. 358.

33 Horowitz, *Ethnic groups in Conflict*, pp. 225–26.

of support. UMNO strove for an all-class ethnic alliance but, as Jesudason points out, workers *as workers* did not figure strongly since ethnic mobilisation made working class organisation redundant. Consequently Malaysia's rapid shift to an export-based economy did not create any major strains in the party. To keep its control over Malay peasants and workers the government set up a national investment fund and a national unit trust to make it possible for them to participate in capital accumulation. As the level of decision-making in executing the NEP moved down to more junior bureaucrats, the role of the MCA as ethnic brokers largely became obsolete. Chinese businessmen began to make their own arrangements, contributing funds to UMNO and dealing directly with Malay politicians and businessmen.[34]

During the early 1990s the most prominent element in UMNO was a big Malay bourgeoisie, many of whom had benefited from the government's privatisation policy and the linkages between bureaucrats, businessmen, politicians, military leaders and religious leaders. UMNO still has by far the most branches of any party and because the party is quite important to the tycoon class it has no shortage of cash at election times. Nevertheless the government apparatus is more important than the party structure in mobilising voters. In marginal seats the government can bring in UMNO supporters under the guise of land projects and unemployment relief to ensure victory.[35] In the meantime UMNO and the alliance which it leads have also become more attractive to non-Malays, particularly those in the private sector. The rapid economic growth of the 1970s and 1980s not only made the Malay economic advance possible but also enabled Chinese to rise in the managerial ranks and the professions. Not only did the economy become less politicised but the government also allowed greater cultural scope to the Chinese. Poverty has been considerably reduced among all the sectors. In the most recent election, the ruling coalition received more Chinese support than ever before. Chinese voters were repelled by the anti-modernist and theocratic elements of the Malay fringe parties and inspired by a new government vision which accepted Chinese more as political co-equals in the Malaysia of the future.

In South Africa the ANC appears to be inspired by the ethnic preference policies of Malaysia, which in a short period of time has become one of the biggest foreign investors in South Africa. But there are major questions around the ANC effort to emulate UMNO in bringing about growth and redistribution and coupling this with increased racial harmony. The main

---

34 Donald Horowiz, "Cause and consequence in public policy theory: ethnic policy and system transformation in Malaysia", *Policy Sciences*, 22 (1989), pp. 249–87.

35 Harold Crouch, *Government and Society in Malaysia* (Ithaca: Cornell University Press, 1996), pp. 62–63.

difference lies in the economy and labour market. Ethnic redistribution in Malaysia was premised on high economic growth rates necessary to allow the incomes of other ethnic groups also to rise. The NEP indeed stipulated that it would take place only if growth rates were around 7 per cent. As Jesudason's chapter makes clear, progress for the poor has come from rapidly expanding demand for labour rather than class-specific redistribution programmes through the state. Furthermore the chief determinant of wage levels has been the market and not the institutional role of unions.[36] Yet despite all this, inequalities in Malaysia are still great although not of the order of those in South Africa.

In South Africa, by contrast, the economy has been languishing with a growth rate that seems unable to go beyond 3 per cent. Furthermore unions have been the key to wage increases since the early 1980s and their advances have come at the price of making it ever more difficult for the poor to get into the formal labour market. The economy is remarkably open with exports and imports representing more than 60 per cent of GDP which means that the dictate of competitiveness under globalisation comes into clear conflict with labour market rigidity. The terms on which this conflict plays out are strongly contested by business and organised labour, making it difficult for the government to find a consensus on the way forward.

Nevertheless black South Africans insist that their government makes it possible for them to catch up materially with the dominant white socio-economic group. This ultimately is what keeps the party together as an all-class black party despite the different ideologies, conflicting interests and clashing programmes of action which are joined under the same roof. The black population entertain strong aspirations to live a middle class life and they expect a black majority government to realise their dream.[37] In a pre-1994 election poll 81 per cent of blacks said that they expect the new government to make sure that "people like me can live like most whites". In another investigation two-thirds of a sample of black youth indicated that they felt that they could get a university degree and wanted the government to make this possible. Two-thirds desired professional work in the new South Africa and more than half of the sample believed that the new government could provide this work.[38]

---

36 Jesudason, *Ethnicity and the Economy*, p. 173.
37 Robert Mattes, *The Election Book: Judgement and Choice in South Africa's 1994 election* (Cape Town: Idasa, 1995), pp. 28–29.
38 Lawrence Schlemmer and Ian Hirschfeld, *Founding Democracy and the New South African Voter* (Pretoria: HSRC, 1994), pp. 48–50.

ANC-supporting blacks are by no means unified about how the dominant party should help them to realise their aspirations. The top strata in black society, jokingly referring to themselves as the patriotic bourgeoisie, accept, albeit reluctantly, the capitalist route, but insist that their advance be facilitated by affirmative action and black empowerment programmes. The leadership of the labour movement pin their hopes on a radical economic alternative with two-thirds of the shop stewards supporting socialism. As long as the ANC is considered as the "Parliament of the African people" there is no prospect of the movement breaking up into its constituent socio-economic blocs. A poll taken before the 1994 election showed that support among blacks for the ANC was equally strong among those who thought their fortunes would improve as among those who believed it would decline. There is as yet no sign of any class solidarity across white–black lines. The white and black unemployed, for instance, vote solidly for historically white and historically black parties respectively.[39]

As Friedman argues in his chapter, ANC dominance is still fragile, both with respect to its control over its black supporters and its dependence on the white-controlled economy. The economy is also much weaker than those of Taiwan and Malaysia. Since the mid-1970s real per capita income has declined by more than 50 per cent and at present the economy seems unable to accelerate its growth rate significantly, despite the promises of the government's macro-economic programme. The ANC's acceptance of a liberal macro-economic framework will force it to retrench state employees and cut back on education and social spending. By contrast, the ANC's most solid constituency at present is the newly emerging black bourgeoisie who are securing state contracts either on their own or in partnership with white businessmen.

Of all the parties surveyed in this volume the KMT has been by far the most successful in developing national self-consciousness in a way that promotes democratic politics and dilutes ethnic tensions. Already during the authoritarian period under mainlander rule ethnic animosities declined as the groups learnt to trust each other and as intermarriage became widespread. There was none of the victim mentality or comprehensive demands for redress prevalent in Malaysia at an earlier stage or in present-day South Africa. The state was tough but not unresponsive to grass roots demands. And as we have seen, its success in narrowing income disparities was almost unparalleled in the world.

---

39 Andrew Reynolds, "The Results", *Election '94*, pp. 190–94.

CORPORATISM AND OPPOSITION POLITICS

South Africa, Mexico and Taiwan are all cases of societies in which a dominant party with a nationalist or populist inclination tries to impose a developmental revolution. The party's professed aim is nothing less than the radical transformation of society. Such a project, if accurately designated, leaves little room for an opposition, which can easily be branded as destructive of the efforts at transformation. But, despite being overshadowed by the dominant party in the political process, opposition parties are by no means bit players on the scene. As Huntington wrote 30 years ago the minor parties play a significant role as "bell-wethers or warning devices". An increase in their support level gives the dominant party directions in which it has to move in order to retain dominance. It could do so either by assimilating new groups or by innovative new policies.[40] Horowitz, in turn, has emphasised the importance of ethnic "flank" parties which challenge a dominant ethnic coalition like the Alliance in Malaysia. Their success or failure is a barometer which the dominant party studies for evidence that it is bending too much in a certain direction.[41]

Thus opposition serves the system. Writing about India in the early 1960s, Morris-Jones notes: "[Government] has continuously to act in the knowledge that the scrutiny of any item may take place and that waste or impropriety may be widely exposed in the House and the press. The fact that government…replies are often vague and cool is less important than that behind the reply there has often been embarrassment and some resolve not to let it happen again."[42] Kothari's depiction of the "Congress system" in India also applies to our dominant parties. He distinguishes the ruling party as the *party of consensus* from the opposition as *parties of pressure*. The latter form no alternative government but they constantly criticise and in doing so exert a latent threat if the ruling group strays too far from the balance of effective public opinion. Both the inevitable factionalism within the dominant party and the idea of a latent threat from the opposition must be considered as necessary parts of the system of dominant party rule.[43]

In Mexico, Taiwan and South Africa the dominant party in all three cases tried to blunt opposition by establishing a form of corporatism. In the case of

---

40   Samuel P. Huntington, *Political Order in Changing Societies* (New Haven: Yale University, 1968), p. 147.
41   Horowitz, *Ethnic Groups in Conflict*, p. 413.
42   W.H. Morris-Jones, "Parliament and Dominant Party: The Indian Experience", *Parliamentary Affairs*, 17 (1964), p. 302.
43   Ranji Kothari, "The Congress 'System' in India", *Asian Survey*, 4, 12 (1964), p. 1162.

Taiwan there was a party–state corporatism in which the dominant party subsidised and controlled an array of interest associations. This contained class conflict, provided an important source of votes for the party and offered a channel for disseminating state policies.[44] It also deprived the different interest groups of their autonomy and stifled the growth of an opposition.

Taiwan's high economic growth rate and the rapid rise of a broadly based middle class to a considerable extent eroded this form of corporatism. These developments would lead one to have expected politics based on class rather than a politicised ethnicity (mainlanders versus indigenous Taiwanese). The opposition in Taiwan, however, developed along ethnic lines. The import-substitution phase in the early years of KMT rule had reinforced the ethnic and political domination of the mainlander minority, who were over-represented in state-owned businesses, government, the universities and cultural life. For the opposition it was easier to mobilise along ethnic lines because the inequality in the distribution of power along ethnic lines seemed greater and more prominent than the power inequality among classes. The thrust of the opposition attack was political reform and ethnic justice rather than the economic grievances of certain classes. Given the fact that the indigenous Taiwanese form more than four-fifths of the population, victory seemed well within the DPP's reach.

This expectation has so far not materialised. The KMT, as Chu's chapter shows, has managed to retain a commanding lead in virtually all occupational categories. This has happened despite a shift to an export-oriented economy in the mid-1960s, which has caused serious tensions in both the PRI and the ANC.[45] The opposition's inability to defeat the KMT must first of all be traced to the remarkable success of the latter in absorbing the indigenous Taiwanese into the party up to the very pinnacles of power. The second reason lies in the KMT's capacity to incorporate into its own platform the opposition's main political plank and ethnic goal, namely the issue of Taiwan's autonomy/independence. It has reconciled the promotion of autonomy with the maintenance of regime stability far more successfully than the opposition could promise credibly to do. While Beijing continues to pressurise Taipei, the KMT's position in the centre is almost unassailable. This allows it to sustain support both from mainlanders, who hope for ultimate reunification but consider it premature, and from the indigenous Taiwanese. An external threat has diminished dissent within the KMT's constituency.

---

44   Ruth and David Collier cited by Shelley Rigger, "Mobilisational authoritarianism and political opposition in Taiwan", *Political Oppositions in Industrialising Asia*, p. 302.
45   Rigger, "Mobilisational authoritarianism", pp. 310–11.

Indigenous Taiwanese have not given up on their ethnic ideals, but are unwilling to support the DPP in greater numbers for fear that its policies may prove to be too extreme. With the possible exception of its counterpart in Botswana, the KMT's strategic acumen is without parallel among all the cases in this volume. It is rare indeed that a dominant party bridges both ethnic and class divisions so skilfully. The KMT success has much to do with the decentralised nature of the private sector, giving neither business nor labour a preponderance of power, and the party's refusal to base itself narrowly on any particular class interests, unlike the labour-based PRI and ANC.

As we have seen, the PRI in Mexico incorporated organised labour, along with the peasant and popular sectors, as the three corporatist pillars of the party organisation. Initially the party pursued populist policies that alienated business, but it was forced to attract business support for a policy of industrial modernisation. During the 1940s the ruling party accordingly reconstituted itself as an all-class, one-party dominant regime. Business now entered into a co-operative relationship with the regime, although it would never come to form one of the corporalist pillars.[46] As Collier explains in her chapter, by the middle of the century the multi-class coalition was cemented by the import-substitution industrialisation model, which relied on local industrial production and tariff protection against manufactured imports. Since the wage level largely determines the domestic market, business and organised labour could forge a class compromise that achieved rising real wages on the basis of an expanding domestic market. The chapters of Kaufman, Collier and Cook all show how Mexico's partial shift in the 1980s away from import-substitution changed the fortunes of the dominant party. Export-oriented industrialisation brought about a substantial real wage decline, the undermining of the strike as a weapon, forced flexibilisation of the labour market and a decline in size of the manufacturing work force. Informally business replaced labour as the main ally of government which increasingly had to act in ways that undermined labour's previously entrenched interests.

The shattering of the business–labour consensus on which the PRI rested during the 1980s impacted strongly on the presidential election of 1988. It produced strong challenges to the PRI both from the left and from the right. The left wanted the regime to return to the principles of the revolution, particularly to re-emphasise the basic objectives of social justice, land reform and economic nationalism. The right-wing National Action Party,

---

46   Ruth Berins Collier and David Collier, *Shaping the political arena: critical junctures, the labour movement and regime dynamics in Latin America* (Princeton: Princeton University Press, 1991), pp. 353–420.

traditionally the party of business, favoured thorough-going political reform that would introduce a liberal democracy based on fair elections and a true multi-party system. It also wanted to end Mexico's form of corporatism, which it depicted as inherently authoritarian and anti-democratic. The PRI use of government funds to massively outspend the opposition and other forms of fraud probably made the decisive difference in the 1988 election in helping its candidate to stave off defeat. But perhaps equally important was the regime's stabilising mechanism of regular presidential succession, and the electorate's hope that the new incumbent would bring the necessary changes. In a system that is genuinely democratic, defeat would have been almost certain.[47]

If South Africa's corporatism is compared with that of Mexico, government–business relations appear at a first glance to be rather similar. As in the case of Mexico, the business establishment was at the outset very suspicious of the new dominant party because of the movement's commitment to nationalising important sectors of the economy. After its unbanning in 1990 the ANC forged a tripartite alliance comprising the party, the South African Communist Party and the Congress of South African Trade Unions (COSATU) on the common commitment to nationalisation and substantial redistribution from whites to blacks. In the run-up to the 1994 founding election COSATU, which proved to be by far the best organised component of the ANC's electoral machine, gave its support on the condition that the ANC implement an ambitious policy of job creation and social welfare, called the Reconstruction and Development Programme (RDP), as the new hegemonic national project.

The Alliance has come under growing strain after the government's abolition of the RDP office and acceptance in 1996 of a liberal macro-economic framework with emphasis on fiscal discipline, privatisation, abolition of exchange control and lowering of tariff walls. The ANC has nevertheless remained firmly committed to affirmative action and the social transformation of society. To discuss macro-economic policy and industrial relations it has introduced a corporatist body in which business, labour and government are represented. The National Economic Development and Labour Advisory Council (NEDLAC) serves as a super industrial relations council where business and organised labour slug it out at the highest level. With South African unionised workers (one-third of formal sector workers) aspiring to rights on a par with Scandinavian social democracies, COSATU continues to press for a more rigid and state-regulated labour market. Instead of arriving at

---

47   Cothran, *Political Stability and Democracy in Mexico*, pp. 161–67.

compromises over a contested Basic Conditions of Employment Bill, organised labour has recently embarked on strikes and demonstration marches while business seeks court interdicts to prevent these actions.

Corporatism in South Africa has some other peculiar features. First, its model of a social partnership is based on that of post-war Germany which was developed in conditions of near-full employment. By contrast South Africa has a labour-surplus economy. Second, the formal corporatist relationship is not underpinned by any social accord or even any informal agreement about the means of achieving growth and redistribution. At a national congress held in September 1997, COSATU pledged itself to socialism and the transfer of power to workers, a programme which is anathema to South African business. Third, although large-scale unemployment is generally regarded as South Africa's greatest crisis, this is not really addressed directly in NEDLAC. The best prospects for job creation lie with small and medium enterprises, but both this sector and the unemployed are not directly represented in NEDLAC.

Apart from the white–black cleavage, the major economic line of division is now between the black employed and unemployed. While the wage and salary income of blacks employed in the formal sector has improved by perhaps as much as a third since the elections of 1994, those of unemployed or informally employed blacks, who make up close to half of the economically active blacks, probably deteriorated even further, having suffered a prolonged decline since the mid-1970s.[48] Some three and a half million economically active people are outside both the formal and the informal labour market and this number is projected to expand by 350,000 per year at existing levels of growth. South Africa's horrific crime levels are partly related to this and to the great length of time it takes the average black youth to find work after leaving school.

In the public debate there are sharply conflicting views about South African corporatism. On the one hand there is the view (represented in this volume by Friedman and Adam) that this form of corporatism can largely compensate for the absence of power-sharing devices and can supplement or even replace the opposition parties' role as representatives of established class concerns. This rests on the conviction on the one hand that the ANC alone is capable of protecting minority interests against the "mortal danger" of dissatisfied blacks, while on the other it is believed that only the NED-LAC style of corporatism with co-operation by government, business and

---

48 Personal communication by Lawrence Schlemmer, 4 October 1997.

labour can launch the country on the high road of fast growth and rapid employment creation. Some take the argument even further in claiming that pacts between labour and business function as a form of racial consociationalism since business is overwhelmingly white and labour black. On the other end of the spectrum stands the liberal South African Institute of Race Relations, which calls for the scrapping of NEDLAC since it reinforces vested interests at the expense of the poor. It also brands as undemocratic the present requirement that all economic and labour legislation be referred to NEDLAC prior to its tabling in Parliament. It provides this remedy: "Were NEDLAC to be scrapped, the government would be able to amend legislation to allow for more flexible labour markets and a lower regulatory burden on small business…and move quickly and decisively to achieve [its] job creation targets."[49]

As editors we tend to agree with the sceptical view of corporatism in South Africa and will return to the debate in our conclusion to the volume (Chapter 14). Here we make only two points. First, we fail to see how corporatism in South Africa can be considered as a form of ethnic or communal power-sharing when business and labour come to agreements about economic and social policy. It is quite unable to resolve issues which hinge on ethnic identity, like language policy or affirmative action. There is little likelihood of a satisfactory balance along Malaysian lines emerging between the new political impotence of the minorities and non-intervention by the state in their economic life. To speed up the improvement in the quality of life of its black constituency in a time of fiscal autonomy, the state will have to cut back heavily on its spending on other communities in the field of education, health and pensions to the point of compromising equality of entitlement. Of the three minority groups, the coloured community is most affected by changes in state expenditure, and it is not clear at all how corporatism is intended to counter their disaffection or indeed that of the much more powerful white community.[50]

The second point is that a party system institutionalising deep cleavages over the longer run leads to polarisation and instability. In the case of Mexico we have had the PRI as a coalition of the whole that institutionalises great inequalities. There is a huge concentration of capital with five conglomerates in Mexico holding half the country's assets. Despite many decades of official corporatism the massive income inequality of Mexico between the top and the lowest quintiles is not much better than that in South Africa with its long

---

49 SA Institute of Race Relations, Press Release, 3 September 1997.
50 This paragraph is based on Charles Simkins, "Will South Africa have a dominant party system?", unpublished paper, 1995.

history of segregation and apartheid. One of the major reasons suggested at the conference is that the corporatist insiders in Mexico and particularly "official" labour benefited disproportionately at the expense of the outsiders. Increasing globalisation in the past two decades has not helped matters. While workers in foreign-linked companies have seen their real wages increase by 30 per cent in recent years, those of employees in firms domestically oriented in their markets (such as textiles) have dropped by 15 per cent. Overall income inequality in Mexico increased by 10 per cent in the second half of the 1980s. By the beginning of the 1990s, 44 per cent of the population was living at or below the government's official poverty line, and the absolute number of people living in extreme poverty (as defined) was higher in 1992 than 1984, when the proportion stood at 15 per cent. While revolts of the urban poor are unlikely, sudden explosions of discontent in remote rural areas can have a major destabilising effect on markets, as the recent history of Mexico has shown.

The ANC is increasingly resembling the PRI in Mexico over the past decade by trying to reconcile contradictory aims. On the one hand it tries to retain its recalcitrant labour support base while seeking "national consensus" and "social balance" between unionised labour and big business. On the other, it hopes to give to the unemployed poor a significant form of social citizenship while protecting the industrial citizenship of the unions that prevents the poor from getting into the labour market. Agreements will almost certainly come at the expense of those not well organised or excluded from the corporatist arena. The costs could be a worsening of structural unemployment, economic stagnation, a growing fiscal crisis and even higher crime levels.[51]

The great temptation for a dominant party could be to try to deflect attention from the cleavages in its own primary constituency by focusing on the wealth and the income of the erstwhile dominant group. In South Africa there are three statistics about white–black income divisions which are particularly relevant. First, the average white household income in 1993 was about five and a half times that of blacks; second, nearly as many blacks as whites find themselves in the highest income quintile; third, the top 20 per cent of black income earners enjoy an average salary or wage ten times that of the lowest 40 per cent.[52] The question is: will the ANC ignore the latter

---

51 For some candid arguments see the comments of Otto Lambsdorff, a previous liberal Minister of Economics in Germany, in *Frontiers of Freedom*, 12 (1997), pp. 13–15 and Paul Perreira, "Privatisation Incognito", *Fast Facts*, April 1997, pp. 8–9.
52 Lawrence Schlemmer, *Investment 2000* (Pretoria: HSRC, 1995), pp. 25–27.

two figures to focus all its redistributive attention on the white–black divide or will all three statistics be given equal consideration? There is as yet no clear and consistent response. There are signs that an important faction in the ANC wants to deflect attention from intra-black cleavages by lumping all blacks into the category of the "majority" and in the name of majority rule call for radical transformation, by which is meant the rapid narrowing of white–black inequalities. The distinct possibility exists, as Simkins points out in his chapter, that this may take the form of a redistribution from the white to the black middle class without improving the position of the rural poor. Nevertheless criticism of government policy (whichever way it turns out) may well be depicted as obstructing nation-building and majority rule.

A study by Levite and Tarrow of the dominant parties in Israel (1948–1977) and Italy has shown how extensive delegitimation can be. Opposition parties can be depicted as devious, fascist and inimical to freedom, the democratic order and national stability. Excluded opposition parties can often do little but to retreat, becoming a cult of true believers, or to accept the dominant party's mores and values at the cost of being seen as its pale imitation.[53] The ANC initially tried to delegitimise both the Inkatha Freedom Party (IFP) and the NP. In the case of the IFP the ANC has recently switched to an attempt at co-optation with offers of a deputy presidency to its leader and other rewards. It demonstrates well the point of Levite and Tarrow that delegitimation is not irreversible when the excluded party proves to be too hard a nut to crack or can help the dominant party to address some intractable problems or meet some major challenges like war. This is indeed true of the IFP which cannot be eliminated in the KwaZulu-Natal area while retaining its strong traditional Zulu base.

In the case of the NP the attempt at delegitimation has taken two forms. First, it is accused of clinging to white privilege and racialising politics. The NP has captured the support of most whites, coloureds and Indians—groups who are most likely to be affected adversely by affirmative action and Africanisation. Nevertheless the NP's success in capturing their support is seen by its critics as a reprehensible exploitation of racial prejudice. Recently an ANC leader in the Western Cape, which is controlled by the NP, called the province a place where "anti-democratic" forces still hold sway and where the road to non-racialism is still blocked.[54]

---

53 Ariel Levite and Sidney Tarrow, "The Legitimation of Excluded Parties in Dominant Party Systems", *Comparative Politics*, (1983), pp. 295–323.
54 *Die Burger*, 30 September 1996, p. 2.

Second, the present NP is projected as still the party of apartheid. Apartheid is depicted as a crime against humanity and a form of genocide. Leading ANC figures accuse NP cabinets and the State Security Council of having issued orders to kill black activists during the final decade of NP rule. In this vein an ANC Deputy Minister brands ex-President De Klerk as a "bald-headed criminal whose hands are dripping with blood". Sometimes the delegitimation takes ethnic forms to which Mandela occasionally also resorts. When an ANC local politician was assassinated he told the black funeral crowd: "Once the *Boere* [a derogatory term for Afrikaners] killed you, but now the Boere use certain black people to murder other black people." He declared in Harare that there is persistent bitterness among the white majority who "finds it difficult to reconcile itself with a black democratic movement which has destroyed white supremacy".[55] In true syncretic fashion such statements are mixed with calls for racial conciliation.

The leverage of the minorities in South Africa lies in their possession of the skills, expertise and capital necessary for the high growth that the ANC needs to be able to meet at least some mass expectations. The democratic transition can be successful only if some compromise can be found between the majority and the minorities, and a willingness on both sides to work for a more equitable distribution of wealth and income. Recently a white ANC member of Parliament urged the Democratic Party, historically the party of the English middle class which won 2 per cent of the 1994 vote, to join the Government of National Unity in the wake of the NP's withdrawal. His argument was that while the ANC has kept the confidence of blacks in a transition that could offer no quick fixes, it needed a partner in government to counteract the growing opposition or apathy of whites, mobilising them "to make mass democracy work".[56] Mandela is known to feel that the opposition parties by pandering to their non-African constituencies have not assisted in consolidating the new democracy. In discussing with Mandela an ANC offer of cabinet seats, the DP discovered that he had in mind the model of the hegemonic party in Zimbabwe. Described by Du Toit in his chapter, this system prevents members of the ruling coalition airing contested issues in public. This was hardly the sort of "coalition arrangement" that would appeal to any opposition party, particularly not the DP, which is accustomed to boldly speaking its mind.[57]

---

55 *Die Burger*, 19 May 1997; *Cape Times*, 22 May 1997 and *Die Burger*, 26 May 1997.
56 Willie Hofmeyr, "DP could make a difference...." *Cape Times*, 27 February 1997, p. 6.
57 Anthony Johnson, "Mandela lets parties off the hook", *Cape Times*, 5 March 1997.

Given the fact that blacks form more than three-quarters of the population, ANC rule seems assured as long as this racial stigma can be attached to any criticism of the government by minority-based parties. Yet the ANC control of a compact black bloc is a phenomenon that dates back only to the early 1990s (or to the 1980s, as said earlier). Opposition parties confidently expect that some major split will eventually occur in the ruling party, particularly once the masses conclude that the ANC and liberation have failed them. A split, however, is unlikely for the present. In his chapter Schlemmer reports on surveys which probed the prospects of a power balance emerging through strengthened black opposition to government. While about one-quarter of blacks have a strong commitment to the principle of opposition and limits on majority rule, at least one half was found to be "hegemonically oriented", a finding that endorses Pempel's observation that a party which has served as a national saviour enjoys long-term benefits. Significantly, high school graduates were found to be less tolerant of opposition influence than rank-and-file voters. Schlemmer comments that the emergence of a new black middle class fed by such graduates will not strengthen democracy for some time to come. This is a subject to which we return in the section on the middle class in Malaysia.

The opposition in South Africa nevertheless still nourishes the hope that a broad black middle class will emerge that by pursuing their class interests will break the racial mould of politics and usher in a system of competitive party politics. The Malaysian experience fundamentally challenges the theory which holds that broad-based economic development produces a middle class that supports a multi-party democracy. While the middle class expanded from 12 per cent of the population in 1970 to 25 per cent in 1995, Malaysia has regressed to a mere semi-democracy. The crunch came in the mid-1980s when a sharp recession hit the economy.[58] There were signs of the new segment of the Malay middle class becoming disenchanted when state patronage began to run short. The question of opposition politics became particularly acute in 1986 when the defeated candidate in a succession struggle in UMNO broke away to form a rival party, Semangat '46. Would economic difficulties cause UMNO to suffer a major loss of support, thus shifting Malaysia from dominant party rule to a competitive system?

For this to happen it was necessary, as Jesudason argues, for the new middle class (i) to strengthen an autonomous civil society, (ii) develop interests that diverge from those of the dominant party and the state, and (iii) construct a coalition and alternative policy programme that competes with the

---

58 For an extended discussion see Jesudason, *Ethnicity and the Economy*, pp. 76–123.

dominant party and its policies. But the Malay middle class stuck to the dominant party.[59] The main reason is that the state's capacity to offer patronage and incorporate a wide range of groups behind the dominant party produces what is called a statist democracy. Particularly if society is also organised ethnically, a middle class does not easily challenge or constrain a party that sponsors and underpins them. It may waver in times of economic decline or when the ethnic elite is split, but will quickly return to the fold once the ruling elites re-consolidate their power.[60] What was also prominent in the minds of the Malay elite was the risks to Malay rule of a three-way split in the Malay vote (UMNO, PAS and Semangat '46) in a first-past-the-post system. Hence in ethnically divided societies there is good cause to question the theory that broad-based economic development goes hand in hand with the rise of a middle class committed to competitive politics. South Africa is unlikely to be an exception.

TYPES OF DOMINANCE WITH DEMOCRACY (OR SEMI-DEMOCRACY)

Taken together our four cases do not display a single pattern. Yet it is possible to draw conclusions about the dominant party as a regime type and highlight both democratic and non-democratic features in its evolution. For present purposes we limit discussion to two critical features of democracy. First, there is the prerequisite that the necessary distinction between the dominant party and the state be maintained. This means the acceptance of constitutionalism and the neutrality of crucial institutions like the state media, security forces, courts and the electoral commission supervising the poll. Second, there is the constraint that power, in principle at least, is temporary, that elections must be both fair and free, and that opponents must be not only tolerated but also given sufficient scope to organise and become an alternative government. This may go as far as advancing the "level playing field" argument of the Taiwanese opposition which contends that the enormous wealth of the KMT violates the spirit of democracy.

The first form of dominant party rule can be summarised as *regime innovation in the direction of a liberal democracy*. The party in this study that most closely resembles dominant parties in advanced industrialised democracies practising a liberal democracy is the KMT. Dominance, as Duverger correctly

---

59 The above two paragraphs are based on William Case, "Semi-Democracy in Malaysia", *Pacific Affairs*, 66 (1993), pp. 183–205.

60 James Jesudason, "Statist Democracy and the Limits to Civil Society in Malaysia", *Journal of Commonwealth and Comparative Politics*, 33, 3 (1995), pp. 334–356.

stresses, goes far beyond electoral strength and this is very much true of the KMT. It depends much more on influence and the ability to reformulate divisive issues, like national sovereignty and economic and social trade-offs, in such a way that its view on them becomes the political consensus.[61] There is in the party a dynamic conservatism, and particularly an ability to draw new groups into the party apparatus and to discard the die-hards. There is also leadership skill in managing the economy and society in such a way that a virtuous cycle of dominance is recognised by all but its inveterate opponents. Undoubtedly the adaptive ability of the present leadership is due to the fact that society is much less fragmented along racial and class lines than, say, that of South Africa. But this is true of the dominant party of Singapore too, which rejects the "Western" notion of democracy. This means that some additional factors must be considered to account for the fact that Taiwan has made such progress in cleaning up the electoral process and bringing about greater separation of state and party.

Taiwan, like apartheid South Africa, demonstrates the capacity of the international community to make a difference. The road to increased international recognition for Taiwan's autonomy goes through the world's recognition of its democracy, one which can be held up as an example to other democratising nations. At the same time Taiwan's evolution in the direction of a liberal democracy has much to do with the KMT's increasing acceptance since the early 1980s of the principle of direct popular elections from the local level up to the highest executive offices. But even in the authoritarian period the KMT encouraged intra-party competition in the form of fostering electoral competition between local factions. In one respect the local factions represented the germ of rejuvenation because they made it easier in the 1980s to expand the principle of electoral competition throughout the system. It may also, however, contain the seed of destruction since the top leadership of the KMT is increasingly driven by the need to pacify local politicians. If these local politicians refuse to co-operate with party strategies the KMT could forfeit its dominant position by losing control of important executive offices or the majority in the legislature. The party's dependence on local factions enables the opposition to attack it persistently for its links to corrupt individuals and practices.[62]

A second pattern of dominance that can be highlighted is *a semi-democracy stuck halfway between authoritarianism and liberal democracy*. In Malaysia the dominant party has been successful, despite the globalisation of

---

61   Maurice Duverger, *Political Parties* (London: Methuen, 1964), p. 308.
62   The paragraph is largely based on a personal communication by Shelley Rigger, 17 June 1997.

the economy, in maintaining its all-class alliance among Malays while at the same time holding the opposition at bay. It has done so by openly utilising authoritarian practices alongside democratic procedures. The power-holders have extraordinary say about the rules of political competition and have designed laws which protect the regime from political challenge. Indefinite detention without trial has been used against leaders of opposition parties and interest groups. The press cannot publish official information without authorisation. The courts have been restructured in the interests of the executive. Gerrymandering is still practised and there have been times when electoral outcomes are not accepted until the victors from the opposition are given the chance to defect to the ruling party.[63]

The regime in fact tolerates the little democracy there is because it presents it with so few difficulties. Indeed, as Case observes, a semi-democracy which borrows "cunningly some features of democracy in order substantively to avoid it" can be a more stable and far less cumbersome system that an authoritarian one. Allowing electoralism but refusing to concede liberal contestation, the dominant alliance may enjoy a long life span, provided growth is high enough for a broad-based system of patronage. It is possible that, in a period of prolonged economic stagnation, the middle class may become impatient enough with the semi-democracy to defect from the present Malay-centred coalition. But of that there is still no sign.[64]

In Mexico the dominant party is greatly weakened in the process of trying to progress from a semi-democracy to a liberal democracy. In recent times the PRI has been unable to incorporate two important new interest groups, namely the middle class and the informal sector, that have grown up outside its corporatist framework. Despite its commitment to the liberal macro-economic framework it has not shed its labour base but remains dependent on it. For its part the old, oligarchic "official" labour faction continues to cling to the party, hoping to revive its populist character. As Cook argues, the PRI needs a new corporatist relationship with organised labour which is autonomous and free of party control. Such an arrangement cannot be a substitute for a liberal democracy but must complement it.

Furthermore, in negotiating with the opposition generally accepted rules for the conduct of democratic competition, the PRI will have to relinquish its position at the commanding heights. But this is precisely the problem. The

---

63 James Jesudason, "Statist Democracy and the Limits to Civil Society in Malaysia", *Journal of Commonwealth and Comparative and Commonwealth Politics*, 33, 3 (1995), pp. 337–38.

64 William Case, "Semi-Democracy in Malaysia: Withstanding the Pressures for Regime Change", *Pacific Affairs*, 66 (1993), pp. 183–205.

PRI has a long history of negotiating pacts with its labour partners, business and opposition parties in which it could largely impose its will, offering only minor concessions that did not undercut its dominance. The kind of trust and mutual recognition required to negotiate new democratic rules and institutions has increased in recent times, but is still in rather short supply.[65] Thus the regime may continue to have its dominance eroded without being able to rejuvenate itself or provide the base for the transition to a liberal democracy.

The third pattern of dominance is that of *presiding over an eroding liberal democracy in the direction of mere majoritarianism and electoralism*. Here we have a regime with many of the features of liberal democracy and the assumptions of a competitive party system acting as a cloak for domination of one group over the other. Well before the transition to democracy van den Berghe, one of apartheid's fiercest academic critics, remarked about the black demand for an "ordinary" democracy: "If your constituency has the good fortune to contain a demographic majority, racism can easily be disguised as democracy. The ideological slight of hand is, of course, that an ascriptive, racially-defined majority is a far cry from a majority made up of shifting coalitions of individuals on the basis of commonality of beliefs and interests."[66] In a study published just before the constitutional negotiations in South Africa began, Horowitz warned of election results which amount to an ethnic census which expresses more the population's ethnic composition than anything else. He made this comment: "If majority rule means Black majority rule and White exclusion something has gone wrong...If democracy is defined as a system of 'rule by temporary majorities', rule by permanent majorities is clearly incompatible".[67]

As we have said, South Africa's new democracy has launched itself with some impressive democratic features including a progressive Bill of Rights, a market-driven economy, an independent judiciary, a vigorous civil society (albeit one that is splintered largely along ethnic lines), a state whose key institutions like the courts and police are not seen as "belonging" to any group, and a free press that reports extensively on corruption. The management of elections is in the hands of an independent electoral commission and legislation is being prepared to regulate electoral funding. The need for foreign investment and the pressure of global markets are so great that

---

65 Laurence Whitehead, "An Elusive Transition: The Slow Motion Demise of Authoritarian Dominant Party Rule in Mexico", *Democratization*, Vol. 2 No. 3 (1995), pp. 246–269.

66 Pierre van den Berghe, "Introduction", Pierre van den Berghe ed., *The Liberal Dilemma in South Africa* (New York: St Martin's Press, 1979), p. 7.

67 Donald Horowitz, *A Democratic South Africa? Constitutional Engineering in a Divided Society* (Cape Town: Oxford University Press, 1991), pp. 96, 98.

government cannot harass the opposition or violate rights, particularly property rights, without incurring serious financial and economic costs.

The system that was negotiated produced the "ethnic census" in the electoral result which Horowitz anticipated and with that a permanent black majority and a permanent white exclusion from political power. In the 1994 election more than 95 per cent of white and black voters respectively opted for the historically white and black parties. The ANC itself relies for over 90 per cent on black support, but has attracted less than a third of the support of the coloured and Indian communities and only 3 to 4 per cent of that of whites. A future in which democracy is not a facade, and the press is independent and free, depends in the first place on countervailing pressures from civil society and opposition parties. But it also depends heavily on an ANC leadership resisting demands in its own ranks to emasculate these institutions.[68]

The ethnic census quality of the 1994 result has given rise to the widespread belief that the ANC's dominance will be prolonged, and this, more than the new government's performance, bolsters the power of the dominant party and saps opposition confidence. Friedman's chapter appropriately highlights the limits to ANC dominance, but one can mention only two factors that will entrench domination: the desire of blacks to catch up collectively with whites and the closed list PR electoral system that will continue to polarise the voters along the fault line of race. The main question about the democratic system is whether the ANC will be able to handle minorities in such a way that they remain committed to the system. Whites, coloureds and Indians, either in an individual or a corporate capacity, pay three-quarters of the total tax.[69] Nevertheless the NP, which in 1994 won 60 per cent of the vote in each of these communities, is no longer in cabinet. There is now no broad-based racial coalition like the one of Malaysia that, symbolically at least, transcends the deep divisions of society and that could legitimise new taxes piled on to an already heavy tax burden. The tax burden and government inability to deal effectively with crime and the perceived ineffectualness of the opposition are likely to produce alienation on the part of the minorities, particularly whites. Since the election of 1994 the proportion of whites who in polls declare that they will not vote or are most unlikely to vote, has risen from 29 to 42 per cent.

---

68 This is a general threat to polities establishing a democracy in conditions of declining or stagnant real income per head. See the editorial conclusion in Stephan Haggard and Robert Kaufman eds., *The Politics of Economic Adjustment: International Constraints, Distributive Conflicts and the State* (Princeton: Princeton University Press, 1992).

69 Personal communication, J.L. Sadie, 2 July 1997.

Many liberals refuse to see the dangers of minorities defecting from a facade liberal democracy. Yet there is clear evidence of an enormous concentration of power at the centre. The ANC's absolute majority in Parliament has produced a political arrangement that in all but name is a Westminster one.[70] The Westminster model is characterised by a highly centralised form of parliamentary government of which the core is the unity of the legislature and executive with the latter clearly predominating. The executive maintains strict caucus discipline and refuses to disperse any significant power to the second and third tiers of government.[71] Westminster makes for parties rigidly controlled by the leadership. While initially there was the hope of a strong and independent ANC legislature, recent developments indicate leadership intolerance of any criticism of an ANC minister by representatives of the party regardless of the charges levelled against him or her.[72] The alternation or potential alternation of government, which is the real (and only) safety valve of the Westminster model, is generally not available in deeply divided societies and certainly not in a dominant party system. For this reason divided societies that have attained stability have moved away from the Westminster model to adopt one whose essence is a sharing of power between parties that essentially represent communities.[73]

The majoritarian principle has come increasingly into play instead of devices that strike a balance between the majority and the minority. In drawing up the final constitution the ANC insisted that appointments to key offices like the Public Protector and the Auditor General are by a simple majority, something which the ANC is likely to have for the foreseeable future. In official commissions, like the Truth and Reconciliation Commission investigating apartheid era human rights abuses, and the Human Rights Commission, the overwhelming number of members appointed by the new government are known to be ANC supporters. None of the judges on the Constitutional Court is known to share the views or have sympathy for the NP or IFP, the main opposition parties. By contrast, several of the judges have appeared to

---

70 Constitution-makers have slightly softened the Westminster variant by making sovereign certain constitutional principles and a special Constitutional Court rather than Parliament. But the principles are so vague and broad that it is essential for the legitimacy of the court's interpretations that there be a proper political balance in the composition of the bench as in the Supreme Court.

71 Graham Wilson, "The Westminster Model in Comparative Perspective", in I. Budge and D. Mackay eds., *Developing Democracy* (London: Sage, 1994), pp. 189–201.

72 One of the first analyses of the functioning of the ANC was presented at the conference on which this book is based. See Richard Calland, "Acclimation, Adaptation and Assertion in a time of institutional change: the ANC's Parliamentary Party, 1994–1996", unpublished paper.

73 Vernon Bogdanor, "Forms of Autonomy and the Protection of Minorities", *Daedalus*, 126, 2 (1997), pp. 65–66.

be either open or tacit supporters of the ANC. The presiding judge has been a long-time functionary of the South African Communist Party which forms part of the ANC alliance. Finally, while whites still occupy half of the middle and top positions of the central state apparatus, there is a steady trend towards the replacement of them by ANC supporters.

At an early stage there is evidence of the erosion of the autonomy of some key institutions. The autonomy of the attorney-general in each province has been removed. Instead a new "super" attorney-general, who will be a political appointment, will lay down policy and ensure compliance. The Minister of Justice has publicly welcomed an ex-ANC leader returning to the country to face criminal charges. Despite an outcry, the minister defiantly declared that "I draw no distinction between the ANC and the government".[74] A cabinet minister has questioned the integrity of the auditor-general despite the constitutional obligation on government departments to assist this office.

The ANC has concentrated power at the centre, particularly with respect to policing, education, health and sport. It seems set to intervene extensively in employment practices in the private sector. Powerful voices insist that semi-state institutions and the private sector be compelled to change their employment practices in such ways that the labour force, right up to top management level, reflect the population composition. The danger here, as the Malaysian case so clearly demonstrates, is of a dominant party invasion into the autonomy of economic and cultural institutions that ends up by creating zones where the party can cut deals, apportion benefits and apply punishments.[75]

Paradoxically, the overall result of an over-concentration of power in South Africa may end up in the ANC getting more and more power over less and less. Unless there is a reversal of policies the result may be a steady deterioration of central state power and the steady parcelling out of state sovereignty of which Kaufman writes in the Mexican case. In South Africa a continuing ANC refusal to devolve policing functions to the provinces and a persistence with the rapid enforcement of affirmative action in the legal system could mean an erosion of legitimacy and an acceleration of de facto power shifting to crime bosses, drug lords and corrupt businessmen. Accompanying problems of legitimacy has been a serious decline in the performance of the criminal justice system. In the past 20 years the crimes reported for every 100,000 South Africans increased by a third but the conviction rate fell by nearly a

74 *Rapport*, 6 July 1997, "Kwaad en verbitter…". He did promise not to interfere in the court case.
75 Martin Woolacott, "Overweening elite that runs Malaysia", *Weekly Mail and Guardian*, March 11 to 17, 1994, p. 25.

third. The odds of a perpetrator of a serious crime being convicted are estimated to be about 20 to 1. The number of criminal convictions in absolute terms is now the lowest in 40 years despite dramatic increases in the population and crime rate. A collapse in the morale of those manning the criminal justice system (partly the result of affirmative action policies) is shown by the resignation of one-third of the total number of state prosecutors during the past two years.[76] Personal security has been substantially privatised; already personnel in the private security industry are double those in the police services.

There has been a growing privatisation of other state services, often occurring in ways cloaked for political reasons. Private schools are growing rapidly in the face of plummeting standards in state schools. Wary of giving significant power to the provinces, the new government has tried to build up local authorities as points of decentralised delivery and accountability. But the capacity of these bodies is suspect. The responsible government department calculated that of approximately 700 local governments one-third can manage, one-third are salvagable and one-third are in varying stages of collapse. Bankrupt local authorities may be forced to privatise many services. In the deep rural areas the problem is even more acute and traditional authority often provides the most important source of stability.[77] Yet the ANC wishes to replace it with elected officials. Overall there is an increasing tendency on the part of important groups and sectors, ranging from white parents and municipal ratepayers to traditional chiefs, to opt out of the state. This may turn the ANC's dominance of it into a hollow shell.

The concentration of power at the centre of government has not been accompanied by a growth of the ANC as party organisation. For the present the ANC can count on a whole array of black civic bodies, student organisations and trade unions to mobilise the masses to support it at election times. But the ministerial/parliamentary wing of the party overshadows the organisational wing. The latter suffers from a declining number of paid-up members, a dwindling number of branches and severe financial problems, necessitating the retrenchment of large part of the party's full-time staff. Compared to, say, the dominant party in India during the first two decades after independence, the ANC as a party does not have nearly the same political

---

76 Colin Douglas "Dit lyk of die staat heeltemal in duie stort", *Die Burger*, 25 June 1997, *Fast Facts*, June 1997.

77 F. van Zyl Slabbert, "Key Issues in Post-Liberation Politics in South Africa", paper presented to a conference of the Konrad Adenauer Foundation on "A Future South Africa", 10–12 September 1997.

substance and penetration to bring about elite–mass integration, and, over the longer run, probably not other forms of political and territorial integration either.[78]

The PR closed list gives the party leadership unrivalled control over the party and its representatives, but the absence of any constituency link produces, particularly in rural areas of developing countries, what has been called the "suspended state". A party that has become driven by power and patronage can offer little to the destitute eking out a living on the land or waiting for remittances from the cities. Grossly neglected by the apartheid state, rural blacks have been most bitterly disappointed by the new ruling party. The traditional elites and particularly the chiefs and headmen feel threatened by the modernist policies of the new government. The populations over which they have control are mass concentrations, remote from infrastructure and notoriously under-policed.[79] Polls show that it is among them that disillusionment is the most severe. While they pose no immediate security threat, it is not far-fetched to see a rural revolt somewhere in the more distant future which can impart a severe shock to the system, like the Chiapas uprising in Mexico that led to large-scale capital flight.

CONCLUSION

Several variables affect the adaptive capacity of the dominant party and its ability to deepen the democratic system over which it presides. Broad-based economic development which narrows inequalities and improves per capita incomes is undoubtedly most desirable for movement in the direction of a liberal democracy with a competitive party system. It is no coincidence that the prospects for democracy are best in Taiwan where inequalities between the top and lowest quintiles were the narrowest in the industrialising world when it embarked on democratisation. By contrast, Mexico and South Africa show the greatest inequality among the countries for which data are available and the prospects for a stable and lasting liberal democracy are uncertain. The ANC is also a racially based party and the great test will be how, in conditions of low economic growth, the party will handle white–black inequalities.

---

78 See the essays in A. Jeyaratnam Wilson and Dennis Dalton, *The States of South Asia: Problems of National Integration* (London: D.C. Hurst, 1982).

79 Lawrence Schlemmer, "Education and Culture: Prospects for Progress and Peace in South Africa", paper presented to the conference "A Future South Africa", held on 10–12 September 1997.

The second variable relates to the character of the dominant party. Of crucial importance is the question whether it contains in its ranks both organised labour and a middle class that has been advanced through ethnic preference policies in the civil service and through state contracts. While these classes serve to consolidate the party's dominance, their incorporation stifles the development of democratic pluralism. For a competitive party system it is particularly important that labour develops political autonomy with respect to the party that initially championed it, but the chance of that is remote in a system that is racially or ethnically based. Finally leadership and contingent choice also play an extraordinary role. Leaders can broaden a democracy as Chiang Ching-kuo did in Taiwan in 1986, fail to institutionalise a liberal democracy as Salinas did in Mexico, or steer the party into a more authoritarian direction as Lee and Mahatir are doing in Singapore and Malaysia respectively. It is ultimately leaders who get the party to submit to at least some democratic procedures while pursuing a national project that they believe will entrench party domination, that push their political system in a more democratic direction.

Chapter 2

STABILITY AND COMPETITIVENESS IN THE POLITICAL CONFIGURATIONS OF SEMI-DEVELOPED COUNTRIES

CHARLES SIMKINS

INTRODUCTION

The purpose of this background study is to locate democracies with dominant parties in semi-developed countries in the context of social, economic and political conditions more generally. Dominant parties in advanced industrial countries have been studied by T.J. Pempel[1], who described them as "uncommon democracies" against the background of competitive democratic systems. It will be seen that dominant party democracies are uncommon in semi-developed countries as well, but that the background is different and more diverse.

THE LIPSET HYPOTHESIS AND SEMI-DEVELOPED COUNTRIES

The Lipset hypothesis relates democracy and development: the greater the level of economic development, the more likely is the political system to be democratic. There are many undemocratic poor countries, while virtually all rich countries are democratic. The relationship is less clear in semi-developed countries; for this reason, some analysts characterise the middle income range as a "zone of transition" in which the prospects for democracy depend more heavily on political history than the level of income per capita.

The World Development Report lists 24 countries with incomes per capita in excess of US$ 9,000 in 1994. Of these, 21 were rated "free" by Freedom House in 1993/94, while three (Kuwait, Hong Kong and Singapore) were rated "partly free". This is the top end of a pattern underlying the Lipset hypothesis of a positive relationship between economic development and democracy.

Immediately below these 24 countries, there is a set of 35 countries with incomes per capita of between US$ 1,800 and US$ 9,000 in 1994. These countries are listed in Table 2.1. A country starting at the bottom of the

---

1 T.J. Pempel, *Uncommon democracies: the one-party dominant regimes* (Ithaca, Cornell University Press).

range, and sustaining a quite rapid per capita income growth rate of 2.5 per cent p.a. would take 65 years to get to the top. During the decade from 1985 to 1994, the median rate of growth in per capita income in the 32 countries for which there are data was much lower—only 0.7 per cent p.a. and 15 suffered declines in real per capita income. Only seven saw incomes per capita rise more than 3 per cent p.a. Apart from the East Asian countries, semi-developed countries have not displayed a pattern of continuous economic progress.

Nonetheless, the Lipset hypothesis would also suggest that middle income countries are the most promising candidates for democracy next to advanced industrial countries. Indeed, 15 middle income countries were rated as "free" by Freedom House in 1993/94, with sixteen rated "partly free" and four (all in the North Africa/Middle East region) as "not free". These ratings are based on two indices: the political rights index and the civil rights index. Both indices range from one (high degree of political and civil rights) to seven (absence of these rights) and Diamond[2] has suggested that one can simply add these up to get an indicator of democratic rule. Free countries have a joint score of less than five and unfree countries a score of more than ten, with partly free countries inhabiting the middle range.

Does the Lipset hypothesis hold across the subset of 34 semi-developed countries for which there were data in 1994? At first sight, it appears not. One can find no significant correlation between the index of democracy on the one hand and income per capita (measured either on an exchange rate or on a purchasing power parity basis) on the other. However, there is a strong correlation between the United Nations human development index (based on literacy and schooling) and the index of democracy. One may also apply a factor analysis to the three measures of development to identify three linear combinations of the measures (the factors), between which there is as little correlation as possible. Most of the correlation between the three measures is captured in the dominant factor, which can be interpreted to represent socio-economic development in general. There is a strong correlation between this factor and the index of democracy, provided that the North African/Middle Eastern countries are left out. The minimum socio-economic characteristics to reach a democracy index of five (the lowest "free" category) seem to be a PPP income per capita of about $ 7,000 and a human development index of 0.825. Table 2 displays the value of these variables for Malaysia, Mexico and South Africa. Of these three, South Africa is least well positioned. Taiwan, on the other hand, lies above all three.

---

2 Larry Diamond, Economic development and democracy reconsidered, *American Behavioural Scientist*, 35, 1992.

Comparable data for Taiwan are not readily available because of its particular international status, but the levels of both indicators are higher than for Malaysia, Mexico and South Africa.

Table 2.1: PPP income per capita and the Human Development Index, 1993/94

Country	Income per capita US$	Human Development Index
Malaysia	8,440	0.826
Mexico	7,040	0.845
South Africa	5,140	0.649

THEORETICAL APPROACHES TO DOMINANT PARTIES

Conceptualising a dominant party

Sartori[3] distinguishes between two types of dominant party system: the "predominant party system" on the one hand, and the "hegemonic party system" on the other. In Sartori's view, the first category refers to the limiting case of a competitive political system, in which one party outdistances its rivals, with the condition that the predominant party can cease, at any moment, to be predominant. By definition predominant party systems must contain more than one party and circumstances must be imaginable in which challenger parties can defeat the predominant party.

The second category refers to a non-competitive situation—not only does alternation not occur, it cannot occur. Sartori makes a further distinction between a "hegemonic party system" and a "one party system proper". In the latter, all but one party is outlawed, whereas peripheral parties exist in the former, but with firm mechanisms to ensure that they are permanently excluded from state power. A hegemonic party system does not allow open contestation or effective dissent. Fraudulent elections, internal repression and a muzzled press are mechanisms for suppressing competition.

Party dominance is not easy to sustain in advanced industrial societies with well-established democratic institutions and a strong civil society. Parties, like other organisations, find it difficult to adapt to changing external circumstances. Party dominance characteristically arises when a coalition of interests develops a successful approach to overcoming a crisis and this programme may keep the party safe from defeat for many years—the Social Democratic Party in Sweden and the Liberal Democratic Party in Japan are two

---

3 Giovanni Sartori, *Parties and party systems: a framework for analysis*, Volume I, Cambridge University Press, 1976.

examples. Party alternation finally happens when the programme on which a ruling party was elected turns out not to be viable and attempts at changing course fail.

The situation is different in semi-developed countries with weaker institutions and civil society. A dominant party can close the circuits of power, using control of the state to keep its existing supporters content and its opponents disorganised. And herein lies the threat of a dominant party to democracy: one of the possible uses of state power is to diminish competition in the electoral arena and to undermine rules supporting competition. Weaknesses of institutionalisation and accountability can reinforce weakness of contestation.

Sartori believed that no examples could be found of a transition between a predominant party system and a hegemonic party system. But there seems no ground for expecting this conceptual distinction to correspond to experience in semi-developed countries with dominant parties. Indeed, an important theme to look for in Malaysia, Mexico and South Africa is precisely the struggle between political competition and closure and the implications of the outcomes for the quality of political systems which are formally democratic.

Sartori also made a distinction between ideological and pragmatic dominant parties; the clearest examples of the former category could be found among formerly communist countries. There was also a less coherent rationale for one-party systems in some post-colonial African states. In the 1990s, the ideological set is empty or almost empty; dominant parties are nearly all pragmatic now.

Freedom House on dominant and one-party systems and political rights

In addition to political rights and civil rights indices, Freedom House[4] offers brief verbal characterisations of political systems round the world. Theorisation of dominant party systems is not Freedom House's long suit and the single sentence of definition in its 1993/94 report is too brief to be adequate: "Dominant party polities are systems in which the ruling party (or front) dominates government, but allows other parties to organise or compete short of taking control of government". A look at the countries classified as one party or dominant party systems reveals rather more about the implicit criteria in use, as the following analysis shows.

---

4 Freedom House, *Freedom in the World: the annual survey of political rights and civil liberties 1993–94*, New York, 1994.

Forty countries are listed as being one party or dominant party systems in 1993. Eighteen of them belong to the World Bank's low income category and a further fourteen to the lower reaches of the lower middle income category. For the purposes of this study, the remaining eight are of interest. They are:

Upper reaches of the lower middle income category: Tunisia
Upper middle income category: Antigua/Barbuda, Gabon, Malaysia, Mexico and Seychelles
High income category: Singapore and Taiwan.
(South Africa is left out of account here because of the political transition in 1993/94.)

Of the forty countries in all income groups, three have a political rights index of 3, six of 4, six of 5, seventeen of 6 and eight of 7. The mean score is 5.5. Since the worst score is 7, Freedom House is effectively using the hegemonic party rather than the predominant party definition of a dominant party system. In other words, there must be evidence of substantial limitations on political rights before Freedom House uses the dominant party characterisation. This is further confirmed by the fact that a country like Botswana, ruled continuously by the Botswana Democratic Party since independence in 1966, is not classified as a dominant party system.

In general, Freedom House's political and civil rights indices are more useful than its brief categorisations of political systems. Its dominant party category conceals as much as it reveals. Its more detailed current accounts of political conditions are of more interest. They need, however, to be complemented by a historically based typology of political conditions in order to illustrate the circumstances in which dominant parties have arisen in semi-developed countries.

COMPARATIVE APPROACHES TO DOMINANT PARTY SYSTEMS IN
SEMI-DEVELOPED COUNTRIES

Introduction
As background to the analysis, political chronologies have been constructed for 24 semi-developed countries[5]. They include all countries with populations of more than a million with incomes between US$ 1800 and $ 9,000 in

---

5 These chronologies were complied from Arthur S. Banks (ed), *Political handbook of the world: 1986*, CSA Publications, State University of New York, 1986 and Europa Publications Limited, *Europa World Yearbook*, 36th edition, London, 1995.

1994. Korea, Singapore and Taiwan have been included, while countries in Eastern Europe and the former Soviet Union have been excluded, as well as South Africa and Namibia. These exclusions are not because the post-communist and post-apartheid countries are uninteresting, but because their political histories following the fall of communism and apartheid are too brief to support the sort of analysis which follows.

Among the 24 countries are five Asian countries (Korea, Malaysia, Singapore, Taiwan and Thailand), ten Latin American countries (Argentina, Brazil, Chile, Costa Rica, Mexico, Panama, Peru, Trinidad, Uruguay and Venezuela), five Middle Eastern/North African countries (Iran, Oman, Saudi Arabia, Turkey and Tunisia), three African countries (Botswana, Gabon and Mauritius) and Greece.

Regime history
The most important dimension of analysis is that of regime type, considered in terms of the following classification:

(a)   stable competitive democracies
(b)   stable dominant parties
(c)   alternation between periods of competitive or dominant party rule, and authoritarian rule of various kinds
(d)   persistent authoritarian rule.

None of the countries has been under continuous military rule since 1960, but nine of them have had one or more spells of it. In addition, two countries have undergone revolutions or non-military coups. Five have had significant states of emergency and one a long standing state of martial law. One is an absolute monarchy.

These leaves only six countries under continuous civilian rule without a spell of martial law or a significant state of emergency. Three have been ruled by the same party (Singapore, Mexico and Botswana). Gabon had a one-party system between 1964 and 1990, and then declared a switch to a multi-party system with a government of national unity, with limited effect, since the legitimacy of the system remains in question. The two countries which most resemble advanced industrial countries with stable party systems and alternation in power are both Latin American: Costa Rica and Venezuela.

Political parties
Military rule, states of emergency, martial law and revolution have all played an important role in reshaping party configurations in subsequent periods of

civilian rule, a phenomenon unknown in advanced industrial countries since 1960. Active state reshaping of the party configuration during a period of authoritarian rule has been common, occurring in Thailand, Korea, Brazil, Panama and Turkey. Suspensions of civilian rule have served to bolster the position of a dominant party in Taiwan, Malaysia and Tunisia. In two countries, military rule changed the balance between right and left, intervening against socialist rule in Chile and Peronism in Argentina. In one case, revolution advanced the cause of Islamic fundamentalism (Iran); in another, a coup dealt with the succession problem in a traditional monarchy (Oman). Only in four cases has military rule or a state of emergency had little impact on parties. Competitive political parties, in short, appear rather fragile in semi-developed countries and are liable to suppression and reshaping by forces other than the will of the electorate.

Dominant parties in semi-developed countries

It is against this rather turbulent and fluid background, with frequent authoritarian episodes, that dominant parties in semi-developed countries need to be interpreted. The authoritarian backdrop invests dominant parties themselves in semi-developed countries with a degree of authoritarianism not present in their advanced industrial counterparts. It is noteworthy that for more than half a century, Mexico has not suffered the military coups affecting large Latin American states—Argentina, Brazil and Chile. Equally, Malaysia has not undergone the military interventions or revolutions seen since 1960 in neighbouring south-east Asian states. And some analysts have suggested that the political transition in South Africa has been eased by a dominant party in the wings; greater political fragmentation might have complicated the transfer of power. Political co-ordination through a dominant party can be seen as substituting for more overt forms of authoritarian control as a bulwark against political instability. The authoritarian strain is also likely to be considerable in cases where there has been no competitive democratic configuration preceding the rule of a dominant party.

Semi-developed countries with dominant parties can be divided into three categories. The first consists of countries with dominant parties which liberalised or have attempted to liberalise in the last decade—Gabon, Taiwan and Tunisia. Of these liberalisations, Taiwan has been the most successful, not surprisingly in the light of the Lipset hypothesis and its now high level of per capita income. The second group consists of countries with non-liberalising dominant parties: Malaysia and Singapore. Mexico is an intermediate case, with the dominant party apparently in terminal decline, but without a coherent programme of liberalisation.

Table 2.2: Key Indicators for Semi-developed Countries

Country	Region	GNP per capita US$ 1994	GNP per capita PPP US$ 1994	GNP per capita growth 1985–1994	Human development index 1993	Freedom House indices Political rights	Freedom House indices Civil liberties	Index of democracy	Expected index of democracy	
Tunisia	NM	1,790	5,020	2.1	0.727	6	5	11	Not free	
Ukraine	FS	1,910	2,620	−8.0	0.719	4	4	8	Partly free	8
Namibia	AF	1,970	4,320	3.3	0.573	2	3	5	Free	7
Peru	LA	2,110	3,610	−2.0	0.694	5	5	10	Partly free	7
Belarus	FS	2,160	4,320	−1.9	0.787	5	4	9	Partly free	7
Slovak Republic	EE	2,250		−3.0	0.864	3	4	7	Partly free	
Latvia	FS	2,320	3,220	−6.0	0.820	3	3	6	Partly free	7
Costa Rica	LA	2,400		2.8	0.884	1	2	3	Free	
Poland	EE	2,410	5,480	0.8	0.819	2	2	4	Free	6
Thailand	EA	2,410	6,970	8.6	0.832	3	5	8	Partly free	6
Turkey	NM	2,500	4,710	1.4	0.711	4	4	8	Partly free	
Croatia	EE	2,560				4	4	8	Partly free	
Panama	LA	2,580	5,730	−1.2	0.859	3	3	6	Partly free	6
Russian Federation	FS	2,650	4,610	−4.1	0.804	3	4	7	Partly free	7
Venezuela	LA	2,760	7,770	0.7	0.859	3	3	6	Partly free	5
Botswana	AF	2,800	5,210	6.6	0.741	2	3	5	Free	7
Estonia	FS	2,820	4,510	−6.1	0.749	3	2	5	Free	7
Iran	NM				0.754	6	7	13	Not free	
Brazil	LA	2,970	5,400	−0.4	0.796	3	4	7	Partly free	6

Country	Region	GNP per capita US$ 1994	GNP per capita PPP US$ 1994	GNP per capita growth 1985–1994	Human development index 1993	Freedom House indices Political rights	Freedom House indices Civil liberties	Index of democracy	Expected index of democracy	
South Africa	AF	3,040	5,130	-1.3	0.649	5	4	9	Partly free	7
Mauritius	AF	3,150	12,720	5.8	0.825	1	2	3	Free	4
Czech Republic	EE	3,200	8,900	-2.1	0.872	1	2	3	Free	5
Malaysia	EA	3,480	8,440	5.6	0.826	4	5	9	Partly free	5
Chile	LA	3,520	8,890	6.5	0.882	2	2	4	Free	5
Trinidad & Tobago	LA	3,740	8,670	-2.3	0.872	1	1	2	Free	5
Hungary	EE	3,840	6,080	-1.2	0.855	1	2	3	Free	6
Gabon	AF	3,880		-3.7	0.557	5	4	9	Partly free	
Mexico	LA	4,180	7,040	0.9	0.845	4	4	8	Partly free	5
Uruguay	LA	4,660	7,710	2.9	0.883	2	2	4	Free	5
Oman	NM	5,140	8,590	0.5	0.716	6	6	12	Not free	
Slovenia	EE	7,040	6,230		0.771	1	2	3	Free	
Saudi Arabia	NM	7,050	9,480	-1.7		7	7	14	Not free	
Greece	SE	7,700	10,930	1.3	0.909	1	3	4	Free	4
Argentina	LA	8,110	8,720	2.0	0.885	2	3	5	Free	4
Korea	EA	8,260	10,330	7.8	0.886	2	2	4	Free	3

Table 2.2 (*contd.*)

Country	Region	GNP per capita US$ 1994	GNP per capita PPP US$ 1994	GNP per capita growth 1985–1994	Human development index 1993	Freedom House indices Political rights	Freedom House indices Civil liberties	Index of democracy	Expected index of democracy
				Average	Average	Average	Average	Average	
East Asia (EA)	3			7.3	0.848	3.0	4.0	7.0	
Eastern Europe (EE)	6			−1.4	0.853	2.0	2.7	4.7	
Former Soviet Union (FS)	5			−5.2	0.776	3.6	3.4	7.0	
Latin America (LA)	10			1.0	0.846	2.6	2.9	5.5	
North Africa/Mid East (NM)	5			0.6	0.736	5.8	5.8	11.6	
Southern Europe (SE)	1			1.3	0.909	1.0	3.0	4.0	
SubSaharan Africa (AF)	5			2.1	0.669	3.0	3.2	6.2	

Sources GNP per capita–World Development Report

Human development index–United Nations, Human Development Report

Political and civil rights indices–Freedom House, Freedom in the World

Note The "expected index of democracy" is predicted from the two measures of GNP per capita and the human development index.

Dominant party projects

Pempel accounts for the persistence of a dominant party's rule in an advanced industrial country by its ability to hold together a majority coalition of interests around a project with enduring appeal. In the case of Sweden, it took the form of economic development under social democratic auspices—a project capable of taking Sweden through the Depression, the war and the post-war expansion under the Bretton Woods system, but not through the more recent phase of globalisation. In Japan, the post-war project was one of peaceful reconstruction and then further export-based growth under the American military umbrella.

Can "projects" be identified for dominant parties in semi-developed countries? It appears that the project in both Singapore and Taiwan has been rapid economic growth; in both countries, fear of the political consequences of poor economic performance in relation to large neighbours (Malaysia and Indonesia in the case of Singapore, China in the case of Taiwan) has helped to promote widespread acceptance of the project. Malaysia's project has changed somewhat over the last twenty-five years: from an initial stress on the incorporation of Malays into the economy to a more conventional East Asian emphasis on economic growth. In the context of a resurgent and politically challenging Islamic fundamentalism, Malay ethnic themes have been somewhat de-emphasised in favour of a "money democracy". In Mexico, the PRI project was initially political stabilisation, resistance of aspects of United States political and economic influence and the incorporation of popular political forces around a labour base. This led to the creation of an extensive patronage system, challenged for more than a decade by a competing programme of liberalisation, entry into the North American Free Trade Area and rapid growth. It is argued later in this book that the PRI project is in terminal decline; the political responses to the decaying programme will determine what is to take its place.

CONCLUSION

In terms of indices of political and civil rights, countries with dominant parties are likely to inhabit an intermediate range between stable competitive party democracies on the one hand and authoritarian systems of rule on the other. Dominant parties in semi-developed countries, however, impose milder restrictions on political and civil rights than dominant parties in poorer countries. To be noted also is the substantial degree of mobility between regime types: examples can be found of both authoritarian and dominant party rule undergoing liberalisation, and of competitive party systems collapsing into authoritarianism.

One might also draw a distinction between the initiation and consolidation of dominant party rule, the maintenance of such rule, and decay of the dominant party project. South Africa is in the first phase, Malaysia and Singapore are in the second, and Mexico and Taiwan in the third. In the first, there are necessarily uncertainties about the implications of dominant party rule for civil and political rights. In the second, it is possible to delineate the forms and limits of dominant party power and to observe the extent of political and civil rights. Uncertainty arises in the third case, because a successful transition to a system which is both competitive and democratic is not assured. The first response to a challenge to a dominant party system can be expected to be a mixture of co-optation and control. Greater toleration of opposition may result, as long as this opposition does not become strong enough to pose a major political threat to the dominant party. Should the opposition burst out of these bounds, only three options are available: to continue liberalisation into a competitive system, to repress, or to pursue a wobbly set of accommodations and controls as an ad hoc and short-term attempt to restabilise the system.

A BRIEF POSTSCRIPT ON SOUTH AFRICA

The comparative picture suggests that the following are the important issues in considering the future of party dominance in South Africa:

1   On the basis of the two measures of income per capita and its human development index, the expected value for the Freedom House combined index of democracy in South Africa is a "partly free" seven. This is lower than the value of nine assigned by Freedom House just before the political change of 1994. But it indicates that socioeconomic development is not sufficient to support an expected "free" classification of five or below; for that, further economic growth and human development are required. Some of the limits to political freedom are apparent: geographical areas in which the rule of law is absent or not assured, limited respect for press freedom, limited political tolerance, and imperfect conduct of elections.

2   Some analysts take the view that it is too early to tell whether South Africa in fact has a dominant party, as only one fully democratic election has been held. Against this view can be cited the fact that in the 1994 election, the African National Congress won three times as many votes as the next

biggest party, and the universal expectation that the ANC will win the 1999 election. Many believe that it is assured of winning at least one further election. Opinion polls since the 1994 election have found little variation in the ethnic pattern of support for the various political parties in South Africa.

3 Like dominant parties in other semi-developed countries, the ANC is pragmatic to the point of somewhat blurring its project. Redistribution is usually stressed as its primary project. One account has been that redistribution should be from the rich to the poor; sceptics suggest that what is actually happening is redistribution from one section of the middle class to another. The evidence to test these competing views is not yet available. For there to be sustained improvement in the conditions of beneficiaries of redistribution, it has to be combined with economic growth. Strategies to achieve it have been debated between business, trade unions and the government, but there is as yet little sign of a wide consensus, with the ANC having to tread a careful path between international economic orthodoxy, business and labour. The timing of measures supporting growth and measures supporting redistribution will shape the coalition of interests in effective support of the government.

4 The experience of a number of semi-developed countries indicates that dominant parties or party coalitions can fall apart while they hold office, forcing the rebuilding of coalitions or early elections. The reasons for this are various, ranging from differential response of factions or parties to policy difficulties, scandals of various kinds, and positioning behaviour by factions and parties ahead of a coming election. In some countries, new party formation is frequent and often built around personalities rather than principles. On the other hand, dominant parties can stay in power for a long time—and opposition to them can be equally long-lived. The pro-business PAN in Mexico has been represented in the legislature since the 1950s and picked up a great deal of strength in the 1994 elections.

5 The most interesting dominant party systems for the purposes of comparison with South Africa are Malaysia and Mexico. The Malaysian government is formed from a front of parties with varying ethnic appeals; in this way, it creates wider legitimacy for the state than if it were governed by a Malay-only party. Given the demography of Malaysia, a Malay-only dominant party would be more vulnerable to intra-Malay political competition than the government is. Malaysian-style political management could be found in South Africa's Government of National Unity as originally constituted, but came to an end with the National Party withdrawal from government and the absence of consociationalist provisions in the

final constitution of 1996. The demographic imperatives for a Malaysian approach are much weaker in South Africa. The contemporary fortunes of the Mexican labour-based system are also of interest in South Africa, given the "triple alliance" of the ANC, the Congress of South African Trade Unions and the Communist Party. Traditional Mexican techniques of political control—manipulation of the media and elections, patronage and other means of abrogating the conditions for free and fair political competition—should be watched for in South Africa. Ultimately, Taiwanese political developments will be of interest, but the preconditions for them in South Africa are not yet met, and how long they will take to emerge is an open question.

Chapter 3

A BORN-AGAIN DOMINANT PARTY?
THE TRANSFORMATION OF THE KUOMINTANG AND
TAIWAN'S REGIME TRANSITION

YUN-HAN CHU

INTRODUCTION

Taiwan's experiences with democratic transition are analytically distinctive from the standpoints of a global crisis of authoritarian regimes and concurrent movements toward democracy. Over the last decade, the incumbent elite has managed to engineer a dual transition: a transition from what Giovanni Sartori termed "a party-state system"[1] (or what Samuel Huntington and Clement Moore termed "a single-party authoritarian system") to what T.J. Pempel termed "a one-party dominant regime"[2] and a parallel transformation of the Kuomintang (KMT) itself from a quasi-Leninist revolutionary party[3] into a voluntary mass-based political party. The two processes were empirically overlapping but conceptually distinctive. One involves the organizing principles of a political system and the other a concrete political organization with its own autonomy and coherence.

The outcomes of Taiwan's regime transition are distinctive in the sense that while the principle of popular accountability and open political contestation are being legitimized and institutionalized, the ruling party has kept its political dominance largely intact through an impressive streak of electoral success. The particular mode and outcomes of the transition pose two sets of perplexing analytical issues for comparative theorists:

First, what made the dual transition possible? How could a quasi-Leninist party, which had been an intrinsic part of the party-state system, not only survive an authoritarian breakdown but capitalize on the crisis to its advantage? Which characteristics of the old regime not only proved to offer the incumbent elite a graceful extrication from authoritarian rule but also enabled it to control its outcomes? What enabling conditions, on the one hand,

---

1 Giovanni Sartori, *Parties and Party Systems* (Cambridge: Cambridge University Press, 1976), p. 47.
2 See Samuel Huntington and Clement Moore eds, *Authoritarian Politics in Modern Society* (New York: Basic Books, 1970) and T.J. Pempel ed., *Uncommon Democracies: The One-Party dominant Regimes* (Itahaca: Cornell University Press, 1998).
3 See Tun-jen Cheng, "Democratising the Quasi-leninist regime in Taiwan", *World Politics*, 42, (1989), pp. 471–99.

prompted the ruling elite to plunge itself into electoral competition, but, on the other hand, favored its electoral fortunes under the new regime?

Second, can Taiwan's transition to democracy ever be considered complete and the new democracy ever be consolidated without a genuine alternation in power? A full transition from a party-state system to democracy requires the development of constitutionalism, the separation of state and party, a realignment of the power relationship among major state institutions, in particular the depoliticizing of the military, security, and law-enforcement apparatus and the hardening of the control of representative bodies and elected officials over the military officers and well-entrenched civil servants or state managers, and the development of organic links between the two opposition camps—autonomous organizations in civil society and opposition parties in political society.[4]

Under a largely incumbent-initiated democratic reform, the ruling party has a natural tendency to confine the scope of democratic reform to what Terry Lynn Karl has termed "electoralism".[5] As a consequence, certain residual authoritarian elements may be preserved and transplanted into the new regime. Furthermore, when a transition process carries a strong element of unilateral imposition over the pace and scope of political reform, it is always questionable if the newly installed institutional arrangements can survive a government turnover. Thus, when a one-party dominant regime is a direct descendant of a party-state system, the properties of this new regime often-times constitute a half-way house between authoritarianism and democracy.

How should we evaluate both the properties and the prospect of Taiwan's emerging political system? The answer lies in, I argue, where the electoral strength of the dominant party comes from. Essentially, we ask to what extent is its newly-acquired (or revitalized) electoral strength no longer dependent on a partisan manipulation of the basic rules of political contestation—constitutional design, electoral system, regulations on campaign financing and media access, judicial independence, political neutrality of the military and civil service, etc. The institutionalization of these practices and arrangements in any competitive democratic regime requires a high degree of consensus among contending political forces. Without the acquiescence of the opposition to these basic rules, the legitimacy of the political system as

---

4   For a more elaborate conceptual exposition along this line, see Hung-mao Tien and Yun-han Chu, "Taiwan's domestic political reforms: Institutional change and power realignment", Gary Klintworth ed., *Taiwan in the Asia-Pacific in the 1990s* (Sydney: Allen and Unwin, 1996).

5   See Terry Lynn Karl, "Dilemmas of Democratization in Latin America", *Comparative Politics* (1990), pp. 1–21.

well as the derived power to govern will be constantly challenged. A dominant party may trespass this boundary in three key areas: employing the coercive power and resources of the state to impede political competition, tinkering with the constitutional design and/or electoral rules for short-term political gain, and awarding itself access to key electoral resources, such as media use and political financing. All these practices and arrangements go much beyond the usual concept of "incumbent advantage" in a competitive democracy. Electoral advantages of this sort can evaporate overnight once a long-running ruling party is thrown out of office. If an emerging dominant party bases its electoral advantage to a substantial degree on a partisan manipulation of these practices and arrangements, this signifies not only an incomplete transition to democracy but an intrinsically unstable regime. None of the four primary cases of "uncommon democracies" investigated by T.J. Pempel and his colleagues fail on these criteria. But a "born again" dominant party always calls for close scrutiny as it is plausibly the usual suspect.

Of course, theoretically speaking, a dual transition from a party-state system does not preclude the possibility of a successful transition to democracy, nor does the institutionalization of a one-party dominant regime necessarily obstruct the prospect of democratic consolidation. We should be open to the possibility that the natural tendency of the entrenched ruling party to limit the scope of democratic reform may be effectively checked by some contingent political constraints and processes. We should be open also to the possibility that a "born again" dominant party, being thoroughly transformed, may manage to build up its electoral advantage in much the same way as other dominant parties in advanced industrial democracies. It may benefit from an electoral system that fosters a multi-party system. It may derive its electoral strength from a rare combination of flexibility and rigidity and uniquely blended symbols and payoffs that enable it not only to retain its loyal core but to garner new blocs of support. It may be able to maintain a pattern of ideological distancing between itself and its principal opponents to prevent the formation of majoritarian counter-coalitions. It may benefit from the fruits of long-term dominance as it has acquired the ability to shape the terms of public policies and the parameters of political conflicts. Or, in a more fundamental sense, some prevailing historical conditions that favored the maintenance of a single-party regime in the past may continue to favor its electoral fortunes. As a result, its ability to achieve its historical projects—security, development, and international legitimacy—could remain largely unhampered under a new regime. In a nutshell, just like other dominant parties in advanced industrial democracies, it may well be the case that it derives its electoral dominance from a peculiar mixture of efforts and luck.

In the following, I shall apply the conceptual framework suggested above to the case of the dual transition from a party-state system in Taiwan. The chapter first examines the historical conditions that have made the KMT's dual transition politically possible.

THE ENABLING CONDITIONS

What made the KMT's dual transition politically conceivable and manageable? There were four key elements: the early indigenization of the KMT leadership, the KMT's accumulated electoral strength in local politics, the built-in adaptability of the official ideology as well as the constitutional arrangements, and an effective economic development program. We will examine these four enabling conditions one by one.

At the dawn of the political opening, potentially the most serious threat to the survival of the Kuomintang was the underlying sub-ethnic cleavage between the minority mainlander and the majority native Taiwanese. Under the old regime, the commanding heights of the party and state had been long dominated by the mainlander elite. Potentially, democratization would have had ignited a broadly-based societal demand for a transfer of political power from mainlander group to native Taiwanese and thus enabled the opposition to deal a fatal electoral blow to the KMT leadership. However, carefully crafted political engineering has complicated the politics of sub-ethnic cleavage. Long before Chiang Ching-kuo initiated political liberalization in 1986, he had first accelerated the Taiwanization of the party power structure since the early 1970s.[6] During Chiang Ching-kuo's tenure, the process of indigenization culminated in his decision to nominate Lee Teng-hui, a native Taiwanese, as his official successor in 1984. As a result, many members of the co-opted native Taiwanese elite have also acquired a high stake in preserving the political dominance of the Kuomintang and the many authoritarian arrangements that had ensured the party's long-term political security. Radical changes in the political institutions posed a grave risk to most native KMT politicians whose gradual ascendancy in national politics was better assured by the KMT-sponsored reform. The acceleration of Taiwanization in the early 1980s helped to partially nullify the mobilization strategy of the opposition along the sub-ethnic line. It also, at later stages, helped to ameliorate the emotionally charged conflict on national identity and pave the way for a compromise.

---

6 See Edwin Winckler, "Taiwan Transition?", Tun-jen Cheng and Stephan Haggard eds., *Political Change in Taiwan* (Boulder: Lynne Riener, 1992).

Next, the KMT regime entered the 1980s with a proven formula for maintaining electoral dominance in a limited popular electoral process implemented at local level. Limited home rule was implemented from 1950. The natives were allowed to elect their representatives up to provincial level and executive heads up to county/city level. Limited electoral opening of national representative bodies was first instituted in 1972 and expanded twice, first in 1980 and again in 1989. The single non-transferable vote (SNTV) system was installed by the *emigre* regime at the local level for co-opting native elites and for incorporating existing local patron–client networks into a superimposed party apparatus. The ruling elite fully recognized that the combination of the single non-transferable vote and multi-member districts would generate formidable intra-party competition. In fact, this was the intended consequence of its initial adoption.[7] Within each administrative district below the provincial level, the KMT nurtured and kept at least two competing local factions striving for public offices, and other electoral offices in many quasi-state organizations, such as farmers' associations and irrigation associations, and more importantly, for a share of region-based economic rents in the non-tradable goods sector to be distributed by the party-sanctioned local spoil system. Thus, the party has effectively functioned as a mechanism of organizing compliance and support among competing local elites.

There existed a mutual dependence between the local factions and the central party leadership. On the one hand, the smooth functioning of the vote-buying mechanism, irregular campaign practices and the local spoil system depended on the indulgence of the various state regulatory and law-enforcement agencies, which were under the influence of the party. On the other hand, the fierce competition among the factions created high entry barriers for the opposition candidates. On top of this, the central leadership could claim the overall electoral victory delivered by disparate local factions. However, the mutual dependence between local factions and central elite had long been an asymmetric one. The fierce competition among rival factions accentuated the balancing role of the party. In each district, the party secretariat controlled a substantial number of swing votes, consisting of loyalist mainlanders, state employees and military personnel. This vote bloc was, in most districts, big enough to tip the balance between competing factions. Thus, the party apparatus enabled the ruling elite not only to keep a limited pluralism, which came with the introduction of electoral process, in check,

---

7   See Yun-han Chu, "The Realignment of Business–Government Relations and Regime Transition in Taiwan", Andrew MacIntyre ed., *Business and Government in Industrializing Asia* (Ithaca: Cornell University Press, 1994).

but also to turn the competitive logic and screening mechanism of the electoral system into an effective instrument of legitimation, political control and selective incorporation. With the electoral rise of the opposition since the late 1970s[8], the above pattern of electoral dominance has been shaken but not undermined. The party and the local factions still retain enormous electoral resources. Also, the party continued to enjoy a firm grip on the organized sectors of civil society and to have under its direct control substantial financial and media resources. The combined electoral capacity of the local factions and the party has consistently delivered an over-two-thirds majority in popular votes and an over-three-quarters majority in seats in elections for representative bodies at all levels before 1986. This inherited electoral advantage gave the party central leadership a certain confidence as well as flexibility in responding to the opposition's demand for democratic reform. A gradual expansion of the electoral avenue did not seem to pose a serious political threat to the security of the national elite.

Furthermore, the political system that the KMT had installed on the island after World War II was never a full-fledged Leninist regime which denies the validity of dissent and open contestation in principle. The official ideology of the KMT does not challenge (or repudiate) the democratic norms in principle. The KMT has defended the authoritarian arrangements on the ground that the country was not ready for a full democracy because of the imminent external threat from the rival Communist regime. Thus, the post-war authoritarianism was founded on a system of extra-constitutional legal arrangements and emergency decrees, which suspended or superseded many important provisions of the ROC Constitution.[9] For the incumbent elite, the ROC Constitution can be frozen but not abandoned because it is the quintessential legal embodiment of the one-China principle. It was adopted when the Nationalist government still exercised effective governance over a majority

---

8 For the gradual electoral rise of the opposition, see Yun-han Chu, *Crafting Democracy in Taiwan* (Taipei: Institute for National Policy Research, 1992), Chapter 2.

9 Ever since 1948, the Temporary Provisions and a series of emergency decrees under the rubric of "During the Period of Mobilization and Combating Rebellion" replaced or superseded many important provisions of the ROC constitution. They threw the country into a permanent state of emergency. These extra-constitutional arrangements were steadily expanded during the 1950s and 1960s (Hu, 1987). In their final form, they provided the president with unlimited emergency power and invalidated the two-term limit on the presidency, suspended the reelection of the three national representative bodies—the National Assembly, the Legislative Yuan and the Control Yuan—extended the tenure of their incumbent members for life, and deferred the election of provincial and municipal heads indefinitely. See Hung-mao Tien, *The Great Transition: Political and Social Change in the Republic of China* (Stanford: Hoover Institution, 1989); Hu Fu, "The Electoral Mechanism and Political Change in Taiwan", Steve Chang ed., *In the Shadow of China: Political Developments in Taiwan since 1949* (London: Hurst and Co., 1993).

part of China, including Taiwan, and was internationally recognized by all major powers.

The very existence of the ROC Constitution, however, brought about many unintended consequences. First, the Constitution had supplied liberal intellectuals and political dissidents with ample ideological ammunition for ridiculing the authoritarian order. The demand for the abolition of the Temporary Provisions and a return to constitutional normality became increasingly credible when the external environment no longer presented itself as an exigency and the besieged mentality of the populace began to subside. A second teetering element in the authoritarian arrangements is the built-in biological clock which set a "natural" limit for the political viability of the "long parliament". The life-long members in the national representative bodies simply faded away after thirty or forty years in office. When this natural elimination process quickened in the late 1970s and early 1980s, there was no politically justifiable way to replace them except for gradually opening up the electoral avenue to the local people. Thus, a political expedience of the past in a quite unintended way forced upon the incumbent elite the issue of democratic opening around the early 1980s. The built-in institutional adaptability also worked in a third sense. In theory, the Temporary Provisions and their auxiliary statutes, which after all were meant to be "temporary", are replaceable and should be replaced by the original provisions of the Constitution once the exigency no long exists. Of course, there is no guarantee that the Constitution can provide the common ground for constructing a political pact between the incumbents and the opposition during regime transition. In fact, as it turns out, the opposition has refused to subject themselves to the legality of the existing constitution on the ground that doing this will create an impression that they are succumbing to the one-China principle. Nevertheless, this institutional safety-valve provides the incumbent reformists with a low-risk exit for extrication from authoritarian order. It is a low-risk exit in the sense that democratic reform will evolve along a prescribed trail and in a predictable direction and that the objections of hard-liners can be diverted when the reform package is presented as nothing but a within-system adaptation.

Finally, on the eve of democratic opening, an export-oriented industrialization (EOI) strategy had been in place for more than two decades. The societal support for the regime-sponsored development program was much more broadly based than the secondary import-substitution strategies launched by many Latin American authoritarian regimes during the same period. The bulk of Taiwan's private sector grew around it and developed a vested interest in it. The export-oriented sectors absorbed a majority of the labor force. More importantly, the EOI strategy addressed both the growth and equity issues with a high degree of effectiveness. In other words, the export-oriented industrialization strategy pursued under the old regime was highly institutionalized.[10] The average annual growth rate between 1961 and 1981 was 9.75 per cent. At the same time, by the early 1980s Taiwan had achieved the most equitable pattern of income distribution among all developing countries.[11] This means that the past authoritarian equilibrium depended mainly, in the words of Adam Przeworski, on equitable affluence, rather than lies and fears.[12]

With an effective development program, the incumbent regime would not be totally discredited even when the popular demand for democratic legitimacy began to gather force. Rather, it could still claim legitimacy of an instrumental nature, and the lineage from the old regime was not entirely a liability for the incumbent elite. The society was relatively free of highly divisive socio-economic cleavages which might be exploited by the opposition and translated into a polarized political cleavage. This, in turn, substantially slowed down the pace of social mobilization and reduced the range of confrontational and mobilizational strategies available to the opposition at the juncture of regime opening. The cohesiveness of the political coalition underlying the development strategy cannot be easily disrupted. Defection *en masse* from the ruling party was unlikely to happen during democratic opening. At the same time, the political opposition lacked the leverage to impose political reforms on the incumbent elite as it has been largely deprived of the option of organizing crippling strikes or large-scale mass rallies. This condition tended to strengthen the hand of the incumbent elite in setting limits on the scope and speed of democratic reform, crafting new political institutions, and working on society's acceptance of a semidemocratic solution.

---

10 See Robert Kaufman and Stephen Haggard, *The Political Economy of Transitions* (Princeton: Princeton University Press, 1995).

11 The difference in income between the top and the lowest quintile in Taiwan shrank from 20 times in 1953 to 4.5 in 1980. This highly equitable distribution of income was accomplished through a series of development policies: an extensive land reform that was introduced at an early stage of industrialization; an export-oriented industrialization strategy which fostered the growth of labor-intensive manufacturing based on small and medium-sized firms; a centralized primary education system which delivered skill-creating opportunities by-and-large equally to the countryside; a conservative credit and fiscal policy which did not discriminate against small and medium-sized firms and a large state-owned sector which preempted many of the monopolistic capital-intensive sectors. See J. Fei, G. Ranis and S. Kuo *Growth with Equity* (New York: Oxford University Press, 1979).

12 Adam Przeworski, *Democracy and the Market: Political and Economic Reforms in Eastern Europe and Latin America* (Cambridge: Cambridge University Press, 1991), pp. 58–57.

CRAFTING ELECTORAL DOMINANCE

Taiwan's transition to democracy reached a point of no return with the convocation of the election of the Second National Assembly in December 1991 and a first reelection of the Legislative Yuan in December 1992. The two events are important historical conjunctures because they not only constitute a necessary first step for a full transition to democracy, i.e., a founding election, but also their outcomes would shape the future course of regime transition. The newly elected National Assembly would be entrusted with responsibility to amend the constitution. The amendments might include a modification of the five-yuan structure, a new procedure for the selection of the president, better delineation of the relationship between the president, the premier, and the Legislative Yuan, and more autonomy for local governments. The Legislative Yuan election, which marked the first time the Kuomintang formally subjected its governing position to a democratic contest, would usher in a new era of legislative assertiveness over the executive power and precipitated an adjustment of the power relation between the KMT parliamentary party caucus and the party central leadership.

In the 1991 National Assembly election, the KMT easily won well over 67.7 per cent of the electoral vote and close to 77 per cent of the new seats (see Table 3.1). This landslide victory gave the KMT leadership absolute control over the legislation of constitutional reform as well as the power of institutional creation in the ensuing four years. In the 1992 Legislative Yuan election, although the Democratic Progressive Party (DPP)[13] expanded their popular electoral support from 28.2 per cent three years earlier to almost a third of the popular vote, the KMT-nominated candidates managed to win a total of 53 per cent of the popular vote and the party as a whole could claim a 60.5 per cent victory when KMT members running as unendorsed candidates were included (see Table 3.1).

From the two founding elections onward, the KMT continued to deliver a stream of electoral victories in all national elections and in many of the most important sub-national elections, albeit with a decreasing degree of effectiveness. The gradual erosion of the KMT's electoral strength seems in many ways inevitable. First, the social transformation brought about by rapid industrialization and the accompanying demographic changes tended to curb the mobilizing capacity of the local factions. The traditional clientelist

---

13   The DPP, as Taiwan's first bona fide opposition party, evolved from a loose coalition of dissidents, known as *Tangwai* (literally outside-the-party). It was formally established on the eve of the 1986 Supplemental Legislative Yuan election in open defiance of the official ban on forming new parties.

networks employed by the local factions could no longer deliver votes as effectively as they used to. Despite the fact that the local factions in the rapidly urbanized areas have all tried to expand their networks to incorporate more secondary associations and regional business concerns, the particularistic nature of local factions proved inimical to the policy demands of the emerging young and urban middle class and the economically disadvantaged groups.

Second, the KMT suffered fierce internal strife following the death of Chiang Ching-kuo in January 1988. The struggle was as much about the (re)distribution of power between the mainlander old-timers and the native Taiwanese elite as about the control of the steering wheel of democratic reform and mainland policy.[14] The formation of two competing power blocs—popularly known as the mainstream faction and the non-mainstream faction[15]—and the ensuing power struggle seriously eroded the KMT's internal coordination mechanism. In the 1992 election, the KMT's much-acclaimed superior vote-equalizing capacity, which had given it a favorable seats to votes ratio under the SNTV system in the past[16], suffered a visible breakdown. Both its capacity in coordinating the party nomination strategy among party nominees and its directing authority over the so-called iron vote (consisting primarily of loyal mainlander party members, state employees, veterans, and military personnel and their dependants) showed signs of cracks. A large number of mavericks, mostly from the non-mainstream faction, entered the race in defiance of the party central directives. Also, the "iron votes" simply became rusty this time. These traditionalists were alienated by the swift Taiwanization of the party leadership and the marginalization of mainlander standard-bearers over the last few years and thus became susceptible to the influence of candidates from the non-mainstream faction. The seat to vote ratio dropped to an all-time low of 1.06.

The power struggle culminated in an open split in August 1993. On the eve of the KMT 14th Congress, some leading figures of the non-mainstream faction decided to break away from the KMT and establish the New Party.

---

14 See Yun-han Chu and Tse-min Lin, "The Process of Democratic Consolidation in Taiwan: Social Cleavage, Electoral Competition and the Emerging Party System", Hung-mao Tien ed., *Taiwan's Electoral Politics and Democratic Transition: Riding the Third Wave* (Armock: M.E. Sharpe, 1995).

15 The formation of two competing power blocs was triggered by the new foreign policy initiatives by Lee. The factionalism became crystallized after Lee's nomination, despite objections from many senior KMT leaders, of Lee Yuan-tsu as his running mate. The coalition centered around President Lee was called the "mainstream faction." The coalition of Lee's opponents, who circled around Premier Hau, became known as the "nonmainstream faction." See Chu and Lin, "The Process of Democratic Consolidation".

16 For example, in 1989, the KMT translated 60.6 per cent of the popular vote into 71.1 per cent of seats, while the DPP translated 28.22 per cent of votes into 21.0 per cent of seats.

Again, the KMT paid a heavy toll for the split in both the December 1995 Legislative Yuan elections and the March 1996 National Assembly elections. The KMT's popular vote in the two elections sank to all-time lows, winning only 46.06 per cent and 49.68 per cent respectively. The setbacks reduced the KMT's margin of majority in the Legislative Yuan to a razor-thin margin of three seats. Also, in the National Assembly, the KMT was deprived of the three-quarter majority required for the passage of constitutional amendment. The electoral surge of the New Party directly accounted for the KMT's setback. In the two elections, the New Party clinched 12.95 per cent and 13.67 per cent of the total popular vote respectively.

Table 3.1: Distribution of popular votes and seats in recent elections for representative bodies

	KMT	DPP	New Party	Independent
1991 National Assembly Election				
Popular vote	71.17%	23.94%	N/A	4.89%
Seats	254	66	N/A	5
Percentage of seats	78.2%	20.3%	N/A	1.5%
1992 Legislative Yuan Election				
Popular vote	52.51%	30.79%	N/A	16.70%[a]
Seats	101	51	N/A	9
Percentage of seats	62.7%	31.7%	N/A	5.6%
1995 Legislative Yuan Election				
Popular vote	46.06%	33.17%	12.95%	7.82%
Seats	85[b]	54	21	4
Percentage of seats	51.8%	32.9%	12.8%	2.4%
1996 National Assembly Election				
Popular vote	49.68%	29.85%	13.67%	6.80%
Seats	183	99	46	6
Percentage of seats	54.8%	29.6%	13.8%	1.8%

Data Source   Central Election Commission, Executive Yuan

Notes

a   The figure includes the votes won by a large number of KMT candidates who entered the race without party endorsement and candidates from small parties, such as Socialist Democrat.
b   Two months later, the KMT expelled one member for his defection in the speaker election.

Using a post-election survey conducted by the National Taiwan University Electoral Study Team, I have disaggregated the popular vote that each party received in the two Legislative Yuan elections into three sub-ethnic components, the Min-nan Taiwanese, Hakka Taiwanese and mainlander.[17] The results are displayed in Table 3.2. The most notable electoral eclipse that the KMT experienced between the 1992 and 1995 elections was among mainlander voters. In 1992, mainlander voters accounted for 24 per cent of the KMT's overall electoral strength. In 1995, they made up only 18 per cent. On the other hand, more than half (54 per cent) of the New Party electoral support came from this traditional KMT stronghold. During the same period, the DPP faced grave difficulty in expanding its foundation of electoral support beyond the Min-nan Taiwanese group as its dependence on this majority sub-ethnic group has actually gone up from 81 per cent in 1992 to 86 per cent in 1995. The DPP has lost favor among the Hakka Taiwanese in part because of the surge of a Min-nan-centric Taiwanese identity among the DPP leadership.

Table 3.2: The subethnic composition of partisan support

| | Subethnic groups | | | | | | |
| | Min-nan | | Hakka | | Mainlander | | |
	Cases	%	Cases	%	Cases	%	Total
1992 Election							
KMT	417	64%	82	13%	155	24%	654
DPP	208	81%	45	18%	3	1%	256
Independent	38	79%	6	13%	4	8%	48
Total	663	69%	133	14%	162	17%	958
1995 Election							
KMT	337	69%	65	13%	86	18%	488
DPP	210	86%	24	10%	11	4%	245
NP	50	37%	11	8%	73	54%	134
Independent	48	86%	3	5%	5	9%	56
Total	645	70%	103	11%	175	19%	923

Data Source   The NTU Electoral Study Team

17 The Min-nan group is the single largest sub-ethnic group among native Taiwanese. Min-nan, literally Southern Fuchien, refers to the Taiwanese who originally came from the southern part of Fuchien province and speak southern Fuchienese. Hakka, a much smaller sub-ethnic group among native Taiwanese, came originally from both Fuchien and Guangdong provinces and speak Hakka.

However, the erosion of the KMT's electoral strength in elections for national representative bodies was balanced by impressive gains in the two newly instituted popular elections for the executive offices—namely the gubernatorial/mayoral election and the presidential election. More significantly, the introduction of the popular election for the provincial governor and the president offered the KMT leadership a chance to redefine the parameters of electoral competitiveness and to move the center of electoral gravity away from representative bodies to executive offices. These newly opened electoral arenas enabled the KMT to reduce its dependence on the local faction and to translate the popularity of its national leadership, especially that of Lee Teng-hui himself, and its incumbent advantage into tangible electoral gains.

The 1994 election for governor of Taiwan and mayors of Taipei and Kaohsiung municipalities represented an important first step of this strategic shift. In the crucial gubernatorial race, the KMT candidate, James Soong, won by a landslide of 56.22 per cent (see Table 3.3), while the DPP candidate, Chen Ting-nan, captured only 38.72 per cent of the popular vote, a marked setback from the 41.4 per cent the party had won in the local election a year earlier. The victory of James Soong signified that the KMT had effectively adapted itself to this brand new electoral arena. An important indicator is that James Soong captured more popular votes than all KMT provincial assembly candidates combined, i.e., 51.03 per cent (see Table 3.3). This is no small achievement. This means that the KMT's overall electoral strength in this first island-wide race for an executive office, which mimics the presidential election a year away in all important aspects, was actually greater than the collective strength of KMT-sanctioned local factions. The Kaohsiung mayoral race revealed the same pattern. The KMT incumbent, Wu Tun-yi, captured 54.46 per cent of vote while the KMT candidates in the city council race clinched only 46.28 per cent (see Table 3.3).

Table 3.3: Distribution of popular votes in the 1994 election

	KMT	DPP	New Party	Indep.
Executive Offices				
Taiwan Area Aggreg	52.05%	39.42%	7.70%	0.83%
Governor of Taiwan	56.22%	38.72%	4.31%	0.75%
Mayor of Taipei	25.89%	43.67%	30.17%	0.28%
Mayor of Kaohsiung	54.46%	39.29%	3.45%	2.80%
Representative Offices				
Taiwan Area Aggreg	49.16%	31.71%	6.09%	13.04%

Table 3.3: (*contd.*)

	KMT	DPP	New Party	Indep.
Provincial Assembly	51.03%	32.54%	3.74%	12.69%
Taipei City Council	39.48%	30.41%	20.83%	9.28%
Kaohsiung City Council	46.28%	24.85%	4.82%	24.06%

Data Source Central Election Commission, Executive Yuan

The ingredients of success for the gubernatorial race were rather different from Legislative Yuan elections. The legislative election essentially consists of, not one nation-wide race, but twenty-six independent races. The dynamics of each race, while affected by national issues and the overall campaign strategy of each party, is decided ultimately by the political configurations and dynamics of each election district at the county level. In these races, traditional vote-getting mechanisms, such as patron–client networks, lineage and communal ties, and vote-buying[18], count a lot for faction-backed KMT candidates. In a way, the KMT's past democratic legitimacy was built more on the aggregate electoral strength of local factions than that of the party itself. In the gubernatorial race, however, given its island-wide magnitude, James Soong could no longer count on the traditional vote-mobilizing mechanisms. The electoral fortune of each candidate in a gubernatorial race is largely shaped by the following three elements: name recognition and favorable media exposure, access to the vote-mobilizing capacity of all types of modern organizations (secondary associations, diversified business groups, and bureaucracy) and policy platform. James Soong enjoyed a clear advantage in all three categories. As an incumbent governor, he received extensive coverage from almost everyone throughout his two-year tenure on the KMT-controlled electronic media. Also, during the campaign season, he easily outspent his opponents in TV and newspaper advertising. His campaign was assisted by the pro-KMT diversified business groups and the KMT-affiliated voluntary organizations (recreational, religious, occupational, etc.) in mobil-

---

18 Faction-backed candidates customarily handed out cash to motivate their potential supporters in the countryside to come out and vote for them. This vote-mobilization practice has prevailed in the local elections for almost three decades. Vote-buying in Taiwan is almost always transacted through interpersonal networks based on existing lineage groups, work units, or communal ties, and is perceived by many voters as an exchange of favor rather than a strict economic transaction. For a further discussion of vote-buying, see Joseph Bosco "Taiwan Factions: Guanxi, Patronage and the State in Local politics", Murray Rubenstein ed., *The Other Taiwan: 1945 to the Present* (Armonk: M.E. Sharpe, 1994).

izing their members or employees. Also, as an incumbent governor, James Soong was able to mobilize most of the 309 administrative units at the town and city level, which depend more on the provincial government than the county government immediately above for fiscal subsidies and project grants. Finally, the DPP's Taiwanese independence platform turned away many stability-minded middle-class voters who worried that a DPP victory in this island-wide contest might trigger both domestic political turmoil and cross-Strait tension. A large number of New Party supporters also came back to the KMT camp because the last thing they wanted to see was a DPP-controlled provincial government.

The 1994 election was a prelude to KMT's victory in the March 1996 presidential election, in which Lee Teng-hui captured 54 per cent of the popular vote in a unprecedented four-way contest. It was no easy victory in light of the fact that the ship of his reelection bid had encountered a series of hidden reefs. When Lee entered the race, he and his running mate, Lien Chan, were not only challenged by two defecting vice-chairmen of his own party, Lin Yang-kang and Hau Pei-tsun, but also by another heavy-weight political figure in the KMT, Chen Lu-an, the then president of the Control Yuan. In addition, the PRC's two missile tests off the Taiwan coast in the summer of 1995 and the ensuing shock waves had sent Taiwan's stock market into a 30 per cent dive and the New Taiwan dollars into a 9 per cent devaluation, and precipitated a wave of capital flight between July and September. These events also provided Lee's opponents with new ammunition for attacking his foreign and mainland policy as well as his leadership.

To appreciate both the magnitude and significance of Lee Teng-hui's victory, we need to compare his electoral support with that of his opponents as well as that of his party in recent national elections. On a number of scores, it was an impressive victory. First, his popular vote was more than twice as large as the second-placed Peng Min-ming, the DPP nominee, who trailed way behind with only 21.13 per cent. Second, it was the KMT's best electoral performance since 1992. His margin of victory was significantly higher than the 46.0 per cent his party won in the recent Legislative Yuan election and visibly higher than the 49.68 per cent his party earned in the concurrent National Assembly election. Third, the Lee-Lien ticket was the highest vote-getter across the board. Even in Taipei city, where the KMT had suffered two humiliating defeats in the 1994 and 1995 elections, Lee-Lien's support surged to 38.9 per cent, the highest of the four (see Table 3.4).

The KMT's revitalized electoral strength was achieved largely at the expense of the DPP, the major opposition. The 1992 election clearly marked the end of the phase of electoral expansion for the DPP. Since then the party's overall electoral strength has apparently reached a plateau. This sign of stagnation first appeared in the 1994 Gubernatorial election, which paved the way for a disappointing showing in the December 1995 Legislative Yuan election. In that election, the DPP registered its smallest gains in both popular vote (2.38 per cent) and seats (3) since 1986. In the presidential election, the large shortfall between the DPP's average electoral support and the poor showing of Peng Min-ming indicated that Lee Teng-hui has managed to carve out at least a quarter (an equivalent of 8 per cent popular vote) or as much as a third of the votes from the traditional DPP constitutencies. The magnitude of the defection from the DPP camp to the Lee-Lien ticket was more than enough to compensate the loss of traditional KMT votes to either the New Party-endorsed Lin-Hau ticket or the independent ticket led by Chen Lu-an. Both Peng's ill-fated campaign and Chen Ting-nan's poor showing before him pointed to the DPP's fundamental dilemma: the closer the contest to the apex of power (and the real contest for governing position), the farther away its candidates are from a victory.

Table 3.4: The 1996 Presidential Election

Party Ticket	KMT Lee-Lien	DPP Peng-Hsieh	New Party Lin-Hau	Independent Cheng-Wang
Overall	54.00%	21.13%	14.90%	9.98%
Taipei City	38.90%	24.34%	24.87%	11.89%
Taiwan Province	56.76%	20.13%	13.42%	9.68%
Kaohsiung City	50.62%	27.32%	12.77%	9.29%
Kinmen-Matsu	41.31%	1.59%	30.64%	26.45%

Data Source   Central Election Commision, Executive Yuan

Note   The New Party didn't nominate its own candidates; it endorsed the Lin-Hau ticket.

THE CONTENTION OVER "A LEVEL PLAYING FIELD"

What accounted for the KMT's revitalized electoral strength? Why is the DPP stagnating electorally just as the regime transition is entering the phase of democratic consolidation?

There is little doubt that the KMT no longer depends on repressive measures to protect its political security. The emerging political system is both open and inclusionary. The electoral process is open to political parties of all ideological stripes, including parties with a communist bent. The social status, as well as the civil rights, was of almost all former political prisoners and dissidents were restored. No more legal restrictions were imposed on the advocacy of Taiwanese independence. Even the leaders of the overseas Taiwanese independence movements, for example Peng Min-ming, after decades of exile, have legally returned to the island and entered the electoral process. The political party system is institutionalized in the sense that the status of the opposition is now formally protected by the relevant state statutes. The legal requirements for the registration of a new political party are minimal. Also, the executive branch no longer exercises the power to dissolve a political party on the basis of its platform. More importantly, the opposition parties have been able to develop grass-root party organs and establish organizational ties with secondary groups. Most citizens and civil groups no longer worry that association with the opposition parties might invite political intimidation from various state agencies.

Nevertheless, contention over the rules of the game lingered on. The opposition simply shifted its emphasis from the openness issue to the fairness issue after the convocation of founding elections. In particular, the opposition parties demanded improvements in three areas: equal media access; political neutrality of the military and security apparatus, the judiciary, and the civil service; and, third, stringent restrictions on party-owned enterprises.

On the issue of media access, the KMT agreed to the allotment of free television time among political parties during elections for national representative bodies as early as 1991 and live television broadcasts of the campaign forums organized by the Central Election Commission during both the gubernartorial and presidential races. However, the KMT had been reluctant to unlock its tight grip on the electronic media. It did make some concessions in the end but only after seeing its regulatory capacity being virtually overtaken by the pace of technological innovation. First came the underground radio stations and unlicensed cable television stations, then the satellites beaming down Chinese-language programs from the sky. The KMT government finally agreed to open up the cable television market and release more spare frequencies for new radio stations and one more network television station.[19] With the arrival of cable television services, KMT's coveted ownership of the three television networks no longer gives itself a preponderant competitive edge. The three networks have since then lost a sizable

---

19 In the summer of 1995, a new network television license was awarded to a DPP-affiliated operator and over a dozen more new radio stations, including many former underground stations operated by DPP and New Party politicians, were licensed.

share of TV viewers to cable television stations as close to two-thirds of all households on the island are now wired.

The opposition also has been able to make some progress on the issue of political neutrality of the military, the security services, the judiciary and the civil service. However, most of the positive changes were precipitated by revolts from the rank and file. The judicial branch has undergone, relatively speaking, the most profound changes. A large number of independent-minded young judges and prosecutors have pushed for sweeping reforms in the judicial system to protect impartiality, eliminate corruption, and nullify political influence since early 1992. Some prosecutors began to crack down on the widespread practice of vote-buying in earnest in recent elections. The security apparatus has become much more cautious and discreet in conducting surveillance on the opposition. This adjustment came about mainly as an unexpected consequence of the KMT's internal strife. The two major agencies, the National Security Agency and the Investigation Bureau, were occasionally embarrassed by intentional leaks by some insiders who sympathize with the KMT non-mainstream faction. In response to the opposition's demand for a "nationalization of the military," the KMT has taken some cosmetic measures to ease the criticism. Instead of abolishing the party cells in the military, the KMT moved them underground and away from the barracks. However, the military continues to dissuade its officers from joining the DPP, and Taiwanese independence is still a taboo. Lastly, the KMT has made little concession over the issue of the political neutrality of the civil service. Blatant violations of the neutrality rule by the KMT were commonplace during the campaign seasons. Many civil servants were instructed by their KMT superiors to help mobilize votes. However, the state employees no longer deliver their votes as obediently as they used to because the New Party has a large number of followers within the bureaucracy. The DPP, with control of a third of the county/city governments, now also enjoys some limited access to public-sector resources.

The KMT, however, has rejected the demand by the opposition to disown its vast party-owned enterprises. The financial stake is simply too high to forego. The KMT business empire currently generates more than NT$ 4 billion (US$ 140 million) of dividends a year. This stalwart financial foundation allows the party to run a huge party apparatus, retain a 4,000-strong full-time staff on its payroll, prop up a strong central leadership, and minimize its dependence on the political donations of the big businesses.

There is no doubt that the persistence of these holdover issues of regime transition will continue to obstruct, if not distort, the normal functioning of Taiwan's newly established representative democracy and pose a series of difficult challenges to the task of democratic consolidation. However, the extent to which they have given the KMT a decisive advantage in electoral competition is open to question. Suffice it to say that if they were indeed decisive, the DPP should have registered steady electoral rise, not stagnation, in recent elections as the protective belts surrounding the KMT have shown growing signs of wear and tear during the regime transition. To unveil the backbone sources of the KMT's electoral dominance we need to move beyond these holdover issues of regime transition and dig deeper into its adaptability and its ability to structure the parameters of political competition. To this we now turn.

The Adaptability of the KMT

At the start of the regime transition, the KMT was racked with a series of deep crises. The DPP challenged the KMT on the issues of power redistribution from the mainlander elite to native Taiwanese, democratic reform, national identity, and Taiwan's sovereign status. All four issues had the potential to arouse widespread popular support. On the other hand, the KMT leadership was seemingly fighting an uphill battle—defending the extra-constitutional arrangements amid a global wave of democratization, insisting on the one-China principle when virtually all major nations have shifted their diplomatic recognition to the PRC as the sole legitimate government of China, and upholding a Chinese identity in the wake of a re-emergence of Taiwanese identity. However, the succession crisis surrounding the death of Chiang Ching-kuo and the ensuing power struggle provided the necessary impetus for a change of course.

When Chiang Ching-kuo suddenly passed away in January 1988, Lee Teng-hui succeeded to his office by constitutional fiat. But he had no tangible power base of his own within the party-state apparatus, and he was surrounded by many senior mainlander leaders, representing various entrenched interests and power blocs. In five years from 1988 to 1993, Lee managed to break up most of the entrenched power blocs, neutralize some conservatives, and assert effective control over the military and security apparatus. He did so with the support of a rousing societal aspiration, the allegiance of like-minded native KMT cadres, timely assistance from the opposition, and a skillful exploitation of the distrust among the older generation of mainlanders.

At first, three entrenched power blocs stood in his way. They were the military, the party, and the economic bureaucracy, in order of importance. Three senior mainlander leaders had built up extensive personal clientelist networks on their respective turf: Hau Pei-tsun, the then chief of general staff, in the military; Lee Huan, the party's secretary general, in the party, and former premier Yu Kuo-hua in the government's finance and economic planning agencies. However, after three rounds of a major leadership re-shuffle in five years, the non-mainstream faction was thoroughly margin-alized from the power center and the mainstream faction moved to dominate the steering wheel of constitutional reform as well as mainland policy.[20] The departure of Hau Pei-tsun from the premier post and the inauguration of Lien Chan, as the first native premier, after the December 1992 election symbolized the end of an era of KMT governance centered on the older generation of mainlanders.

More significantly, during the intra-party power struggle, Lee skillfully shifted the burden of defending these orthodox lines to his rivals—the non-mainstream faction. During Hau Pei-tsun's three-year tenure in premiership, the issue of how to handle the DPP's open challenge to the legitimacy of the Republic of China became a recurring clash point between the mainstream and non-mainstream factions. The conflict was as much about national iden-tity as about the scope and pace of democratic reform. The two issues simply became entangled. The non-mainstream faction considered the proponents of Taiwan independence as secessionists and urged the government to take legal action against them. President Lee, however, resisted the pressure from the conservative camp and managed to hold off any immediate legal action against the DPP. The non-mainstream also insisted that leaders of overseas Taiwanese independence movements should remain barred from entering the country. Lee, on the other hand, pushed steadily for eradicating the so-called black list system that had previously denied many overseas dissident leaders entry permits. Lee also engineered the abolition of the stringent art-icle on treason and sedition, known as Article 100 of the Criminal Code, and thus removed a major legal restriction on the advocacy of Taiwanese inde-pendence.

Lee's efforts to seek ideological accommodation with the opposition repeatedly ran into strong resistance by the non-mainstream faction. How-ever, the accumulation of animosity and distrust simply hardened the resolve of Lee and his allies to accelerate institutional reform, especially in the direc-tion that would effectively undermine the power base of his rivals. The con-flict soon reached a point of no return in the second half of Hau's three-year tenure. Hau's ally in the Legislative Yuan, notably the New KMT Alliance, began openly questioning Lee's commitment to Chinese nationalism. In

---

20 See Hung-mao Tien and Yun-han Chu, "Building Democratic Institutions in Taiwan", *China Quarterly* 148 (1996), pp. 1103–1132.

response, members of the mainstream faction in the Legislative Yuan, notably the Wisdom Club, attacked the non-mainstream faction as a conservative group interested only in preserving its past prerogatives and identifying more closely with mainland China than with the 21 million people on the island.

Between 1989 and 1992, the two camps clashed over almost every major policy issue. The non-mainstream faction suspected both the wisdom and motivation underlying Lee's new foreign policy initiatives, which marked a clear departure from the one-China principle. Over mainland policy, the non-mainstream faction favored broader economic and cultural exchange across the Taiwan Straits, while Lee resisted the pressure for lifting the ban on direct trade and direct air and sea links with mainland China. On constitutional design, the non-mainstream faction opted for a minimum change to the ROC Constitution. Lee, instead, was for a more extensive revision of the Constitution. The mainstream faction pushed for a series of constitutional amendments, all aimed at expanding the power of the president. The locus of contention eventually came down to the electoral system for the election of the president. The non-mainstream faction preferred indirect election, akin to an electoral college system, and opposed popular election, which was favored by Lee. Popular election was viewed by the non-mainstream faction as a pretext for further expansion of presidential power and potentially a vehicle for self-determination. This was deemed not only a necessary step to transform the Constitution from a parliamentary to a semi-presidential system but imperative to safeguard Taiwan's national interests.

The logic of strategic alliance compelled the DPP to side with Lee Teng-hui at all crucial junctures of the power struggle between the mainstream and non-mainstream factions. Within the DPP the goal of Taiwanese independence became the only consensual benchmark against which all political strategies were evaluated. In this light, the non-mainstream faction was regarded as the primary foe because it represented the major obstacle to the DPP's nation-building cause. This tacit grand coalition between the DPP and the mainstream faction culminated in their joint effort to oust Hau. At the same time, the DPP obtained from the KMT mainstream faction satisfactory answers to their various political demands: alleviating past grievances such as the February 28th incident, a commitment to hold direct popular elections for the presidency by 1996, a steadfast position on refusing party-to-party talks between the CCP and the KMT, continuing the ban on direct air and sea links between Taiwan and mainland China, and lastly a concerted diplomatic effort to join the United Nations and its related agencies. Most importantly, a sense of Taiwanese solidarity fostered a steady convergence of the DPP and the KMT mainstream in three key issue areas—constitutional design, mainland policy and foreign policy. It was a shared belief between the KMT mainstream faction and the DPP that a popular election for the highest executive office would not only boost Taiwan's international visibility but also strengthen the government's position in either cross-Straits negotiation or domestic political bargaining.[21] Both shared the worry that full-scale economic integration with mainland China would eventually compromise Taiwan's political autonomy. Both believed that UN membership for Taiwan could provide a permanent multilateral guarantee of Taiwan's political autonomy and territorial security.

Of course there is a limit to this tacit alliance. The downfall of Hau and the marginalization of the non-mainstream faction precipitated a shift in the parameters of political conflict. First, the logic of electoral competition set the two political camps on a collision course as their common major political adversary, the KMT non-mainstream faction, had already been forced out of the ring. Second, the process of the displacement of conflicts set in. After the convocation of founding elections and a thorough Taiwanization of the KMT leadership, the appeal to democratic ideals and Taiwanese identity exhausted its electoral utility. Suddenly the DPP found that it could put forth a few new demands for democratic reform that could arouse widespread popular support. Also, it could no longer characterize the KMT as an "emigre regime" as the ruling party was now in the firm grip of President Lee. While its formal position on the question of the future of Taiwan is in stark contrast with the KMT's official stance for reunification, the DPP found it increasingly difficult to put forward a distinctively different mainland policy and foreign policy. Even its once powerful campaign for joining the UN quickly lost steam as soon as Lee decided to act on a UN membership drive and took control over foreign policy agenda-setting away from the DPP. Lee has been able to harness the zeal for independence with a call for the formation of a sense of shared destiny among the 21 million people and a gradual de-emphasis of the so-called one-China principle. In a nutshell, the DPP became the victim of its own success.

To break out of this predicament, the DPP has been eager to walk out of the shadow of Lee Teng-hui and to line up voters on new issues on which the incumbent KMT mainstream leadership appear vulnerable. On the eve of the 1992 election, the DPP rediscovered the potential of the socio-economic justice issue, which it had ignored during its founding years. In the 1992

---

21   The DPP pushed strongly for it also in the hope that an island-wide popular election would help foster the growth of Taiwanese nationalism. See Yun-han Chu, "The Security Challenge for Taiwan in the Cold War Era", East Asia Institute Report, Columbia University, 1995.

election, the DPP formally introduced its "welfare state" platform, which promised an extensive array of entitlement programs including universal health insurance, subsidized housing, and government-guaranteed retirement income for the elderly. Also, the DPP candidates launched vigorous attacks on the problem of widespread political corruption which had existed for a long time in local politics and was recently transmitted into the national arena.

To gauge the extent to which the DPP's new platform has improved its electoral fortunes, I again turn to post-election surveys conducted by the National Taiwan University Electoral Study Team. Here, I examine the changes in the level of electoral support within various socio-economic groups between the 1992 and 1995 Legislative Yuan elections for the three major parties. In Table 3.5, the respondents are grouped into ten different occupational categories: business owner, management/professional, office workers, self-employed labor, farmer, labor, state employee, college students, housewife, and unemployed.[22] The figures clearly show that in the 1992 election the KMT won overwhelming support among the managerial/professional class, state employees and college students. As a matter of fact, in that election the KMT enjoyed a commanding lead in virtually all occupational categories with one qualification and one exception: The only qualification is that the DPP managed to win a substantial share of labor support (37 per cent). The only exception is that the DPP received more support from the business-owning class than the KMT.[23] Overall, the KMT continued to enjoy broadly based socio-economic support.[24] The DPP was, in a way, a mirror image of the KMT. It, too, drew support across the socio-economic spectrum and enjoyed no firm grip on any major socio-economic group. Three years later, the DPP's anti-corruption and social welfare platform did little to expand its electoral base. Among the targeted groups, the DPP made a small gain among the self-employed[25] (from 29 per cent to 36 per cent) and farmers (from 25 per cent to 29 per cent) while suffering a visible electoral setback among office workers (from 28 per cent to 16 per cent)

---

22 The definition of the ten categories are mostly identical across the two surveys except for the following: First, for the 1992 election, the business owner category included only owners of companies and enterprises; for the 1995 election, the category was broadened to include owners of small shops (with nine employees or more). Second, for the 1992 election, office workers included sales clerks, while for 1995 election sales clerks were counted as labor.

23 However, the number of cases in this category is too small to draw a statistically meaningful conclusion.

24 For a comparative analysis of the socio-economic foundation of the KMT in earlier elections, see Yun-han Chu, *Crafting Democracy*, pp. 70–77, and Hu Fu, "The Electoral Mechanism".

25 This category includes primarily owners of small shops, street vendors, taxi drivers, craftsmen, etc. This group constitutes the bulk of the urban informal sector.

Table 3.5: Partisan support among occupational groups: 1992 and 1995 elections

Occupation	1992 Election						1995 Election							
	KMT		DPP		Independent		KMT		DPP		NP		Independent	
	Cases	%	Cases	%	Cases	%	Cases	%	Cases	%	Cases	%	Cases	%
Business owner	7	44%	8	50%	1	6%	31	46%	21	31%	11	16%	4	6%
Manager/professional	72	77%	18	19%	4	4%	26	35%	19	25%	24	32%	6	8%
Office workers	101	68%	41	28%	7	5%	63	54%	19	16%	26	22%	8	7%
Self-employed labor	87	68%	37	29%	4	3%	73	55%	48	36%	6	5%	5	4%
Farmer	51	67%	19	25%	6	8%	27	64%	12	29%	2	5%	1	2%
Labor	88	58%	56	37%	9	6%	84	51%	51	31%	19	11%	12	7%
State employee	103	85%	15	12%	3	2%	56	60%	15	16%	18	19%	4	4%
College student	26	76%	5	15%	3	9%	8	24%	17	52%	7	21%	1	3%
Housewife	107	64%	52	31%	9	5%	99	61%	37	23%	15	9%	11	7%
Unemployed	17	71%	6	25%	1	4%	18	56%	6	19%	4	13%	4	13%
Total	659	68%	257	27%	47	5%	485	53%	245	27%	132	14%	56	6%

Data Source   The NTU Electoral Study Team

and labor (from 37 per cent to 31 per cent). The DPP did win over one group from the KMT—college students—who are more receptive to its anti-corruption and anti-Mafia politics campaign than any other social group. The level of electoral support for the DPP here has jumped from 15 per cent to 52 per cent! In a nutshell, the DPP's new emphasis on anti-corruption and socio-economic justice issues did not trigger a visible partisan realignment along the socio-economic cleavage. The KMT has managed to retain an all-class appeal, albeit with a lesser degree of effectiveness. The KMT continued to enjoy majority support among major socio-economic groups in the 1995 election: office workers (54 per cent), self-employed (55 per cent), farmers (64 per cent), labor (51 per cent), state employees (60 per cent) and house-wives (61 per cent).

There is no doubt that the KMT has not lost its firm grip on any of the major socio-economic groups, not even among state employees. The level of electoral support that the KMT received dropped substantially across the board between 1992 and 1995. However, the KMT's recent setback has much more to do with the New Party than the DPP. The New Party accounted for much of the KMT's electoral decline among the managerial/professional class, office workers, labor and state employees (see Table 3.5). However, the New Party did not carve out its electoral slice simply from the KMT's stronghold, such as state employees. It also ran into head-on competition with the DPP among business owners, the managerial and professional group, office workers and college students. The New Party actually became more popular than the DPP among the managerial and professional group, office workers and state employees. The New Party, on the other hand, is much less capable than the DPP of attracting support beyond the urban middle class. Its electoral strength was very flimsy among farmers and the self-employed (constituting the urban lower-middle class) and not much stronger among factory labor.

In summary, the KMT has managed to be all things to all people. Its extens-ive socio-economic foundation has eroded but not disintegrated. Three short-term factors account for the KMT's electoral resiliency and the DPP's stagnation. First, the KMT leadership responded to the rising demand for entitlement programs with its own version of a social welfare platform. The budget earmarked for the assistance of veterans, elders, farmers, the unem-ployed and families below poverty line was dramatically increased, from 12.2 per cent of the net expenditure of all levels of government to 18.3 per cent in 1994. Also, in 1995, the government formally introduced universal health insurance. Second, the DPP has to compete vigorously with the New Party over the socio-economic justice and anti-corruption issues. The New

Party, being eager to expand its electoral base beyond the traditional KMT loyalists and mainlander voters, places much of its emphasis on catering for the policy demands of the post-war generation and urban middle class. Third, and most importantly, the KMT mainstream faction continues to extract considerable political mileage out of a popular sentiment anchored on Taiwanese identity. Lee Teng-hui has come to be viewed by a majority of native Taiwanese as the protector of the island's autonomy from the PRC and the embodiment of the glory and honor of the Taiwanese people. The media has actually coined a phrase, the so-called Lee Teng-hui complex, to describe this emerging popular sentiment. The projection of Lee as a saint-like figure makes him virtually beyond the reach of criticism despite many manifestations of the arrogance of unfettered power and an apparent reluctance to clamp down on corruption. The call for Taiwanese solidarity continues to gather steam after the downfall of Hau Pei-tsun. This time, the common adversary is no longer the KMT non-mainstream faction but the PRC and its so-called collaborators on the island.

Another long-term factor which has so far worked in the KMT's favor is Taiwan's unique industrialization process. Beneath Taiwan's long-running economic prosperity and full employment is a very fluid class structure. There exists a highly decentralized private sector, which generates a large number of owner-operators as well as a sizable temporary working class. A large portion of the male population experienced vertical social mobility, i.e., class mobility, during their life cycle or within their family. The economic structures inhibit the growth of independent union movements in an even more decisive way. Most companies and work-units are relatively small. This means that most laborers do not enjoy much collective bargaining power over their employers to begin with. Also, the majority of industrial workers are first-generation working class. Their social identity is still heavily shaped by their primary bonds rather than class status. By the time the second-generation working class arrived on the scene around the early 1990s, Taiwan's economy was already in the process of moving into a service-based and brain-intensive economy. Thus, in Taiwan, there never existed a politically activated working class which might have provided the opposition with a solid social foundation. On the contrary, just like the farmer movements, the independent union movements were in most cases preempted by the state-sanctioned union organizations. While political opening might encourage the politicization of distributional issues, especially the labor–capital disputes and growth–environment clashes, the incumbent elite in Taiwan can prevent these issues from spilling over into partisan competition. As long as its capacity to make credible policy commitments is not hampered, new social groups are more likely to look to the incumbent elite rather than the opposition for solutions.

The Shifting Pattern of Ideological Distancing

Just as the KMT mainstream leadership has registered remarkable success in narrowing the ideological distance between it and the DPP, Beijing's suspicion about Lee Teng-hui's hidden agenda of creeping independence grew sharply. Beijing was especially alarmed by Taipei's recent bid for UN membership. This bold move is increasingly viewed by Beijing as a preparatory step to seeking formal independence. Beijing responded first with the issuing of the "White Paper on the Taiwan Problem and China's Unification" in mid-1993, in which Beijing put forward a clear rejection of all the proposals raised by Taipei to participate in the international community, including "One China, two seats". Also, the PRC mobilized all diplomatic resources at its disposal to block Taiwan's attempt to reopen the debate on Chinese representation in the General Assembly and, at the same time, put pressure on all major powers to reiterate their observance of the one-China principle. Furthermore, to send a strong warning signal, the PLA conducted a series of extensive military exercises in autumn 1994.

The cross-Strait tension finally reached boiling point when the White House granted President Lee Teng-hui a visitor visa for his trip to his alma mater in summer 1995. In retaliation, Beijing launched a week of missile tests off Taiwan's northern coast in late July to remind the United States, Japan and Taipei of the dire consequences of sponsoring (or pursuing) the Taiwanese independence cause. It was then followed by a second round of missile tests near a Taiwan-controlled off-shore island on the eve of the KMT Congress for presidential nomination in late August 1995. As we have seen above, the missile tests and the shock waves sent Taiwan's stock market and the New Taiwan dollar plummeting and precipitated a wave of capital flight. Apparently, the hard-liners in Beijing had hoped that, through a series of threatening moves, Beijing would be able to disrupt Lee's reelection bid and bring Taipei to its knees. Along this line of reasoning, Beijing decided to extend the military threats well on to the election day. However, to the disappointment of Beijing's hard-liners, the latest rounds of live-ammunition exercises did little to stop Lee's campaign momentum. The crisis in the Straits might have actually helped Lee Teng-hui's reelection as many traditional DPP supporters shifted their support because of worry that Taiwan might lose ground to the PRC if the majority could not speak with one voice. A vote for Lee Teng-hui has become a "No" to the PRC.

The tension in the Straits revived the national identity issue as the predominant cleavage dimension. During the campaign, foreign and mainland policy issues dominated the public debate and virtually shut out all other policy concerns. The deterioration of cross-Strait relations also inadvertently helped the KMT mainstream to consolidate its centrist position on this most salient issue. The KMT effectively painted the DPP and the New Party into their respective corners. The KMT's propaganda characterized the DPP's independence cause as dangerous and irresponsible and the New Party's pro-reunification platform as disloyal to the Taiwanese people. On the other hand, it promoted the so-called Republic of China on Taiwan formula anchored on a two-China model while being ingeniously evasive, flexible and ambiguous on the issue of national reunification. The PRC's sabre-rattling strategy also seriously disrupted the momentum of the Taiwanese independence movement and pushed more and more voters into a centrist position, where protecting the status quo and resisting the PRC's hostile reunification campaign are favored over either independence or reunification.

In Figure 3.1, I present the telephone survey data from Taiwan's two leading newspapers on the issue of Taiwan–mainland relations. The data series reveals the shift in public opinion from October 1991, on the eve of the 1991 election, to August 1995, the date of the PLA's second missile test. It is evident that the Taiwanese independence cause reached a plateau around mid-1994 and suffered a mild setback in 1995. The most dramatic shift was the decline in support for reunification, from a high of 36 per cent to 19 per cent, as a growing number of native Taiwanese took their cue from the president's wavering position on the One-China principle.

A face-to-face island-wide survey conducted by the National Taiwan University electoral study team during the presidential campaign provides more direct evidence demonstrating how the shifting pattern of ideological distancing decisively favors the KMT mainstream, and in particular Lee Teng-hui himself. In Figure 3.2, I compare the popular perception of the KMT's policy position collected in the 1996 survey data with the same data collected in a survey conducted after the 1992 election. The chart clearly shows how dramatically the KMT mainstream has repositioned itself on the issue of Taiwan–mainland relations. In the early part of 1993, 68.7 per cent of the respondents perceived the KMT as being firmly pro-reunification. Only 12.6 per cent of the respondents thought that the KMT did not take a clear position on the issue and almost no one considered it as being pro-independence. Three years later, the perception of being firmly pro-reunification dropped to 27.1 per cent for the KMT party and to only 20 per cent for Lee Teng-hui.

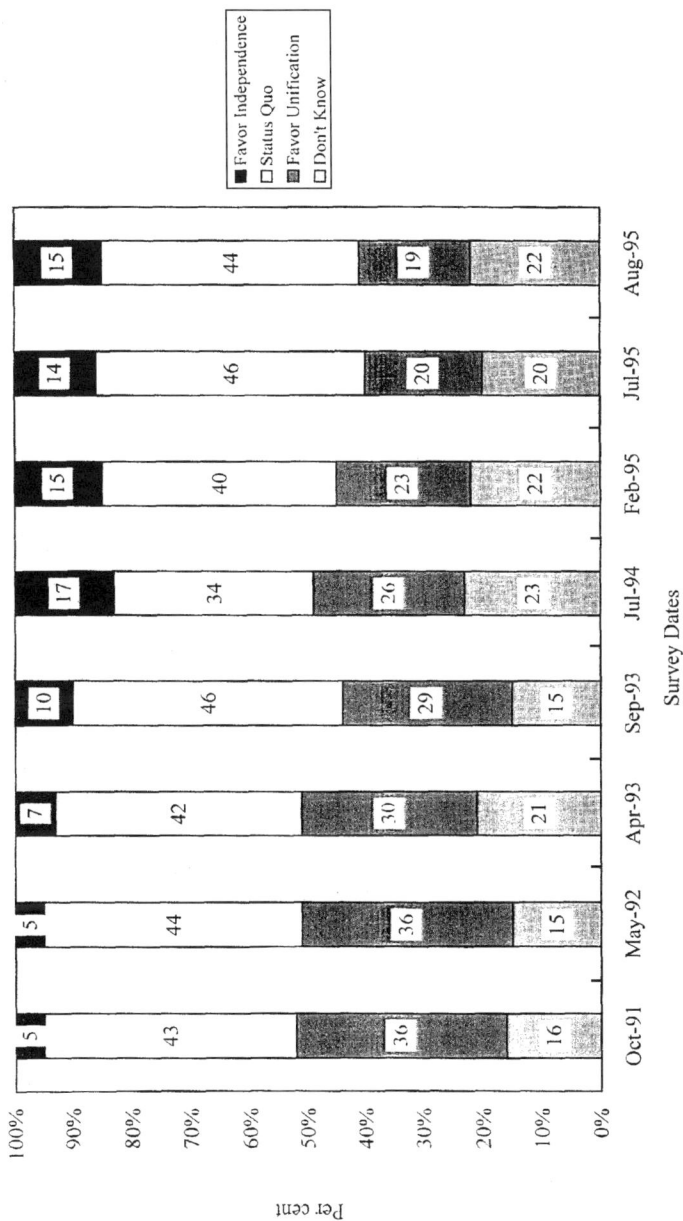

Figure 3.1: Preferences over the issue of future mainland–Taiwan relations
Data Sources: 1991–93, China Times; 1994–95 United Daily

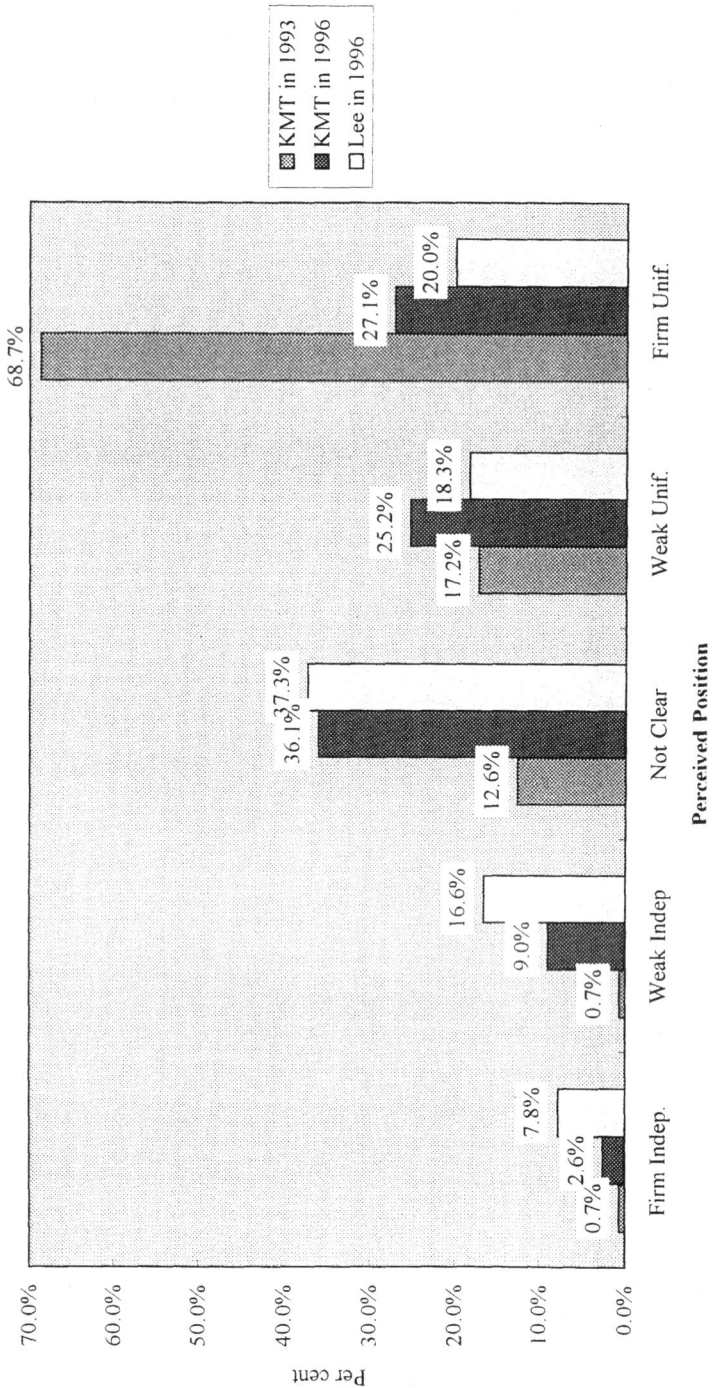

Figure 3.2: Shift in perceived policy position between 1993 and 1996

Legend:
- KMT in 1993
- KMT in 1996
- Lee in 1996

Data values by Perceived Position:

Firm Indep.
- KMT in 1993: 0.7%
- KMT in 1996: 2.6%
- Lee in 1996: 7.8%

Weak Indep
- KMT in 1996: 0.7%
- KMT in 1993: 9.0%
- Lee in 1996: 16.6%

Not Clear
- KMT in 1993: 12.6%
- KMT in 1996: 36.1%
- Lee in 1996: 37.3%

Weak Unif.
- KMT in 1993: 17.2%
- KMT in 1996: 18.3%
- Lee in 1996: 25.2%

Firm Unif.
- KMT in 1993: 68.7%
- KMT in 1996: 20.0%
- Lee in 1996: 27.1%

Y-axis: Per cent (0.0% to 70.0%)

X-axis: Perceived Position

At the same time, 36.1 per cent of the respondents don't see the KMT as taking a clear position and slightly more of them (37.3 per cent) see Lee Teng-hui in the same light. Furthermore, the KMT's wavering position was ambiguous enough to lead 8 per cent of the respondents to consider it pro-independence, albeit not firmly. The proportion of respondents who see Lee Teng-hui in a pro-independence light is even higher (16.6 per cent).

This new image of the KMT as well as of Lee Teng-hui is in stark contrast to that of the DPP and the New Party. In Figure 3.3, I compare popular perceptions toward the three major parties and Lee Teng-hui. The image of being firmly pro-independence remains the trademark of the DPP despite the recent efforts by some DPP leaders to soft-pedal its position on pursuing formal independence. This reflects the perception of more than four-fifths (80.2 per cent) of the respondents. The New Party, on the other hand, is perceived by 41.5 per cent of the respondents as being firmly pro-reunification and by 21.8 per cent as being pro-reunification despite its strategy to downplay the national identity issue and to project itself as essentially an anti-independence force.

The popular perception that the two opposition parties are positioned on the two polar ends of the issue spectrum not only gives the KMT a decisive competitive edge but also constrains the possibility of the formation of an anti-KMT coalition between the DPP and the New Party. Recently, a growing number of DPP leaders have recognized the party's predicament and openly concede that it is virtually impossible for the DPP to build up a winning electoral majority on the issue of Taiwanese independence. In particular, after the missile crisis, the independence option is seriously discredited in the minds of the stability-minded business elite and the middle class by the PRC's demonstrated resolve to use military means. However, the very existence of a sizable bloc of pro-independence zealots (estimated to be around 15 per cent of the electorate) has prevented the DPP from making a marked shift away from a pro-independence platform.[26] The bold suggestion of a "Grand Reconciliation (with the New Party)" by the outgoing party chairman, Shih Ming-Teh, in the early part of 1996 almost ignited a revolt by the radical wing, the so-called fundamentalists.

Thus, the DPP, seemingly the only viable alternative to the KMT on the political horizon, has almost become a captive of its institutionalized position on Taiwanese independence. Its recent efforts to shift the focus of policy debate away from national identity issue to issues related to socio-economic

---

26 Some leaders of the pro-independence zealots formed a new party, the Nation-Building Party, to check the DPP leadership who signaled a softening of its independence claim.

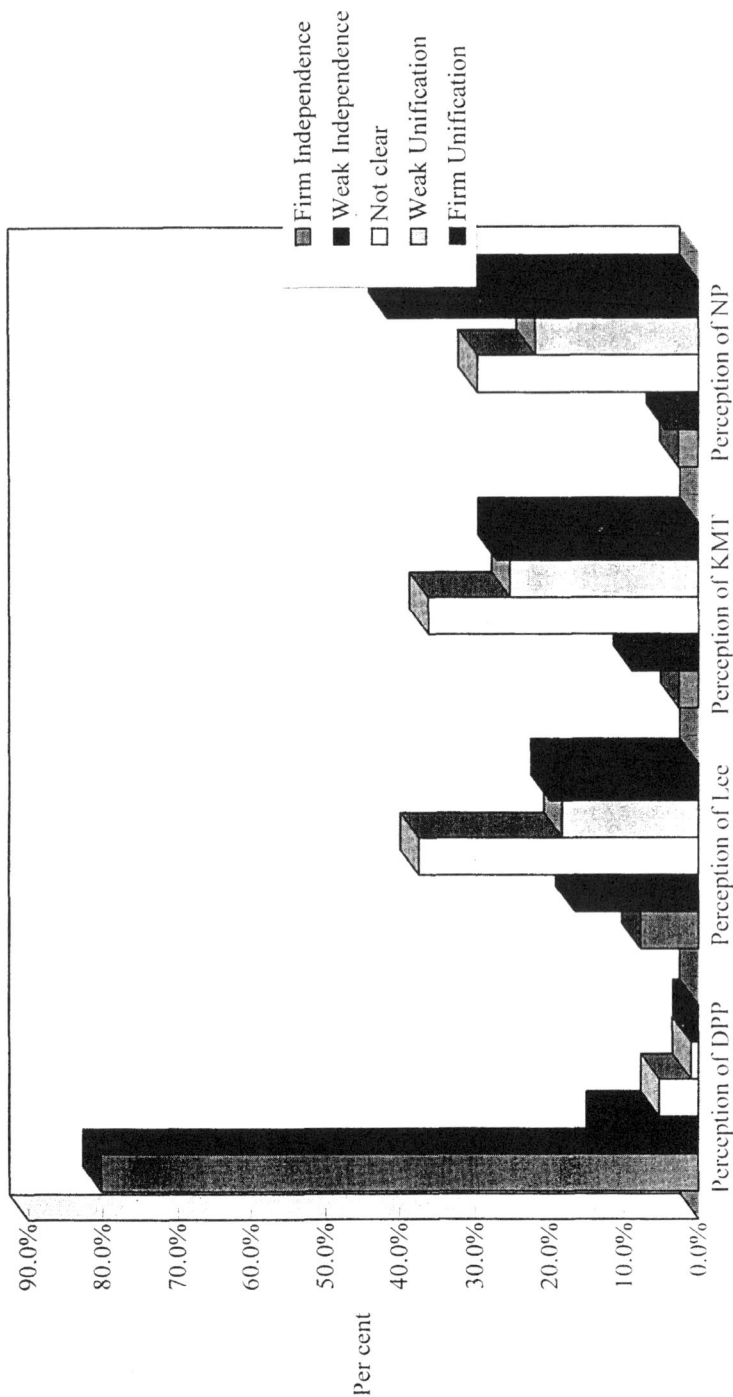

Figures 3.3: Citizens' perceived policy positions (survey 1996)

Legend:
- Firm Independence
- Weak Independence
- Not clear
- Weak Unification
- Firm Unification

Per cent axis: 0.0%, 10.0%, 20.0%, 30.0%, 40.0%, 50.0%, 60.0%, 70.0%, 80.0%, 90.0%

Categories: Perception of DPP, Perception of Lee, Perception of KMT, Perception of NP

justice and anti-corruption were not entirely successful. In fact, as long as the KMT controls the tempo of cross-Strait political interaction, it will continue to accentuate the salience of the national identity issue and delegitimate both the DPP and the New Party in its favorite game.

Finally, the international context looks increasingly unfavorable to the Taiwanese independence cause. Around the early 1990s, the proponents of Taiwanese independence were encouraged by the way in which the political and territorial integrity of many existing states was seriously challenged following the break-up of the Eastern bloc. In many instances, the international community was seemingly receptive to the claims of certain collective entities of their rights to self-determination, autonomy or secession. At the same time, the CCP was treated by most of the Western governments as an outcast regime following the Tiananmen crackdown. However, this window of opportunity turned out to be ephemeral. It did not take long for Taiwan to learn that the so-called new world order presents as many new constraints as new opportunities.

As the prospect of an imminent collapse of the communist regime on the mainland quickly diminished around 1993–94, the economic sanctions and diplomatic boycott undertaken by the West against the PRC were soon replaced by a policy of constructive engagement and enlargement. As the world starts to reckon with the implications of the rise of China as a superpower in the 21st century, it seems increasingly unlikely that the United States, Japan or major European countries will recognize the claim of the Taiwanese people to their right to self-determination in the face of a possible military confrontation with a PRC equipped with nuclear arms. The two missile crises in the Taiwan Straits have also shown the people of Taiwan that President Lee Teng-hui has already pushed the strategy of creeping independence to its realistic limit. A further push for *de jure* independence will guarantee nothing but a disastrous outcome. Thus, from the mid-1990s onward, the Taiwanese independence movement has lost its momentum despite the fact that the DPP now enjoys a much freer political space for ideological mobilization.

BY WAY OF CONCLUSION

Taiwan's dual transition from a party-state system was not only facilitated by a number of enabling historical conditions—the early indigenization of the KMT leadership, the party's accumulated electoral strength in local politics, the built-in adaptability of the official ideology as well as the constitutional arrangements, and an effective economic development program—which made a peaceful extrication from a single-party authoritarian regime politically conceivable and manageable. This was complemented by a crucial contingent factor, the succession crisis and intra-party power struggle which accelerated the indigenization of the power structure, provided the impetus for policy redirection, and restrained in a limited way the natural tendency of the entrenched incumbent elite to restrict the scope of democratic reform.

The fact that a former quasi-Leninist party can deliver a stream of electoral successes after the convocation of founding elections is no small achievement in itself. Although a partisan grip on the state apparatus remains an important ingredient of its electoral fortune, it is no longer the most decisive element. Increasingly, the born-again KMT builds up its electoral strength in much the same way as other dominant parties in advanced industrial democracies. It builds a winning majority on a rare combination of flexibility and rigidity and a unique blend of symbols and payoffs. This involves taking an ambiguous centrist position on a predominant cleavage dimension and practicing eclecticism and pragmatism on socio-economic issues. Its ingenious program of gradually consolidating Taiwan's sovereign claim without endangering the status quo enables the KMT not only effectively to reconcile the seeming contradiction between the popular aspiration for a separate identity in the international community and the prevailing concern for stability and prosperity, but also virtually to chain the two opposition parties to the two polar ends of the spectrum. More fundamentally, it benefits from the fruits of long-term political dominance. It has acquired the ability to shape the terms of public policies and the parameters of political conflicts. The power of institutional creation enables the KMT to direct the center of electoral gravity away from the elections for representative bodies to the contest for top executive offices and, thus, reduce its dependence on the local faction as well as on the practice of vote-buying.[27] A firm grip on the steering wheel of mainland and foreign policies enables the KMT to extract extra political mileage out of both the deep-seated aversion to a rupture in cross-Strait relations and the popular sentiment of Taiwanese solidarity. Also, the KMT can, in a limited way, introduce a shift in the popular allegiance in the direction of either pro-reunification or Taiwanese nationalism by employing state power to erect a new cultural hegemony and impose its own vision of nation-

---

27 The disappointing seat-to-vote ratio in the recent Legislative Yuan election prompted the KMT to consider initiating an overhaul of the existing electoral system. As the KMT has lost its competitive edge under the SNTV system, the party leadership resolved during the campaign of the recent National Assembly to introduce a new system based on single-member district and plurality rule. The proposed reform theoretically will foster the growth of a two-party system and put the New Party at a severe disadvantage.

building. Finally, as long as its ability to achieve its historic projects—security, development, and international legitimacy—remains unhampered under a democratic regime, a majority of social groups are more likely to look to the incumbent rather than the two opposition parties for solutions. In this sense, the expectation of long incumbency itself loads the electoral dice in favor of the incumbent party.

Chapter 4

NO EASY STROLL TO DOMINANCE: PARTY DOMINANCE, OPPOSITION AND CIVIL SOCIETY IN SOUTH AFRICA

STEVEN FRIEDMAN

Since South Africa's first non-racial election produced an electoral majority of almost two-thirds for the African National Congress—40 percentage points ahead of its nearest rival—it has become almost a conventional wisdom to assume that the ANC will monopolise government for many years.

This probability is based on assumptions about the salience of racial identity in South African politics. The ANC, the world's oldest "liberation movement"[1] has consolidated its status as the premier vehicle of black African aspirations, a seemingly sure-fire formula for electoral victory in a society with a history of racial polarisation, which prompts an inevitable tendency by the electorate to vote on largely racial lines.[2] While the ANC brings together a wide array of interests and perspectives, it is held together by a common (largely black) response to racial domination, a point acknowledged by deputy President Thabo Mbeki who predicted, a year after the 1994 general election, that the ANC would dissolve only after the effects of racial supremacy and division were eradicated.[3] He did not say, but no doubt assumed, that this would take at least a generation, during which the only credible challenge to the ANC would be likely to come from a black-led alternative with impeccable "liberation" potential—a credible rival of this sort is not currently on the horizon.

The rigidity of political loyalties is also seemingly confirmed by a strong territorial tendency in South African politics: the 1994 general and 1995 and 1996 local elections tended to confirm the extent to which, particularly but

---

1   The ANC was formed in 1912 and has dominated "liberation" politics since then, despite some challenges, including the 1959 breakaway of "Africanists" who formed the Pan-Africanist Congress. See, for example, Edward Roux, *Time Longer Than Rope: The History of the Black Man's Struggle for Freedom in South Africa* (Madison, Wisconsin: University of Wisconsin Press, 1972).

2   Various estimates have been offered of racial voting trends in the 1994 founding general election. While these clearly cannot be definitive, what is known of the results taken together with various opinion surveys suggests overwhelming black African support for the ANC, with whites tending to vote for white-led parties such as the NP, Freedom Front and Democratic Party. See, for example, Steven Friedman, *Yesterday's Pact: Power-Sharing and Legitimate Governance in Post-Settlement South Africa* (Johannesburg: Centre for Policy Studies, 1995).

3   *The Star*, 27/4/95.

not exclusively in formerly black residential areas, support for political parties is geographically concentrated: it was not uncommon for parties (the ANC and Inkatha Freedom Party particularly) to win up to 97 per cent of the vote in particular magisterial districts.[4] This geographic dominance is in some cases evidence of identity politics since, despite apartheid's end, residential areas are still often largely racially homogenous. But it was, at least until 1994, often maintained by force as parties and interests across the spectrum created "no go" areas where opponents dared not tread.[5] There are signs of a weakening of this trend since then—the ANC and IFP committed themselves to allow each other to campaign in their respective strongholds during the 1996 local election campaign in the KwaZulu/Natal province. But the local elections certainly confirmed a tendency to fixed party loyalties, which usually find geographic expression.

These realities have prompted the view that post-apartheid South Africa is developing—or has already developed—into a "party dominant system". Some analysts are, in anticipation of this possibility, revisiting the study of these systems in an attempt to gain a greater understanding of the likely development of the South African polity.

At first glance, the anticipation of ANC hegemony seems to rest on irrefutable logic. It has, over more than eight decades, established itself as the almost unchallenged symbolic vehicle of majority aspirations for "liberation". The reality that racial identities and interests will play an important role in politics for a good while yet, and the overwhelming—and growing—black majority make it difficult to imagine a serious threat to the ANC's parliamentary majority in the next two elections and, quite possibly, the two after them. While some analysts regularly predict a split in the ruling party, attempts to establish a credible challenge to its hegemony within the "liberation" camp have repeatedly foundered.[6]

Nor do we lack examples of parties or movements who, after leading a battle for national "liberation", have insulated themselves from electoral challenge for very long periods. In these cases, the dominant party relies primarily on the symbolism accrued in the "struggle" against colonial or

---

4 Steven Friedman and Louise Stack, "The Magic Moment" in Steven Friedman and Doreen Atkinson (eds)., *The Small Miracle: South Africa's Negotiated Settlement* (Johannesburg: Ravan, 1995).

5 ibid.

6 During the period of anti-apartheid "struggle", attempts to establish a worker's movement independent of the ANC failed. See Steven Friedman, *Building Tomorrow Today: African Workers in Trade Unions, 1970–1983* (Johannesburg: Ravan Press, 1987). After the 1994 election, an attempt by Rocky Malebane-Metsing, an ANC member of the NorthWest provincial executive, to establish a rival party was an electoral disaster.

minority rule and is perceived by the electorate as an expression of a nation or group's desire for "self-determination".[7] The most obvious one is drawn from (white) South Africa's own past: the National Party which—within the confines of the white minority to which the apartheid-era franchise was restricted—won every election from 1948 until the end of the racial franchise in 1994. Other striking examples, under conditions in which the franchise was or is enjoyed by all adult citizens, are India's Congress Party and, much closer to home, the Botswana Democratic Party.

But the deduction that a "party dominant system" in South Africa is foreordained is, as this chapter will try to show, far less self-evident, for this term refers to far more than the expectation that one party will win repeated electoral victories. If that was all it did mean, these systems would hardly be exceptional—they would include many of the planet's democracies, including some which have never been labelled dominant party systems, such as Britain under the Conservative Party and Gaullist France. Far more is required before we can categorise a political system as "party dominant"— and, since dominance is achieved over time, it is misleading to assign that label to South Africa yet.

This chapter will, therefore, discuss the likelihood of South Africa becoming a "dominant party system" and will then examine the implications of this analysis for both opposition parties and the organisations of civil society.

SOME CONCEPTUAL ISSUES

The essential point about "party dominant systems" is that they are democracies: there is regular and open electoral contest, opposition parties are free to organise and civil liberties are, at least in the main, respected. Within this context, however, one party monopolises power.

Insistence on this point is important for two reasons. First, it distinguishes between systems in which, despite regular elections, party domination is achieved in whole or part by undemocratic means and those in which it is an accurate expression of the will of the electorate, expressed in democratic procedures. Singapore, where party dominance was achieved in part by arresting the left-wing opposition[8], or Mexico, where mechanisms were,

---

7 The ANC's non-racialism ensures that it is concerned to project itself as an expression of national aspirations, not purely black ones. Whether this self-image is accurate is the subject of much scholarly debate.

8 Chan Heng Chee, *The Dynamics of One Party Dominance: The PAP at the Grassroots* (Singapore: Singapore University Press, 1976), pp. 197ff.

until 1994, used to guarantee electoral outcomes[9], are in the former category (as is South Africa under NP rule); the latter spans a range of democracies from India and Botswana to Sweden, post-independence Israel, and, until recently, Italy and Japan.

This raises the second point—that, because it is won within democratic rules, party dominance cannot be achieved simply or even predominantly by force or fraud. This applies to some extent even in our first category of authoritarian party dominance within electoral rules since the minority parties are entities which "the dominant party cannot ignore in its political calculations".[10] It is, therefore, forced to take voter preferences more seriously than a military junta or one-party regime. But it applies far more so to a dominant party which is constrained by democratic rules.

In a celebrated formulation, Duverger thus categorised a dominant party as one which is "identified with an epoch": domination is "a question of influence rather than strength".[11] This implies that dominance stems from the dominant party's ability to establish itself in the minds of the electorate as the "natural" party of government. As Duverger notes, dominant parties are able to convince not only their own supporters of this reality, but the opposition too: "Even...citizens who refuse to give it their vote, acknowledge its superior status and its influence; they deplore it, but admit it".[12]

Achieving this status within democratic rules is, to state the obvious, hardly automatic: maintaining it is far less so. On the first score, it has been suggested that "it is virtually necessary for a party to preside over the establishment of the polity" for it to achieve the necessary "identification with the epoch".[13] But while so presiding may be virtually necessary, it is not remotely sufficient.

However identified with the epoch dominant parties may be, democracies provide constant channels for the expression of diversity, which do not dissolve once a party has achieved dominant status. In many cases, dominant parties achieve dominance by winning a bare majority or less of the popular vote: India's Congress (like Italy's Christian Democrats and, since 1963, Japan's Liberal Democrats) did not, at the high point of its dominance, win 50 per cent of the vote in any election[14]—Sweden's Social Democrats have

---

9   Jorge Castaneda, *The Mexican Shock*.

10   Chan, op. cit., p. 4.

11   Maurice Duverger, *Political Parties* (London: Methuen, 1959), p. 308.

12   ibid.

13   Alan Arian and Samuel H. Barnes, "The Dominant Party System: A Neglected Model of Democratic Stability," *The Journal of Politics*, Volume 36, 1974, p. 594.

14   Stanley A. Kochanek, *The Congress Party of India: The Dynamics of One-Party Dominance* (Princeton: Princeton University Press, 1968), p. 408.

done so only twice.[15] Given this, dominant parties cannot afford complacency about their dominance.

This point holds even where dominant parties win a large majority since even identification with an epoch may not prove permanent. The ability to translate potential into actual dominance depends on creating what has been called a "virtuous cycle of dominance", where government office achieved through a dominant position is used to ensure further dominance.[16]

Some of the methods used to achieve this goal sail close to the wind of liberal democratic practice. The use of patronage or what LaPalombara has labelled "parentela" or kinship contacts between government and citizens—in which the state is at the very least a good deal more open to the dominant party's "family" than to opposition voters[17]—is a common device. Where dominant parties accede to power as an expression of group aspirations, in a context in which there are very clear divides between the "we" it represents and the "they" against which it fought, *not* using patronage to reward "us" at the expense of "them" may be seen as a betrayal of its constituency. So too is a gradual blurring of the divide between party and state, which may be achieved either by the exclusion of opposition party supporters from bureaucratic posts[18] or simply by virtue of the fact that state officials serve only one party for a protracted period. And, in some dominant party systems, effective delegitimation of the opposition is a powerful dominant party tool.[19]

It is, however, misleading to conclude from this that dominant parties can always rely on these methods. Delegitimation of opposition parties, for example, is not automatically within the gift of dominant parties: "An excluded party's delegitimation is a function not only of its enemies' actions but of the cultural understandings of the mass public and…the way in which international and domestic conditions support or deny its basic view of reality".[20] Dominant parties cannot delegitimate the opposition by *fiat*: conditions must exist in which the electorate is open to delegitimation. Thus, while Israel's first premier, Ben-Gurion, invested much effort in delegitimating his

---

15   Gosta Esping-Andersen, "Single-Party Dominance in Sweden: The Saga of Social Democracy" in T.J. Pempel (ed.), *Uncommon Democracies: The One-Party Dominant Regimes* (Ithaca and London: Cornell University Press, 1990), p. 45.

16   Pempel, op. cit., p. 16.

17   Joseph LaPalombara, *Interest Groups in Italian Politics* (Princeton: Princeton University Press, 1964).

18   Ariel Levite and Sidney Tarrow, "The Legitimation of Excluded Parties in Dominant Party Systems", *Comparative Politics*, April, 1983, pp. 295ff.

19   Levite and Tarrow, ibid and Arian and Barnes, op.cit., analyse the effective use of this strategy in Italy and Israel.

20   Levite and Tarrow, op. cit., p. 297.

opposition as "fascist", he would have been unable to do so had it not behaved in a way which gave credence to that claim.[21] Nor might Italy's Christian Democrats have succeeded in delegitimating the Communist Party had there been no Cold War—or examples of behaviour by European Communist states—in voters' minds.

Equally importantly, the strategies described here are never enough, in a democratic system, to ensure continued dominance. Parties with potential for dominance are usually if not invariably alliances of diverse interests: they have "ties, often formal ones, with many diverse groups and interests which (they) must somehow reconcile, pacify and reward"[22]. This reality "make(s) it difficult to maintain party cohesion by means of strict party discipline. Rather, cohesion emerges from the mutual desire to share the fruits of power…".[23]

It follows that dominant or potentially dominant parties which do not recognise this and who therefore seek to impose strict internal discipline—or fail to maintain the often delicate balance between their varying interests— run the risk of ceasing to dominate. A short period in the life of the post-independence Indian Congress Party illustrates this. An attempt by a faction to dominate leadership positions prompted the departure of several senior leaders to form a rival party.[24] This threat to its dominance was removed by Nehru's intervention which set a subsequent pattern in which internal pluralism became a key principle in Congress—one which has been maintained in varying degrees ever since.[25] The result was an ability, at least for a period, to hold differing interests within the party and, therefore, to ensure dominance.

Nor is internal pluralism necessarily enough to ensure continued dominance. The dominant party does need to govern and that requires it to make decisions which will inevitably favour some interests over others. Unless a dominant party can achieve the very difficult feat of ensuring that all its factions are confident that they can win at least a significant proportion of the battles, it is likely to shed sections of its support base. It is then essential, if it wishes to maintain its dominance, that it seek support from new interests to compensate for its losses. A celebrated case is the Swedish Social Democratic

---

21 Levite and Tarrow, p. 300. Violent protests by the opposition in the immediate post-independence period helped to make Ben-Gurion's point for him.
22 Arian and Barnes, op. cit., p. 602.
23 ibid.
24 Kochanek, op. cit., pp. 35ff.
25 Ashutosh Varshney, "India" in S.M. Lipset, ed., *The Encyclopedia of Democracy* (Washington: Congressional Quarterly, 1995), Volume II, p. 604.

Party, which shed its agrarian supporters and successfully recruited white collar workers as a substitute support base.[26]

More generally, dominant parties, by definition, cannot represent only a narrow band of interests: "The dominant party ensures its continued success by effectively spreading out among many social strata rather than concentrating on only one; it mobilises support from all sectors of society...."[27] While this claim is perhaps a little overstated since some sectors remain beyond the reach of even dominant parties, it expresses the reality that dominant parties must stress inclusiveness—at least in their natural support base —if they are to remain dominant.

Similarly, the conditions which ensure dominance never endure indefinitely. Even the most stable dominant parties face the threat of "generational" change, in which the next generation of voters does not recall with the same enthusiasm the heroic deeds which ensured the party its dominance. This is particularly so in cases, such as India and Israel, in which a dominant party owes its status to its role in the founding of the state: "Population replacement...creates difficulties for a dominant party that has built its legitimacy on the 'myth of the founding'".[28] Even before generational factors come into play, however, dominant parties are sure to face "moments of crisis" in which new circumstances threaten their dominance. They are only likely to continue if they have the strategic flexibility to adapt: "The politician of the dominant party can rely on electoral stability *if he makes the appropriate decisions...*".[29]

More specifically, the fact that dominant party systems are democracies means that they remain vulnerable to inevitable changes within society and politics and must retain "flexibility of manoeuvre" if they are to survive: "The dominant party must adjust to changes in the society, and the greater the fragmentation of the society, the greater the difficulty it experiences in doing so".[30] Since fragmentation—or diversity—are inevitable features of societies, particularly if they are reasonably industrialised, remaining dominant is difficult, however many advantages the dominant party enjoys.

It is, therefore, not axiomatic that access to government office inevitably ensures continued dominance. The "virtuous cycle" is by no means guaranteed and dominant parties must ensure that they use state power to maintain

---

26 Pempel, op. cit., pp. 17/18.
27 Arian and Barnes, op. cit., p. 603.
28 Levite and Tarrow, op. cit., p. 305.
29 Arian and Barnes, p. 614. My emphasis.
30 ibid, p. 597.

and extend the alliances which underpin their dominance. A dominant party must, for example, distribute enough to its support base to retain its loyalty, while ensuring that its opponents' supporters derive enough from public administration to ensure their continued loyalty to the democratic order: a politics of pure particularism would ensure that, while party dominance might survive, a stable democratic order would not. Dominant parties may be more prone to corruption and maladministration, since they are partly insulated from voter rejection.[31] But they are not immune from the need to build or preside over a state which commands broad public loyalty. It is therefore reasonable to conclude that "long-term dominance by a single party involves clever tactics of electoral mobilisation, tactical positioning and governance…" and that domination is "an art far more than it is an inevitability".[32]

These points are illustrated by the fact that, contrary to scholarly belief two decades ago, party dominance is not a permanent state. While Duverger's insistence that "every dominance carries within it the seeds of its own destruction" because the dominant party "wear(s) itself out in office",[33] seemed implausible then, it seems undeniable in a world in which very few "classic" dominant parties remain in office.[34] Dominance may, if the dominators are skilled and flexible, and enjoy favourable political and social conditions, last for decades: it is becoming apparent that it does not last for ever.

SOUTH AFRICAN APPLICATION

This background suggests strongly that the African National Congress's status as dominant party is by no means guaranteed.

It is, to be sure, extremely difficult to imagine the ANC failing to win a majority in 1999. It is equally hard to predict its defeat in 2004 or even, perhaps, in 2009. But this would merely ensure it a term of office as lengthy as that of Britain's post-1979 Conservative government: it would not guarantee dominant party status, in the sense that it would firmly insulate itself from effective political challenge.

---

31 In the mid-1970s, the Italian Christian Democrats remained dominant despite surveys showing that voters, by large majorities, saw the opposition Communists as both more efficient and more honest. Levite and Tarrow, op. cit., p. 317.

32 Pempel, op. cit., p. 32.

33 Duverger, op. cit., p. 312.

34 Among the many examples of ex-dominant parties are India's Congress, Italy's Christian Democrats, and Israel's Labour. Even Japan's Liberal Democrats have experienced their first period out of the office which seemed theirs by right.

More importantly, as this chapter implied earlier, dominance requires that the dominant party dominate the polity in general, the public policy debate in particular. Sweden's Social Democratic Party, for example, maintained dominance even while in opposition during the mid-1970s, since the government which replaced it largely pursued its programme.[35] The dominant party "sets the mood of the political scene" and is able to ensure that policy inputs "are filtered through structures dominated by the party and are thereby softened, purified and domesticated".[36] If South Africa is indeed moving towards a dominant party system, the ANC must be able to turn electoral victory into a means to achieve a monopoly or near-monopoly of the public policy agenda.

There is no doubt that the ANC enjoys strong advantages—indeed, it meets many of the criteria advanced here for dominant status. It has a powerful "founding myth" on which to rely: its role in spearheading the demise of apartheid and the creation of a non-racial democratic state makes it an ideal candidate for identification "with an epoch". Indeed, if we follow Duverger, it may already be so identified: brave statements by the National Party and the leftwing Azanian People's Organisation notwithstanding, the behaviour of political and social elites, and, perhaps, the assumptions which underlie public opinion, already appear to assume ANC dominance.[37] Despite the turbulence of many aspects of the country's transition, voting the government out of office is not an option seriously broached by its opponents.

But the ANC has some way to go if it is to establish dominance. Whether it is using the instruments of state to create a "virtuous cycle" is open to serious doubt. It has, to be sure, presided over a reasonably swift change in the racial composition of the upper echelons of the public service[38] and it may be assumed that the new incumbents are a loyal support base. But its avowed intention to retrench up to 300,000 public servants, most of whom will be lower-paid black officials in two of its provincial strongholds, the Northern Province and Eastern Cape,[39] suggests that it may (unlike the National Party) be unable to turn public service jobs into a source of mass support.

---

35 Pempel, op. cit., p. 18.

36 Arian and Barnes, op. cit., pp. 611, 601.

37 The NP has declared publicly that it does not expect to win the 1999 election, but has suggested that it has a reasonable prospect in 2004.

38 Richard Humphries and Khehla Shubane, *Situation Analysis: Public Service Transformation*, paper commissioned by United Nations Development Programme, 1/95 (unpublished).

39 Briefing by Minister of Public Administration to Centre for Policy Studies, 11/95; Humphries and Shubane, ibid.

More importantly, the ANC has not yet succeeded in ensuring that the state delivers resources effectively to its support base. To name but two examples, its mass housing policy has resulted primarily in deep disaffection among the beneficiaries;[40] and pension provision, a key source of economic sustenance in rural areas particularly, is subject to severe administrative disruption.[41] Links between the governing party and its support base are more tenuous than supposed, a point illustrated by its continued inability to persuade supporters to pay for municipal services. While there are contrary examples, it is far too early to suggest that the ANC in government is able to use the levers of power to solidify its support base. This is part of a wider problem—the limited reach of the new South African state over which the ANC presides. Dominant parties do not have to govern strong states to remain dominant—Italy is a clear example—but it certainly helps if they do.

It is beyond the scope of this chapter to analyse the reasons for this. Besides obvious administrative inexperience, the current administration may be hampered by an elite bias which prevents it delivering effectively to a mass constituency.[42] Equally if not more importantly, changes in the global economic environment create pressures for fiscal discipline which limit (but certainly do not eradicate) opportunities for social spending in general, patronage in particular: witness criticism within the ANC camp of spending cuts which are eroding social infrastructure such as hospitals.[43] This may support the view that creating a "virtuous cycle" of dominance is not purely a matter of strategy: "…party strategy is only primary within the limits of political opportunity, which in turn is dependent on the structural parameters within which politics operates"[44]. What is important for our purposes is that the effect is to threaten prospects for dominance. If this context persists, ANC voters may opt out of politics rather than voting for an alternative.[45] But this would erode its dominance of society, if not the formal polity.

Secondly, for much of its history (with the exception of the exile period), the ANC has conformed to a key survival principle of dominant parties by avoiding strict party discipline. Some analysts have mistaken the movement's often loud diversity for a sign of imminent dissolution. However, the

---

40 Mary Tomlinson, *From Rejection to Resignation: Beneficiaries Views on the Government's Housing Subsidy Scheme* (Johannesburg: Centre for Policy Studies, 1996).

41 *The Star* 2/10/96.

42 See my analysis of government priorities, *Business Day* 30/10/96.

43 *Business Day* 30/10/96.

44 Levite and Tarrow, op. cit., p. 315.

45 This possibility is suggested by focus group research. See Craig Charney, *Voices of a New Democracy: African Expectations in the New South Africa* (Johannesburg: Centre for Policy Studies, 1995).

conceptualisation offered here suggests that it has been a sign not only of an ability to cohere, but also of potential dominance, since it indicates an ability to accommodate an array of interests and values. Were that to change, however—if the ANC leadership was indeed to insist on imposing discipline on its divergent interests—fissiparous tendencies might well emerge.

There are signs that such an attempt may be made. The clearest example is ANC leadership reaction to leftwing criticism of its macro-economic strategy. Initially, the leadership reacted by insisting that the strategy's fundamentals were not negotiable, but that the critics remained valuable allies.[46] Later, however, the Minister of Finance attempted to persuade an ANC member of the Western Cape's provincial executive to desist from public criticism,[47] while leadership figures are said to have sought to remove a leftwing critic of the plan from the ANC's National Executive. On the opposite end of the ANC spectrum, Chief Patekile Holomisa has been disciplined by the movement for publicly opposing its position on traditional leadership—in one case, on a platform he shared with Inkatha Freedom Party leader Mangosuthu Buthelezi.[48] In principle, the constitution offers ANC leadership (and that of other parties) a device which gives it great latitude to discipline dissidents—a clause which stipulates that members of parliament who leave, or are expelled from, their parties cease to be legislators.[49] But this serves only to maintain discipline within the ANC—it is no guarantee against defections. Indeed, since dissidents would much prefer to remain within a party virtually ensured of an electoral majority if they possibly can, it is, if used often, an invitation to them.

It is as well not to make too much of these examples: it is far too early to assess whether the ANC will seek to narrow dramatically its parameters for internal diversity. But, were it to attempt this, it could face, over the next few years, a splinter to its left, if trade unionists and socialists believe they are no longer free to pursue their interests within the ANC, and to its right, if traditional leaders and their supporters reach the same conclusion.

Of the two, that to the left would probably be more significant. The ANC's shift to a more market-oriented economic strategy has alarmed its two

---

46 See address by Mandela to SA Communist Party Congress, *Business Day* 3/6/96.
47 *Business Day* 30/10/96.
48 *The Star* 28/9/96.
49 This clause is seen by some analysts as evidence of authoritarian tendencies within the majority party. But it is hard to understand why the ANC should be singled out here since the Democratic Party was the only parliamentary party engaged in constitutional negotiations (which the IFP boycotted) to oppose this stipulation. In any event it is, arguably, a logical consequence of a closed list proportional representation system in which voters elect parties, not people.

alliance partners, COSATU and the SA Communist Party. While the leadership of both allies are extremely eager to continue the alliance arrangement, COSATU's leadership in particular might well face irresistible pressure for the formation of a separate workers' party if it was not at least permitted to articulate opposition to the new economic stance while remaining within the alliance. Neither this development nor a breakaway by supporters of traditional institutions (who might prefer to mobilise outside the representative system) would threaten its prospect of an electoral majority: but either or both would dent perceptions of its present and future dominance.

A similar constraint on dominance is a strong centralism among ANC national leadership which may operate to weaken its links with its support base. The best-known manifestation is the tendency, which became evident in 1996, to impose leadership choices on ANC provinces. ANC Free State premier Patrick Lekota was removed—in effect by national leadership after its attempts to resolve a leadership battle in the province failed: the evidence suggests that Lekota enjoyed substantial popularity within the province and, in particular, within the provincial ANC. National leadership also attempted to prevent a challenge to the Northern Province ANC chair (and premier) Ngoako Ramathlodi by prevailing on his challengers not to contest the position. The unpopularity of this decision was illustrated when a little-known "stalking horse" Senator George Mashamba, challenged Ramathlodi after his better-known rivals withdrew—and won narrowly. These events suggest that centralism may be not a source of dominance but a signal to rebellion.

Ironically, the long-standing assumption in the ANC that national government is the sole centre of power (which, for the entire apartheid period, it was) has led to a tendency by national leadership to neglect the provinces: its national ministers and MPs, as a rule, do not play a great role in provincial ANC branches. This might be seen as a sign of respect for provincial initiative and autonomy were it not for the tacit assumption within the ANC that, with the exception perhaps of Premiers, the strongest leadership is assigned to the national tier. It is, however, at the provincial level that voters experience parties: neglect of provinces is, therefore, costly to the ANC. This—and a gulf between leadership and base—may explain one of the most eminent developments for the ANC, a sharp decline in membership in provinces such as Eastern Cape, where its support base has always been assumed to be the strongest, and Gauteng, where its organisation has been regarded as superior.[50]

---

50   Centre for Policy Studies, *Quarterly Trends*, Prepared for the National Business Initiatives, January, 1997.

A final point should be mentioned here. Dominant parties who derive their dominance primarily from a "founding myth"—their role in establishing the state—have usually been able to rely on lengthy tenure by a charismatic founding figure. Examples range from India's Nehru and Israel's Ben-Gurion to Botswana's Seretse Khama. The ANC's founding figure is scheduled to govern for five years only and its ability to continue to capitalise on this advantage may depend on Nelson Mandela's willingness and ability to exert at least symbolic influence after his formal withdrawal from politics.

Nor is this prospect made more appetising for the ANC by the knowledge that Mandela's presumed successor, Thabo Mbeki, has acquired a reputation, whether deserved or not, for intolerance to internal opposition and for driving opponents out of key positions.[51] If the ANC's second state president does prove hostile to pluralism in the movement, its status as a dominant party in a representative democracy could be threatened.

In sum, despite its manifest advantages, the assumption that dominant party status will accrue to the ANC regardless of how it responds to the challenge of internal diversity and effective governance may be deeply flawed. It may well have much to do before it is assured of dominant party status.

But, precisely because the ANC has governed for so brief a period, none of this means that the prospect of ANC dominance is remote. Indeed, given its "natural" advantages, little may be required of it beyond tolerably effective governance and an ability to refrain from silencing internal dissent. While it will inevitably face crises, it may weather them. Given this, what prospects face opposition parties and civil society?

OPPOSITION UNDER ANC DOMINANCE

An implication of the argument developed in the previous section is that challenges to ANC dominance, if they are to arise, are likely to emerge from within its constituency, not the current opposition. There are good reasons for asserting this.

The most obvious stems from an aspect of the legitimacy question discussed earlier. Not all dominant party systems depend on delegitimation of the opposition, but the ability to achieve this is a potent weapon in the hands of an aspirant dominant party. And the ANC's major opponents suffer from severe real or potential legitimacy problems, a reality flowing from the

---

51 ANC general secretary Cyril Ramaphosa's departure from politics is seen by some within the ANC as a response to manoeuvering by Mbeki. Centre for Policy Studies, *Quarterly Trends*, commissioned by National Business Initiative 8/96, p. 2.

country's racial history. In the case of the National Party, while the ANC has at times sought actively to delegitimate the NP[52], this strategy has more to do with a desire to preserve unity within the ANC than with a strategy to beat off an electoral challenge. History has, in effect, delegitimated the NP as a contender for mass support, given its role in introducing and implementing apartheid.

While it is clearly impossible to "prove" that this NP disability will endure, it may be worth noting that public disenchantment with Robert Mugabe's Zimbabwean government, while deep, has never translated into a willingness to vote for an alternative even vaguely associated with the Rhodesian Front or its successor, the Conservative Alliance of Zimbabwe. The Freedom Front is, given that the height of its aspiration is to speak for the white Afrikaner minority, even more clearly ruled out as a contender for power. In theory, the Democratic Party's legitimacy barrier—the fact that many voters see it as a "white party"—is not terminal, since it could recruit a black leadership. Even if it did, however, the prospect of a majority opting for classical liberalism in South African conditions is implausible for the foreseeable future.

This leaves the opposition to the left of the ANC, currently hampered not by delegitimation, but by an apparent voter perception that its programme is implausible, and the Inkatha Freedom Party. At present the IFP's stress on Zulu tradition sharply curtails its available support base, since it excludes both non-Zulus and Zulu speakers who identify with modernity. Could this change? Probably not, since the IFP's association with ethnic particularism and traditional structures is so central a feature of its *persona* that it is hard to imagine it being shed any time soon.

It must be stressed, however, that legitimacy, although the literature fails to define it clearly, may mean something other than the ability to challenge for an electoral majority. While legitimacy is a necessary component of this capacity, parties may be legitimate even if they lack it. Britain's Liberal Democrats are but one example of a party which enjoys legitimacy, but whose prospects of ever winning a majority are extremely remote. Legitimacy should, therefore, be seen not as the capacity to secure majority support, but a status in which the party is regarded as a legitimate participant in the polity, whose views need to be taken into account and which is, at least in principle, a potential partner in a governing coalition. Nor need delegitimation be permanent: opposition parties which have experienced delegitimation have, on occasions, found themselves readmitted to the circle of legitimate particip-

---

52 See for example Centre for Policy Studies, *TransAct*, vol. 2, no. 10, 11/95. See also statements by ANC Department of Information and Publicity.

ants in politics—indeed, a couple have eventually won elections.[53] The common thread between recent cases in which delegitimated parties have been relegitimated has been a severe national crisis which has prompted the dominant party to invite its opposition to play a role in governing or policy-making.[54]

Relegitimation has, to be sure, tended to occur only in societies far less polarised than South Africa and is thus far less likely here. Nevertheless, what the South African transition lacks in democratic bonhomie it more than makes up for in pragmatic accommodation. A development of this sort is thus possible: severe economic crisis or a collapse of public morale could prompt the ANC to invite some or all of its opponents into government. And in principle, this prospect is enhanced by the fact that delegitimation is rather more complex here than in some of the "classic" cases such as Italy and Israel.

Whether there is a uniform ANC attempt to delegitimise the NP, DP and IFP is debatable. Harsh rhetoric is not necessarily delegitimation: to fulfil the latter criterion, ruling party denunciations must question the opposition's loyalty to the democratic order. ANC statements portraying the NP as corrupt and bigoted, or attacks labelling the DP a representative of white business are not necessarily delegitimation—attempts to imply that opposition parties are not committed to democratic rules are. Both the IFP and NP (although not the DP) have been subject to attacks of this sort—the NP has on occasions been portrayed as an enemy of democracy—but it is too early to identify a uniform pattern: in his 1997 speech opening Parliament, Mandela was at pains to stress that there were "good people" committed to the new society in all parties: he explicitly mentioned the NP. This suggests that, for the present, delegitimation is uneven enough to permit the governing party to revitalise a new accommodation with the opposition if it felt moved to do so.[55]

There are also counter-trends. The Freedom Front has not been the target of delegitimation, partly because it has been willing to deliver to the new

---

53 The rightwing opposition in Israel and the Communists (renamed the Party of the Democratic Left) in Italy. See Levite and Tarrow, op. cit., for an account of this process in Israel.

54 ibid, p. 319.

55 This treatment doggedly refuses to address the delegitimation issue as a normative one for two reasons. Firstly, the moral debate is complex. While some argue that ANC "delegitimisers" show scant regard for democratic tolerance, it could be argued that it is unreasonable of a party which presided over more than forty years of racial domination, with its attendant human rights abuses, to expect its opponents never to refer to this fact. Secondly, this chapter has suggested that delegitimation is less a normative issue than a consequence of peculiar historical circumstances which give the majority party fuel for delegitimation attempts. That abundant fuel exists in South Africa is hardly in doubt.

constitutional order a rightwing white constituency whose violent resistance the ruling party feared and because it has displayed a willingness to co-operate with the ANC in the hope that this will secure concessions for its goal of achieving a degree of "Afrikaner self-determination".[56] Nor is rhetoric the only measure of delegitimation: so too is majority party propensity to recognise opponents as participants in decision-making.

On this measure, delegitimation of the opposition has been, at most, partial. The DP has been given the chair of the important parliamentary Public Accounts committee and a role, albeit junior, in constitution-making. Ruling party responses to the IFP have been ambivalent at times: its return to the constitution-making process was hailed by the ANC[57] and its role was described by the ANC's constitutional development minister as "a constructive attempt to find solutions".[58] And, despite NP delegitimation, the ANC continues to initially co-operate with it in the Western Cape provincial executive—and to negotiate constitutional compromises with it.[59] Its presence in a post-settlement unity government itself conferred a degree of potential legitimacy. Whether the opposition is taken more seriously as an influence on policy than its equivalents in other democracies is an issue for research—but it clearly has not yet been excluded from any influence at all.

These examples suggest that opposition parties may not be forced to rely on national crises—which they either cannot create or, if they do seek to act as a loyal opposition, cannot be seen to be attempting to create—to ensure a degree of influence. Their prospects may depend on a perception by the ruling party that it cannot resolve some problems on its own and that they have something to contribute to the solution. The Freedom Front may, as suggested above, already be in this position and the threats to stability posed by ANC-IFP conflict may be propelling the latter towards it. The NP may be hampered by the reality that it is not a real or perceived interlocutor of the key interests outside the ruling party's ambit.[60] The DP is in a similar position, but the fact that it is harder to delegitimise may give it some influence despite that.

This claim about the NP is open to objection, given its strong electoral base among white and coloured people. It is suggested, for example, that the ANC lacks the capacity to persuade white ratepayers to contribute their

---

56 See for example interview with Gen Constand Viljoen in *TransAct*, op. cit., vol. 2, no. 4, 4/95.

57 ANC Department of Information and Publicity, statement, 3/10/96.

58 SABC Radio interview, 4/10/96.

59 See, for example, *The Star* 3/10/96.

60 See Steven Friedman, *Yesterday's Pact*, op. cit.

dues[61] and that, by implication, only the NP can do this. But, while the NP is the electoral choice of an important section of the society, this does not mean that they rely on its presence in government to bind them to the democratic order. In not a single dispute between minority interests and the ANC government since 1994 have the former relied on the NP to represent them—this includes white ratepayers who, in 1996, refused to pay rates increases levied by an ANC council. And one reason for the NP's departure from the Government of National Unity in 1996 was the view of a section of its leadership that it was unable to represent its constituency effectively within the Cabinet. Certainly, the NP has not demonstrated the control over the actions and attitudes of its constituency which would easily convince a reluctant ANC government that the co-operation of key minorities can be ensured only by inviting the NP back into the government.

It is worth stressing here that the fact that the ANC's opponents have little chance of assembling an electoral majority give it latitude to allow the opposition into the political mainstream. It has been argued that dominant party calculations on this question in Israel and Italy played a crucial role in shaping the fate of party dominance in the two societies. Israel's Labour brought its rightwing opponents into the government during the 1967 war, legitimating it as a component of government, while Italy's Christian Democrats allowed the Communists a role in decision-making during the economic crisis of the 1970s, but did not invite them into the cabinet, prolonging both the perception that they were not fit for a role in government—and Christian Democratic dominance.[62] In South African conditions, however, even a Labour-style calculation by the ANC would be unlikely to offer its opponents the prospect of majority support, and this sharply reduces the risk to the ANC of doing so.

To some extent, opportunities for minority parties depend on factors outside their control: the extent to which the governing party succeeds in entrenching its own dominance—resolving problems which might otherwise require minority party assistance—and the degree to which it sees co-operation with minorities as a means of resolving those problems if they do arise. But this does not imply that minority parties are helpless.

Firstly, their prospects do not rely purely on their ability to catch the governing party's attention at the national level. If viable subnational levels of government exist, and minority parties are able to control some of these, they do enjoy a degree of leverage in a dominant party system: the Italian

---

61 Personal communication to the author, Hermann Giliomee, 7/2/97.
62 Levite and Tarrow, op. cit., p. 322.

Communists' control of local government is a key example: "… (it) sustained a link between it and the noncommunist left and provided jobs for thousands of party militants who might otherwise have left politics altogether".[63] At present, this presents opportunities for both the NP and IFP to play an active role in the polity.

This begs an obvious question: will sufficient powers for subnational government be retained to allow opposition parties sources of power or influence? This remains in the balance. The introduction of a system of "cooperative governance" which gives provincial governments a greater say in national legislation through representation in a National Council of Provinces with significant powers to shape legislation, particularly that affecting the provinces, but which grants provinces very limited exclusive powers, could greatly reduce the leeway of opposition-controlled provinces since it is possible for the seven ANC provinces to outvote them, forcing them to operate within legislation imposed upon them by the majority party. But this is by no means an inevitability since the ANC provinces can only approve legislation diminishing the power of their opposition-run counterparts if they are willing to diminish their own power as well. And the Council's impact will depend on whether the ANC is able to exert sufficient party discipline to ensure that its provinces vote routinely on party lines rather than on provincial interests: if they do the latter, of course, the opposition provinces may find themselves in the majority on some issues. Even if they do vote on party lines, it is possible that the laws imposed on provinces will give enough leeway to the opposition provinces to exert influence in their areas.

Local government is subject to a host of pressures from a central government eager to see it implement its agenda. There is also no tradition of autonomous local government in South Africa on which opposition-held municipalities could rely. Nevertheless, the 1996 constitution does give local governments bent on claiming a degree of autonomy significant room to manoeuvre.[64] While autonomy will certainly not be handed to municipalities on a platter, there is significant space open to those with the will to claim it and the political skill to press their claims.

Secondly, opposition parties are presented with options: the way in which they respond could shape their future. Two elements seem crucial here. Firstly, they do need to ensure that they represent constituencies whose co-operation the governing party needs. Racial cleavages in South Africa may constrain some democratic options by dooming some parties to permanent

---

63 Levite and Tarrow, op. cit., p. 313.
64 See Chapter 7, *RSA Constitution, 1996.*

minority status, but they guarantee that significant constituencies will remain outside the governing party's orbit. If they are effectively captured and retained by minority parties, the governing party may need to co-operate with those parties. As noted above, the NP's failure to be seen as a credible gatekeeper to key minority constituencies has sharply constrained its options: to remain effective, opposition parties will need to consolidate their support among key minority constituencies.

But this requires a particular sort of politics. The literature suggests that minority parties in dominant party systems have three options if they experience delegitimation (real or perceived). One is "…becoming a cult of true believers", the second is adopting "the dominant mores and values of the society" and the third to attempt to "extend (their) influence with new sections of the population…or to ally with legitimate participants…".[65] While these choices are partly determined by governing party behaviour, only the third offers prospects of growth and influence. And it is "not at all contradictory to the second but apparently incompatible with the first…".[66]

Whether the current opposition will be able to gain the loyalty of new sections of the population is unclear: certainly it cannot be guaranteed. But this analysis has implied that opposition parties have some prospect of co-operating with—if not allying with—legitimate participants. They can do this only by moving some way towards accepting the dominant mores.

This presents minority parties with a difficult but achievable challenge: to solidify their representation of excluded constituencies, but to do so in such a way that their loyalty to a non-racial order is not in question. Their incentive to meet the second criterion is not only that this would enhance prospects of working with the majority camp, but that it would reduce the danger of an outcome ignored by the literature—that "sectarian closure" could be self-defeating since it may result in the withdrawal of their constituency from politics.

The danger that minority constituencies may opt out of the new polity is very real. Evidence can be found in constant talk of white emigration, in the refusal by white ratepayers in Johannesburg suburbs to pay for municipal services[67] and in surveys indicating general disaffection with the political process.[68] Nor is this purely a minority problem: withdrawal from politics

---

65   Levite and Tarrow, op. cit., p. 298.
66   ibid.
67   See, for example, my analysis in *Business Day*, 16/9/96.
68   IDASA, "Parliamentary Ethics and Government Corruption: Playing with Public Trust", *Public Opinion Service Report No. 3*, 2/96.

may be the reaction of some majority constituencies if the new order fails to meet their expectations.[69] An opposition strategy which rests on solidifying minority constituencies' disaffection is, therefore, more likely to promote a flight from the polity by supporters than increased influence. Minority parties' two strategic imperatives are, therefore, to solidify their constituencies and to enhance their loyalty to the democratic order. Unless they achieve both, the outlook for minority parties may be bleak.

If the majority party does squander its opportunities and force dissident constituencies into new parties, minority parties would enjoy new possibilities for influence since alliances with legitimate parties and with the ANC itself would be possible. A left breakaway would offer opportunities for parties to the ANC's left only, but might create new openings for co-operation between the opposition to the ANC's right and the ANC itself. Rightwing breakaways (prompted by attitudes towards, for example, traditional leadership) or centrist disaffection would, while less likely, offer greater opportunities for co-operation with the breakaway party, less for a new relationship with the ANC.

Whether these occur is, of course, not within the gift of minority parties. But they do have options for extended influence even if there are no breakaways.

CIVIL SOCIETY AND ANC GOVERNMENT

Power in democracies does not flow purely from the formal representative system: since dominant party systems are democracies, the same point holds for them too.

Parties with overwhelming majorities in the legislature may confront organised interests who are able to exert independent influence on decision-making. This reality constitutes—in principle—a brake on the dominant party's power since these interests are, or can be, a countervailing force.

This is not automatic. Where, as in South Africa, dominant or potentially dominant parties are movements too, they are invariably buttressed by a network of organisations who operate in civil society but are in alliance with, affiliated to or sympathetic to, the dominant party. Dominance is clearly enhanced if they are able to ensure that the ruling party dominates not only in the formal polity, but in civil society too.

---

69 Charney, op. cit.

The National Party's rule was underpinned not only by a church, universities, cultural organisations, business associations, trade unions[70] (at least for a time) and sporting bodies. They were bound to the ruling alliance by a secret society, the Afrikaner Broederbond,[71] which played an important role in ensuring that the NP's hold extended long and deep into Afrikaner civil society. But dominance may not be achieved only or even primarily by manipulation—it may express Gramsci's notion of "hegemony",[72] in which an alliance of interests becomes dominant in civil society because it expresses the *zeitgeist*, or the dominant ethos within society.

At first glance, the ANC seems to have established a firm hold over that portion of civil society which shares its values. It is an explicit ally of the Congress of South African Trade Unions and an almost explicit one of the SA National Civic Organisation.[73] An association of hereditary chiefs, the Congress of Traditional Leaders (Contralesa), supplied members of the ANC's first parliamentary caucus. Persons sympathetic to the ANC are assumed to dominate the SA Council of Churches, key black-owned businesses, and a host of non-governmental organisations working in areas ranging from development or culture to advocacy issues such as the environment. ANC concern to ensure that universities—or at least predominantly black ones—are within its fold may be illustrated by claims that ANC politicians intervened to dissuade the University of Durban Westville from appointing a former president of AZAPO as its vice-chancellor.[74]

Whether or not a democracy develops into a dominant party system, the relationship between interest groups and the state is sharply influenced by party alignments—those within the ruling party fold will enjoy greater influence than those outside it. The point may seem trite, but is often ignored in literature on corporatism in democratic societies, which discusses relations between the state and interest groups without conceptualising political parties

---

70 For the National Party's role in building a trade union support base, see ES Sachs, *Garment Workers in Action* (Johannesburg: Eagle Press, 1957).

71 Ivor Wilkins and Hans Strydom, *The Super-Afrikaners: Inside the Afrikaner-Broederbond* (Johannesburg: Jonathan Ball, 1978); Hennie Srefontein, *Brotherhood of Power: An Expose of the Secret Broederbond* (London: Rex Collings, 1979).

72 Antonio Gramsci, *Selections from Prison Notebooks*, edited by Hoare and Nowell Smith (London: Lawrence and Wishart, 1971).

73 While SANCO is ostensibly politically unaligned, it routinely endorses the ANC at election time and many of its activists have been elected to office on ANC tickets. See, for example, Steven Friedman and Maxine Reitzes, *Democratic Selections?: State and Civil Society in Post-Apartheid South Africa* (Midrand: Development Bank of SA, 1995).

74 *Quarterly Trends*, op. cit.

as an intervening variable[75]. Clearly, this variable takes on added force if the ruling party presides over a society with sharp social and political divisions.

If past experience is a guide, therefore, it would seem reasonable to assume that the ANC is in the process of building a formidable presence in civil society through this network of associations which, like those which under-pinned NP dominance, will buttress its rule. Similarly, we may expect inter-ests outside the ANC camp to be deprived of access to the state—again, as they were under the NP. The remainder of this chapter will, however, sug-gest both that the ANC's civil society constituency is likely to counter-balance as well as buttress majority party dominance—and that interest groups outside the ANC camp have not been left without resource.

Then and Now: From "Volksbeweging" to Fractious Alliance
Two clear and related differences between the ANC and the National Party in government present themselves to even the casual observer—the fact that the ANC has no Broederbond to impose the dominant movement's stamp on civil society[76] and the fractiousness of the ANC alliance compared to the homogeneity of the NP's camp during its heyday.

This does not mean that ANC leaders necessarily harbour a deep respect for civil society's autonomy. Attempts to ensure that the section of civil society most likely to provide an ANC constituency is thoroughly monopolised were legion, particularly during the period of anti-apartheid "struggle".

From the mid-1970s, the ANC was concerned to ensure that the nascent independent trade union movement was led by ANC activists and it was par-ticularly concerned when, in the early 1980s, the Federation of SA Trade Unions seemed intent on maintaining organisational and strategic independ-ence.[77] The formation in 1983 of the United Democratic Front, the legal, internal, bearer of the ANC tradition, was heralded as an attempt to unite and coalesce a wide range of anti-apartheid civil society organisations but was as much, if not more, an attempt to ensure that they operated under leadership sympathetic to ANC ideals and willing to accept its leadership.[78]

---

75 For a critique of this literature which asserts the role of parties as "active participants in the role of building bridges...between interest associations and state actors", see Miriam Golden, "Inter-est Representation, Party Systems and the State: Italy in Comparative Perspective", *Comparative Politics* 18, no. 3, 1986.

76 *Sunday Times* 6/10/96 reports an attempt among black business people to establish an "African Bond", partly inspired by the Broederbond. It is, however, clearly far too early to assess its effects—or even whether it will be established.

77 Friedman, *Building Tomorrow Today*, op. cit.

78 Steven Friedman, "Bonaparte at the Barricades: The Colonisation of Civil Society", *Theoria*, 79, May 1992.

The civic movement and youth congresses which operated alongside it during the 1980s were not, as their own and UDF rhetoric insisted, a spontaneous attempt to represent the local concerns of the grassroots. By far the majority were established by UDF activists who were later to occupy senior positions within the ANC. Equally importantly, beginning in the late 1980s and persisting to this day, an ideology grew up around the civic associations which portrayed them not as a particular interest or pressure group, but as the voice of entire "communities"—an explicit claim to dominance.[79]

But, despite this, many organisations in the ANC camp have displayed significant independence. In many cases, it is difficult to determine whether this is so because ANC-aligned organisations are headed by free spirits or whether statistical probability ensures that black-led organisations are likely to be sympathetic to the ANC. But it is worth noting that, whatever the rationale of the UDF's formation, internal resistance to apartheid by the ANC camp in the 1980s was characterised by a strong ethos of accountability which was not purely rhetorical—and that the imperatives of attempting to organise constituencies legally force a degree of democratic practice.

The second factor, the fractiousness both of the ANC and of those civil society organisations sympathetic to it, is in marked contrast with the pattern under NP rule. In that case, both the party and the associations allied to it showed an almost monolithic unity. Dissent or difference was expressed privately, within the inner circle, if it was expressed at all. The ANC camp is far more of a loose alliance united by a set of common symbolic goals and the result is difference over policy and goals, a high degree of rivalry for position and, at times, public criticism of the movement's actions.

It is as well not to overstate this phenomenon. There is a clear tendency to close ranks on particular issues and, inevitably, given that they share a common symbolic framework and broad view of the world, the network of ANC civil society associations agree on much. But it is difficult to imagine components of the NP camp during its period of dominance denouncing its economic policy, as COSATU is currently doing, or to conceive of NP-aligned cultural organisations criticising the disbursement of public funds by an NP government, as cultural groups aligned to the ANC did during the controversy over health department spending on an AIDS awareness play.[80] And the idea of NP leaders and activists in its allied civil society organisations fighting pitched gun battles over the legitimacy of a local authority—as ANC

---

79   ibid and Steven Friedman, *The Elusive "Community": The Dynamics of Negotiated Urban Development* (Johannesburg: Centre for Policy Studies, 1993).

80   See, for example, radio and television interviews by Ivan Toms, Zakes Mda.

and SANCO leaders did in a North Cape town[81]—would clearly have been an impossibility.

Despite the clear similarities, then, the ANC alliance is not, as the NP and its constituency was, a united, coherent, *volksbeweging* or national movement. It is an umbrella for a range of disparate interests and values which has, at least to a degree, defied co-ordination.

This is, however, the starting point rather than the end of analysis. How does this organisational form—or lack of it—work to support and constrain concentration of power? What limits are there to civil society independence and influence within the ANC alliance? How ephemeral is this relative autonomy of ANC civil society organisations? And does the existence of substantial civil society interests outside the ANC alliance pose a significant obstacle to the concentration of power?

A Bounded Autonomy?

A useful prism through which to view the nature of ANC-aligned civil society and its likely future is the Reconstruction and Development Programme, the platform which the ANC alliance unveiled shortly before the 1994 election and which became a unfiying programme after it.

The RDP was, initially, the idea of the Congress of SA Trade Unions, which was concerned to bind an ANC government to redistributive and development goals; other left groups within the ANC, equally concerned that the movement in office would turn its back on some of its popular constituencies, endorsed this attempt.[82] This initiative was, however, constrained by a desire among ANC economic thinkers to align its economic programme with perceived international realities. The result was a complicated internal process in which just about every interest group in the ANC, from environmentalists through to the black business lobby, inserted a clause of their own in the document.[83] The result was both contradictory[84] and vague.

This process can be viewed as a successful attempt to paper over divisions between the movement's leadership and its civil society interest groups. By fudging divisions, the ANC alliance arguably ensured that all the interest

---

81 The battle took place in Colesberg, over the appointment of a councillor who had held office in a Black Local Authority to chair its transitional council. *Sunday Times* 18/12/94.

82 Graeme Gotz, "Reconstruction and Development: Shifting the Goalposts", *SA Labour Bulletin*, Johannesburg, vol. 20, no. 3, June 1996, pp. 10/11.

83 African National Congress, *Reconstruction and Development Programme: A Policy Framework*, 1994.

84 The document contains, for example, commitments both to tougher environmental control and enhanced industrial development.

groups remained within the camp and that real interest divisions would remain concealed, allowing the leadership to dominate. On the other hand, the need to accommodate varying interests by inserting their concerns confirms that the political leadership does not have unlimited latitude to dictate the policy agenda.

It is also important to stress that interests outside the ANC camp, although not present at the negotiations, did exert some influence on the finished product since the stance of the economic planners owed something to an assessment of business interests. This became more pronounced when the RDP base document became a white paper: to name one key example, a reference in the former to the nationalisation of mine land was removed in the latter, after a period in which the mines lobbied vigorously against the clause. Whether the change was negotiated directly with the mining industry is less relevant than the fact that its interests were accommodated in the policy process.

To be sure, there is compelling evidence that shifts in ANC economic policy owe more to the influence of international business than its local equivalent.[85] But, as the market becomes increasingly globalised, international civil society[86] has become a factor in domestic politics and this dynamic does create strategic openings for local business. As long as an ANC government remains aware of international economic dynamics—and it is hard to see how it can ignore them—this opportunity for an interest group outside the ruling camp will remain.

This dynamic may explain the new government's interest—or at least that of some of its members—in negotiated economic policy-making, expressed by the creation of the National Economic Development and Labour Council[87] and attempts to cement partnerships between it and white business. While both strategies have encountered significant difficulties, they do attest to an acknowledgement of a need to take note of interests outside the ruling alliance. This tendency to deal with significant interests outside the ruling camp has been a key feature of the negotiation period of the early 1990s.[88]

---

85 President Mandela, to name but one example, announced his movement's commitment to privatisation after a visit to Germany, where he met key business figures.

86 For a discussion of international civil society see Mervyn Frost, "The Globalisation of Civil Society: What Impact on South Africa?" in Richard Humphries and Maxine Reitzes (eds), *Civil Society After Apartheid* (Johannesburg: Centre for Policy Studies, 1995).

87 Nedlac is a statutory bargain forum, comprising organised business, labour and government: one of its four chambers also includes "community" interests. Friedman and Reitzes, op. cit.

88 Khehla Shubane and Mark Shaw, *Tomorrow's Foundations?: Forums as a Second Level of a Negotiated Transition in South Africa* (Johannesburg: Centre for Policy Studies, 1993).

Two reservations about this dynamic need to be addressed. The first is that a trend towards quasi-corporatism may bode ill for democracy in general, and minority parties in particular since it removes policy negotiation from the formal polity and ensures that the governing party sees organised interests as more plausible bargaining parties than minority parties.[89] But, as a preceding section has argued, if these parties are unable to represent strong interests, they are unlikely to wield any influence in policy-making whatever arrangements the governing party makes with those interests. In this context, quasi-corporatism may extend, rather than narrow, access to decision-making. And, if they do acquire this ability, negotiation between political parties would need to become at least an important supplement to this form of policy-making.

The other is the oft-cited point that bargaining of this sort may do less to invigorate democracy than to ensure that a cartel of elite interests buttresses majority party dominance. When a major insurance company refuses to pay its rates to an ANC local council,[90] it may be safely argued that this day is yet to dawn. Nor is a relationship of this sort between the ANC and white business inevitable. Structuring a relationship with white business which commits the latter to the new order is a challenge which still faces the ruling party—indeed, its ability to do so is one of the factors which will determine its capacity to entrench its dominance. For its part, white business has some leverage to shape the terms of any bargain of this sort. The outcome will, therefore, depend on the strategic decisions taken by key actors in both camps. Nor, of course, would a relationship between government and white business necessarily preclude democratic politics—whether it does will depend on the nature of the relationship, in particular the extent of its openness and the degree to which it excludes other interests.

At least some arrangements with interests outside the majority camp can, of course, alienate or worry interests within it: at a time when relations between the ANC and COSATU are subject to severe stress, the point need hardly be belaboured. These tensions are a graphic illustration of the extent to which civil society interests within the ANC have not been co-opted into a compliant relationship with it. Nor is this the only example: two others may be briefly cited.

The first is the tension since 1994 between the ANC in government and non-governmental organisations, including those within its camp. It centres on ANC ministers' insistence that donor NGO funding be channelled

---

89 Friedman, *Yesterday's Pact*, op. cit.
90 Liberty Life, which refused to pay increased rates to Johannesburg's Eastern Metropolitan Sub-structure, in protest at what it saw as unacceptably large increases.

through it[91] and that a structured council of NGOs be established to regulate the relationship. This fairly straightforward exercise in co-option has not been an unqualified success: NGOs have lobbied with some effect to curb government plans, and many have proved too fractious to be incorporated into the ruling elite.

The second is hypothetical. If any interest is both indispensable to, and in principle available for, a strong alliance with the ruling party, it is black business. And yet this outcome is not assured, certainly once, as seems likely, Mandela is succeeded by Mbeki. Not only does the heir apparent face the uncomfortable prospect that his best-known political rival, Cyril Ramaphosa, is a key figure in a major black business conglomerate: it is worth noting that an advisory committee established by Mbeki, in which black business people are prominent, includes no representative of any of the most important black-owned companies:[92] a cosy cartel is, therefore, hardly guaranteed.

In sum, an ANC government is not yet able to use its components of civil society to underpin its power: they do act, to some degree, as a countervailing force to the power of the majority party's leadership. It is as well to stress that this does not necessarily mean that civil society organisations sympathetic to the ANC are always vigorous watchdogs over the government. A key indicator is the series of corruption controversies which have emerged since the ANC took office. To be sure, as noted above, some of these interests did voice their concerns at the health ministry's role in funding the AIDS awareness play. But, in general, civil society organisations within the ANC camp have been less than vigorous in their concern to watch over public money: COSATU's silence has been particularly significant. But to say that these interests will constrain government power on some issues only is not to say that they do not constrain it at all.

As for interests outside the ANC camp, electoral arithmetic and a history of racial polarisation certainly limit their influence, particularly where they are seen to be led by, or to serve the interests of, whites: despite his vigorous pursuit of reconciliation, Mandela has more than once dismissed criticism of the ANC as an expression of white concerns. But, as our treatment of business suggests, uncomfortable realities, if not ruling party intentions, offer them a significant degree of real and potential influence.

---

91 See, for example, *Mail and Guardian* 13/4/95; RDP Office, *Report to Parliament: Taking the RDP Forward*, 8/6/96.

92 Among the notable omissions from Mbeki's council are representatives of New Africa Investments (NAIL), Real Africa Investments (RAIL), Kunene Investments, Thebe Investments and National Sorghum Breweries. *Mail and Guardian* 19–25/7/96.

The evidence gathered here suggests that it is possible to outline—albeit tentatively—the degree to which civil society interests, within or outside the ruling camp, are able to constrain government actions. Direct and public challenges to the new governing elite's probity or competence have little effect, as evidenced both by the corruption controversies and by unsuccessful pressure for the removal of Cabinet ministers whose competence is questionable. The reasons are in some cases too detailed to permit of thorough treatment here: suffice it to say that, in a context in which the governing party is aware that it is expected to fail by most outside its camp, and in which it suspects, with some justification, that racial bias lies behind this expectation, the tendency to close ranks when its governance is challenged is very high. This is particularly so given a long-standing ANC political culture in which disloyalty to the movement is interpreted—or portrayed—as hostility to non-racial democracy. Whatever the reasons, however, civil society influence on the quality of government, while it clearly exists,[93] is of limited effect.

But, as this section has argued, interest groups have real and potential influence over policy outcomes, whether these relate to the future of NGOs, social and economic policy or the advisability of anti-trust legislation.[94] This influence is not beyond the reach of groups who are seen by the ruling alliance to be relatively hostile—if they are able to find allies (in some cases, tacit ones) with reasonable credibility within the ANC camp—and international opinion, to which the ANC is sensitive. Thus the SA Institute of Race Relations, a frequent and vocal critic of the ANC, with other liberal organisations, successfully led a fight against a proposed Bill which would have severely restricted non-governmental organisations.[95] It was, however, probably able to do this because the Bill elicited considerable opposition from NGOs within the broad ANC camp—and, perhaps, among foreign aid donors.

Not surprisingly, perhaps, where civil society organisations are campaigning for causes which elicit little support from interests credible to the ANC or to foreign opinion, they are less likely to succeed: the SA Agricultural Union has had little success in altering significantly legislation aimed at protecting

---

93 One obvious example is that the Press has far greater leeway to report on corruption than it did in the past.

94 The ANC has, since 1994, promised to introduce legislation curbing economic concentration but has not done so, presumably because either realities or business lobbying or both deterred it.

95 The import of this example is, on the surface, weakened by the fact that the Bill was proposed not by the government but a group of lawyers commissioned, ironically, to draft legislation to enhance the legal status of NGOs. Initially, however, the ANC chair of non-profit organisations National Assembly's welfare committee welcomed the Bill, which suggests that it might have reached the legislature had a campaign not been mounted against it.

farm tenants from eviction. This, however, is not particularly significant: the power of civil society clearly cannot be measured by the ability of every civil society interest to win every issue. Their ability to do so depends on their ability to assemble a strong coalition in support of their aims or to bring sufficient pressure to bear to prompt a government rethink. It is possible in principle that even conservative interests such as the SAAU may find issues on which this becomes possible.

Confidence that this reality will persist stems from the probability that this influence has—particularly in the case of non-ANC interests—less to do with the preferences of political leaders than with the reality of a society in which push-button governance from the centre is particularly implausible.

There is, of course, no guarantee that political leadership will heed the evidence and accommodate those interests whose co-operation it needs to govern effectively. This means that an authoritarian attempt to silence civil society interests within and without the ANC remains possible. But, in conclusion, two points may be made about this possibility.

The one is that such an attempt, if the essentials of democracy are to be maintained, seems destined to fail. It was argued earlier that an attempt to silence the ANC left could prompt its withdrawal from the ANC camp and, therefore, a significant threat to its dominance: this point applies with equal or more force to an attempt to silence the trade union movement.[96] And, of course, if democratic essentials were not maintained, the question of party dominance would become irrelevant since this chapter has argued that it makes sense to use this categorisation only of democratic systems.

The other is that, if it took this course, the ANC would still face perhaps the most serious threat to its dominance—one which resides, at least partly, outside the formal polity and civil society. This is the limited reach of the current government—a feature which it shares with the last years of the reign of its predecessor. Many of the most serious challenges faced by the new order have stemmed not from overweening governance, but its opposite, a tendency, which this society shares with many others, for much of social life to remain outside the orbit of government: if the point requires evidence, high crime rates, low tax payment levels, formal or informal tax and service charge boycotts, and unauthorised use of public services should suffice.

There is little evidence that the governing party enjoys the capacity to reverse this trend by force or manipulation, still less that it can do so by edict.

---

96 COSATU and the SA Communist Party, for example, requested a meeting of the ANC alliance to discuss concerns that the unions in particular were not consulted on policy initiatives. *Weekly Mail and Guardian* 4–10/10/96.

If the ANC is to attempt to secure dominance over the society, let alone the polity, it will be forced to exercise the same strategic judgement, pragmatism and adaptability as successful dominant parties elsewhere. If it succeeds while remaining within the parameters of constitutional democracy, its dominance will be richly deserved—even if, as in all other societies in which one party has dominated a democracy, its dominance will not endure indefinitely.

Chapter 5

THE RESILIENCE OF ONE-PARTY DOMINANCE
IN MALAYSIA AND SINGAPORE

JAMES V. JESUDASON

INTRODUCTION

The political systems of Malaysia and Singapore stand out in Southeast Asia
in that their military forces have never participated directly in politics. Their
citizens have not experienced harsh authoritarian rule, and the opposition
parties are allowed to exist legally. The leaders of both regimes do appreciate
the benefits of electoral competition for regime legitimacy, and have stead-
fastly held elections within constitutionally prescribed time frames. However, within this broad electoral framework, the ruling parties in Malaysia
and Singapore have sought actively to dominate the political process in their
countries, taking it for granted that they should rule with at least a two-thirds
majority in Parliament, which allows for constitutional changes to be made
with ease. The ruling coalition in Malaysia, initially called the Alliance but
restructured and renamed as the Barisan Nasional (BN) or National Front in
1974, has been in power since independence in 1957 and in Singapore, the
People's Action Party (PAP) has ruled since 1959. Neither party has shown
any sign of losing its predominant position in the polity. Considering that a
number of long-standing dominant parties, such as the Liberal Democratic
Party of Japan, the Congress Party of India, and the PRI of Mexico, have
either lost power or have weakened over time, it is worthwhile to ask why
the PAP and the Barisan have remained so hegemonic. In Malaysia, the question is also tantamount to asking why the United Malays National Organisation or UMNO, the core party in the Barisan, has been in power for so long.
Just as the main opposition parties revolve around the Barisan Nasional in
the general political system, the non-Malay component parties revolve
around UMNO in the ruling coalition.

At first sight, juxtaposing the PAP and the Barisan Nasional might seem
out of place because the two countries differ in size, economic levels, and in
their demographic profiles. Singapore is a highly urbanised city-state with a
population of 3.5 million, and a per capita income of around US$ 22,500,
putting it in the income bracket of rich industrialised countries.[1] Malaysia's

---

1   World Bank, *World Development Report* (New York: Oxford University Press, 1996), Table 1, pp. 188–9.

population is about 20 million and, unlike Singapore, has a significant but diminishing rural sector. Malaysia's per capita income of US$ 3,480 puts it in the upper-middle income category of countries as classified by the World Bank, one whole category below Singapore. The ethnic distribution in Singapore is about 78 per cent Chinese, 14.1 per cent Malay, and 7.1 per cent Indian. The Chinese majority have higher average incomes than the other two groups. In Malaysia, the politically loaded category "Malay and other indigenous groups" comprises 60 per cent of the population while the Chinese and Indian groups are 30 per cent and 10 per cent of the population respectively. The Malay majority has historically had and continues to have a lower average income than the other two groups, making the management of ethnicity one of the more challenging aspects of the country's politics.

Despite these differences, the political systems in Malaysia and Singapore provide important insights into the nature of dominant parties in general. Their similarities, such as the relatively coherent and capable bureaucracies inherited from colonialism, and the high dependence on export-oriented manufacturing, suggest that there are some interesting prerequisites for sustaining one-party dominance. Firstly, the cases indicate that the political party which first controls a well-developed, top-down colonial bureaucracy, and continues to manage society relatively well, has tremendous longevity in the polity. Secondly, globalisation, rather than threatening the dominant party, may indeed have facilitated its consolidation in Malaysia and Singapore. The ruling parties have been able to manage dominance by combining labour control and success in the global economy effectively. This is an interesting counterpoint to the view that international economic pressures have caused the decline of the Social Democratic Party in Sweden, Europe's long-standing dominant party, and the weakening of Mexico's PRI. It appears globalisation can put pressure on the dominant party only when dominant parties relying on the critical link with the working class pursue polices that are at variance to international market expectations in order to preserve this relationship. The regimes in Malaysia and Singapore, by their particular economic policies and links to labour, have so far escaped the threats economic globalisation can pose to the dominant party.

Both the dominant parties also demonstrate that there are a variety of state–society linkages possible to establish one-party dominance. The PAP has been described as having a "cadre party in a mass party guise", in which there is tight control in recruiting higher-echelon cadres to the party, a weak desire to seek large grassroots membership, and a fear of internal party pluralism.[2] The party's main mode of linkage with society, such as with the labour movement and ethnic groups, is through corporatist arrangements, relying on an ideology of ethnic neutrality. In contrast, UMNO is a mass-mobilising ethnic party that seeks a broad membership base. UMNO symbolically privileges the Malay group and has numerous clientelist relations with the different social classes in Malay society, although it also seeks a modicum of accommodation with the non-Malays.

The resilience of both parties has attracted the attention of Southeast Asian scholars, but no consistent account has been put forward. Some analyses focus on control and coercion in accounting for their hegemony. In general, scholars do not describe the Barisan and the PAP as either unambiguously democratic or authoritarian. Crouch, for example, terms the Malaysian regime as a repressive-responsive one, while Chan Heng Chee, in describing the PAP, has used words such as paternalistic, good government, and authoritarian in the same breath.[3] Given the multifaceted nature of both regimes, it is not surprising that some recent works have preferred to highlight the role of repression in the polity, highlighting media bias, gerrymandering, patronage, coercive legislation, and politically motivated arrests of oppositional figures.[4] Unfortunately, these accounts fail to distinguish between the following two possibly very different cases: that the illiberal characteristics of the regimes merely act as an added lever for dominance, or that they are fundamentally responsible for party rule.

Another genre of explanations has been based on the failure of the middle class to play its historical role in making the political system more competitive and pluralistic. Girling, who strongly subscribes to Lipset's wealth-democracy thesis of seeing economic development as breeding democracy, finds Singapore and Malaysia to be anomalies to his general position.[5] While the middle class has played an important democratising role in Thailand and Philippines, they have failed to do so in Singapore and Malaysia. Girling finds it paradoxical that both these countries are the most advanced economically, have the largest middle class, and in the 1960s were the most

2   Chan, Heng Chee, "Political Parties", Jon Quah, Chan, and Seah, eds., *Government and Politics of Singapore* (Singapore: Oxford University Press, 1985), pp. 159–60.
3   Harold Crouch, *Government and Society in Malaysia* (Ithaca: Cornell University Press, 1996), p. 240; Chan Heng Chee, *The Dynamics of One-Party Dominance: The PAP at the Grassroots* (Singapore: Singapore University Press, 1976), p. 230.
4   For example, Anne Munro-Kua, *Authoritarian Populism in Malaysia* (Houndmills: Macmillan Press, 1996) and Christopher Tremewan, *The Political Economy of Social Control in Singapore* (Houndmills: Macmillan Press, 1994).
5   John Girling, "Development and Democracy in Southeast Asia", *Pacific Review*, 1, 4 (1988), pp. 332–333.

democratic in Southeast Asia, but have over time regressed in their democratic development. In Girling's view, the ethnic divisions in Malaysia between the Malays and the Chinese have forestalled any unified middle class or working class action against the dominant regime, while the PAP's dominance is based on its skill in keeping a tight control over the population and obtaining the "materialistic acquiescence of most Singaporeans".[6] Some recent works have also mentioned the failures of the middle class to act progressively. Jones and Brown, in their article on "Singapore and the Myth of the Liberalizing Middle Class" portray the middle class as beset by self-doubt and anxiety, an outcome of confusion produced by the state's mixture of incompatible languages.[7] Crouch sees the weak democratic role of the middle class as a product of ethnic divisions, and the dependence of the Malay bourgeoisie on the state.[8] These ideas tell us that the middle class is not born in a liberal swathe, but they fail to distinguish between the middle class as a product of the regime and as a cause of the regime, often threading both lines of argument. Here we want to use a more regime-focused approach that examines how the dominant parties meet the grievances and anticipate the needs of the middle class, since failure to do so might indeed produce a less acquiescent middle class.

Case's study of "semi-democracy" in Southeast Asia—which he calls halfway houses because they permit electoral participation while denying liberal rules of contestation—is also concerned with why the dominant parties of Malaysia and Singapore have been so long in power.[9] Although he makes the interesting comment that semi-democracies are able to borrow "cunningly some features of democracy in order substantively to avoid it", his main explanation focuses on group rivalries in a divided society.[10] He tries to show that the key constituents of a regime may not be as much interested in empowerment or motivated by the state's authoritarian harshness as by their own violent rivalries with other social constituencies. The regime aligns itself with a core constituency, such as the Malay ethnic group in Malaysia or the English-educated middle class in Singapore, whose members in turn support the regime because of the protection offered against rival ethnic and class groups. In other words, enduring conflict among social groups in society

---

6 Girling, "Development and Democracy," p. 333.
7 David Jones and David Brown, "Singapore and the Myth of the Liberalizing Middle Class", *Pacific Review*, 7, 1 (1994), p. 79.
8 Harold Crouch, *Government and Society*, p. 243.
9 William Case, "Can the Halfway House Stand?—Democracy and Elite Theory in 3 Southeast Asian Countries", *Comparative Politics*, 28, 4 (1996), pp. 437–460.
10 Case, "Can the Halfway House Stand?", p. 438.

leads to mutual distrust, and refuge is sought in a semi-democratic Leviathan. However, this view does not differentiate carefully enough between the historical roots of the dominant parties in social divisions and the actual role of social divisions at present. One can argue that the nature of social divisions in Malaysia and Singapore has changed in the last 30 years, but the dominant-party state remains entrenched for other reasons.

From the above discussion, we see that there is no shortage of variables that are seen to produce dominant parties. They include the role of internal social divisions, coercion, economic growth as well as the missing role of the middle class. In my view, dominant parties are complex institutions in which none of these factors, considered alone, are sufficient to explain their functioning. In some sense, all of the explanations above play a key role in our understanding of the dominant parties under consideration. But what is more important to consider is that dominance is a self-conscious process and the dominant party cannot be ignored as a strategic actor in society. We cannot be social-structural determinists in understanding the dominant party, nor can we merely see coercion as the key device used by the ruling elites.

Pempel's work on *Uncommon Democracies* in Western Europe contains useful ideas for this study because he understands dominant parties as institutions that shape the social structure as much as they are constrained by it. He demonstrates that dominant parties are dynamic organisations that do not necessarily decline over time. They are adept at creating new social bases of support or abandoning old ones in order to stay in power.[11] The Barisan and the PAP have made significant shifts in their bases of support to stay in power and have been effective in responding to the grievances of key constituencies of the party. They have not been static institutions.

Pempel's other important insight is that dominant parties often make a serious ideological effort to be the embodiment of the nation. Parties that have played the role of national saviour or have delivered the nation from serious crises are able to derive long-lasting benefits from presenting the party and nation as coterminous. In addition, the very longevity of rule allows the dominant party to acquire "the opportunity to re-shape the nation's society and politics to its liking".[12] Turning to Malaysia and Singapore, we observe that the dominant parties invest much effort in shaping the identities and interests of large sections of the population, not least in their attempts to influence how individuals think about the very meaning of politics. Citizens

---

11 T.J. Pempel, ed., "Conclusion: One-Party Dominance and the Creation of Regimes", *Uncommon Democracies: The One-Party Dominant Regimes* (Ithaca: Cornell University Press, 1990), p. 352.

12 Pempel, "Conclusion", p. 352.

have been asked to see politics not as an arena for open-ended negotiation or for contesting the cultural options of society but as a means for giving the mandate to good leaders to deliver economic growth and political stability. Both the Barisan and the PAP have portrayed themselves as the true defenders of the nation and citizens are reminded that there are no real options to their rule.

There is little doubt that economic growth has also been critical for underpinning the dominant one-party state in Malaysia and Singapore. There is evidence from Malaysia that a period of weakened growth, by threatening redistributive and clientelist arrangements, can put pressure on the unity of UMNO and pose a threat to the dominant party system. On the other hand, growth should not simply be seen as the regimes' attempt to "buy off" citizens, but, more importantly, it can be viewed as the vital basis for the dominant parties to hold multi-class constituencies. The pressures for obtaining a broad class spectrum of voters are all the greater when overwhelming control of the legislature and political process is desired. One can in fact modify the argument that economic growth is important for legitimacy by saying that it is the imperative of maintaining a multi-class constituency for dominance that drives the growth process.

The dominance of a single party over a sustained period of time produces a political culture that is detrimental for opposition parties. Citizens come to expect that they should behave like the dominant party if they want to stand any chance of getting broad support. As Duverger tells us, a dominant party is identified with an epoch: "its doctrines, ideas, methods, its style, so to speak, coincide with those of the epoch."[13] There are not many incentives to vote for the opposition, and the internal fragmentation of the opposition does not inspire confidence that they are serious advocates for an alternative government. Thus, although the Barisan and PAP have frequently been accused of transgressing the principles of fair political competition by employing many measures that go beyond the normal advantage of incumbents in a competitive democracy, the chief characteristic of these regimes is the enfeeblement of the opposition not by outright and sustained coercive means but by leaving them with narrow bases of political power. The dominant parties, by occupying an expanded and flexible ideological terrain, make it difficult for the opposition to pose a clear ideological alternative to it. However, the opposition is in some ways useful for the dominant parties because it acts as an early warning system of growing disenchantment against

---

13 Maurice Duverger, *Political Parties: Their Organisation and Activity in the Modern State* (London: Methuen & Co. Ltd, 1962), p. 308.

the regime and gives legitimacy to the principle of the sovereignty of the people.

It is important to point out that there are tensions and challenges in maintaining one-party dominance. Each party is faced with unique problems, as a result of their different principles of organisation, which can have a potential impact on the political system. UMNO has to contain internal factionalism and ensure that the non-Malays do not become too alienated from the political system, while the PAP has to seek ways of preventing political apathy in a highly technocratic society. It is not as if these problems cannot be overcome, but often they can be put aside when economic growth is high. One important point to consider in Malaysia and Singapore might be the impact of a low growth environment on the dominant one-party state, because it is likely to be poor economic conditions rather than the actions of the opposition parties that will produce change.

ELECTORAL RECORD

Both the PAP and the Barisan Nasional have been able to muster votes far in excess of 35 per cent of the total vote that Pempel regarded as the norm for the dominant parties in Western, liberal democracies. UMNO and its allies have managed to get around 55 to 65 per cent of the total vote in the last two decades. The PAP has seen a gradual decline in its share of the total votes since the late 1960s but it appears to be stabilising at around 60 to 65 per cent in recent elections. However, too much importance should not be given to the PAP's vote share because the opposition parties have not contested the majority of seats in recent elections, choosing to focus on contests where they have the most chance of winning. What is significant in both systems is the vast over-representation of the government parties in Parliament in relation to the total electoral votes received. The PAP's share of Parliamentary seats has never fallen below 95 per cent since 1969. The Barisan has won more than 80 per cent of the seats in five of the last six elections held. The use of the first-past-the-post system, based on the British model rather than the proportional representation system of Continental Europe, has undoubtedly contributed to this lop-sided situation.

Behind the picture of overall dominance of the Barisan and PAP, there are nonetheless some interesting variations in the electoral results over time. The PAP and Barisan have faced critical junctures during which their authority was put to the test but also times when they extended their dominance. From the vantage point of the late 1950s and early 1960s, it would not have been a foregone conclusion that the PAP would end up becoming a hegemonic

Table 5.1: Results of Parliamentary Elections in Malaysia and Singapore

	Malaysia				Singapore		
Year	Government	Per cent of votes	Per cent of seats won (Total seats)	Year	Government	Per cent of votes	Per cent of seat won (Total seats)
1959	Alliance (precursor to the Barisan National)	51.8	71.1 (104 seats)	1959	PAP (legislative council)	53.4	84 (51 seats)
1964	Alliance	58.4	85.5 (104 seats)	1963	PAP	46.5	72.5 (51 seats)
1969	Alliance	48.4	64 (103 seats)	1968	PAP	84.4	100 (58 seats)
1974	Barisan	60.7	87.6 (154 seats)	1972	PAP	69	100 (65 seats)
1978	Barisan	55.3	84.4 (154 seats)	1976	PAP	72.4	100 (69 seats)
1982	Barisan	60.5	85.7 (154 seats)	1980	PAP	75.5	100 (75 seats)
1986	Barisan	55.7	83.1 (177 seats)	1984	PAP	62.9	97.4 (79 seats)
1990	Barisan	53.4	70.5 (180 seats)	1988	PAP	61.8	98.7 (81 seats)
1995	Barisan	65.0	84.3 (192 seats)	1991	PAP	59.3	95 (81 seats)
				1997	PAP	63.5	97 (83 seats)

Source   Liak Teng Kiat, "Malaysia: Mahathir's Last Hurrah?", *Southeast Asian Affairs 1996* (Singapore: Institute of Southeast Asian Studies, 1996), Table 1, p. 223;

Gordon P. Means, *Malaysian Politics: The Second Generation* (Singapore: Oxford University Press, 1991), Table 1.1, p. 6;

Christopher Tremewan, *The Political Economy of Social Control in Singapore* (Houndmills: Macmillan Press, 1994), Table 6.5, p. 181.

party. During that period, the PAP was plagued by a deep chasm between two sets of leaders, an English-speaking, social democratic group without a mass base but which had been acceptable to the colonial authorities, and a pro-Communist group of leaders with powerful connections to the left-leaning, Chinese-speaking, urban working class.[14] After the PAP won the first elections during self-rule in 1959, this opportunistic alliance could not withstand the test of time, and the party split along ideological lines in 1961, with the left-wing group forming a new party called the Barisan Sosialis (BS) or Socialist Front. The moderates, feeling vulnerable about a take-over, had established a top-down system in which their carefully chosen cadres would vote for the top leadership. As a result, the radicals could not take control of the party from within, and decided to break away to challenge the PAP as a separate party. Such a strategy must have seemed entirely reasonable to them given the high level of support they received from the Chinese-speaking population. However, in a government crackdown against alleged subversives in 1963, most of the Barisan's leaders, along with left-wing trade unionists, journalists, and students, were arrested.[15] Despite these actions and the sudden calling of the elections in 1963, the Barisan Sosialis managed to win 33.3 per cent of the vote and obtain 13 seats. The party's performance left some analysts thinking that Singapore would quite definitely develop into a two-party system. All such expectation evaporated very soon when the Barisan Sosialis, facing numerous political obstacles, made a highly controversial move in 1966 to quit parliamentary politics and concentrate on mass political agitation.[16] The party boycotted the 1968 elections, but this political gesture, rather than de-legitimise the government, only surrendered political space to the PAP. The PAP leaders, having lost their mass base, were forced to re-create a new one through effective policies, and used their overwhelming strength to generate rapid economic development and to ensure national survival. This last fact was a matter of great concern after the country, which had joined Malaysia in 1963, was ejected in 1965.

From 1968 to 1980 the party enjoyed total control of Parliament. However, the aura of PAP invincibility was punctured in 1981 when a long-time opposition figure won a by-election. From the mid-1980s to the mid-1990s,

---

14 C.M. Turbull, *A History of Singapore 1819–1975* (Singapore: Oxford University Press, 1977), p. 253.

15 R.S. Milne and Diane K. Mauzy, *Singapore: The Legacy of Lee Kuan Yew* (Boulder: Westview Press, 1990), p. 59.

16 Chan Heng Chee "The PAP and the Structuring of the Political System", K.S. Sandhu and P. Wheatley, eds., *Management of Success: The Moulding of Modern Singapore* (Singapore: Institute of Southeast Asian Studies, 1989), p. 73.

the PAP's vote share declined and the small opposition parties managed to win a few seats. In the 1991 elections, which saw the party's vote fall just below 60 per cent, new questions were raised about the party's ability to dominate society, leading one local analyst to write a book called *Whither PAP's Dominance?*.[17] Just when many expected the trend of voting against the government to continue, the PAP made a comeback in the 1997 elections and enhanced its position electorally, increasing its share of the vote after 10 years of incipient decline, and conceding only two seats to the opposition parties.

The dominant party in Malaysia has also had its share of challenges and opportunities. The Alliance, comprising moderate ethnic leaders from the UMNO, Malaysian Chinese Association and the Malaysian Indian Congress, enjoyed prestige as the party that had brought independence and that could work out elite compromises, through consociational mechanisms, to preserve ethnic peace.[18] Both the Alliance and its successor, the Barisan, have had to balance with some delicacy the Malay assumption of political primacy (such as giving official status to the Malay language and Islam, preserving the monarchy, and upholding Malay special rights allowing for privileged access to bureaucratic jobs, educational scholarships, and business licenses) while preserving the legitimate economic and cultural interests of the Chinese and Indian groups. Toward the mid-1960s racial outbidding began to hurt the Alliance. The main Malay opposition party, the Parti Islam Se-Malaysia (PAS) attacked the UMNO for selling out Malay interests to the Chinese, while the non-Malay opposition parties attacked the government for failing to advance the idea of equal citizenship. In the watershed elections of 1969, the Alliance performed far below its expectations and lost its coveted two-thirds majority in Parliament. In an atmosphere of uncertainty, paranoia, and intense ethnic suspicion, riots broke out and the country suffered its worst episode of racial violence. For one and a half years, Parliament was suspended and the nation was placed under emergency rule.[19]

UMNO was presented with an historic opportunity to consolidate its position during the changed political conditions. A massive affirmative action programme was put in place for the Malays, and various laws, such as the Sedition Act and the Sensitive Issues Act, were enacted to remove explosive

---

17 Bilveer Singh, *Whither PAP's Dominance?: Analysis of Singapore's 1991 General Elections* (Petaling Jaya: Pelanduk Publications, 1992).

18 For a further elaboration of consociationalism in Malaysia, see Arend Lijphart, *Democracy in Plural Societies* (New Haven: Yale University Press, 1977), pp. 150–3.

19 Zakaria Haji Ahmad, "Malaysia: Quasi-Democracy in a Divided Society", Larry Diamond *et al.*, eds., *Democracy in Developing Countries: Asia. Volume 3* (Boulder: Lynne Rienner, 1989), pp. 360–1.

ethnic issues, such as Malay special rights and the symbols of Malay predominance, from public debate. UMNO also redesigned the Alliance framework to incorporate opposition parties into an expanded coalition called the Barisan Nasional or National Front. Even PAS, UMNO's main rival in competing for Malay votes, joined the Front for a brief period from 1974–1977. UMNO's level of support increased among the Malays, while PAS gradually found itself as a party with regional influence relying on a narrow platform of making Malaysia an Islamic republic.

As UMNO became the definitive party, the new challenges to the party came from within rather than from outside the party. As UMNO's patronage role expanded, the party had to satisfy a wider set of interests, leading to factions and latent fissions. In the late 1980s UMNO split into two, after an ambitious Cabinet minister, Tengku Razaleigh Hamzah, tried but failed narrowly to dislodge Dr Mahathir Mohamad, the prime minister since 1981, as President of UMNO. He subsequently formed a rival party called Parti Semangat 46. The formation of Semangat gave rise to much euphoria about the possibility of a two-party system emerging in Malaysia. Some observers felt that the dominant party system was slowly crumbling as voters became disillusioned with the corruption and authoritarian tendencies of the prime minister.[20] One scholar made the interesting argument that UMNO and the Barisan were aggregating too many diverse interests for their own good, suggesting that overwhelming dominance would be increasingly difficult to manage.[21] But as in the case of Singapore, the elections of 1995 proved that the dominant party had great rejuvenating powers. The Barisan disappointed all those who wished to see a more competitive party system, obtaining the largest share of the popular vote in its history.

SHIFTING PARTY BASES

Both the PAP and the Barisan have selectively demobilised and cultivated groups according to pressures put on them by opposition parties and key internal constituencies. This ability to make the necessary shifts and respond to their key constituencies has been important in rejuvenating the dominant parties. However, it is important to understand the different institutional contexts in which both parties operate because it shapes the manner of

---

20 Hari Singh, "Political Change in Malaysia: The Role of Semangat 46", *Asian Survey*, 31, 8 (1991), pp. 727.

21 Gordon P. Means, *Malaysian Politics: The Second Generation* (Singapore: Oxford University Press, 1991), p. 316.

response to political pressures. Political management in Malaysia can be said to fit the model of ethnic patronage. In this model, ethnic elites act as patrons and sponsors to their respective ethnic groups. The UMNO is the foremost ethnic patron, possessing superior resources and power to channel rewards and privileges to its broad constituents. UMNO has been willing to work with the moderate elites of the other ethnic groups, provided they recognise UMNO's hegemony.[22] The centrality of ethnicity for the Barisan means that ethnic mobilisation is considered legitimate in the political system, and opposition parties are free to make their own ethnic and religious appeals within certain circumscribed limits.

The PAP, on the other hand, eschews overt political mobilisation, whether based on ethnicity or class. The legacy of the PAP, having to compete against Chinese nationalism and left-wing, working class agitation, has left a strong mark on state–society relations in Singapore. The PAP's preferred linkages with society fits best with the model of corporatism. Without going into all the complexity implied by the concept, corporatism is used here to mean the state's important role in regulating social groups and influencing the nature of interest articulation, with the aim of realising a rational outcome.[23] The PAP plays a central role in influencing the leadership of the peak trade union body, key ethnic organisations, as well as a host of associations, and is able to powerfully shape the nature of legitimate demands made by them. The top leadership's great degree of insulation from the pressures of its own ordinary members and branch leaders further facilitates the PAP's relative autonomy from social groups in society, including the interests of local Chinese capital.[24]

Thus ethnic patronage and corporatism provide the institutional parameters within which the UMNO and the PAP have shaped their respective bases of support. The UMNO has revitalised itself as a party by making lateral shifts along ethnic lines, varying the degree of favouritism shown towards the Malays in response to external and internal pressures. The wider Barisan coalition has been aloof, even hostile, towards the labour movement because ethnic mobilisation has made working class organisations redundant for political

---

22 Zakaria, "Malaysia: Quasi-Democracy", p. 373.

23 For a useful overview of the concept, see Douglas A. Chalmers, "Corporatism and Comparative Politics", in Howard J. Wiarda, ed., *New Directions in Comparative Politics* (Boulder: Westview Press, 1985), especially p. 62.

24 Chan Heng Chee, *The Dynamics of One-Party Dominance: The PAP at the Grassroots* (Singapore: Singapore University Press, 1976), p. 225. On domestic Chinese capital, see Ian Chalmers, "Loosening State Control in Singapore: The Emergence of Local Capital as a Political Force", *Southeast Asian Journal of Social Science*, 20, 2 (1992), pp. 63.

support. The main trade unions, containing members with diverse ethnic backgrounds and political orientations, are themselves constrained from allying with any political party openly for fear of tearing themselves apart.

The PAP, on the other hand, bases its legitimacy on its impartiality in mediating ethnic and class interests. The claim to neutrality within a top-down corporatist structure gives the party enormous leverage to reshape the activities of groups to meet the central national goals of economic growth and stability. The essential logic of the PAP is to position itself effectively between the interests of labour and capital, and create a widespread middle class as a way of obtaining support. The party does not make pronounced lateral shifts along ethnic lines nor along class lines to maintain its political base. Rather, grievances are met incrementally in response to shortfalls in electoral support, but in ways compatible with long-term economic growth.

Let us examine each of the cases in turn. In the 1960s, the Alliance party thought that stable support would come from successfully maintaining the independence bargain. The Malays were accorded symbolic primacy in the polity while the Chinese economic position would be protected. UMNO focused its attention on retaining the support of the party's large rural Malay base. State patronage took the form of providing access to land for underemployed Malay agriculturists, supporting prices for rice production, subsidising re-planting schemes in cash crops for small-holder farmers, and pouring in development funds, especially in UMNO-controlled constituencies, for road construction, electrification, and the building of mosques.

Toward the late 1960s, there were fundamental internal and external challenges to the independence bargain.[25] The bureaucratic Malay middle class, which had grown through preferential polices, became increasingly frustrated with the laissez-faire system, which was dominated by foreign and Chinese companies, because of their difficulty in taking up entrepreneurial roles.[26] As a strategic group inside UMNO, their grievances put pressure on the ability of the top leaders of UMNO to hold on to a large multi-class Malay constituency. A further problem for the UMNO was that despite its rural policies, Malay peasants were suffering from worsening incomes as a result of growing rural underemployment. The PAS party supplied the external attack on the UMNO, accusing it of failing to defend Malay interests more strongly. The Alliance coalition, however, was not able to offset growing

25 Donald L. Horowitz, *Ethnic Groups in Conflict* (Berkeley: University of California Press, 1985), pp. 584–5.

26 Jomo K. Sundaram, *A Question of Class: Capital, the State, and Uneven Development in Malaya* (New York: Monthly Review Press, 1988), p. 248.

Malay disillusionment by getting the support of lower and middle class non-Malays. These groups gave their allegiance to the opposition parties, such as the Democratic Action Party (DAP) and the Gerakan, which attacked the moderate ethnic leaders in the Alliance for acceding too much to Malay symbolic and political hegemony.

After the ethnic crisis of 1969, UMNO, rejuvenated by a younger, Malay nationalist leadership, sought to regain UMNO dominance by re-aligning the political system. With the long-term aim of building a solid urban clientele for future support, UMNO was prepared to alienate the non-Malays to a greater extent than before, and calculated that greater dividends would be reaped for the party in making the switch. To regain dominance, the leaders re-asserted Malay hegemony in language and cultural matters, and promulgated the New Economic Policy (NEP), 1970–1990, a 20-year policy to redistribute wealth along ethnic lines. Through state intervention, and the modification of the laissez-faire system, the planners aimed to create a Malay industrial and commercial class, and to shift large numbers of Malays from agriculture into urban jobs.[27] Although the rural sector continued to be important politically, and received vast new state funds for rural projects, the key political goal became the elevation of Malays to positions that were the symbols of modernity. As UMNO's hegemony increased, the other component parties in the Barisan lost effective power to bargain hard with the party, and began to act more like sounding boards for outstanding grievances in their ethnic communities. Lower class and middle class Chinese voters did not support the Barisan strongly, routinely voting for parties that championed the cause of equal cultural and political rights for all communities.

UMNO protection and patronage was vital for the creation of the new urban clientele of businessmen and corporate men. The government imposed new administrative rules on economic activity and expanded bank lending to Malays. State enterprises were promoted to counterbalance Chinese and foreign domination, and various bodies provided training and financial schemes to promote small Malay entrepreneurs. Regulatory bodies pressured private Chinese and foreign companies to open up ownership opportunities for Malay entrepreneurs at substantial share discounts, and to hire more Malay managers and workers. The NEP provided many rent-seeking opportunities for an inter-connected elite group in Malay society, comprising bureaucrats, politicians, military officials, royal families, and religious

---

27 For an extended discussion of the NEP, see James V. Jesudason, *Ethnicity and the Economy: The State, Chinese Business, and Multinationals in Malaysia* (Singapore: Oxford University Press, 1989).

functionaries, to became rich and influential.[28] In the first half of the 1990s, when the government modified the NEP and came up with the New Development Policy, 1991–2000, shifting the emphasis somewhat from redistribution with growth to growth with redistribution, the key mechanism for the expansion of the big Malay bourgeoisie became the privatisation policy of the government.[29] Government companies and government-run services were hived off to well-connected individuals, who obtained their assets cheaply in non-competitive bids, and paid for them through bank borrowings pledging their new assets as collateral.

The political leaders, however, did try to get broad political support and to blunt criticisms that the state's policies were concentrating wealth in a few hands by allowing ordinary Malays to become shareholders in various state-sponsored unit trusts. The middle class managed to obtain generous educational scholarships and high-paying jobs through affirmative action, while the working and agricultural classes also had more job opportunities in the urban sector than previously. By expanding its role as an ethnic patron to a broad range of groups, UMNO was able to consolidate its position, and push aside its rivals, such as the Islamic PAS party, to focus on a more narrow religious platform.

There are tentative signs that a new re-alignment might be in the making. As UMNO's patronage role expanded, more diverse interests became ensconced in the party. It became a challenge to maintain internal unity. In 1987, UMNO split into two, and its off-shoot, Parti Semangat 46, offered greater competition, at least for a while. The Chinese constituency, especially its middle class stratum, who had benefited so much from years of economic growth, was a natural candidate for buttressing the Barisan, and weakening potential challengers to UMNO. During the 1990s, the UMNO made new overtures to the Chinese, such as agreeing to permit more privately-run tertiary institutions to form, and promising increased government aid to Chinese education. But this lateral shift was facilitated by the changing class nature of the key party brokers in UMNO. The grassroots leaders in the 1960s tended to be Malay rural schoolteachers and local government officials. For example, the percentage of teachers among UMNO delegates in the 1981 party elections was 41 per cent, but in 1987, their numbers had fallen to 19 per cent. The group that came into ascendancy were people with business

---

28 Ozay Mehmet, *Development in Malaysia: Poverty, Wealth and Trusteeship* (London: Croom Helm, 1986), p. 136.

29 Jomo K.S., *U-Turn? Malaysian Economic Development Policies After 1990* (Townsville: James Cook University of North Queensland, 1994), p. 80.

backgrounds.[30] This group, a product of the NEP, has been more willing to find accommodation with the Chinese and Indian business and middle classes.[31] At the elite level, there have been more business tie-ups between Malay and Chinese businessmen, and so the economy has become less politicised ethnically. The general Chinese middle class are a potential ally of the corporate elite in UMNO because both share a distaste for the theocratic and anti-modernist stance of opposition parties such as PAS. The vast increase in support for the Barisan in the 1995 elections was in no small part due to the non-Malay middle class feeling that the UMNO for the moment had become more inclusive and ethnic boundaries were losing their distinctness.

Unlike the UMNO's and Barisan's explicit reliance on ethnicity for dominance, the PAP has been extremely wary of this approach and has curbed opposition parties from politicising communal feelings. Seeing themselves as the rational organisers of society, the PAP leaders have put themselves above the interests of the ethnic groups, as well as those of labour and capital, claiming to act solely in the national interest.

The PAP has sought to contain ethnic political loyalties but has signalled its concern for the ethnic groups by recognising those interests that accord with PAP goals.[32] When merger with Malaysia failed, the PAP explicitly assumed an ethnically neutral stance *vis-à-vis* the Chinese, Malays, and Indians. To differentiate its approach from UMNO, and not wanting to engage in a similar affirmative programme for the Singaporean Malay population, the PAP strongly articulated the notion of meritocracy and even-handed multi-racialism. While initially prepared to see Malay as the *lingua franca*, the PAP, after 1965, promoted English as the common language of meritocratic achievement, often in opposition to Chinese educational and business groups that wished to see Mandarin as the common language. To combat any view that it was merely a party that catered to the English-educated, and undercut the position of Chinese nationalists, all students were expected to be bilingual, in English and in their "mother tongue", which referred to Mandarin, Malay, and Tamil.[33] Thus, while claiming ethnic neutrality, the PAP was able to signal its interest and respect for the respective cultures in the following way:

---

30 Edmund T. Gomez, *Political Business: Corporate Involvement of Malaysian Political Parties* (Townsville: James Cook University of North Queensland, 1994), p. 56.

31 James V. Jesudason, "Chinese Business and Ethnic Equilibrium in Malaysia", *Development and Change*, 28, 1 (January 1997), p. 135.

32 David Brown, *The State and Ethnic Politics in Southeast Asia* (London: Routledge, 1994), p. 103.

33 Sharon Siddique, "Singaporean Identity", K.S. Sandhu and P. Wheatley, eds., *Management of Success: The Moulding of Modern Singapore* (Singapore: Institute of Southeast Asian Studies, 1989), p. 566.

"each official 'racial culture' was promoted through the schools and portrayed on television dramas, in 'cultural shows' and as an 'instant Asia' display for tourists."[34] In later years, each of the languages, in particular Mandarin, was strongly promoted as a way to preserve culture and combat insidious Western values. Mandarin was elevated to first-language status, on par with English, in selected schools, and English-educated Chinese families were keen that their children become effectively bilingual. Thus by the 1990s, it became difficult to sustain the view that there existed a cultural chasm between the English-educated and Mandarin-educated, or that such a chasm sustained the dominant party-state.

After 1980, ethnically-based corporatist structures began to be institutionalised to manage certain grievances. The government's meritocratic principles made it difficult for the lower income groups to catch up with the professional classes. The Malays, in particular, began to complain that meritocracy did not prevent discrimination against them and that they were falling behind the Chinese group.[35] But it was not just a Malay problem, as the grievances of the lower classes manifested themselves in the decline of votes received by the PAP in the 1980s and early 1990s. Not wanting to institutionalise an affirmative action programme for the minorities or a more extensive welfare system, which would either violate the neutrality of the state or hurt the economy, the PAP converted the external pressures on it into an internal ethnic responsibility.[36] The PAP began to promote community self-help groups which were headed by prominent ethnic members trusted by the PAP. In 1981, Mendaki (Council for the Education of Muslim Children) was formed to enhance the academic performance of Malay students and to allocate scholarships. In 1989, before the 1991 elections, a similar organisation for the Indians, the Singapore Indian Development Agency, was set up to help low-achieving students in the community. After realising that the Chinese lower classes also had their grievances, the government established the Chinese Development Assistance Council to aid the Chinese poor in 1992. The ethnicisation of welfare tackled many issues at once for the PAP: to signal to the ethnic groups that it was a protector of cultural bonds, to show its concern for civic-mindedness by getting co-ethnics to contribute funds and volunteer their time towards their organisation, to make low achievement a communal rather than a state responsibility, and to

---

34 Brown, *The State and Ethnic Politics*, p. 83.
35 Brown, *The State and Ethnic Politics*, p. 87.
36 Chua Beng Huat, "Racial-Singaporeans: Absence after the Hyphen", *Social Scientist*, 24, 7–8 (July–August 1996), p. 58.

deploy social organisations for enhancing the competitiveness of individuals in the labour market. Such an ethnic corporatist strategy fits Brown's insight into how the PAP is able to contain and yet utilise ethnicity to gain legitimacy. In affirming the cultural values of the diverse population, the PAP makes it difficult for oppositional groups to mobilise against the party on the basis of its indifference to ethnic cultures, or even to claim that it is ethnically biased.

The state has also contained the working class through corporatist controls. Given its historical struggles, the PAP has been fearful of opposition groups penetrating the labour movement. When the PAP won the 1959 elections, the prime minister, Lee Kuan Yew, swiftly distanced himself from his radical populist support. Left-leaning unions allied to the Barisan Sosialis were demobilised by not granting them legal recognition and arresting their leaders. The PAP then set up an alternative body, the National Trades Union Congress (NTUC) in 1961. The NTUC became the only legitimate channel through which labour could be represented and over time the corporatist linkages between party and union deepened as Cabinet ministers routinely took up the position of secretary-general of the union body.[37]

While the UMNO has been happy to see the labour movement languish, the PAP has tried to prevent trade union membership numbers from falling as jobs shift from manufacturing to services. The number of union members as a percentage of the total labour force in 1990 was about 14 per cent in Singapore and 10 per cent in Malaysia.[38] To control and yet reward the labour movement, the PAP has had to position itself skilfully between labour and capital. The chief strategy has been to set the conditions for high levels of efficiency and economic growth, which has been facilitated by the PAP's autonomy from ethnic, religious, and class groups.

The PAP's other lever to get working class support has been using the state's plentiful fiscal resources from economic growth to make social provisions that are compatible with a strong work ethic and a good investment climate. As we shall examine later, the most celebrated effort has been to facilitate near-universal home ownership among the population. The Barisan, being less committed to the working class, has failed to provide cheap and adequate housing to Malaysian workers, resulting in illegal squatter settlements in the major cities. Singapore's housing policy has made workers

---

37 Garry Rodan, *The Political Economy of Singapore's Industrialization: National State and International Capital* (Kuala Lumpur: Forum, 1989), pp. 30, 160.

38 Calculated from Jomo K.S. and Patricia Todd, *Trade Unions and the State in Peninsula Malaysia* (Kuala Lumpur: Oxford University Press, 1994), pp. 15, 34; Ministry of Labour, Singapore, *Singapore Yearbook of Labour Statistics* (Singapore, 1997), p. 83.

feel that they lead middle class lifestyles, and has allowed the PAP to have a base in the working class. However, within the broad multi-class approach, the PAP has made incremental shifts in the degree of emphasis paid to the different classes, depending on the party's perception of their electoral importance. In the 1980s, the PAP focused on co-opting the middle class politically through various feedback channels, seeing them as potential agents of liberalisation. The government also pursued its strong belief that market principles would make for a stronger economy, and the working classes found themselves having to pay more for basic social services. But as working class grievances increased, reflected in opposition strength in the poorer constituencies, the PAP began in the 1990s to channel more resources to them, mainly in the form of using fiscal surpluses to top up the funds in individual retirement and medical accounts.

In conclusion, it is worthwhile to point out that social divisions in both societies were more pronounced in the 1960s than in the 1990s. We need to qualify the argument of a tight link between social divisions and the dominant one-party state. Both the UMNO and the PAP are strategic actors that aim to dominate politics, and actively shape the social structure to that end. To maintain support, the UMNO has made lateral shifts along ethnic lines to rejuvenate the ruling coalition while the PAP, working within a corporatist structure, meets grievances by steering the allocation process along class lines.

THE MANAGEMENT OF DOMINANCE: ECONOMIC GROWTH AND REDISTRIBUTION

In both Malaysia and Singapore, rapid economic growth has been a critical aspect of managing one-party dominance. By making possible high levels of social mobility, and channelling resources to key constituencies, both regimes have been able to obtain the support of broad multi-class constituencies. Opposition parties are thereby neither able to build a large alternative multi-class constituency nor to cultivate a particular class to pose a strong threat to the dominant parties. There is circumstantial evidence to indicate that lower growth rates would have hurt these regimes. For example, during the pronounced recession in the mid-1980s in Malaysia and Singapore, there was a relative fall in support for the parties. In 1987, amidst continuing economic difficulties, UMNO split into two, but the party recovered with economic growth.

Although the mix of clientelism and developmentalism is significantly different in Malaysia and Singapore, both countries have enjoyed high growth rates over a sustained period of time. From 1965 to 1987, the average annual growth of GNP per capita grew at 7.2 per cent in Singapore and 4.1 per cent in Malaysia.[39] In the more recent period, from 1985 to 1994, the average annual growth rate was 6.1 per cent in Singapore and 5.6 per cent in Malaysia.[40] It is unlikely that these dominant parties could have enjoyed such durability if not for these growth rates.

A key basis for development in Malaysia, despite pronounced clientelist arrangements, has been the importance placed by the government on the role of the private sector. Even during the New Economic Policy (NEP), when the state imposed new regulations on the private sector, the planners were careful to design in-built mechanisms to prevent excessive damage to the economy by stipulating that ethnic redistribution would take place only if growth rates were around 7 per cent per annum. Multinationals were actively solicited and ownership requirements on them were carefully structured according to their importance for manufactured exports. Preserving a strong private economy was not only a recognition by UMNO that mobility and job creation for non-Malays was important for political stability but the party itself needed high economic growth to obtain the support of the growing Malay working class. Whenever the investment climate has been seriously threatened, such as in the mid-1980s, the state was flexible enough to liberalise the economy, cut public expenditure, and moderate excessive regulations on foreign and Chinese enterprises.

Economic growth in Malaysia has also been facilitated by the weakness of labour. The destruction of the communist-inspired, anti-colonial movement in the late 1940s and 1950s was a mortal blow to the labour movement, and accounts for Malaysia's ability to shift smoothly from import-substitution industrialisation to vigorous export-oriented industrialisation in the late 1960s. Unlike the labour-based regimes of Latin America, populist politics and working class mobilisation did not constrain national economic decision-making. Both import-substitution industrialisation and export-oriented industrialisation did not arise from the play of social interests but were governmental decisions to promote growth. Following independence, the ruling coalition continued to weaken working class organisations through numerous labour regulations, specifying the conditions for the registration of unions and the procedures for collective action, all of which have effectively

---

39 World Bank, *World Development Report, 1989* (New York: Oxford University Press, 1989), Table 1, pp. 164–5.
40 World Bank, *World Development Report, 1996* (New York: Oxford University Press, 1996), Table 1, pp. 188–189.

nullified the strike as a weapon. In the all-important foreign-dominated export-oriented zones, the Ministry of Labour has the power to disallow the formation of trade unions, and has used his powers to prevent federations of unions from developing in the critical electronics sector. Union membership, not surprisingly, has been low and unions have been relatively powerless to block the huge influx of foreign labour into the country.[41] The freedom of capital to shape the working environment and wage levels of workers has allowed Malaysia to be a recipient of a high level of foreign direct investment, and helped transform Malaysia from a raw materials-exporting country to one in which manufacturing exports make up 80 per cent of export revenues.[42]

General economic growth and state sponsorship of Malay mobility have been vital in allowing UMNO to maintain its multi-class constituency. The Malay middle class expanded greatly, from about 12 per cent of the population in 1970 to 25 per cent in 1995. In 1970, the professional and administrative class comprised 4.8 per cent of the Malay population but this had grown to 14.3 per cent in 1995.[43] Perhaps what was most striking was the visible increase in the Malay corporate and capitalist class, which enlarged its ownership of share capital from 2 per cent of the total in 1970 to 20.6 per cent 1995.[44] The agricultural population decreased from 65 per cent in 1970 to only 25.3 per cent in 1995 as Malays moved into new industrial and clerical jobs. The state has been critical in the transformation of Malay society. A rough indicator of the state's importance as an ethnic patron can be gauged from the average income of the ethnic groups. The average Malay household income was 44 per cent of the Chinese in 1970 but had increased to 55 per cent in 1995.[45] As a counterpoint, the Indian community, which did not receive state patronage and aid, saw its average income fall from 77.6 per cent to 74 per cent of the average Chinese income in that period.

The growth generated in the private sector was also important in containing Chinese working class and middle class disaffection against the state. Non-Malays were able to move into more professional and middle class positions with economic expansion. The general fall in the poverty rates for all the ethnic groups also tempered overt resistance among the non-Malay poor against the state. By the government's measure of poverty, the overall

41 Jomo and Todd, *Trade Unions*, pp. 149–150.
42 Rajah Rasiah, *Foreign Capital and Industrialization in Malaysia* (New York: St. Martin's Press, 1995), p. 198.
43 *Fourth Malaysia Plan 1981–1985* (Kuala Lumpur: National Printing Department, 1981), p. 59; *Seventh Malaysia Plan 1996–2000* (Kuala Lumpur: Percetakan Nasional Malaysia, 1996), p. 82.
44 *Seventh Malaysia Plan*, p. 87.
45 *Fourth Malaysia Plan*, p. 46; *Seventh Malaysia Plan*, p. 91.

incidence decreased from 49.3 per cent of households in 1970 to 9.5 per cent in 1995.[46] However, inequality remains high in Malaysia—not as high as in Brazil and South Africa, but in the vicinity of countries such as Mexico and Costa Rica.[47] High growth rates are important for regime legitimacy because the progress that the poor have made had largely come from improvements in the labour market rather than class-specific redistribution programmes.

An interesting test to determine the effects of low growth for one-party dominance was provided in 1987. In the aftermath of the 1985 and 1986 recession, UMNO encountered difficulties in holding its broad multi-class alliance within the Malay community. Government expenditure cutbacks hurt the government's patronage system as contracts, licences, and scholarships, all critical for keeping different groups loyal to UMNO, became less available. The brewing restiveness among the Malay middle class provided Mahathir's rival, Tengku Razaleigh, who otherwise had no real ideological difference with the prime minister, with the opportunity to challenge the premier for the party presidency. According to Khoo, small businesses teamed up with bureaucrats to side with Razaleigh to oust the more pro-tycoon Mahathir.[48] Razaleigh narrowly failed in his attempt, but the after-shocks led to a split in the party and Razaleigh ended up forming his own party called Parti Semangat 46. Semangat formed loose alliances with the existing opposition parties and campaigned nation-wide for the necessity of a two-party system. In the period leading up to the 1990 elections, Semangat helped forge a public discourse which focused on accountability, the inde-pendence of the judiciary, the restoration of workers' rights, and the elimina-tion of business investments by political parties.

By the late 1980s, the economy had become stronger as commodity prices improved and the flow of direct foreign investment increased. As Case notes, this enabled the UMNO to replenish its patronage funds and reincorporate bureaucratic managers and businessmen, "revealing that the middle-class Malays were less interested in mounting strong political opposition than sharing in boom cycles".[49] In the 1990 elections, Semangat won only 8 seats out of the 59 parliamentary seats it contested and subsequently petered out as a party. In the 1995 elections, Semangat suffered from a humiliating rout,

---

46 *Fourth Malaysia Plan*, p. 32; *Seventh Malaysia Plan*, p. 72.

47 World Bank, 1996: Table 5, pp. 196–7.

48 Khoo Kay Jin, "The Grand Vision: Mahathir and Modernization", J.S. Kahn and Francis Loh, eds., Fragmented Vision: Culture and Politics in Contemporary Malaysia (Sydney: Allen & Unwin, 1992), pp. 61–65.

49 William Case, "Semi-Democracy in Malaysia: Withstanding the Pressures for Regime Change", *Pacific Affairs*, 66, 2 (Summer, 1993), p. 198.

and in a complete about-turn, Razaleigh decided to join UMNO in 1996, along with the majority of his 200,000 party members. Khoo notes wryly that the UMNO exiles were "unable to weather the prospect of long-term political marginalization and exclusion from the economic advantages of belonging to UMNO".[50]

The UMNO split clearly revealed that one-party dominance could be threatened by low economic growth. A section of the Malay middle class was capable of looking for alternative parties to UMNO to further their economic interests. They were not seeking a democratic alternative but a better patron that could continue to channel benefits to them in constrained circumstances. This class could threaten UMNO, but in the final analysis, were not able to cut the psychological and economic umbilical cord to UMNO.

Singapore represents an alternative model of obtaining a multi-class constituency for dominance. The ethnic neutrality of the PAP, its corporatist control of the working class, and its autonomy from the local Chinese business class have minimised clientelist relations with any social group. The regime single-mindedly focuses on economic achievement, and is a quintessential developmentalist state.[51] The local bourgeoisie and petty bourgeoisie are relatively weak in Singapore, whose economy is based on large-scale foreign multinationals and state-owned enterprises (known as government-linked companies). Foreign companies produce as much as 75 per cent of manufacturing output and 85 per cent of manufacturing exports, while state enterprises in Singapore, unlike in most other countries, are notable in their drive for profits, and efficient management.

Without any natural reliance on ethnic appeals, the PAP has had to create its political support by promising a middle class lifestyle to large sections of the population. The middle class in particular has made impressive gains in the last 30 years. In 1970 the stratum in professional, administrative, and managerial jobs was 11 per cent of the population but it had grown to 24 per cent in 1990.[52] Besides enjoying rapid mobility and relatively low levels of taxation, the middle class is favourably treated in the government's compulsory savings scheme, the Central Provident Fund (CPF). At present, both the employer and employee are required to contribute 20 per cent of the

---

50 Khoo Boo Teik, "Malaysia: Challenges and Upsets in Politics and Other Contestations", *Southeast Asian Affairs 1997* (Singapore: Institute of Southeast Asian Affairs, 1997), p. 199.

51 For a good overview, see W.G. Huff, "The Developmental State, Government, and Singapore's Economic Development Since 1960," *World Development*, 23, 8 (1995), pp. 1421–1438.

52 Department of Statistics, Singapore, *Singapore Census of Population 1990: Economic Characteristics* (Singapore: SNP Publishers, 1993), p. xvii; Department of Statistics, Singapore, *Economic and Social Statistics Singapore 1960–1982* (Singapore: SNP Publishers, 1983), p. 38.

employee's salary to a retirement fund, which can be used for making house purchases. The contributions are tax free, leading some analysts to say that it is the world's best tax shelter for the higher earning groups in society.[53] Politically, the middle class is marked by a low level of political activism. In a survey of middle class attitudes, Leong discovered that the members of this class make a "conscious effort to distance themselves from public, especially political, issues".[54] Rodan has hypothesised that one reason for middle class apathy is the compatibility of the PAP worldview with the ethos of this class. The ideology of meritocracy accords the middle classes a high social status, and "fosters mutual interests and values between the development-minded PAP and large sections of the middle class".[55]

The dominance of the PAP would not be possible, however, without the support of the working and lower classes. One of the feats of the PAP has been its ability to constrain and yet reward the labour movement. Through legal regulations, ranging from limiting the issues over which workers can strike to compulsory arbitration procedures, the strike rate has decreased markedly since the 1960s, becoming almost non-existent in the 1980s and 1990s.[56] Through the workings of the National Wages Council, a tripartite body comprising employers, the NTUC, and the government, wage increases have generally been pegged below productivity increases in order to attract high foreign investment.[57] But these restrictions have been compensated by large increases in the living standard of workers, partly resulting from the full employment economy but also through incessant efforts by the NTUC and the government to increase worker skills and productivity. The result has been the embourgeoisment of workers, who are able to acquire visible middle class symbols, such as washing machines, insurance policies, air-conditioners, overseas travel and microwave ovens.[58] The NTUC itself has been at the forefront of fostering middle class respectability, running supermarket chains and resorts with golfing memberships, selling a plethora of insurance schemes, and building high-end condominiums.

53 Quoted in M. Ramesh, "Social Security in Singapore: Redrawing the Public–Private Boundary," *Asian Survey*, 32, 12 (December, 1992), p. 1104.
54 Leong Choon Heng, "The Construction of a Contented and Cautious Middle Class", unpublished paper presented at the International Conference on East Asian Middle Classes and National Development in Comparative Perspective, December 19–21, 1994, Taipei, Taiwan. 60 pages. p. 41.
55 Garry Rodan, ed., "State-Society Relations and Political Opposition in Singapore", *Political Oppositions in Industrialising Asia* (London: Routledge, 1996), p. 99.
56 Data obtained from *Straits Times*, 29 April 1996.
57 W.G. Huff, "The Developmental State", p. 1425.
58 Yao Souchou "Consumption and Social Aspirations of the Middle Class in Singapore," *Southeast Asian Affairs 1996* (Singapore: Institute of Southeast Asian Studies, 1996), p. 339.

Perhaps the most important symbol of middle class status for the less well-off is their ability to acquire a flat or apartment in public housing estates. The sale price, which is lower than comparable dwellings in the limited private housing market, covers the costs of building and land acquisition. The type of flat purchased is dependent on the household's ability to pay, including the funds available in an individual's Central Provident Fund account.[59] The flat can be sold after five years, and the capital gains retained or used to purchase another flat. The government's decision to base its housing policy on ownership rather than on rentals was a conscious strategy to give people a stake in stability and undercut radical sentiments in the working class. Home ownership figures in Singapore are the highest in the world. In 1990, 87.5 per cent of households owned their own homes.[60] The psychological effect of this is that 75 per cent of the population say they enjoy a middle class lifestyle.[61] There are ideological benefits for the regime—the overwhelming presence of dwelling units in the Singapore landscape "acts as a powerful sign of the existing regime's ability to fulfil its promise to improve the living conditions of the entire nation".[62]

The public housing programme has also helped compensate for the economically weaker position of the minorities in Singapore. There is no affirmative action policy for them, and since the fate of individuals is left to the marketplace, it is difficult for many minorities to maintain their relative position in society. For example, in 1980, the average Malay household income was 73.8 per cent of the average Chinese income, while the average Indian household income was 93.4 per cent. In 1990, the divergence increased. The average Malay and Indian household income had become 69.6 and 88.9 per cent respectively.[63] But the figures for home ownership have vastly improved for the minority groups. In 1980 the level of home ownership was 62 per cent for the Chinese, 50 per cent for the Malays, and 42 per cent for the Indians but in 1990, the figures had increased for all, but most impressively for the minorities, reaching 88, 92, and 81 per cent respectively.[64] Home ownership is probably the key to understanding why the ethnic minorities describe themselves as enjoying middle class lifestyles to an even higher degree than the

---

59 Chua Beng Huat, *Communitarian Ideology and Democracy in Singapore* (London: Routledge, 1995), p. 134.

60 Department of Statistics, Singapore (1993), p. xiv.

61 Information from Yao, "Consumption and Social Aspirations", p. 339.

62 Chua, "*Communitarian Ideology*", p. 139.

63 Calculated from Department of Statistics, Singapore, *Singapore Census of Population 1990: Households and Housing* (Singapore: SNP Publishers, 1992), Table 7, p. 8.

64 Ibid; p. 19.

Chinese—the figures for the Malays, Indians and Chinese are 78, 75, and 74 per cent.[65] But in addition to creating a sense of well-being, the housing programme has been used to undercut explicit ethnic and class politics.[66] Established minority communities and the different Chinese dialect groupings were broken up and re-mixed in the housing estates, diluting the possibilities for ethnic, especially Malay, mobilisation. There has also been a dampening effect on class politics because the estates contain a mix of dwelling types, from rental flats for the poorest groups to more luxurious units for the middle class.

The political importance of housing has not been lost on the PAP. The government is now, after having provided wide access to housing, embarking on an upgrading programme for the housing estates, starting with the older areas. Depending on the type of dwelling, the government subsidy ranges from Sing $ 33,700 to $ 38,900, with owners paying between 8 and 21 per cent of the total costs. Upgraded estates fetch a premium in the housing market. This fact gave the PAP a high degree of leverage to influence the voters' choice in the 1997 elections. One of the concerns of the PAP has been that constituencies, while generally supportive of the government, vote for the opposition just to have balance in the Parliament. The government sees this behaviour as a form of extortion, and has come up with the following response. In the elections voters were told that the upgrading programme would be tied directly to the support received by the PAP.[67] This stark choice caused much consternation, but in the end the voters put their economic interests ahead of any desire to see more opposition MPs.

In conclusion, both the UMNO and the PAP have managed to build large multi-class constituencies through economic growth. In Malaysia, the ruling coalition has built up a large Malay clientele, but has made sure that the non-Malay middle class and the working class have a minimal allegiance to the political system. In Singapore, the PAP has placed itself between capital and labour, and has successfully balanced both sets of interests, generating broad, though not necessarily zealous, multi-ethnic and multi-class support.

MANAGING DOMINANCE: IDEOLOGIES AND IDENTITIES

The UMNO and PAP have put in a major ideological effort to shape the very meaning and ends of politics. Both ruling parties place themselves as the only

---

65 Information from Yao, "Consumption and Social Aspirations", p. 339.
66 Chua Beng Huat, "Not Depoliticized but Ideologically Successful: The Public Housing Programme in Singapore", *International Journal of Urban and Regional Research*, 15, 1 (1991), pp. 36–7.
67 *Sunday Times*, October 23, 1996.

legitimate embodiment of political activity, and raise the spectre of chaos if politics were to become more open or if opposition parties obtained more power. Perhaps their greatest ideological role is the setting of the agenda on thinking about the future of the nation, and their promise of elevating the nation economically and culturally in the global system. The leaders deride the liberal vision of open democratic politics as an obstacle to the national aspirations and political stability. Through the use of the media, the governmental perspective is powerfully purveyed to the population, resulting in the constriction of alternative secular visions of politics.

David Jones and David Brown have argued that the managerial vocabulary of the Singapore elite has left the middle class—and presumably the wider electorate—without a firm political identity. They argue that the middle class has become linguistically incoherent by being bombarded with a mixture of languages used by the state—a utilitarian liberalism that asks them to stand on their own feet and not depend on state welfarism and a concocted communitarianism that asks citizens to put community above self.[68] In their confusion, the middle class have turned to the managerial certainties provided by the state, and have found meaning in the anxious pursuit of material self-interest and conformity to the political system.

The government's role in shaping cognition has indeed been fundamental, but the propagation of ideology has not been a total ideational construct. Historical experiences have given a certain plausibility to the idea of the state as the stable and certain manager of society. When merger failed with Malaysia, there was much anxiety among the population about Singapore's ability to survive as a small entity in the global economy.[69] The ethnic tensions that surfaced during the merger period also led to a garrison mentality in which Singapore was portrayed as a small Chinese-dominated society surrounded by potentially hostile Malay neighbours. These conditions led to a strongly articulated ideology of survival and pragmatism which gave little room for liberal politics. A persistent fear was that a high degree of internal pluralism could bring out domestic ethnic issues with regional ramifications. Further anxiety over the survival of the state and the economy was fuelled in 1968 when the British government announced it was withdrawing its military bases from Singapore.

In the 1960s and 1970s, the discourse on survival and pragmatism did allow for eventual democratic practice when the society reached "maturity",

---

68 Jones and Brown, "Singapore and the Myth", p. 85.
69 See Chan Heng Chee, *Singapore: The Politics of Survival 1965–1967* (Kuala Lumpur: Oxford University Press, 1971).

an interesting concept that Singaporeans use to discuss their readiness for the loosening of controls over their lives.[70] Since the 1980s, however, the PAP has embarked on a strong attack of liberal democracy. Asian values or shared values have been consciously enunciated as an antidote to creeping Western individualism. The values of Asia are seen as superior in providing social order, strong families, and high-growth economies because they are collectively oriented rather than premised on an ineffectual liberalism.

The senior minister and ex-prime minister of Singapore, Lee Kuan Yew, has played a powerful role in calling into question the benefits of Western democratic practice, and has even gone on to export his views regionally. In 1992, Lee urged the Filipinos to concentrate on economics rather than politics if they wanted to join the ranks of the newly industrialised countries:

> Contrary to what the American political commentators say, I do not believe that democracy necessarily leads to development. I believe that what a country needs to develop is discipline more than democracy.[71]

Lee has also disparaged Indian democracy: "(T)he Indians just love an argument. That is why it is a wonderful time in India. They never get a consensus. What you have is more debate. The Western democracy practised in India may make an enjoyable campaign but I am not sure we need that in Singapore."[72]

The general population, from the young to the old and from the working class to the middle class, share the view that liberal systems produce gridlock, uncontrolled welfarism, and economic decline. Newspapers in Singapore portray the problems of the welfare state, unemployment, crime, and family breakdown as one inter-related phenomenon occurring in the West, and most Singaporeans will say unhesitatingly that the cause is too much freedom.

The PAP has also pre-empted thinking on the future by always defining a desirable model along which the society will be engineered. In the past the models were foreign but in the last 15 years, Singapore has begun to see itself as an international model in its own right.[73] Israel was the model in the 1960s because it had a strong military, and was seen as an oasis of competence in the middle of backwardness and poverty. In the 1970s, Japan and Switzerland provided the models to emulate. Singaporeans were urged to

---

70 Chua, *Communitarian Ideology*, p. 57.
71 *The Times of London*, Nov. 19, 1992.
72 *New Straits Times*, June 15, 1996.
73 Jean-Loius Margolin, "Foreign Models in Singapore's Development and the Idea of a Singaporean Model," Garry Rodan, ed., *Singapore Changes Guard: Social, Political and Economic Directions in the 1990s* (Melbourne: Longman Cheshire, 1993), pp. 85–9.

follow the voluntary discipline of Japanese workers while aiming for Swiss standards of living. The Swiss were positively evaluated because they were the richest people in the world and were tame, respectful and worked hard. The present goals for Singapore are to be the richest nation in the world, develop a world-class transportation system, and spawn a gracious and caring society.

The managerial ideology of the state has not, however, resulted in everyone thinking that oppositional politics is a liability. Many think that the opposition is necessary to counter-balance state power and make the government attentive to their views. For example, in a recent survey of 418 young Singaporeans in their twenties, it was reported that most felt that it was necessary to have an opposition in Parliament, with only 23 per cent disagreeing. However, there was basic agreement with the way the government was managing the society.[74] Eighty-seven per cent considered Singapore to be the best place to make a home, 95 per cent regarded Singapore as a safe place, 93 per cent considered the economy stable and strong, and 89 per cent thought the government was a good one. Only 11 per cent of the respondents thought there were too many government controls while a mere 7 per cent mentioned the lack of political freedom in Singapore as a problem.

In Malaysia, the regime cannot derive the same level of legitimacy from pure technocratic managerialism because the presence of clientelism makes it difficult for the UMNO and the Barisan to claim, as the PAP does, that it rules without corruption. The greater degree of internal factions within UMNO and the acceptance of ethnic political activity make for a greater degree of divergence about how the country should be run. Even regarding democracy, there is no consensus within government that democratic practice is an encumbrance on economic growth. While the prime minister, Dr Mahathir, has railed against the West for its democratic extremism, his deputy, Anwar Ibrahim, has spoken out against authoritarianism in Southeast Asia and the "condescending attitude of Asian leaders toward their citizenry".[75]

Yet the leaders of UMNO and the Barisan have strongly articulated the idea that the ruling coalition is the only means of achieving long-term political stability in the country. The memory of "May 13" (1969), when ethnic peace broke down, is frequently evoked as the latent danger lurking in the Malaysian polity. In fact, so powerful is the imagery of the event that the government has often obtained support for the use of the Internal Security Act by evoking "May 13" to arrest those deemed to be a threat to national security.

---

74 *Straits Times*, June 27, 1996.
75 *Asian Wall Street Journal*, Aug. 26, 1996.

The legitimacy of the Barisan, in particular the UMNO, is based on a number of pillars, among which ethnicity is fundamental. Ethnicity has served as a fundamental link between the state and the Malay society, although this link has been flexibly reconstituted from time to time. Initially UMNO's role was to defend Malay political and symbolic supremacy amidst threats from non-Malays. Later the UMNO saw itself as modernising the Malay and giving him pride in his economic achievements. Presently, the rhetoric has shifted to the global level. UMNO aims for Malays to become global actors, ready to face the next century culturally and psychologically. The UMNO image of the Malay is not necessarily positive, and contains many of the stereotypical elements that the British had of him, such as his conservatism, lack of drive, and inferiority complex. This dialectic of Malay leaders disparaging the Malay and then purporting to rescue him has been a long-standing theme in Malay politics. Dr Mahathir's controversial book, *The Malay Dilemma* written in 1970, had many negative things to say about Malay capabilities, tracing their deficiencies to weak genes resulting from frequent cousin marriages.[76] In a recent book by Muhammad Taib, the ex-chief minister of Selangor entitled *The New Malay*, the same themes of Malay incapacity and the need for deliverance are highlighted. Unlike the old Malay, who is seen as passive, uncreative, non-competitive and dependent on others for technology, the New Malay will be self-reliant and confident. The author went on to say that such a goal can be "realistically achieved with an appropriate and comprehensive strategy" through the efforts of leaders with the ability to think, plan and act in far-reaching ways.[77]

The UMNO has also organically linked itself to the religious orientations of the Malay population. Facing other claimants to religious salvation, such as PAS' theocratic state, the UMNO over time has moved Islam to a central place in its ideology. But UMNO's version of Islam is to help in the process of modernity and bring material progress to the Malays.[78] The UMNO leadership has exhorted Malaysian Muslims to be a model for the rest of the Islamic world and give Islam a good name, rejecting the Middle Eastern heartland as representing the true possibilities of the religion. UMNO's religious programme is wrapped up with the interesting attempt to tie economic interests to broader moral and national causes.

---

76   Mahathir bin Mohamad, *The Malay Dilemma* (Singapore: The Asia Pacific Press, 1970).

77   Muhammad Taib, *The New Malay* (Petaling Jaya: Visage Communication, 1996), pp. 4, 7.

78   T.N. Harper, "New Malays, New Malaysians: Nationalism, Society and History", *Southeast Asian Affairs 1996* (Singapore: Institute of Southeast Asian Studies, 1996), p. 244.

In contrast to the above focus on Malay identity, lately the UMNO has also added to its ideological arsenal a more multi-ethnic understanding of nationhood. Since there are inherent political problems in explicitly advocating equal rights for the non-Malays, the future has been used creatively to project a community appealing to all. The national slogan that emerged in the 1990s is Vision 2020, articulating Dr Mahathir's view of a future, open-minded community.

By the year 2020, national evolution will have led to an ethnically integrated society living in harmony made up of one race, *Bangsa Malaysia* (Malaysian race). The new national community will be liberal and tolerant, with full and fair partnership among all ethnic groups, who will be able to practise their own customs and religions, and yet feel that they belonged to one nation. This new formulation was a far cry from previous notions of nationalism, which always had a Malay thrust to it. This new vision does not make UMNO's ideology of Malay supremacy redundant, but is one more symbolic repertoire that UMNO is able to employ when political conditions warrant.

THE POLITICAL OPPOSITION AND ITS POLITICAL CONTAINMENT

The political opposition in both Malaysia and Singapore has not been able to pose a serious challenge to the dominant parties. One can point to the negative sanctions and constraints that weaken the opposition, but from the discussion so far, it should be apparent that the positive acts of the ruling parties also explain their hegemony. I have argued elsewhere that what is particularly damaging for the political opposition in Malaysia is the syncretic nature of the state. The regime is able to combine a variety of approaches in the economic and ideological realms, such as mixing clientelism and development, democratic procedures and selective coercion, and ethnic and religious consciousness with national feeling, leaving only limited bases for the opposition to cultivate.[79] The PAP appears to have a less syncretic approach since it claims to be secularist and ethnically neutral, but even here the PAP tries, at the ideological level, to combine what it believes to be the best of Western pragmatism and Asian values. Except for religious parties, such as PAS, which rejects the whole secular and moral order, the opposition parties in both societies find it very difficult to offer a better alternative, particularly when they do not control state resources.

---

79 James V. Jesudason, "The Syncretic State and the Structuring of Oppositional Politics in Malaysia", Garry Rodan, ed., *Political Oppositions in Industrialising Asia* (London: Routledge, 1996), p. 131.

A general feature of both political systems is that no one opposition party or even a coalition of opposition parties can secure a majoritarian basis of rule. For example, the two or three main opposition political parties in Malaysia and Singapore have to share the 30–40 per cent of the votes cast for the opposition. No single opposition party has the potential to form an alternative government, but there are inherent constraints in forming a more effective amalgamation to challenge the ruling parties.

Although there are important differences in the nature of the opposition in Malaysia and Singapore, such as their greater vibrancy in Malaysia, the common feature is that they appear as stunted variants of the dominant party. The ethnic and religious properties of the Barisan have been transposed over to opposition parties, which also rely on ethnicity and religion for their appeal. The elitist and top-down nature of the PAP and its multiracialism also contributes to opposition parties having elitist structures.[80] All the opposition parties in Singapore, with one exception, are multi-ethnic in principle. The weakness of the opposition centrally arises from the fact that the dominant party sets the terms of operation of the opposition, to the extent of influencing its organisational features.

The main opposition parties in Malaysia act as flank parties, a term used by Horowitz to describe the mobilisation of constituencies at the more extreme poles of the dominant party.[81] Their party platforms push more vigorously issues such as the extension of Chinese or Malay ethnic rights, the Islamisation of the country, and in some instances a stronger redistribution policy. UMNO's chief rival, PAS, is an Islamic-based party that controls the state government of Kelantan, one of the 13 states that make up the federation. It was a serious challenger to UMNO in the 1960s, mobilising the Malay peasantry and poorer segments of the Malay population against UMNO's alleged over-generosity to Chinese economic and cultural interests. When UMNO swung to promote Malay capitalism, the Malay language, and the symbols of Islam more vigorously, PAS was forced to shift ground, advocating the literal interpretation of Islam as the basis of Malaysian society. Presently, the austere lifestyle of PAS' leaders does have moral appeal among the poorer stratum of Malay society and those who see UMNO politicians as self-seeking.[82] But barring an economic crisis or an UMNO becoming hopelessly

---

80 Garry Rodan, ed., "State-Society Relations and Political Opposition in Singapore", *Political Oppositions in Industrialising Asia* (London: Routledge, 1996), p. 116.

81 Horowitz, *Ethnic Groups*, p. 413.

82 Shamsul A.B., *From British to Bumiputera Rule: Local Politics and Rural Development in Peninsula Malaysia* (Singapore: Institute of Southeast Asian Studies, 1986), pp. 238–9.

corrupt, the appeal of PAS is likely to be limited to the poorer pockets of Malay society and certain regions in the country.

The Democratic Action Party (DAP), which has had the same leader for more than three decades, is almost the mirror image of PAS. It has strongly campaigned for non-Malay rights and interests and has managed to attract lower and middle class Chinese support, although there was a swing away from the party in the 1995 elections. Since non-Malay mobility and life chances are determined fundamentally by market opportunities rather than state largess, there are fewer risks for the Chinese to vote for the opposition. However, the DAP cannot become a more significant party without greater Malay support. Despite trying to reach out to Malays by advocating causes that transcend ethnicity such as the high prices charged by privatised government companies, the DAP has not been able to shed its label as a Chinese chauvinist party inflicted on it by the Barisan, thereby making little headway with the Malay population.

Under the best conditions, the DAP and PAS are able to win 20 per cent each of the votes cast in a general election. It is only through a wider coalition that they could possibly pose a threat to the Barisan. Yet such a wider coalition will have to aggregate a wider set of ideological and ethnic interests than found in the dominant party. Thus when Semangat 46, the presently defunct party that broke off from UMNO in 1988, tried to form a united alliance with PAS and the DAP against the Barisan in 1990, the experiment failed and showed up the dilemma of opposition politics in Malaysia. The unlikely partnership could not articulate a vision of democracy going beyond attacking the specific malpractices of the regime and few voters believed that the parties were ideologically cohesive. Malay voters, in particular, were not willing to abandon the Barisan for some abstract notion of a two-party system without being sure that there would be economic benefits in making a switch. This alliance did help the opposition win a few more seats than in the previous election and did capture the imagination of the non-Malay middle class over the possibility of an effective counterweight to the Barisan. However, Semangat 46 itself did not do as well as it wished, winning only 8 of 59 parliamentary seats it contested. But instead of persevering to popularise the concept of a two-party system, it made a complete switch and began to push for greater Malay rights. The party now attacked the UMNO for being too close to Chinese interests, returning to an old battle cry of Malay opposition parties that worked in the 1960s but began to have less plausibility when UMNO re-established itself as an effective ethnic sponsor. Semangat was effectively wiped out as a significant political force in the 1995 elections.

The opposition in Singapore has been in a more precarious position than in Malaysia. When the Barisan Sosialis boycotted electoral politics in the 1960s, its surrender of political space has never been recovered by the opposition. Only the Workers' Party (WP), the Singapore Democratic Party (SDP), and the Singapore People's Party (SPP), a recent off-shoot of the SDP, have won a handful of seats since 1981. The membership of the parties is extremely small, estimated at 280 for the SDP and 2,600 for the Workers' Party, and an even smaller number, fewer than 100, are believed to be active members.[83]

Unlike in Malaysia, communal opposition parties are basically non-existent. Only the Pertubohan Kebangsaan Melayu Singapura (PKMS), a party that started as a branch of the UMNO during the merger, lingers on as an ethnic party. The official ideology of multiracialism, government action against communal and chauvinist appeals, and the redistribution of the Malay population from *kampong* (villages) to public housing have neutralised the PKMS. The main opposition parties are to the left of the PAP, favouring greater economic redistribution and a more democratic society. There are no right-wing parties promoting bourgeois and middle class interests against the workers, attesting to the ability of the PAP to also cater to elite interests in society. The Workers' Party, which has been headed by the persistent J.B. Jeyaretnam, a lawyer, since 1971, is a social democratic party that has tried to get working class support by asking for more extensive welfare measures.[84] However, the party basically campaigns on political and legal issues, such as the need for more political and civil rights, repealing the provision allowing the prime minister to appoint the judge of the Supreme Court for a fixed period, greater press freedom, and the removal of the climate of fear in the country.[85] The Social Democratic Party was founded in 1980 by another lawyer, Chaim See Tong, who was subsequently ejected from his own party, after which he went on to become the leader of the Singapore People's Party. The SDP stands for more health benefits for the population, and speaks out against the unfair advantages enjoyed by the middle class, and the excessive social and political restrictions in the society. There is little divergence between the WP and the SDP. The support for these parties is predominantly the working class, tapering off as one moves toward the higher reaches of society.

---

83 Rodan, "State-Society Relations", p. 116.
84 Milne and Mauzy, *Singapore*, p. 92.
85 Chan, "Political Parties", p. 165.

The opposition parties are highly dependent on a main leader, through whom the party becomes known to the public. As with the opposition parties in Malaysia, the Singapore opposition tends to chip away at PAP polices at the margin, concentrating on the supposed failures of the PAP. The SPP leaders have even said that the party does not have any deep ideological conflict with the PAP.[86] One consequence of personality-dominated politics is that opposition parties are not able to amalgamate, although it would seem logical given their political weakness and their basic similarity in ideology. Co-operation amongst them does not extend beyond election strategies not to compete against each other in the same constituency.

Tocqueville's view that a democracy, by providing security for the majority, can curtail liberty helps elucidate the constraints faced by the opposition in Malaysia and Singapore. By controlling the media and legally circumscribing the sphere of legitimate political activity, the Barisan and the PAP have made it difficult for the opposition to grow and for alternative ideas to percolate in the society. Using the language of demand and supply, we can say that the demand for an alternative governing party, or even a powerful opposition, has been lowered by the effectiveness of both dominant parties. But it is necessary to examine the supply side of the equation, and to show the risks and barriers to individuals wishing to gain political influence and advance their ideas and criticisms. The leaders of the ruling parties do think an opposition is useful, not to replace them, but to keep the government on its toes. Maintaining this state of political affairs requires strong efforts in political monitoring and control.

The Malaysian regime tolerates autonomous civil society activity to a greater extent than in Singapore. The UMNO and the Barisan are more internally differentiated than the PAP, and following Sartori, we observe more pluralism in the political system as a whole.[87] As long as ideas and disagreements do not become mobilised into strong oppositional activity, the government is willing to tolerate oppositional activity in civil society, preferring to ignore rather than weaken the civil society groups.

Nonetheless, the government is able to protect itself from strong challenges to its rule and weaken the opposition through a variety of devices. The main newspaper groups are controlled by groups and business interests linked to particular political parties and leaders in government.[88] In addition,

---

86 Rodan, "State-Society Relations", pp. 117–9.
87 Giovanni Sartori, *"Parties and Party Systems: A Framework for Analysis* (Cambridge: Cambridge University Press, 1976), p. 66.
88 Crouch, *Government and Society*, pp. 86–87.

all newspapers must obtain a licence for publication, which is reviewed annually. The few critical publications in Malaysia are limited to select audiences. The publications of the opposition parties, such as the DAP and PAS, are restricted by law to party members only and cannot be sold to the general public. *Aliran Monthly*, a critical magazine put out by an intellectual reform group, is freely available in most book stores, but its readership is confined to a select middle class group. All radio stations and two of the three national T V stations are government monopolies.

Overt forms of political control include the Societies Act, which requires every association and interest group to get government permission for its establishment, and empowers the Registrar of Societies to de-register a society on security or moral grounds. The Official Secrets Act gives the government punitive powers to prosecute any journalist who publishes official information without authorisation. The Internal Security Act (ISA) empowers the Minister of Home Affairs to detain a person without trial if he is deemed to act in a way prejudicial to the security of the country or the maintenance of essential services. The courts have been stripped of their power to oversee ISA cases except in purely procedural matters. In 1987, during the time of the UMNO split, which led to a new boldness among opposition groups, 106 social and political activists were arrested under the ISA. In 1994, the Shia-inspired Al-Arqam sect was banned, and the government used the ISA to detain its leaders for propagating views which went against the teachings of official Islam.

The leaders of the Barisan, in particular Dr Mahathir, believe that elected representatives of the people possess the sole mandate to rule. This has led to control over the courts as well. As Crouch observes, when "court decisions have threatened fundamental government interests, the government has taken whatever action necessary to defend its position".[89] In 1988, the Lord President was impeached after a period of growing tension between the prime minister and members of the judiciary, who had made some decisions in favour of opposition parties and journalists.

Electoral procedures and the demarcation of constituency boundaries also disadvantage the opposition. Open-air election rallies have been banned since 1974. In 1990, the Elections Act was amended to allow for vote counting to be conducted in local polling stations rather than in a central counting area. The number of polling stations has been increased so that in some places only 700 voters can be registered in a polling station.[90] The reward

---

89   Crouch, p. 142.
90   Crouch, p. 61.

and punishment of voters can now be done with more precision. Means also notes how gerrymandering is blatantly practised in Malaysia.[91] Historically, Malay-majority constituencies, especially in the rural areas, were vastly over-represented compared to urban Chinese areas, where the Barisan has enjoyed far less support. Interestingly, Gomez finds that with the Chinese becoming more supportive of the Barisan, the re-delineation exercise before the 1995 elections actually favoured constituencies that were evenly divided between Malays and non-Malays.[92]

The most fascinating aspect of Singapore, as an educated and rich society, is the surprising under-supply of professional and articulate candidates willing to join the opposition. The opposition is unable to field a full list of candidates to contest every constituency in Singapore. This failure is only partly a result of the opposition strategy not to contest in more than 50 per cent of the seats in Parliament, thereby assuring voters that the PAP will not be thrown out in a freak election. Opposition members, if they want to take on the PAP aggressively, must be prepared to be totally blameless as individuals and be armed with masses of correct information. This high requirement, and the risk of offending PAP notables through the lack of caution, makes the rewards too little and the risks too high for talented and educated people to join the opposition in general.

Singapore has many of the same rules and laws as Malaysia, such as the Internal Security Act, the Official Secrets Act, and the Societies' Act. The Internal Security Act was last used in a major way in 1987 to arrest 22 relatively young middle class professionals and Catholic social workers alleged to be involved in a Marxist conspiracy to overthrow the government. Another prominent instance was the detention of Francis Seow in 1988. He was a former Solicitor-General, and later, as President of the Law Society, had collided with the government when his society offered a dissenting opinion on a legislative proposal to restrict the circulation of foreign publications carrying negative reports on the country. Seow joined the Workers' Party to stand for the 1988 elections but was arrested under the ISA for conspiring with a US diplomat to organise an opposition group of English-educated professionals.[93] Upon his release, he stood in the elections, and narrowly lost. He subsequently fled the country when tax evasion charges were brought against him, and now criticises the regime from his base in the United States.

---

91 Means, *Malaysian Politics*, p. 316.
92 Edmund T. Gomez, *The 1995 Malaysian General Elections: A Report and Commentary. Occasional Paper No. 93* (Singapore: Institute of Southeast Asian Studies, 1996), pp. 7, 10.
93 Milne and Mauzy, *Singapore*, p. 68.

The PAP, however, also employs a set of unique mechanisms to contain the nature of political expression in the society. The sphere of proper political speech and writing has been circumscribed by the PAP using legal procedures against opposition members who defame them. The leader of the Workers' Party, J.B. Jeyaretnam, has been found guilty of numerous defamation cases against him brought by PAP ministers and members. The most publicised instance of a defamation suit against an opposition member involved a Chinese lawyer, Tang Liang Hong, who had joined the Workers' Party for the 1997 elections. In the election campaign in late December 1996, PAP stalwarts labelled him an anti-Christian Chinese chauvinist who threatened to undermine racial harmony in Singapore. He retorted by calling his accusers liars in the *Straits Times* newspaper, upon which he was slapped with 13 defamation suits launched by 11 politicians of the PAP, including the prime minister, Goh Chok Tong, Senior Minister Lee Kuan Yew, the two deputy prime ministers, and other top politicians.[94] Tang fled the country, but the courts in Singapore judged that there were sufficient grounds for the PAP to describe him as an anti-Christian Chinese chauvinist, awarding his plaintiffs damages amounting to around US$ 5 million.

Opposition politicians must be careful not only about what they say about the PAP, but also in how they analyse government policy. Chee Soon Juan, as the leader of the SDP, wrote a book, *Dare to Challenge: An Alternative Vision for Singapore*, in 1994 as the basis of his party's platform.[95] In it he produced statistics on health to claim that the government had dramatically cut down on public expenditures on health. In August 1996 the government convened hearings of the Select Committee on Health Care to examine spending on health. Chee was invited to present his views, and was pinned down on his faulty figures and careless research. Later Chee and three other SDP members were brought before the Committee of Privileges to face charges of contempt of Parliament, and were found guilty and fined.

The PAP has also modified the system of Parliamentary representation in ways that substantially depart from British practice. After the 12 per cent vote swing against the government in the 1984 elections, the PAP introduced an act providing for the appointment of up to three non-constituency MPs (to ensure a minimum of three opposition MPs in Parliament) from opposition candidates with the highest losing percentage of votes. One of the concerns of the leadership was that young voters might think they are missing something

---

94 *Asiaweek*, February 28, 1997.
95 Chee Soon Juan, *Dare to Change: An Alternative Vision for Singapore* (Singapore: The Singapore Democratic Party, 1994).

from not having strong political competition, and might vote for the opposition just for the sake of having an alternative voice in parliament.[96] In 1989, an equally novel scheme was introduced through constitutional amendment to provide for the appointment of up to six (now increased to nine) non-elected, nominated MPs for two-year terms. The team chosen for 1997 had three managing directors of companies, two lawyers, one partner of an accounting company, and an NTUC leader. The choice of these individuals seems to accord with the PAP's view that Parliament should debate public matters in practical, informed, and business-focused terms. Some of the nominated MPs have been judged to be more articulate and impressive than the regular MPs, further inculcating the view that political candidates ought to behave like technocrats. Another modification which has displeased the opposition is the introduction, since the 1988 elections, of the Group (multi-member) Representative Constituency. Under this system, existing constituencies have been combined and re-arranged to produce a single voting bloc, and a group of candidates standing together would all be voted in *en masse* if they polled the most votes. The number of MPs standing in each of these super-constituencies has increased from a maximum of three (with at least one minority candidate) in the 1988 elections to four in 1991 and to six in the 1996 elections.[97] The opposition leaders have complained that this scheme has hurt their chances of victory.[98] For one thing, some of their single constituency strongholds have been combined into these larger units. Milne and Mauzy also argue that opposition parties, as "parties of personalities", are likely to suffer from having the appeal of the leader being diluted by relatively unknown team-mates.[99] Opposition leaders also say that lesser-known or weaker PAP candidates can now get in on the coattails of prominent ministers.

However, despite the sometimes dismissive attitude of the leaders of the Barisan Nasional and PAP toward the opposition, the latter has nonetheless performed some useful roles for these dominant parties.

When Semangat entered politics and tried to build a multi-ethnic alliance to compete more intensively against the Barisan, the dominant coalition was forced to rethink its own political platform. The party began to appeal to Chinese interests and feelings, and UMNO leaders began to support Chinese cultural events more openly.[100] Just as PAS showed up some political

96 Milne and Mauzy, *Singapore*, p. 68.
97 *Business Times*, Oct. 2, 1996.
98 *Straits Times*, Oct. 2, 1996.
99 Milne and Mauzy, *Singapore*, p. 70.
100 Crouch, *Government and Society*, p. 124.

weaknesses in UMNO in the 1960s, the opposition in the late 1980s and 1990s pushed UMNO toward a more racially accommodative stance, helping it to consolidate its position in the society.

The opposition in Singapore has also played the role of an early warning system for grievances building up in the polity. In the early 1980s, the government of Lee Kuan Yew introduced the "graduate mothers' scheme" which provided generous inducements for women with tertiary education to produce more children. This policy was extremely unpopular with the lower classes, and even its beneficiaries did not like to be treated so instrumentally. This scheme was believed to be one factor that caused the vote swing against the government in the 1984 elections. In 1985, the policy was dropped, and more acceptable pro-natal policy was put in place. Toward the late 1980s, the government began to cut back on social security provision, expecting citizens to pay more for services rendered.[101] The opposition capitalised on the perceived inequality developing in Singapore, and managed to sustain its share of the vote in the 1991 elections. Fearing lower-class alienation, the PAP focused more carefully on inequality after the elections, and has promised to provide a minimum social safety net for the poor, in contradistinction to its strong anti-welfare ideology in the 1980s. The opposition in Singapore has therefore helped a technocratic and highly developmentalist state remain responsive to the population.

PROSPECTS FOR CONTINUED HEGEMONY

It would be wrong to think that there are no internal tensions in the management of political dominance in Malaysia and Singapore. The weaknesses of the dominant parties can be traced to those very structures and practices that have made them successful. There is no reason to believe that the dominant parties will inevitably decline, but the task of managing and controlling society is a perpetual challenge.

In Singapore, the chief problem for the PAP is its own technocratic approach to politics and its highly economistic orientation in society. Having successfully solved many of the basic economic problems of the citizenry, the incremental gain in political support from extra-economic growth has grown smaller. The economic pay-off for the citizen's political support has become very high, as evidenced by the large subsidies given for the upgrading programme in housing. As Hirsch acutely pointed out in his book, *The Social*

---

101 Ramesh, "Social Security in Singapore", p. 1103.

Limits to Growth, achieving affluence has its in-built contradictions.[102] The sense of well-being shifts from enjoying basic amenities to obtaining positional goods conferring status, such as obtaining a superior education or a private bungalow with a sea-view. These goods are inherently scarce because as they become widespread, the more devalued they become. The survey of young Singaporeans in their twenties reveal the mix of anxiety and high expectations that come with the pursuit of positional goods. Given land scarcity, the government has said that it would be difficult for more than 25 per cent of the population to live in private condominiums, regarded as more prestigious than living in public housing. However, 60 per cent of the young report that having private property is either very important or quite important to them.[103]

For all of Singapore's success, as many as 18 per cent of the population have thought about migrating to another country.[104] The number that actually does is very small but the above figure reflects a certain unease about life in Singapore. For the people who have contemplated migrating, the main reasons are the high cost of living, the stressful life, the high prices of houses and cars followed by the excessive number of rules and regulations in existence. It is interesting that it is the respondents in the middle third of the class spectrum that think most of migrating rather than the affluent or the poorer groups, reflecting the status anxiety of the middle class.

It may be argued that increasing the realm of participation and opening public discourse could actually help the PAP maintain support and get a higher level of moral approval. There are limits to how far the party can continue to offer the carrots while brandishing the big stick, or to keep modifying the electoral system, before legitimacy is seriously affected.[105] Even if liberal sentiments are not strong, there is still a greater desire for pluralism than the political system allows for, judging from the gap between the votes the opposition receives and its actual representation in Parliament. However, the party so deeply fears that pluralism could quickly slip into a situation producing policy grid-lock and economic ruin that it is not willing to risk providing more in the country. The result is that while the regime desires for its citizens to have stronger social bonds and identification with Singapore, it finds it difficult to produce an energising moral vision and a genuine participatory

---

102 Fred Hirsch, *Social Limits to Growth* (Cambridge: Harvard University Press, 1978), p. 173.

103 *Straits Times*, June 28, 1996.

104 *Straits Times*, Aug 15, 1997.

105 This interesting insight is provided by Diane K. Mauzy, "Singapore's Dilemma: Coping with the Paradoxes of Success", *Southeast Asian Affairs 1997* (Singapore: Institute of Southeast Asian Affairs, 1997), p. 275.

framework to capture the imagination of the society.[106] One could imagine the PAP employing the language of social rights more to its advantage, given the adequate levels of social provision in the country, but its fear that the concept of rights will produce excessive individualism, liberalism, and welfarism prevents the construction of a more salutary ideology. Instead, the government has preferred to build national feeling on the more negative symbolism of the vulnerability and uncertainty facing the nation.

One challenge facing the PAP is maintaining the support of its multi-class constituency. While the leaders have argued that inequality has been kept within bounds, they have been concerned that inequality will increase with the globalisation of the economy. The more capable Singaporeans will have to be paid at levels comparable to the best globally while the unskilled will have to compete with their low-wage counterparts from elsewhere. Salient polarisation of this sort will pose problems to the party's desire to have overwhelming dominance in Parliament. Interestingly, the government has come up in recent years with innovative programmes based on market-compatible logic to deal with creeping inequality. In the "A Share for All" programme, periodic redistribution of the country's wealth will take place not through minimum wages or high taxation but through asset-enhancement schemes.[107] Singaporeans will be given a stake in the shares of large profit-making government-owned companies and the huge surpluses of the government will also be used to top up the funds available to individuals for retirement, medical, and educational purposes.

UMNO is less technocratic, more pluralistic internally, and the leadership more dependent on the grassroots for support than the PAP. It is prone to factions and employs patronage mechanisms to reward politically connected individuals as well as to secure general support. As a result of UMNO's close links to business cliques, the party can suffer from deep divisions and fissures as factions vie for influence. Contests for leadership positions are invariably linked to different economic factions. So great is the potential for divisions in UMNO that in its most recent party elections in 1996, Dr Mahathir Mohamad imposed the rule that the posts for the President and Deputy President of UMNO, occupied by himself and his deputy, Anwar Ibrahim, would not be contested.[108] Observers in Malaysia believe that Mahathir was trying to prevent Anwar's supporters from trying to oust

---

106 Khong Cho-Oon, "Singapore: Political Legitimacy through Managing Conformity", Muthiah Alagappa, ed., *Political Legitimacy in Southeast Asia* (Stanford: Stanford University Press, 1995), p. 132.
107 Mauzy, "Singapore's Dilemma", p. 267.
108 *New Straits Times*, Oct. 12, 1996.

him. Both men have different economic visions, with Anwar more in favour of a broader spread of the Malay capitalists, while Mahathir likes to promote a few chosen tycoons. Some of Dr Mahathir's grandiose projects, such as erecting the two tallest buildings in the world, constructing a mammoth hydroelectric scheme in the middle of rich tropical rain-forests, and building the world's longest shopping mall on a river, are believed to stem from this nexus of power, patronage, and business.

The top leaders do acknowledge occasionally the role of "money politics" or vote-buying in UMNO and do seem concerned that such activities would ultimately deplete UMNO of its strength and coherence. The Malay middle class has become more willing to express its dissatisfaction over corruption and the closed-door deals in which the allies and relatives of politicians enrich themselves. As a beneficiary of UMNO policies, the Malay middle class has traditionally been quiescent, but there is more audible disquiet over tight links between top Malay corporate tycoons and the Mahathir regime. An UMNO riddled with money politics will make political and religious management in the broader political arena even more contentious as the regime's Islamic detractors attack UMNO for using religion as merely a cloak for advancing narrow, materialistic interests.

Economic growth has served as a major factor in resolving different interests within UMNO as well as containing broader political conflict. It is difficult to predict the consequences of low economic growth, but we can certainly expect internal struggles within UMNO to increase. It is unlikely that UMNO will split again unless Dr Mahathir refuses, even in a bad economic situation, to make way for other aspirants to office. The UMNO elite has drawn lessons from the split in the 1980s and will want to avoid such open warfare again. But what is more likely to happen is a reconfiguration of power within UMNO rather than a factional challenge from without.

UMNO has shown itself capable of internal change, and there are voices within the party calling for more party discipline and transparent procedures. An economic slowdown could provide new opportunities for the party to shift to other bases of legitimacy, which has been made redundant by the current economic boom. Dr Mahathir's support of the Malay tycoon class stems more from his own predilection rather than the logic of UMNO political power. A lot of resources have been used inefficiently as a result of the political nature of the privatisation programme and the pursuit of grandiose projects. There is therefore slack in the allocation process to spread resources to a larger group of small Malay capitalists for patronage purposes and to better deliver services to the lower classes. It is therefore possible for

UMNO to reconsolidate even in an economic crisis by more redistributive policies and more transparent procedures.

There is little prospect for a movement away from the dominant party model in Singapore, even in a period of pronounced economic crisis. Such a crisis would probably stem from external shocks rather than discredited internal mismanagement. An economic crisis might de-mystify PAP claims to technocratic expertise and embolden the middle class to press for a less restrictive political climate. But in the final analysis, the population will turn to the PAP for solutions because of its track record of economic management. The swing against the PAP could increase, and make a slight dent in its overwhelming control of Parliament. However, even if the political system became more pluralistic, the PAP is likely to remain dominant, and in a more competitive situation, could actually generate increased popular enthusiasm for itself. The PAP has not used all its cards in managing dominance, and the trump card, when needed, is the legitimacy to be gained from greater pluralism.

CONCLUSION

Both the Barisan and the PAP have been able to build upon the top-down structure of the colonial state to remain as long-lived dominant parties. By maintaining electoral mechanisms and sustaining economic growth, both the parties have been able to build broad multi-class constituencies as a basis of support. Their paths of doing so have been different. The UMNO, the core party in the Barisan, has played the role of an ethnic patron to build up a Malay multi-class constituency, receiving fluctuating support from the non-Malays. The PAP, using a corporatist framework, has remained ethnically neutral, and has built its multi-class constituency by positioning itself carefully between the interests of capital and labour.

I have indicated that the dominant party cannot be seen merely as a product of internal divisions in society, where mutual distrust is resolved through support of a dominant party acting as an electoral Leviathan. The division between Malays and the Chinese in Malaysia and between the English-educated and Chinese-educated in Singapore could, hypothetically speaking, have initially prevented the forming of cross-class and cross-ethnic alliances for a competitive democracy. But there has been a blurring of these divisions in Singapore and to some extent in Malaysia, but instead of weakening the dominant party, both parties may have been strengthened by it. I have also pointed out that the politically restrictive measures employed by the Barisan and the PAP are only one element in their tool-kit. It is necessary to consider the broader institutional dynamics of the dominant party as a key ingredient in its longevity. The UMNO and the PAP have demonstrated their ability to shift their bases of support and to be responsive when conditions have warranted. Having attained a position of dominance, they have had strong incentives to enact long-term polices that produce economic growth and sustain multi-class constituencies. The irony in Malaysia and Singapore is that the regimes' control of the labour movement, through active neglect or corporatist arrangements, has improved the position of the general working class more than in places such as South Africa and Guyana, where a labour aristocracy has been influential in politics. Performance legitimacy, in turn, has provided the leverage to shape perceptions about what constitutes politics, and the criterion for judging good political leadership. In Singapore, politics has been propagated, not as an arena of contention between different moral or cultural options, but as a mechanism for allowing citizens to choose the leaders best equipped to secure a better economic future in a world filled with uncertainty. In Malaysia, politics has an important economic dimension, but in addition it has been about inculcating the proper path to ethnic salvation and national self-esteem. In short, the dominant parties have the ability to occupy large stretches of the ideological terrain and absorb diverse interests, leaving limited bases of support for the opposition to cultivate.

The limited ideological spaces available to the opposition parties has led them to attack particular state policies and practices or to reject the whole political and moral order. Neither are compelling enough to gain large support, and so no opposition party has inspired confidence that they can form an alternative government. In Malaysia, the opposition parties are highly polarised from one another ideologically and are not able to combine effectively. In Singapore, they are poorly organised and, while they are quite similar to one another, are not able to amalgamate because the parties are based on individual personalities. But by contesting in politics, sometimes with inexplicable tenacity, the opposition in both countries have given legitimacy to the dominant parties as expressions of popular sovereignty, and have helped them detect grievances before these become too serious. Thus far, the expansion of the middle class has not helped the opposition develop a more competitive political system or a broader liberal framework of politics. This class is intrigued by the idea of having greater opposition in the society but its members do not seem to be willing to take active steps in bringing the result about. The case of Malaysia and Singapore suggests that when the state is able to meet the economic interests of the middle class and electoral procedures give credence to the rule of the majority, large sections of the middle class have few incentives to challenge the dominant party and embrace liberty as a political ideal. In Malaysia, the direct dependence of the Malay middle class on the state makes them even less desirous of seeking major changes to UMNO's predominant position in the polity.

The UMNO and PAP, however, are not free from internal tensions. UMNO has salient patronage features which can lead to internal factions and collusive business–political links. The PAP's technocratic orientation commits the party to emphasise economic pursuits but the expectations generated can never quite be satisfied. A prolonged economic crisis could well test the legitimacy of these parties, although no one can be clear about what the political alternatives would be. Yet it is worth remembering that the dominant parties in Malaysia and Singapore are capable of flexibility and have the option, if pressed, to rely on new bases of legitimacy. One can envisage the PAP shifting the polity to a more participatory system, gaining legitimacy in the process while continuing to maintain dominance in a more liberal-pluralistic context. Perhaps with greater difficulty, but still within the realm of possibility, one could imagine UMNO becoming more ethnically neutral and technocratic in its economic policies, while preserving itself as the best available party to lead a complex society.

Acknowledgements
I would like to thank my colleagues, Habibul Khondker and Lam Peng Er, for their helpful suggestions and encouragement.

Chapter 6

DOMINANT PARTY AND OPPOSITION PARTIES IN MEXICO: FROM CRISIS TO REFORM TO CRISIS

ROBERT R. KAUFMAN

The dominant-party regimes explored in this volume differ widely in terms of the way they relate to state and society, but for much of their histories, most of them have been characterized by complex combinations of autocracy and political inclusion. With the current exception of the leaders of South Africa's ANC, the rulers of these countries have, at least in the past, used the coercive and financial resources of the state to limit serious electoral challenges to their political power. Even during their authoritarian periods, however, the dominant-party regimes of Mexico, Taiwan, and Malaysia also extended representation to a variety of competing groups, both within and outside the framework of the ruling party itself. This "limited pluralism", as Juan Linz argued several decades ago, is among the features which distinguish "authoritarian regimes" from the "totalitarian" party-states that once dominated many Communist societies.[1]

Where dominant-party systems combine cooptation and inclusion with "undemocratic" constraints on the electoral process, they can have ambiguous, even contradictory implications for the governance of their respective polities. On the one hand, in deeply divided societies, the restricted channels of representation provided by dominant-party regimes may serve as mechanisms for the peaceful management of ethnic, regional, or economic conflicts—conflicts that in more democratic and competitive systems could erupt in violence or undermine effective macroeconomic policy. But dominant parties can also be vehicles of predation and rigidity, through which privileged groups capture economic rents and political power at the expense of the larger society. Sooner or later, they pose the classic question of "who guards the guardians?"

The double-edged character of dominant-party regimes raises a number of perplexing issues. How and under what conditions are they able to maintain a relatively stable mix of cooptation and coercion? Under what conditions do they contribute to the peaceful governance of divided societies, and when do

---

1 Juan Linz, "Totalitarian and Authoritarian Regimes," in Fred Greenstein and Nelson Polsby, eds., *Handbook of Political Science*, vol. 3 (Reading, Mass.: Addison-Wesley, 1995), pp. 174–411.

they compound the problems which these societies face? What are the possibilities for regime change and democratic transitions?

A cross-national examination of these issues is well beyond the scope of this chapter. In particular, it is important to note at the outset that many of the challenges faced by the democratically-elected government of South Africa are markedly different from those which confront dominant parties that have been the pillars of authoritarian regimes. The experiences of such parties in Mexico and elsewhere, however, can help to highlight what is distinctive about these challenges and provide points of reference for opportunities and problems that may arise in the future.

In this chapter, I provide an overview of the structure and transformation of Mexico's dominant-party regime. During the last two decades, this regime has been hailed as a model of enlightened economic and political reform, and condemned as an authoritarian system hopelessly permeated with rents, privilege, and corruption. As implied, both characterizations contain important elements of truth. From the debt crisis of 1982 to the end of the Salinas administration in 1994, the elites at the head of the dominant party were able to implement wide-ranging market adjustments well in advance of most other Latin American countries, and to initiate a gradual process of political liberalization "from above".

In pursuing this course, however, authorities relied heavily on corporatist bargains and clientelist networks that were becoming increasingly ineffective as means of legitimation and social control. The underlying weaknesses of the regime came fully into view during the turbulent 1994 presidential transition and peso crisis which followed shortly afterward. By the middle of the decade, the oldest dominant-party system in the world at last appeared to be in a process of disintegration.

In the following pages, I trace the way the Mexican regime has moved from crisis to economic and political reform and back to crisis. The first section outlines a number of important institutional and political characteristics of the system and the strains which began to emerge during the 1970s and early 1980s. The second part analises the political and economic reform efforts launched between 1982 and 1994. In the third section, I discuss the collapse of these reform efforts, the destabilization of the old regime, and the possibilities for a democratic transition.

THE MEXICAN SYSTEM

The role of ruling parties depends to a large extent on the circumstances in which they come to power. In Mexico, the dominant party was formed in

1929, about a decade after the military and economic elites of the old order had been destroyed or weakened by a long civil war (1911–1920). The revolutionary generals and middle-class politicians who emerged in the wake of the civil war had to contend with each other for power, and were continuously subject to pressures from their powerful neighbor to the north. But unlike in South Africa, they were not constrained by the veto of a strong private sector or an independent military establishment. Under these circumstances, the party evolved into an instrument of authoritarian rule, with strong corporatist links to peasant and union organizations and a capacity to manipulate the electoral process on behalf of governmental elites.

Unlike in revolutionary communist systems, on the other hand, the new elites in Mexico were less interested in radical social transformations than they were in ending deadly internecine struggles for access to office. They thus tended to use the party as a means of negotiating with each other, and with non-party groups, over access to state office and public resources. By the 1940s, norms of mutual toleration had been firmly established among competing party factions; and the party elite as a whole had begun to establish a cooperative, if sometimes tense, relation with the emerging domestic private sector and with the United States.

There have been many changes, of course, during the nearly 70 years that the ruling party has been in existence. Nevertheless, at least five relatively enduring features of the regime are relevant to understanding contemporary problems of economic management and political democratization.

1 *Presidential authority* Until at least the mid-1990s, the Mexican system was characterized by highly concentrated presidential authority, limited by a strict prohibition against reelection at the end of a six-year term (the *sexenio*).[2] The no-reelection principle was established explicitly to prevent the long-term dominance of a single individual, and to offer rival power contenders a periodic opportunity to advance; it has been a bedrock of political stability in Mexico since the late 1920s. During their tenure in office, however, presidents exercised enormous personal power. As heads of both the state and the ruling party, they controlled access to all major bureaucratic and elective offices, dominated the policy-making process, and named their own successors. They also exercise significant influence over public opinion, both through the quasi-monopolistic and pro-regime television networks and through private newspapers that depend on public advertising and government-supplied newsprint. This concentration of power was crucial, as

---

2 On presidential authority see Jorge Carpízo, *El presidencialismo mexicano* (Mexico City: Editorial Siglo XXI, 1983).

we shall see, in the initiation of economic reforms during the 1980s and 1990s.

2   *The corporatist alliance with unions and peasant organizations*   As in South Africa, the political elite's proclaimed support for goals of social just-ice and racial equality initially facilitated the establishment of strong political links to unions and peasant organizations. These links were consolidated during a period of social and political reform in the 1930s.[3] In subsequent decades, however, corporatist organizations—and particularly the official union movement—became mechanisms of social control. As interlocutors between the government and organized workers, official union leaders retained some bargaining leverage with respect to long-term wage and employment benefits for their rank and file; real industrial wages did in fact grow steadily from the mid-1950s until about the late 1970s. On the other hand, union leaders were themselves highly dependent on government elites for career advancement and access to material rewards, and they collaborat-ed closely in maintaining industrial peace and the political support of their followers.[4]

3   *Understandings with business elites*   With the onset of industrializa-tion during the 1940s, political accommodation with an expanding private sector became an increasingly important feature of the political system. Through back-channel understandings or more formal negotiations with corporatist chambers, key segments of the business elites were offered favor-able economic treatment in exchange for financial support and political qui-escence.

As successive presidents sought to respond to signs of popular unrest dur-ing the 1970s, this pattern of accommodation began to erode. Business lead-ers began to provide support for the opposition National Action Party (the PAN), and relations between the state and private-sector organizations became more politicized and confrontational. Even during this period, how-ever, conflict between the private sector and the regime remained limited in important ways. Large financial–industrial conglomerates continued to derive benefits both from the government's overall policy stance and from their ability to exploit particularistic links to authorities. With the economic reforms and privatization of the 1980s and 1990s, state–business relations

3   See Ruth Berins Collier and David Collier, *Shaping the Political Arena: Critical Junctures, The Labor Movement, and Regime Dynamics in Latin America* (Princeton, New Jersey: Princeton Uni-versity Press, 1991), pp. 196–271.
4   Ruth Berins Collier, *The Contradictory Alliance: State–Labor Relations and Regime Change* (Berkeley: Institute of International Studies, University of California, Berkeley, 1992).

again came to be characterized by high levels of mutual accommodation and support.[5]

4 *The financial bureaucracy* The Central Bank and Finance Ministry in Mexico, and after the mid-1970s, the Planning and Budget Ministry, constituted especially powerful centers of technocratic decision-making and bureaucratic coordination. These agencies sometimes faced significant challenges from other factions of the party and the bureaucracy and were by no means immune to political interference from the President himself. Nevertheless, the "financial bureaucracy" in Mexico maintained high standards of technical competence and was allowed to exercise extensive control over macroeconomic policy for long periods of time.[6] The highpoint of technocratic influence came during the long period of "stabilizing development" in the 1950s and 1960s, and again during the period of economic adjustment in the 1980s and 1990s.

5 *The electoral connection* Historically, the ruling party typically relied on semi-competitive elections to legitimate its political authority and to provide a safety-valve for opponents of the regime. Small opposition parties were tolerated, and at times, even subsidized, but privileged access to public patronage and the mass media allowed the PRI to maintain overwhelming hegemony within the electorate. As head of the party, the president was thus assured control of the congress and state governments, despite formal provisions for a federal system and a division of legislative and executive powers. It should be noted that threats to the PRI's near electoral monopoly—and thus to the regime as a whole—had become increasingly evident throughout the post-war period. The most important point of vulnerability was the growth of middle-class and urban-informal sector groups that were not incorporated into the PRI's traditional corporatist machines. Over time, opposition parties appealing to these groups began to make significant inroads into the PRI's electoral strength. The most durable of these challenges came from the PAN (the National Action Party); by the 1980s, the PAN began to gain significantly in state and local elections, and during the 1990s, it became the largest opposition party.

---

5 See Sylvia Maxfield and Ricardo Anzaldúa, eds., *Government and Private Sector in Contemporary Mexico* (San Diego: Center for U.S.–Mexican Studies, Monograph Series 20, 1987); Robert Shafer, *Mexican Business Organizations: History and Analysis* (Syracuse: Syracuse University Press, 1973); Roderic A. Camp, *Entrepreneurs and Politics in Twentieth Century Mexico* (New York/Oxford: Oxford University Press, 1970); Carlos Arriola, *Los empresarios y el Estado, 1970–1982* (Mexico: UNAM/Miguel Ángel Porrúa, 1988).

6 Sylvia Maxfield, *Governing Capital* (Ithaca: Cornell University Press, 1990).

During the presidential elections of 1988, a strong challenge also came from a left-of-center opposition, led by Cuauhtémoc Cárdenas's breakaway faction of the ruling party. To fend off a Cárdenas upset, PRI officials resorted to widespread fraud. And although the populist opposition grew weaker during the 1990s, the ensuing protest over the legitimacy of the election provided an important spur to new initiatives for political reform.

Until the outburst of the debt crisis in the 1980s, however, Mexico's loosely-structured authoritarian regime did relatively well in managing the social and political tensions it faced. For much of the post-war period, the party's claim to represent the nationalist and egalitarian aspirations of the 1910 revolution provided an important foundation of legitimacy. And although profound social inequalities persisted, or even worsened during that period, the regime did provide mobility opportunities for members of the large mestizo majority and channels of representation through which major power contenders could exert influence. Thus, for much of its history, Mexico experienced stable and relatively non-repressive government, while many other countries of Latin America were dominated by far more coercive military dictatorships or were ravaged by civil war.

The regime's economic performance was also impressive, compared to most other semi-industrialized countries of Latin America. This was especially the case during the 1950s and 1960s—the decades of so-called stabilizing development. Technocrats within the financial bureaucracy dominated macroeconomic policy making, and the period as a whole was characterized by a combination of very high rates of import-substituting growth, and very low rates of inflation.

The pressures which eventually led to the debt crisis started to mount during the 1970s, as reformist factions of the political elite became increasingly concerned about income inequality, rural poverty and unrest, and bottlenecks generated by rapid economic growth. Under Presidents Luis Echeverría (1970–1976) and Jose López Portillo (1976–1982), the government attempted to address these issues through a series of political and social reforms, including subsidized consumption benefits for low-income groups, increased expenditures on health and education, support for wage demands of unions, and the opening of new electoral spaces for leftist political forces.

These efforts helped to reduce the potential for anti-system protest, but also increased distributive conflicts within the system. On the one side, there was pressure from conservative business interests, which successfully blocked tax reforms throughout the 1970s despite a comparatively low tax burden.[7] On the other side were the advocates of increasing both social expenditures and industrial investment. Over the course of the decade, these cross-pressures led to severe macroeconomic disequilibria and rendered the country extremely vulnerable to the decline in petroleum prices, the sharp rise in interest rates and the decline in lending that occurred in the early 1980s.[8]

These problems, it should be noted, were in some respects exacerbated by the lack of accountability and entrenchment of vested interests that characterized the dominant-party regime. The absence of institutionalized checks on presidential authority allowed both Echeverría and López Portillo to commit serious policy blunders, including a sudden initiative to nationalize the banks in 1982. At the same time, competing positions on fiscal policy typically reflected interests that had acquired substantial political leverage within the regime. By the mid-1990s, as I shall argue below, these features of the system had become important impediments to continuing political and economic reforms.

We must be cautious, however, in casting the political and institutional structure of the regime as the main culprit in the run-up to the debt crisis. Growing balance of payments deficits and external indebtedness plagued all of the import-substituting economies in the region, and both democratic and authoritarian political regimes experienced severe macroeconomic crises. Mexico, to be sure, gained a temporary respite from these problems from the oil boom of 1978 to 1981. But oil riches created problems of their own in the form of a badly overvalued peso that squeezed out opportunities for other export activities and encouraged very high rates of protectionism for domestic industry.

While the regime was unable to forestall the explosion of a macroeconomic crisis in 1982, finally, it did respond quickly to this challenge during the next decade. Policy was at times characterized by false starts and improvisation; but the scope of the changes introduced in Mexico were matched in Latin America only in Pinochet's Chile and were implemented with far less repression. The crisis that again hit Mexico at the end of the Salinas period should not obscure the significance of these achievements, which we examine in the following section.

---

7   Leopoldo Solís, *Economic Policy Reform in Mexico: A Case Study for Developing Countries* (New York: Pergamon Press, 1981), pp. 67–78.

8   For a discussion of the run-up to the debt crisis, see Carlos Bazdresch and Santiago Levy, "Populism and Economic Policy in Mexico, 1970–1982," in Rudiger Dornbusch and Sebastian Edwards, eds., *The Macroeconomics of Populism in Latin America* (Chicago and London: University of Chicago Press, 1991), pp. 223–63.

FROM CRISIS TO REFORM (1982–1994)

The process of reform in Mexico proceeded through several phases. Under Miguel de la Madrid (1982–1988), the government focused mainly on economic adjustment, beginning with a very tough stabilization program initiated in 1982. Between 1985 and 1988, the government introduced a series of trade reforms that opened the Mexican economy and a concerted wage-price agreement (the Economic Solidarity Pact) that helped bring inflation under control.[9] During Carlos Salinas's presidency from 1988 through 1994, the government extended the process of economic reform and began an ambitious project of political liberalization.

The economic changes introduced under Salinas included major new privatization initiatives, normalization of relations with external creditors, and a deepening of earlier steps toward trade liberalization. By the early 1990s, the government had begun the sale of virtually all state enterprises outside the oil sector and concluded Brady plan agreements to reduce the external debt. These steps, in turn, paved the way for Mexico's reentry into private foreign credit markets; and the inflow of portfolio investment accelerated dramatically. The program was capped, finally, by the completion of the NAFTA treaty, which was viewed by the government as a means of assuring that Mexico's economy would remain open under future administrations.

Political reforms received little attention under De la Madrid and were deliberately allowed to lag behind economic adjustment under Salinas. As noted, however, Salinas's tainted victory in the 1988 elections provided a strong impetus for new efforts to broaden the political base of the regime. These efforts involved three interrelated sets of measures.

In the first place, the government attempted to establish more cooperative relations with the conservative PAN opposition. The PRI and the PAN joined in passing electoral reforms aimed at reducing fraud in registration and voting procedures; and even more important, Salinas responded to post-election protests by agreeing to seat PAN governors in four of Mexico's 31 states.[10] Such moves, the government hoped, would serve not only to coopt the conservatives but to marginalize the more populist Cárdenas movement, reorganized as the PRD (or Party of Democratic Revolution) after 1988.

---

9 See Robert R. Kaufman, Carlos Bazdresch, and Blanca Heredia, "Mexico: Radical Reform in a Dominant Party System," in Stephan Haggard and Steven B. Webb, eds., *Voting for Reform: Democracy, Political Liberalization, and Economic Adjustment* (New York: Oxford University Press, 1994), pp. 360–411.

10 For an important discussion of the reform process in Mexico, see Juan Molinar Horcasitas, *El tiempo de la legitimad: elecciones, autoritarismo, y democracia en México* (México, Cal y Arena, 1991).

Salinas also sought ways to arrest the long-term decline in the electoral strength of the ruling party, particularly among low-income and middle-class urban voters not linked to the traditional corporatist sectors. Initiatives to "modernize" the PRI centered on shifting the balance of power away from conservative union and peasant sectors and establishing territorially-based party organizations that would presumably be more responsive to the urban electorate.

The third component was the initiation of the National Solidarity Program (PRONASOL), and the organization of a massive new anti-poverty bureaucracy with hundreds of thousands of community-based committees throughout the country. PRONASOL served simultaneously to build personal support for the president in low-income communities, to reduce his dependence on the traditional party hierarchy, and to recruit new political leaders who might spearhead the reform of the PRI itself.[11]

In one way or another, this combination of economic and political reforms threatened virtually every traditional constituency of the Mexican regime. Fiscal adjustment, trade reforms, and privatization launched during this period hurt organized workers; import-substituting industrialists; low-income beneficiaries of government consumption subsidies; public employees within the middle-class. Opposition was also strong among party activists. Cuauhtémoc Cárdenas himself had been governor of the state of Michoacán before breaking with the PRI, and was the son of one of the party's most popular leaders, Lázaro Cárdenas, the reformist president of Mexico during the 1930s.

New bases of support generated through Salinas's political reforms helped somewhat to offset defections from the PRI's more traditional constituencies; the PRONASOL campaign was especially popular and did much to undercut Cárdenas's strength within the urban-informal sector.[12] But Salinas's efforts to reform the PRI deepened the divisions with PRI old-guard activists, who reacted strongly and sometimes violently against efforts to dislodge them from positions of power. In many parts of the country, Salinistas were in fact impelled to accommodate old-guard factions which had captured control of newly-established territorial organizations. Control of the

---

11 Denise Dresser, "Bringing the Poor Back In: National Solidarity as a Strategy of Regime Legitimation," in Wayne Cornelius, Ann Craig, and Jonathan Fox, eds., *Transforming State–Society Relations in Mexico: The National Solidarity Approach* (La Jolla, Calif: Center for U.S.–Mexican Studies, University of California, 1994), pp. 143–66.

12 Juan Molinar Horcasitas and Jeffrey A. Weldon, "Electoral Determinants and Consequences of National Solidarity," in Cornelius, Craig, and Fox, "*Transforming State–Society Relations in Mexico*, pp. 123–142.

government and the dominant party, on the other hand, allowed both De la Madrid and Salinas to deploy powerful institutional weapons against such opposition. The enormous concentration of authority in the office of the presidency was clearly the most crucial of these weapons. De la Madrid— and even more Salinas—used extensive powers of appointment to purge old-guard and protectionist factions of the party from virtually all major positions of authority within the executive branch, and to replace them with technocrats recruited from within the financial bureaucracy.[13] The new elite was by no means fully united around a detailed strategy of economic reform, but it did share a common perspective about the urgency of fiscal and monetary retrenchment, and played a major role in initiating the broader structural adjustments which followed.

Despite the opposition of old-guard union leaders to party restructuring, the corporatist structure of the ruling party also provided a major power resource in deflecting protest against the economic reform initiatives. Official union leaders voiced strong objections to these initiatives, sometimes publicly, but they could not engage in sustained confrontations against these initiatives without jeopardizing their own positions of authority. For the most part, therefore, they cooperated with the government in keeping their members in line.[14]

Long-standing modes of accommodation also provided the foundations for enlisting the cooperation of the business elite, ending the adversarial relations of the 1970s. Although many sectors were fearful of trade reforms, they generally welcomed the stabilization program, and supported the institution of wage and price controls after 1988. More important, for a small and politically well-connected segment of the private sector, the privatization program became the source of major financial windfalls and the accumulation of substantial new wealth. Thus, as during the "stabilizing development period," back-channel ties remained an important segment of the business–government relationship.[15]

Throughout this period, finally, the government could count on the backing of United States government and international financial institutions. This backing, to be sure, was contingent in part on the "good behavior" of the Mexican regime, and disagreements over the pace and timing of reforms

---

13 Miguel Ángel Centeno, *Democracy within Reason: Technocratic Revolution in Mexico* (University Park: The Pennsylvania State University Press, 1994).
14 See Ruth Berins Collier, this volume; Kevin J. Middlebrook, "The Sounds of Silence: Organized Labor's Response to the Economic Crisis in Mexico," *Journal of Latin American Studies*, 21 (1989): 195–220.
15 See Kaufman, Bazdresch, and Heredia, "Mexico: Radical Reform in a Dominant Party System".

sometimes produced serious tensions between the regime and its northern creditors.[16] Nevertheless, the United States government had a strong interest in maintaining the financial and political stability in Mexico, and generally encouraged favorable treatment by private creditors, the World Bank, and the IMF. As noted, new financing began to flow into Mexico in the late 1980s, and accelerated substantially during the run-up to the NAFTA accords.

As of the early 1990s, it could plausibly be argued that Mexico had successfully surmounted the crisis of the 1980s and that it was on a smooth path toward economic and political reform. An upturn in growth during the first half of Salinas's term provided some indication that the adjustment efforts were bearing fruit. From 1989 through 1992, Mexico's GDP expanded at an annual rate of 3.8, while inflation dropped almost to single digits. Though the economy slowed in 1993 and 1994, the general public continued to be positive about the reforms and relatively optimistic about the future— perhaps as a result of the government's sustained propaganda campaign in the press and media. In a national survey conducted in 1994, a staggering 83 per cent of the respondents from virtually all occupational, income, and educational categories expressed full or partial support for the government's economic reform program. Despite the economic slowdown, moreover, almost 45 per cent expected their personal situation to improve in the following year, whereas only 12 per cent expected it to decline.[17] Partly as a consequence of perceived or expected economic successes, the political reforms undertaken under Salinas also appeared to be paying off, both in terms of more solid support for the ruling party and with respect to Salinas's own personal popularity. Notwithstanding continuing factional struggles within the party, the PRI won a smashing victory in the mid-term elections of 1991, which unlike in 1988 were generally free of fraud. Votes for the ruling party candidates, it should be noted, correlated closely with the distribution of expenditures for Salinas's anti-poverty program.[18]

The 1994 presidential transition occurred under black clouds of political violence, including the Zapatista uprising, the assassination of Luis Donaldo

---

16 During a tense standoff with the IMF in 1986, the De la Madrid government came close to declaring a moratorium on its external debt payments.

17 Robert R. Kaufman and Leo Zuckermann, "Attitudes toward Economic Reform in Mexico: The role of Political Mediations," *Papers on Latin America #42* (Columbia University: Institute of Latin American and Iberian Studies, 1996). Eighteen percent felt their situation would remain the same, and about a quarter of the sample answered "don't know."

18 Juan Molinar Horcasitas and Jeffrey A. Weldon, "Electoral Determinants and Consequences of National Solidarity," in Cornelius, Craig, and Fox, "*Transforming State–Society Relations in Mexico*", pp. 123–142.

Colosio, Salinas's chosen successor, and the post-election killing of PI leader Ruiz Massieu. Nevertheless, the elections themselves were conducted under the most impartial and stringent supervision in Mexican history, and the outcome was widely interpreted as a success for Salinas and the ruling party. Colosio's replacement, Ernesto Zedillo, gained a strong 50 per cent of the vote, outdistancing his nearest rival, the PAN's Diego Fernandez de Cevallo, by about 15 per cent.

Salinas himself left office as one of Mexico's most popular presidents, with approval ratings of more than 80 per cent in 1994.[19] As his term drew to a close, his approach to reform was often contrasted with the sequence of political and economic changes introduced under Gorbachev in the Soviet Union. The collapse of the USSR, it was argued, could be attributed to the mistake of allowing democratization to outpace the consolidation of market-oriented reforms. The outgoing Mexican president, in contrast, had deliberately reversed this sequence: first, a successful economic reform, implemented through the power of a highly centralized regime; then more gradual political reforms in which a restructured PRI would come to occupy the pivotal center of a more competitive multiparty system.[20] Despite the political violence and other danger signals, the road ahead appeared to be leading in this direction at the onset of the new sexenio.

FROM REFORM TO CRISIS (1994–?)

The event that most immediately precipitated the collapse of the Salinista project was the peso crisis of December 1994, which hit only three weeks after the inauguration of the Zedillo government. Although Salinas's failure to devalue earlier left the incoming government with a difficult policy problem, the Zedillo government seriously mismanaged the devaluation announcement and triggered a panicky stampede of funds out of the country. The free-fall of the peso during ensuing months had a devastating impact on the real incomes of virtually all sectors of Mexican society, shattering the high expectations for economic improvement that had been built up during the Salinas period. While there was much finger-pointing among officials about responsibility for the crisis, the main effect was to discredit the technocratic elite as a whole—and especially Salinas himself.

As these shocks unfolded, it also made a significant difference that the new president was Zedillo, rather than the murdered Colosio. Under Salinas,

---

19 Kaufman and Zuckermann, "Attitudes toward Economic Reform".
20 Centeno, *Democracy within Reason*.

Colosio had at different points headed both the PRI and PRONASOL, and the political capital he accumulated along the way would have provided resources for relatively strong presidential leadership. Zedillo, in contrast, was a technocrat, with few ties to either the party organization or the PRO-NASOL bureaucracy. Faced with crisis and protest, he concentrated during the first years of his term on the management of the austerity program, while otherwise showing an unprecedented inclination to shrink the authority of the presidency. Zedillo's disinclination to assume personal command of the PRI had an especially disorienting effect within the ruling party. In the absence of presidential leadership, factional struggles became increasingly bitter and intense.[21]

Bad judgment and bad luck thus had a considerable amount to do with the pressures that battered the regime in the post-Salinas era; the course of events might have been quite different if the new government had been more skillful in adjusting the exchange rate, or if the attempted assassination of Colosio had failed. But these accidents of *fortuna* and *virtu* were themselves linked to more enduring features of the old order; and their devastating effects revealed how fragile this order had in fact become.

To begin with, it is clear that the insulated technocracy which had guided the recovery had miscalculated badly in its decision to delay exchange rate adjustments in 1994. Exchange rate appreciation had posed serious dilemmas throughout the recovery of the late 1980s and early 1990s. On the one hand, a strong peso served as an anchor for the stabilization program. Yet peso appreciation also constituted a major impediment to the growth of the export sector and impelled the government to rely on high interest rates and large capital inflows to finance trade deficits. This is not a tradeoff that can be easily managed through wide-ranging public debate. Nevertheless, some serious policy errors that became evident in hindsight might have been avoided in a regime less extensively dominated by the personal ambitions of the incumbent president.

The best time for an exchange rate adjustment was probably during the second half of 1994, after the PRI had won the election but before the new government took office. The failure to take action at that point can be attributed at least in part to Salinas's reluctance to take measures that might hamper his bid to be named head of the World Trade Organization at the end of his presidential term. These ambitions also contributed to the even more serious blunder of contracting short-term dollar debt (tesobonos) in order to

---

21 For an analysis of internal PRI politics in the Zedillo period, see the contribution of Maria Lorena Cook, this volume.

maintain reserves. This course was determined exclusively by the President and his Finance Minister, without input from other members of the economic team. It is an error that probably would not have been committed in a more institutionalized and accountable policy-making context.

The president's capacity to manipulate public opinion also proved a double-edged weapon. Through most of Salinas's term, government influence over television and most print journalism had, as noted, been an invaluable asset in building support for its market reforms. But expectations formed in the absence of a more thorough public discussion of the policy alternatives crumbled quickly in the face of the new reality. In opinion surveys conducted in November 1994 and March 1995, opposition to the government's program climbed from only 10 per cent to almost one-half the population.[22]

Colosio, as noted, might have dealt with such problems more forcefully than Zedillo, his emergency replacement. Nevertheless, as discussed, the factional struggles that surfaced after 1994 had been mounting throughout the 1980s and 1990s and it is likely that Colosio would have been far more constrained in managing these conflicts than his immediate predecessors. Indeed, it is plausible that factional rivalries played a role in his death and the subsequent murder of Ruiz Massieu—although the full story of these murders will probably never be known.

Finally, the unexpected promotion of Zedillo to the presidency posed challenges that were also rooted in long-standing features of the system. Zedillo's inclination to disconnect the presidency from the ruling party stemmed in part from his conviction that the president should act as a more neutral guarantor of the rule of law. To strengthen the credibility of this commitment, Zedillo appointed a PANista as his Attorney General and authorized him to investigate fully the charges of corruption that swirled around the ruling party. The problem, however, was that in a system organized through dense clientelistic networks, a genuine commitment to the rule of law threatened to undercut the very basis of political authority which the president needed to govern.

Predictably, therefore, Zedillo was quickly drawn into bitter conflicts with Salinistas, old-guard activists, and other segments of the ruling party. Conflicts with the Salinistas centered on the widening investigation into earlier political assassinations and corruption, leading to the arrest of Salinas's brother, Raúl. Federal attempts to guarantee the probity of state gubernatorial elections in turn led old-guard politicians into open

---

22 Kaufman and Zuckermann, "Attitudes toward Economic Reform".

political rebellion against the president in an effort to defend their claims to victory.

Additional challenges to the president surfaced in 1996. A number of important presidential initiatives—including a proposal to privatize part of the petroleum industry—was voted down by the PRI majority in Congress. Problems for Zedillo also arose during the 18th General Assembly of the party, held in the aftermath of a series of defeats in state and local elections. Rebellious delegates passed resolutions which criticized the government's economic policies and placed restrictions on opportunities for technocrats in the executive branch to run for governorships and the presidency under the PRI banner.

For Zedillo, such challenges posed unpleasant choices between political isolation and strategic retreat, and by the beginning of his third year in office, the president began to move toward a more openly partisan role. In an effort to reassert control over the ruling party, Zedillo replaced the top leadership in the executive committee and began to take a more direct hand in the nomination of PRI congressional and gubernatorial nominees. Not entirely coincidentally, Antonio Lozano, the PANista Attorney General, was also sacked. Although his replacement was a politically-neutral civil rights activist with a reputation for integrity, the move was widely interpreted as a sign that Zedillo's "non-partisan" anti-corruption drive was losing momentum.[23]

But the central question posed by the economic and political crises of the Zedillo era is whether—in terms of progress toward a more democratic multiparty regime—the glass is half full or half empty. Economic crisis, political violence, and pervasive corruption are hardly causes for encouragement. Yet the old authoritarian order has clearly unravelled, and there are important signs of change in a positive direction. Ironically, these changes result partly from Salinas's currently discredited program of political liberalization, as well as from the loss of centralized control which Salinas attempted to maintain. They offer some hope that over some medium term—say, by the year 2000—Mexico might complete a transition to a troubled, but reasonably stable multiparty democracy.

A positive irony of the current economic crisis is that it has expanded opportunities for the contending party forces to negotiate new, more democratic and transparent rules of the game. De la Madrid and Salinas paved the way for these changes, both through earlier electoral reforms and by providing the main opposition party, the PAN, with opportunities to gain valuable

---

23 In the eyes of some, one such sign was the replacement of PANista Attorney General Lozano in October 1996.

experience in state and municipal government.[24] Yet the trend toward a genuinely multiparty system accelerated dramatically after 1994.

The most important beneficiary has been the PAN, which is reaping the payoff from years of organization at the local and state level as well as of backing important segments of the business community. As noted, the party temporarily gained a crucial position in Zedillo's cabinet, and currently controls six state governorships and numerous mayoralties throughout the country. The PAN's electoral prospects for the 1997 congressional elections are also very good, and there is a reasonable chance that the party could capture a majority of the Chamber of Deputies.

The left-oriented PRD has also resurfaced as an important player in the political process. While the party's electoral strength continued to be undermined by severe internal factionalism and limited financing, the open hostility that characterized its relations with Salinas dissipated under Zedillo, and the PRD participated extensively in the negotiations over electoral and constitutional reform.

The parties involved in such negotiations are predictably beset by internal conflicts between hardliners and moderates, and the uncertainty has been increased by Zedillo's refusal to speak for the PRI. Despite conflict and backsliding, however, the leaders of the three parties have taken major steps to consolidate and deepen electoral reforms instituted during the earlier period of political liberalization. Agreements reached among the three parties in 1996 included provisions for closer federal supervision of state and local elections and a new formula that reduces the distortions in the assignment of congressional seats. Provisions for limiting campaign expenditures were also incorporated into the original agreements, although these were later watered down by the PRI majority in the Congress.

Electoral reforms—even ones which might eventually include stricter regulation of campaign finance—do not guarantee a stable democracy. They do, however, provide the foundation of a far more competitive party system as well as for much stronger legislative and federal checks on executive authority. Relations between the federal government and local authorities have already undergone substantial change. Since 1994, governors, mayors, and members of congress acquired a degree of political autonomy unmatched since the early years of the revolution, and they have pressed within the framework of the federal constitution for increased control over tax revenues and public programs. This has had a variety of effects throughout the

---

24 Alonso Lujambio, *Federalismo y Congreso en el Cambio Político de México* (México: UNAM, 1995).

country. In some regions it has increased the leverage available to the PAN, while in others, conservative PRI governors have successfully pressed for greater autonomy as well. Decentralization, finally, has also lowered the threshold of participation for an array of grass-roots and reform movements that had previously had only limited access to politics.[25]

As in other presidential democracies, multipartyism and a functioning constitutional division of power carries the risk of policy stalemate or incoherence; this could have serious implications for the capacity of the Mexican government to deal with pressing social problems.[26] As already mentioned, a number of presidential policy initiatives have been defeated or watered down in the Congress. Ending the rubber-stamp character of legislative institutions does not necessarily eliminate the capacity to govern, however.[27] It is of some significance, in this respect, that although the PRI's more independent legislators have defied the president on some issues, they were persuaded to back the tough austerity program that constituted the centerpiece of the strategy for recovery.

The construction of broad-based governing coalitions would also be facilitated by renewed economic growth; among other things, this would enhance the feasibility of compensation for interests that are harmed by market reforms. In this regard, there are also some hopeful signs. With strong financial backing from the United States and the IMF, the government appeared to have edged the economy away from the financial brink during 1996. More important, the current crisis should not obscure the importance of the structural changes instituted under De la Madrid and Salinas. Trade liberalization, privatization, and formalized access to the huge North American market have created opportunities for a strong and sustained expansion.

In many respects, the most troubling issue of an optimistic scenario involves the future role of the PRI. On the one hand, if a democratic transition is to be consolidated in Mexico, it is important that the PRI undergo electoral defeat. It is not enough, in other words, for the ruling party to forgo its privileged access to public resources; if it is to adapt to democracy after almost 70 years in power, the PRI must also learn to function as an opposition. On the other hand, the PRI continues, as it has for decades, to occupy

---

25 Robert R. Kaufman and Guillermo Trejo, "Regionalismo, transformación del régimen y Pronasol: la política del Programa Nacional de Solidaridad en cuatro estados mexicanos", *Política y gobierno* vol. III, num. 2, segundo semestre de 1996, pp. 245–281.

26 Juan J. Linz and Arturo Valenzuela, eds., *The Failure of Presidential Democracy* (Baltimore: Johns Hopkins University Press, 1994).

27 See especially Matthew Shugart and John M. Carey, *Presidents and Assemblies* (New York: Cambridge University Press, 1989).

the political center of the Mexican electoral spectrum, and a disintegration of the party would leave a dangerous vacuum.

Unfortunately, the biggest failure of the Salinas reform project lay in its effort to modernize the PRI and prepare it for a role in competitive multiparty politics. Old-guard opposition was not the only reason for this failure; it stemmed as well from the fact that Salinas and his allies continued to view the party as an instrument which would allow them to retain the control of the state. It was to be a "democratic party", but one that would continue to win elections and dominate representative institutions. The prospect of defeat thus poses both an unprecedented challenge and opportunity for PRI activists. Because a significant fraction of voters continues to identify with the party, competing factions have an incentive to remain united under the party label. Long-term cohesion as a party of the center, however, is likely to depend on whether impending electoral defeats stimulate further fragmentation or renewed and more successful efforts to democratize the internal party structure.[28] As with the Communist parties of Central Europe, internal party reforms would substantially increase the chances that the party could rise from the ashes and recapture power on a new basis.

CONCLUSION: PROSPECTS FOR A DEMOCRATIC TRANSITION IN MEXICO

To sketch the positive opportunities in the Mexican transition is not, of course, to deny the significance of the many things that could go wrong. Further assassinations of high-level political governmental and political leaders, for example, are distinct possibilities, with unpredictable consequences.

Even in the absence of further assassinations, it is also possible that sectors of the government, the military, and the business elite might attempt to reduce political uncertainty with an effort to restore authoritarian controls. A "Mexican Fujimori" would by no means be out of the question, although in Mexico's highly politicized society, such a figure would probably be more repressive and less successful than the original version.

Perhaps a more likely scenario is that the power of the central state would continue to deteriorate. The "parceling out of sovereignty" is already well under way; and in some parts of the country, the state apparatus has been captured or displaced by political bosses, drug mafias, or guerrillas. This pattern of instability could well stall or reverse current efforts to revive the economy, and we could then see a reverse of the hoped-for virtuous cycle

---

28 See Maria Lorena Cook, this volume.

sketched above: a narrowing of opportunities for the construction of broad-based coalitions and an increase in the destabilizing effects of political conflict.

While these dangers are very real, however, anxieties about the future of Mexico stem in part from the predictable uncertainties that characterize a political transition, especially in a society that had been so thoroughly dominated by highly centralized structures of power. In Mexico, the old rules of the dominant-party regime can no longer be counted on to regulate contestation, but there is not yet a clear agreement on new ones. These uncertainties might have been reduced if the Salinista project of liberalization from above had not crashed so suddenly; but it is not clear whether the new rules that might have evolved from that project would have allowed Mexico to cross the line from a liberalizing authoritarian regime to a genuinely democratic one. Democracy, as Adam Przeworski has written, is the institutionalization of uncertainty; it is an agreement on rules which leaves open the question of which contenders and policies will prevail.[29] For Salinas and his chosen successors, achieving this kind of institutionalization would sooner or later have required them to negotiate with their opponents on a more equal basis, and to demonstrate a far greater willingness to relinquish the position at the commanding heights of power. While the costs of the current crisis have been depressingly high, it has nevertheless served to push the Zedillo government precisely in this direction. A Luis Donaldo Colosio, governing under more favorable economic circumstances, might also have followed this course; but we have no way of knowing.

---

29 Adam Przeworski, "Some Problems in the Study of the Transition to Democracy", in Guillermo O'Donnell, Philippe C. Schmitter, and Laurence Whitehead, eds., *Transitions from Authoritarian Rule: Prospects for Democracy* (Baltimore and London: The Johns Hopkins University Press, 1986), pt. 3, *Comparative Politics*, pp. 58–61.

Chapter 7

BRIDGE OR BRIDGEHEAD? COMPARING THE PARTY SYSTEMS OF BOTSWANA, NAMIBIA, ZIMBABWE, ZAMBIA AND MALAWI

PIERRE DU TOIT

INTRODUCTION

The aim of this chapter is to compare the party systems of selected Southern African States in order to assess the likelihood of the emergence of multi-party democracies. The conceptual framework being used is that of one-party dominant democratic systems, relevant to those systems which evolved in post-war Japan, Israel, Sweden and Italy. This is augmented by the distinction drawn by Diamond between *electoral* democracies (where even genuinely competitive elections remain somewhat disconnected from the contest for and exercise of power), and *liberal* democracies (where elected officials are at the centre of power, and elections allow for real contests for power). Both these regime types need to be distinguished from *pseudodemocracies*, where elections do take place, but are empty rituals where results are foregone conclusions, and are thus almost completely removed from the actual contest for power.[1] Diamond argues that many of the Third Wave democracies need to be reclassified into the ranks of the electoral or pseudodemocracies. This chapter examines some Southern African Third Wave cases, and considers whether the dominant party rule in each case warrants such a reclassification.

ONE-PARTY DOMINANT SYSTEMS: PATTERNS IN INDUSTRIALIZED DEMOCRACIES, AND EXPECTATIONS FOR EMERGING AFRICAN DEMOCRACIES

The principal cases of one-party dominance in modern industrial democracies, according to T.J. Pempel, are the Labor Party in Israel from pre-independence until 1977, Sweden's Social Democratic Party from 1932 until 1976, Japan's Liberal Democratic party from 1955 onwards, and the Christian Democrats in Italy from 1945 (up to 1996).[2]

---

1 Larry Diamond, "Is the Third Wave Over?", *Journal of Democracy*, vol. 7, no. 3, July 1996, pp. 20–38, at 21–25.
2 T.J. Pempel, "Conclusion. One-Party Dominance and the Creation of Regimes", in T.J. Pempel, (ed.) *Uncommon Democracies—The One-Party Dominant Regimes* (London: Cornell University Press, 1990), p. 333.

Pempel's overall assessment of the role of dominant political parties in these democracies is that they serve as "pivotal bridging and shaping mechanisms", echoing Miriam Golden who finds dominant parties to be "…active participants in the process of building bridges of cooperation, however fragile, between interest associations and state actors"[3]. This positive assessment must be read with caution, however. Neither Golden nor Pempel spell out the necessary organizational requirements for such a bridge-building project. The work of Huntington is especially important in this regard. He has argued that in modernizing societies the ability of one-party dominant systems to perform this bridging function is closely tied to both party strength and party system strength. Strong parties outlive charismatic founding leaders, exhibit organizational linkages with interest formations in society that subordinate these associations to party leadership, and are able to secure party allegiances which harness the ambitions of party activists without making the parties vulnerable to the opportunism of such individuals[4]. Strong parties, assembled in a party system which produces effective competition, yield a strong party system, crucial to the assimilation of new entrants to politics through institutionalized channels, and therefore linking state and society in a way that contributes to political stability.[5]

There are a number of reasons why the benign bridging effect of dominant parties in one-party dominant systems is unlikely to be found in the emerging democracies of African states. First, the cases discussed in this chapter are all culturally diverse, and are potential, incipient or actually divided societies. With the exception of Israel, the principal cases of Italy, Sweden and Japan are most certainly not divided societies.[6]

Secondly, all these African cases occupy a distinctly peripheral position within the global political economy in contrast to that of the principal cases who are all located within the core of the modern global economy. Thirdly, the state-building process in Southern Africa, via colonialism, is a far more recent project than the European cases, with Israel again as the exception.

---

3   Pempel, "Introduction. Uncommon Democracies: The One-Party Dominant Regimes", in Pempel, (ed.) *Uncommon Democracies*, p. 15; Miriam Golden, "Interest Representation, Party Systems, and the State: Italy in Comparative Perspective", *Comparative Politics*, vol. 18, no. 3, 1986, pp. 179–301, at 298.

4   Huntington, *Political Order in Changing Societies*, (New Haven: Yale University Press, 1968), pp. 409–412.

5   *Ibid.*, pp. 412–433.

6   One-Party dominance in European divided societies have in some cases led to most unfortunate results. In Northern Ireland, for example, Unionist Party dominance from 1921 to 1972 ended in the collapse of the Stormont parliament, the imposition of direct rule and the onset of civil violence and insurgency warfare.

The result is that states are still relatively weak in the African cases, while even Israel can be considered a strong state, despite its young status.[7] Finally, these weak African state structures were imposed onto relatively strong societies, where antecedent ethnic loyalties still exert a countervailing source of identification to the more recent identity of citizenship offered by the modern state.[8]

Can these African dominant parties, representing voting blocs in strong divided societies, and embedded in weak states with a precarious peripheral economic position, be expected to function as benign *bridges* between society and the state, able to pave the way for consolidated liberal democracies? Or is it more likely to expect them to act as *bridgeheads* to single party hegemony, either through a sustained period of electoralism, or in the form of elections which amount to pseudodemocracy? The general proposition examined in this chapter is that the outcome will be shaped by the strength of the dominant party, the strength of the party system, the nature of the ruling ideologies, the calibre of leadership, and the changing character of the international system.

The classic cases of European dominant party systems all exhibited a so-called cycle of dominance. This entailed the ascendant party being able to emerge from a crisis of mobilization, taking a "major historical bloc" of voters with it, effectively delegitimizing the opposition, and holding onto its ascendancy through decisive leadership. Dominance was lost, in turn, through a combination of factors, including changes in the international system, leadership circulation, the exhausting of ideological causes, and the emergence of new crises of mobilization.[9] In the following section the above framework of analysis will be employed in analysing the selected African cases.

Botswana

Democratic politics in Botswana have been heavily influenced by the colonial policies (or lack of them) of Britain. Firstly, the country was virtually colonized by request, when Khama III of the Bamangwato sought protection from the Transvaal Republic (ZAR) across the Limpopo, and from the German

---

7   Joel S. Migdal, *Strong Societies and Weak States—State–Society Relations and State Capabilities in the Third World* (Princeton: Princeton University Press, 1988), pp. 269–277.

8   *Ibid.*, pp. 33–41.

9   Ariel Levite and Sidney Tarrow, "The Legitimation of excluded parties in Dominant Party Systems—A Comparison of Israel and Italy", *Comparative Politics*, vol. 15, no. 3, April 1983, pp. 295–327.

presence in the east.[10] Secondly, the reluctant colonizers ruled the Bechuana-land Protectorate from 1884 with corresponding lack of enthusiasm, accurately described as "benign neglect". This neglect resulted in the minimal dislocation of traditional authority structures, centred on the eight Tswana chieftaincies,[11] and the maintenance of the rural cattle economy to the extent that by the late 1960s more than 70 per cent of the rural population still owned cattle, albeit highly unequally distributed.[12] The overall result was that, by independence, indicative of its level of underdevelopment, Botswana was the third poorest country in the world.[13] The third important characteristic of the colonial era was the early establishment of an "administrative state". Expatriate officers occupied key decision-making positions in the colonial regime from the outset, thus setting in motion the momentum of administrative decision-making and policy initiatives being generated from the centre, coupled to a preponderance of talent and expertise being concentrated in the ranks of the officials of the state.[14]

Reluctant colonization instead of coercive conquest resulted in the emergence of a moderate indigenous nationalism, leaving the society largely unpolarized; benign neglect delivered a traditional society, unscathed by social upheaval and modernization, exceptionally poor, yet unequally so, existing parallel to the new democratic institutions; and the administrative state provided a stable, effective set of institutions for the new state leaders to command.

The 1965 elections at the eve of independence found three major parties contesting the vote. The Botswana Democratic Party (BDP) led by Sir Seretse Khama assembled a wide coalition of interests: the traditional Tswana leadership, and with them, the rural population (Khama was a former Chief of the Bamangwato), the white and black commercial cattle farmers (Khama and his party leaders were mostly commercial farmers themselves), the colonial bureaucrats at the core of the state (Khama skilfully promised not to Africanize the state at the expense of established expertise), and an ethnic core of Bamangwato tribal members (about one-third of the population). The BDP policy position was that of middle-class nationalism, aiming to take power in such a way that capitalist practices, technocratic priorities, and

---

10 Richard P. Stevens, *Lesotho, Botswana & Swaziland—The Former High Commission Territories in Southern Africa* (London: Pall Mall Press, 1967), pp. 115–12.

11 Louis A. Picard, *The Politics of Development in Botswana—A Model for Success?* (Boulder, CO: Lynne Rienner, 1987), pp. 36–38.

12 H.A. Fosbrooke, "Land and Population", *Botswana Notes and Records*, vol. 3, 1971, pp. 172–187, at 176.

13 Mike Sill, "Sustaining a success story", *Geographical Magazine*, February 1993, pp. 37–42, at 37.

14 Picard, *The Politics of Development in Botswana*, pp. 71–95.

traditional values and institutions would be strengthened. Opposing the BDP were the Botswana Peoples' Party (BPP), representing a militant Pan-Africanism, initially at least, and the Botswana National Front (BNF), who positioned themselves as a socialist party.[15] The election resulted in an easy victory for the BDP, capturing 28 of the 31 contested seats with 80.4 per cent of the vote. The BPP was the only other party to succeed, capturing 3 seats with 14.2 per cent of the vote.[16]

A number of constitutional rules have subsequently favoured the BDP, as the incumbent majority party. These include the first-past-the-post electoral system within single member constituencies; the minimum voting age of 21 years; stringent citizenship qualifications; registering procedures which entail that a new voters' roll be drawn up for every election; and the fact that no provision is made for absentee votes. These rules have influenced voting turnout in all subsequent elections, with only the 1984 election having exceeded the 1965 turnout of a 74.5 percentage poll.[17]

However, the major reasons for BDP electoral victories in every sub-sequent election, up to and including the 1995 election, are to be found in party performance. Indicative of Botswana's underdevelopment, at independence the country had only 25 km of tarred road, only 8 secondary schools, of which only one was a government school, opened only the year before independence, and a GNP per capita of US$ 14.[18] In 1965 infant mortality was 122 per 1000 live births, life expectancy at birth for women stood at 49 years, for men at 46, and there was one medical doctor for every 27,450 people. However, such "benign neglect" proved to be an asset, instead of a liability.[19]

Starting from this very low base of social delivery and pervasive scarcity, the BDP was able to implement a wide range of policies aimed at providing public goods. These included a programme to extend the rural infrastructure, to upgrade the urban infrastructure in the emerging shantytowns, and also

---

15　John D. Holm, "Elections in Botswana: Institutionalization of a New System of Legitimacy", in Fred. M. Hayward, (ed.) *Elections in Independent Africa* (Boulder, Co: Westview Press, 1987), pp. 132, 133; R. Nengwekhulu, "Some Findings on the Origins of Political Parties in Botswana", *PULA*, vol. 1, no. 2, 1979, pp. 47–75 at 59, 74, 75.

16　James H. Polhemus, "Botswana Votes: Parties and Elections in an African Democracy", *The Journal of Modern African Studies*, vol. 21, no. 3, 1983, pp. 397–430, at 415.

17　John D. Holm, "Elections and Democracy in Botswana", in John D. Holm and Patrick Molutsi (eds.), *Democracy in Botswana—the proceedings of a symposium held in Gaborone, 1–5 August 1988* (Athens, OH: Ohio University Press, 1989), pp. 189–202.

18　Christopher Colclough and Stephen McCarthy, *The Political Economy of Botswana—A Study of Growth and Distribution* (Oxford: Oxford University Press, 1980), pp. 207–208; Sill, "Sustaining a Success Story", p. 37.

19　World Bank, *World Development Report 1991* (New York: Oxford University Press, 1991), pp. 259, 261.

for education, health care and drought relief. This was done on a largely equitable basis, across the various regions of the country, and yielded favourable election results for the BDP in 1974 and 1979, allowing it to recapture losses sustained in the 1969 election.[20]

The governing BDP was able to finance these programmes from tax revenues initially drawn from the cattle industry, having obtained an export quota to the then European Community. This was later supplemented largely through the revenue gained from diamonds, discovered after independence, and first exploited from the Orapa mine which came into production in 1971. The overall impact has been spectacular growth, with GDP growing annually at a rate of 13.9 per cent from 1965 to 1980, and at a rate of 11.3 per cent from 1980 to 1990.[21] The impact on society was also highly visible, with a dramatic decline in infant mortality rates, a surge in primary and secondary school enrollment, and an increase in life expectancy.[22]

Through its many years in power the BDP has managed to affect the structure of both state and society in a number of ways. Regime changes were not undertaken, but rather, strenuously resisted. (A hotly contested issue, for example, is whether the voting age should be lowered to 18 years, from the current 21 years.) The emergent ideological divide, with the socialist oriented BNF, and the radical nationalist BPP set up against the moderate technocratic BDP in 1965, has virtually dissolved in favour of the development priorities of the latter. The character of the state, especially with respect to policies of Africanization, was profoundly affected by the BDP policy of gradualism, and of maintaining a corps of expatriate officers, who are employed on a short contract basis. As transient foreign employees of the state, these expatriates comply with the conditions of *gelding*, insulated and autonomous from society, and loyal only to their employer, the state.[23] This autonomy has been decisive in allowing state institutions to provide public goods on such an equitable basis, one of the key factors in explaining the BDP's sustained electoral success. Finally the BDP has managed to elevate the society from the ranks of the "low" to that of the "medium" category in terms of the United Nations Human Development Index (HDI).

What the BDP has been unable to do is, firstly, to maintain this high level of governing performance. Declining performance by the BDP can be

---

20 Pierre du Toit, *State Building and Democracy in Southern Africa—Botswana, Zimbabwe and South Africa* (Washington DC: United States Institute of Peace Press, 1995), pp. 54–57.
21 World Bank, *World Development Report, 1991*, p. 207.
22 *Ibid.*, pp. 259, 261.
23 Du Toit, *State Building and Democracy in Southern Africa*, p. 59.

measured in rising unemployment, which stood at 30–35 per cent by mid-1993.[24] Economic growth which still stood at 10 per cent in 1985/86 plummeted to –0.3 per cent in 1992/93, recovering somewhat to 4 per cent by 1993/94.[25] At the same time the income inequalities widened even further, amid a firm insistence by the government not to extend the social safety net.[26] Rising corruption, indicative of a corrosion of the internal cohesion and discipline of the long-ruling coalition, resulted in both the Vice-President and Agriculture Minister having to resign.[27]

Secondly, the BDP has been unable to extend its own voting support into the ranks of newly emerging categories of voters. The BDP has been able to hold onto its original core of voters, among the rural traditionalists, the state bureaucrats, and its ethnic heartland among the Bamangwato and Bakwena. Thus far it has not succeeded in gaining votes from the newly emerging urban, working-class voters.

The impact of both sets of factors is revealed by the 1994 election results. The BDP drew 54.6 per cent of the vote, capturing 27 seats in parliament—21 of these constituencies being primarily within the Bamangwato, Bakwena or Barolong rural tribal bases (together about 47 per cent of the population). The BNF emerged with a strong challenge, drawing 37.1 per cent of the vote, and 13 of the seats. It won 5 of the 6 most densely populated urban constituencies, with significant support from among the rural Bangwaketse.[28]

The 1994 result confirms a gradual trend of declining support for the BDP, which had peaked at 76.7 per cent in the 1974 election. This decline was hitherto obscured by the distorting effects of the single member constituency first-past-the-post electoral system, and by malapportionment, but should this trend continue, the likely prospect is that the BNF can gain power within the medium term. The question of whether the BDP will relinquish power will be taken up in the last section of the chapter.

Namibia

Namibian politics of this century were largely shaped by three sets of crucial historical events, each reinforcing the other. The first was the genocidal

---

24 *Africa South of the Sahara 1996* (London: Europa Publications, 1996), p. 186.

25 *Ibid.*, p. 183.

26 Kenneth Good, "At the Ends of the Ladder: Radical Inequalities in Botswana", *The Journal of Modern African Studies*, vol. 31, no. 2, 1993, pp. 203–230; Kenneth Good, "Towards Popular Participation in Botswana", *The Journal of Modern African Studies*, vol. 34, no. 1, 1996, pp. 53–77.

27 Kenneth Good, "Corruption and Mismanagement in Botswana: a Best-Case Example?", *The Journal of Modern African Studies*, vol. 32, no. 3, 1994, pp. 499–521.

28 Stephen Rule, "Electoral trends in Botswana—A geographical perspective", *Africa Insight*, vol. 25, no. 1, 1995, pp. 21–30.

Herero War of 1904 and Nama War of 1905, waged by the German colonial forces.[29] This effectively left the northern regions far more populous for the rest of the century (with the ethnically unrelated Ovambo, Kavango and Makololo groups accounting for close to two-thirds of the entire population). This also meant that the emerging industrial and mining sector of the modern colonial economy was, from the outset, reliant on northern black labour, who eventually came to form the core of the industrial labour unions.[30] Finally, it ensured that the majority of voters in democratic politics would come from the north.

The second formative event was the South African colonial government's attempt to implement apartheid in the country, primarily based on the blueprint of the so-called Odendaal Commission.[31] This raised the issue of apartheid, i.e. institutionalized white domination by South Africa as the salient political dividing line, even into the first democratic elections.

The third factor is that of resistance by SWAPO (South West African People's Organization) which escalated into an armed insurgency war, conducted in the north of the country. SWAPO, from the outset an organization with an Ovambo support base, having evolved from the OPO (Ovamboland People's Organization) naturally selected the north as their base for infiltration.[32] The populous north thus became the centre of the anti-apartheid resistance. The effect after 23 years of war was that the north also ended as the most destabilized, radicalized and politically mobilized partisan supporters of SWAPO, who positioned themselves as *the* organization of liberation from apartheid-style colonial rule.

The long drawn out process of international negotiations to bring about the independence of Namibia through the implementation of UN Security Council Resolution 435 did not change the basic structure of the colonial society, or soften the salient political divisions and issues which would

---

29 The Herero population was reduced from about 80,000 to 15,000 and the Nama from about 20,000 to 9,800, according to André du Pisani, *SWA/Namibia: The Politics of Continuity and Change* (Johannesburg: Jonathan Ball, 1986), p. 45, footnote 45. See also Tilman Dedering, "The German-Herero War of 1904: Revisionism of Genocide or Imaginary Historiography", *Journal of Southern African Studies*, vol. 19, no. 1, March 1993.

30 Colin Leys and John S. Saul, "Introduction", in Colin Leys and John S. Saul (eds.) *Namibia's Liberation Struggle—The Two Edged Sword* (London: James Currey, 1995), p. 9. See also W.G. Clarence-Smith and R. Moorsom, "Underdevelopment and Class Formation in Ovamboland, 1945–1915", *Journal of African History*, vol. 16, no. 3, 1975, pp. 365–381, esp. pp. 377–378; and Richard Moorsom, "Labour Consciousness and the 1971–72 Contract Workers Strike in Namibia", *Development and Change*, vol. 10, 1979, pp. 205–231. esp. pp. 207, 209.

31 Du Pisani, *SWA/Namibia: The Politics of Continuity and Change*, pp. 159–177.

32 Richard Dale, "Melding War and Politics in Namibia: South Africa's Counterinsurgency Campaign, 1966–1989", *Armed Forces and Society*, vol. 20, no. 1, Fall 1993, pp. 7–24, esp. pp. 14, 15.

dominate the inaugural election. SWAPO projected itself as the only untainted party, thus delegitimizing the other parties even before it took power: "SWAPO rallies emphasized the need to reject collaborationist parties, projecting an image as the only truly nationalist party, one consistently opposed to South African rule".[33] By contrast, the main opposition to SWAPO, the Democratic Turnhalle Alliance (DTA), tried to escape from its history of taking part in the South African sponsored interim government by emphasizing an instrumental ability, a message almost devoid of symbolic content. "DTA's central message seemed to be to project an image of a patron sufficiently experienced in government and with enough access to resources to be trusted with people's security and welfare".[34]

The 1989 election was held under the supervision of the United Nations Organization, acting in terms of Resolution 435. A proportional representation electoral system in which the entire country was treated as a single constituency was used, without any threshold, requiring a party to poll 1.39 per cent of the vote to capture one of the 72 seats.[35] The turnout of 95.65 per cent yielded a result in which SWAPO gained 57.3 per cent of the vote (and 41 seats) leaving the DTA as a distant second with 28.6 per cent of the vote and 21 seats. The other 8 parties shared the remaining 14.1 per cent of the vote.[36]

The most remarkable aspect of the result is the Ovambo support for SWAPO. In the Ovamboland electoral district 92.3 per cent of the vote went to SWAPO. (The adjacent Kavango district registered a 51 per cent SWAPO vote.) Given the numerical dominance of this region (close to half of the entire population) the Ovambo vote contributed to 70 per cent of the overall SWAPO vote. What remains unclear is whether they did so in their capacity as Ovambos, Namibians, workers or as Africans.[37] Significant support for SWAPO was also registered in those major towns with an organized

---

33 Lionel Cliffe et al. The Transition to Independence in Namibia (Boulder: Lynne Rienner, 1994), p. 160.
34 Ibid., p. 161.
35 Ibid., pp. 250–252.
36 Ibid., p. 183; P.J.J.S. Potgieter, "The Resolution 435 Election in Namibia", Politikon, vol. 18, no. 2, June 1991, pp. 26–48, at 34, 35.
37 Attempts to establish either ethnicity or class or interests as the causal factor in shaping voter preference have thus far been rather weak. See for example, Potgieter, "The Resolution 435 Election in Namibia", and William Lindeke, Winnie Wanzala, and Victor Tonchi, "Namibia's Election Revisited", Politikon, vol. 18, no. 2, June 1992. Both these efforts suffer from being theoretically uninformed, empirically shallow and methodologically crude. For the theoretical, empirical and methodological criteria of establishing the causal status of independent variables see Pierre du Toit, State Building and Democracy in Southern Africa—Botswana, Zimbabwe and South Africa, pp. 92–96. The most balanced assessment of causal factors in this election is found in Cliffe et al., The Transition to Independence in Namibia, pp. 185–195.

working-class population, but still short of persuasively being able to claim to be a truly national party.

Namibia achieved independence with a constitution featuring a Presidential executive, and a proportional electoral system which allows for multi-party democracy within a unitary state. SWAPO has thus far adhered to this constitution without amendments, and crucially, retaining the PR electoral system.

The legacy of inequality which confronted the new rulers was most noticeable with respect to land: about 44 per cent of the total land area at independence was owned by about 4000 farmers, most of them white, 41 per cent was communally owned by 150,000 black families, and the remaining 15 per cent was owned by the state.[38] An overall indication of inequality is the calculation that the most affluent 5 per cent of the population in 1989 were estimated to control 71 per cent of the GDP, and the bottom 55 per cent of the population about 3 per cent of the GDP.[39] By the early 1990s less than half (43 per cent) of the total labour force were in paid employment in the formal sector.[40]

The overall approach of SWAPO in dealing with this legacy has been extremely cautious. The economic policy is the orthodox one of operating within the parameters of the capitalist domestic (and international) system with the hope of inducing enough growth with which to expand the tax base of the state rather than to radically redistribute what there is. The plans for major land redistribution have been all but abandoned (instead soft loans at low interest rates are made available to blacks for buying land), and affirmative action measures in the public service have been conducted within the constitutional limitation of article 141(1) protecting public servants who entered employment under the South African regime prior to 1990.[41] The most visible expansion of services has been in education and welfare services, without operating beyond budgetary constraints.[42] Overall racial income inequality remains high (22:1 in the commercial sector), and the housing backlog (at 40,000 units in 1991) is increasing.[43]

38 André du Pisani, "Rumours of Rain: Namibia's post-independence experience", *Africa Insight*, vol. 21, no. 3, 1991, pp. 171–179, at 175.
39 Chris Tapscott, "National Reconciliation, Social Equity and Class Formation in Independent Namibia", *Journal of Southern African Studies*, vol. 19, no. 1, March 1993, pp. 29–39 at 30.
40 *Ibid.*, p. 33.
41 Ibid., p. 34; Du Pisani, "Rumours of Rain", p. 174; Denis Herbstein, "Jobs and Land", *Africa Report*, vol. 38, no. 4, 1993, pp. 52–55.
42 Madeleine Lass (ed.) *Africa at a Glance, 1995/6*, Pretoria: Africa Institute of South Africa, 1995, pp. 25, 35.
43 Stef Coetzee, "Namibia after two years of independence", *Africa Institute Bulletin*, vol. 32, no. 6, 1992, pp. 1, 2.

Other attempts at restructuring the society have also been taken up with extreme caution. Public rhetoric by SWAPO politicians have repeatedly voiced the need to dismantle ethnic traditional authorities, to depoliticize ethnicity in general and to promote a non-ethnic national identity. No formal policy on the official status of the many traditional leaders has as yet been formulated though, and instead, what has been implemented is "…an *ad hoc*, issue-by-issue, day-to-day *informal* ethnic-regarding policy by regional and national government leaders that prioritized pragmatic accommodation" (original emphasis).[44]

Despite this limited success in effecting fundamental changes to state and society, SWAPO has succeeded in extending its electoral support base substantially beyond its core of Ovambo supporters. In the 1992 regional elections for lower tier authorities it managed to gain more than two-thirds of the vote.[45] In the 1994 National Parliamentary and Presidential elections this trend continued with SWAPO securing 73.89 per cent of the Parliamentary vote, and Sam Nujoma, the incumbent President, taking 76.34 per cent of the vote in a two-way contest for the Presidency.[46]

SWAPO now clearly commands the position of an electorally dominant party, and is well positioned to establish a "cycle of dominance" where elections have less and less to do with actual contests for power. This position was achieved by virtue of the following factors. Firstly, in the words of André du Pisani: "The opposition parties, both large and small, were up against a clientalist state with a loyal flock and a benign shepherd".[47] Under conditions of scarcity, control over state institutions and resources assumes vital importance, and makes patronage a very persuasive method of gaining support. Secondly, the symbolic capital of being not only the principal agent of decolonization and liberation, but now also of national reconciliation, again served as the basis for delegitimizing the opposition. Thirdly, performance legitimacy, especially in the field of foreign politics (such as regaining Walvis Bay from South Africa) could offset the retention of the domestic economic status quo. The major questions now are whether SWAPO will use its dominance to try to effect regime changes of a fundamental nature, and how it

---

44 Joshua Bernard Forrest, "Ethnic–State Political Relations in Post-Apartheid Namibia", *Journal of Commonwealth & Comparative Politics*, vol. 32, no. 3, November 1994, pp. 300–323, at 319.

45 William A. Lindeke and Winnie Wanzala, "Regional Elections in Namibia: Deepening Democracy and Gender Inclusion", *Africa Today*, 3rd Quarter, 1994, pp. 5–14, at 8.

46 *Africa South of the Sahara*, 1996, p. 682.

47 André du Pisani, "Limited Choice: The 1994 national and presidential elections in Namibia", *Africa Institute Bulletin*, vol. 35, no. 1, 1995, p. 1.

will respond to ethnic demand-generation by factions within the Ovambo population, especially those within the Kwanyama group.[48]

Zimbabwe

The precolonial social upheaval of the *Mfecane* resulted in the settlement of the isiNdebele-speaking people in the western regions of contemporary Zimbabwe by the mid-nineteenth century, adjacent to the resident Shona speakers, thus establishing the major cultural cleavage among the African population with a 4:1 numerical ratio in favour of the Shona speakers.[49] This came to be superimposed by the white settlers, who assumed formal control of the region in 1898.[50] From these communities the three major stakeholders in modern politics would emerge.

British colonial policies ensured white settler control, enacted through an elected parliament who implemented apartheid-style policies.[51] Efforts to extend electoral participation to Africans resulted in the Unilateral Declaration of Independence in 1965, soon to be reciprocated by the start of an armed rebellion by the African nationalists in 1966. Crucial to this civil war was the split in nationalist ranks in 1963, leading to the formation of the Zimbabwe African National Union (ZANU) (under the leadership of Robert Mugabe from 1975), which broke ranks with the Zimbabwe African People's Union (ZAPU) led by Joshua Nkomo. Initially the split was about leadership matters, but it soon consolidated into a replication of the Shona/Ndebele ethnic divide.[52]

These two forces, with their respective armies, remained distinct bodies throughout the war, operating from different bases (Zambia for ZAPU, and Mozambique for ZANU), into different regions (the northwest by ZAPU, the east by ZANU). They collaborated only reluctantly at the Lancaster House Conference in 1979, forming a tenuous alliance under the banner of the Patriotic Front (PF), renaming themselves as ZANU-PF and PF-ZAPU

48   Forrest, "Ethnic–State Political Relations in Post-Apartheid Namibia", pp. 316–319.
49   J.D. Omer-Cooper, *The Zulu Aftermath—A Nineteenth-Century Revolution in Bantu Africa* (Evanston, IL: Northwestern University Press, 1966), p. 151.
50   Robert Blake, *A History of Rhodesia* (New York: Alfred A. Knopf, 1978), pp. 42–154.
51   Claire Palley, "Law and the Unequal Society, Discriminatory legislation in Rhodesia under the Rhodesian Front from 163 to 1969, part 1", *Race*, vol. 12, no. 1, July 1970, pp. 15–47, and "Part 2", *Race*, vol. 12, no. 2, October 1970, pp. 139–167.
52   Masipula Sithole, *Zimbabwe: Struggles within the Struggle* (Salisbury: Rujeko, 1979); and "Ethnicity and Factionalism in Zimbabwe Nationalist Politics", *Ethnic and Racial Studies*, vol. 3, no. 1, January 1980, pp. 17–39.

respectively. At this Conference, under the stern chairmanship of Lord Carrington, a peace agreement was reached, and a democratic constitution and transitional procedures negotiated.[53]

Provision was made for the first elections to be conducted under a party-list proportional representation system, without any regional voting districts. The inaugural elections of 1980 delivered close to a 94 per cent turnout, and was easily won by Mugabe's ZANU-PF, receiving 63 per cent of the vote (57 of the 80 seats), drawn mostly from the numerically dominant Shona-speaking population of the eastern highlands.[54] Nkomo's PF-ZAPU got 24.1 per cent of the vote (20 seats), mostly from the western Matabeleland region. The remaining 3 seats were taken by the United African National Council (UANC), while the 20 seats reserved for whites (in terms of the Lancaster House agreement) were all captured by Ian Smith's Republican Front (RF).[55] The white population had declined dramatically from 275,000 in 1979 to about 80,000 in 1983.[56]

The first decade of ZANU-PF rule was marked by numerous constitutional changes. This included changing the electoral system from party-list PR to the constituency-based first-past-the-post plurality system, thus already favouring the incumbent party in the 1985 election. In 1987 the Westminster-type executive was changed to a presidential system, and minority protection was scrapped. The most striking continuity was the extending of security measures (including 60 new emergency regulations in the first four years of independence).[57]

These changes were complemented by the major ZANU-PF policy initiatives of the first ten years of rule. The most important were the Matabeleland campaigns of 1983 and 1985. These military incursions, conducted by the Fifth Brigade, were ostensibly to subdue "dissident" actions of a criminal nature, but resulted in widespread atrocities against the civilian population, and were clearly aimed against PF-ZAPU.[58] The second policy initiative was

---

53 Jeffrey Davidow, *A Peace in Southern Africa: The Lancaster House Conference on Rhodesia* (Boulder: Westview Press, 1984); Stephen John Stedman, *Peacemaking in Civil War—International Mediation in Zimbabwe, 1974–1980* (Boulder: Lynne Rienner, 1991).

54 Sithole, "Ethnicity and Factionalism in Zimbabwe Nationalist Politics", p. 21.

55 D.S. Tevera, "Voting Patterns in Zimbabwe's Elections of 1980 and 1985", *Geography*, vol. 74, no. 2, 1989, pp. 162–165.

56 W.J. Breytenbach, "Transition in 'Settler' societies in Africa: Problems and parallels revisited", *Plural Societies*, vol. 22, no. 1 and 2, November 1992, pp. 85–123, at 88.

57 Ronald Weitzer, "In Search of Regime Security: Zimbabwe Since Independence", *The Journal of Modern African Studies*, vol. 22, no. 4, 1984, pp. 529–557.

58 Lawyers Committee for Human Rights, *Zimbabwe: The Wages of War—A Report on Human Rights* (New York: The Lawyers Committee for Human Rights, 1986).

to create a one-party state. Having subdued PF-ZAPU militarily, the next step was to merge the two parties, which was duly achieved in April 1988, with the hope of formalizing this power consolidation in a one-party state. The third policy initiative was to assume control over the economy so as to effect the distribution of public goods in a programme of delivering "social-ism-for-the-blacks".[59] This entailed both the rapid Africanization of the public service and accelerated land redistribution.

The election results of 1985 and 1990 have revealed the effects of these constitutional changes and policy programmes. The 1985 elections, held in the aftermath of the Matabeleland campaign, revealed a deepening of the ethnic division, which first appeared in the 1980 election. With a very high turnout of 97.02 per cent, ZANU-PF increased its share of the votes to 77.19 per cent (64 seats), while PF-ZAPU held on to 19.31 per cent of the vote, taking every one of the 15 seats in the Matabeleland region. The original ZANU, led by Sithole, won the remaining seat. The UANC failed to get any seat, drawing only 2.24 per cent of the vote.[60]

The 1990 election, the first to be held after the party merger, removed the institutional framework for expressing this divide. Turnout dropped sharply to 54 per cent, with the unified ZANU-PF taking a landslide victory, capturing 78 per cent of the vote, and, with the help of the electoral system, 117 out of the 120 contested seats. The new opposition party, the Zimbabwe Unity Movement (ZUM), took only 2 seats, but almost 20 per cent of the vote.[61]

What has been the impact of this overwhelming dominance of ZANU-PF on the character of the regime and society? In 1984 at the ZANU party congress the formal ideological objective was defined as the project of the pursuit of "…a socialist state in Zimbabwe based on Marxist–Leninist principles".[62] This entailed, firstly, the establishment of a one-party state. Although energetically pursued, this objective was eventually abandoned, when the merger between ZANU and ZAPU proved to result in a *de facto* one-party state. The second dimension of this project, to limit civil liberties in favour of state security, was easily achieved, with ZANU legislating

---

59 Jeffrey Herbst, *State Politics in Zimbabwe* (Berkeley: University of California Press, 1990), pp. 227–231.

60 Anthony Lemon, The Zimbabwe General Election of 1985", *Journal of Commonwealth and Comparative Politics*, vol. 26, no. 1, March 1988, pp. 3–21.

61 Sam Kongwa, "Zimbabwe's 1990 general election and the search for direction", *Africa Institute Bulletin*, vol. 30, no. 3, 1990, pp. 6–8.

62 William H. Shaw, "Towards the One-Party State in Zimbabwe: A Study in African Political Thought", *The Journal of Modern African Studies*, vol. 24, no. 3, 1986, pp. 373–394 at 374.

extensive additions to the state security grid left by the white colonists who preceded them.[63] The least headway was made with the third objective, that of securing state control over the economy, and of eliminating capitalist rules in favour of socialist ones.

Large-scale intervention by the state into society, so as to eliminate racial backlogs left by the white rulers of Rhodesia, and to provide public goods equitably, was implemented, with visible effect in the fields of education, minimum wages, health services, and agricultural producer prices.[64] All of these fell short of textbook socialism, but eliminated the white/black discrepancies (which was facilitated by a mass emigration of whites). These policies nonetheless limited economic liberties and inhibited growth. Average GDP for the first 12 years of independence stands at 2.8 per cent, and unemployment in 1995 was over 50 per cent, with real incomes in 1994 at 68 per cent of their 1990 levels.[65] The official striving for socialism was abandoned when Zimbabwe capitulated to the forces of global economic liberalism by submitting to an extensive Economic Structural Adjustment Programme in 1991.

The most recent election of 1995 was therefore held amidst conditions of economic stagnation, and control of state resources and institutions (such as the media) by the ruling ZANU-PF, who had extensive security measures and personnel at their disposal, and who made ample use of state funds. The latter was made possible through a controversial constitutional rule which gives parties an annual allocation of Z$ 32 million from state funds, *only for parties with more than 15 seats in parliament!*[66] Not surprisingly, 8 opposition groups boycotted the election, only half the eligible voters did register, and of them only 57 per cent turned out to vote. Fifty-five of the candidates (all ZANU-PF) were unopposed, and ZANU-PF won 63 of the remaining 65 seats.[67] With ZANU-PF hegemony thus secured, the regime now clearly conforms to a pseudodemocracy. The dynamics of party politics now moves to power struggles within the ruling party, amid speculations about the emergence of ethnic factions within the Shona-speaking support base of ZANU-PF.[68]

---

63 Ronald Weitzer, "Continuities in the Politics of State Security in Zimbabwe", in M.G. Schatzberg, *The Political Economy of Zimbabwe* (New York: Praeger, 1984), pp. 81–118.

64 Du Toit, *State-Building and Democracy in Southern Africa*, pp. 251–254.

65 *Africa South of the Sahara 1996*, p. 1070.

66 Norman Aphane, "Democracy—Zimbabwean style", *Africa Institute Bulletin*, vol. 35, no. 3, 1995, p. 9.

67 Simon Baynham, "Zimbabwe's elections: A hollow victory", *Africa Institute Bulletin*, vol. 35, no. 3, 1995, p. 3.

68 "Zimbabwe: Lining up for tomorrow and beyond", *Africa Confidential*, vol. 35, no. 14, pp. 3–5.

Zambia

The campaign for independence in the British colony of Northern Rhodesia was initially led by the Northern Rhodesia African National Congress (ANC), established in 1951 under the leadership of Harry Nkumbula. His leadership was later eclipsed by Kenneth Kaunda who formed the United National Independence Party (UNIP). The 1964 independence elections were easily won by UNIP, who gained 55 of the 65 seats on the main roll, with the ANC taking the other 10. A further 10 seats were reserved for the white settlers, whose National Progress Party (NPP) took all 10. In 1966 the NPP dissolved itself, thus ending the white/black divide in Zambian politics.[69]

From the outset Zambian electoral politics has been closely interwoven with the ethnic composition of the country. Ethnicity in Zambia is primarily expressed in a combination of linguistic and regional identities. The major groups are the Bemba (the largest group at 34 per cent of the population and living primarily in the northeast), the Tonga (16 per cent, in the south and central areas), the Malawi (14 per cent) and the Lozi (9 per cent, concentrated in the south and west of the country).[70] In the 1964 elections UNIP drew its core support from the Bemba, as well as from other groups/regions with the exception of the Tonga (who stayed loyal to Nkumbula's ANC), and the Lozi in the south. UNIP's multi-ethnic coalition was nonetheless wide enough to assemble 70 per cent of the African vote.[71]

Thereafter the dominant issue for UNIP was how to retain such a winning coalition amidst continual ethnic splintering and fragmentation. Kaunda took measures to counter accusations of Bemba hegemony within UNIP and to contain the eroding effect of ethnic splinter parties by restricting open electoral competition. This culminated in the December 1972 legislation formalizing the Zambian one-party state. In the subsequent 1973 one-party elections voter turnout slumped badly to 39.80 per cent, but recovered to 66.9 per cent in 1978 and 63.9 per cent in 1983.[72] Overt ethnic mobilization was duly curtailed, submerging but not changing the underlying structure of basic loyalties.[73]

---

69 Marcia M. Burdette, *Zambia—Between Two Worlds* (Boulder, Colorado: Westview Press, 1988), p. 65.
70 Brian Hunter, (ed.) *The Statesman's Yearbook, 1995–1996* (New York: St. Martin's Press, 1996), p. 1621.
71 James R. Scarritt, "Communal Conflict and Contention for Power in Africa South of the Sahara", in Ted Robert Gurr *et al.*, *Minorities at Risk—A Global View of Ethnopolitical Conflicts* (Washington DC: United States Institute of Peace Press, 1993), p. 266; Donald L. Horowitz, *Ethnic Groups in Conflict* (Berkeley: University of California Press, 1985), p. 430.
72 Bornwell C. Chikulo, "The Impact of Elections in Zambia's One Party Second Republic", *Africa Today*, 2nd Quarter 1988, pp. 37–49, at 38, 39.
73 Scarritt, "Communal Conflict and Contention", p. 268.

In order to consolidate its dominance UNIP resorted to a number of policies. The first was the rapid expansion and Africanization of the public service (already initiated in 1964), followed by the extension of educational and welfare services. Most crucial, however, was Kaunda's strategy of constantly shuffling and reshuffling the top positions in the public service and cabinet, coupled to a steady rise in the number of cabinet positions. This made virtually every appointment a function of personal preference of the President, and prevented every incumbent from establishing autonomous executive competence. Personal loyalty became the decisive criterion for career advancement, thus establishing the basis of patron/client politics and the creation of a small indigenous Zambian middle class.[74] This trend came to be fine-tuned with the arithmetic of ethnic balancing within the ranks of UNIP, aimed at pre-empting the kind of splintering which took place when Kapwepwe left UNIP.[75] However, the effect of these strategies in securing UNIP hegemony through patron/client politics were eventually decisively undercut by Zambia's economic crisis.

Zambia, like Botswana, inherited a single commodity economy, at the mercy of international market prices, and thus extremely dependent on global economic forces. Unlike Botswana's beef (and later, diamonds), Zambia's copper economy did enter a very volatile price regime in the 1970s, and, again unlike Botswana's state leaders, Zambia's leadership were ill equipped to deal with this crisis.

Under these conditions of increased vulnerability, Kaunda in 1968 announced the nationalization of major industries, extending this plan in 1969 to include the copper mines. This effectively ended any prospect of further foreign investment, inhibited technological modernization of the plants, and amounted to the process of "state capitalism" replacing that of "African Socialism". The result was that the structure of the economy remained essentially unchanged, and continued state solvency and societal prosperity hinged ever more on the maintenance of the international copper price.

In 1975 this fell dramatically so that external borrowing became imperative to fund populist programmes and to oil the wheels of the patronage system. This eventually brought the Zambian government into borrowing from the IMF, which by 1981 imposed its strict guidelines of "stabilization" onto the

---

74 Carolyn L. Baylies and Morris Szeftel, "The Rise of a Zambian Capitalist Class in the 1970s", *Journal of Southern African Studies*, vol. 8, no. 2, 1982, pp. 187–213; Ian Scott, "Middle Class Politics in Zambia", *African Affairs*, no. 308, July 1978, pp. 321–334.

75 Burdette, *Zambia*, pp. 65–72.

domestic economy: devalue the currency, lower imports, reduce price controls on essential commodities and cut subsidies on others, and limit wage increases.[76]

The effect was to impose hardship on those least able to afford it, thus widening the inequalities between the few beneficiaries of patronage and the rest. The share of national income accruing to the top 5 per cent of the population rose from 35 per cent to 50 per cent between 1975 and 1983, while average wages, in real terms, declined by close to 40 per cent between 1974 and 1983.[77] The public had to cope with immense price increases: in 1986 the price of maize meal rose by 120 per cent, that of petrol rose by 500 per cent in 1990, and when another 100 per cent rise in the maize meal price was announced in 1990 widespread riots erupted in Lusaka.[78]

Opposition to Kaunda grew despite the formal one-party state under the control of UNIP. The informal extra-parliamentary opposition came from the ranks of the churches, students, and labour unions, as well as independent entrepreneurs outside the patronage network.[79] These opposition forces coalesced into a new, potentially winning multi-ethnic and multi-regional coalition, which, as soon as Kaunda conceded to hold new multi-party elections, registered as the Movement for Multi-Party Democracy (MMD), under the leadership of trade unionist Frederick Chiluba.

The 1991 elections were contested mainly between UNIP and the MMD, with MMD emerging as the clear winner, taking 71.96 per cent of the vote, as opposed to the 23.6 per cent of UNIP. This converted into 125 parliamentary seats for the MMD and 25 for UNIP from a low turnout of 43 per cent. MMD swept all regions, with the exception of the Eastern, where UNIP took 68.17 per cent of the vote. Chiluba also trounced Kaunda in the Presidential election, drawing 75 per cent of the vote.[80]

The general assessment of this re-democratization of Zambia is that it amounts to "...a transition from a *de jure* to a *de facto* one-party state".[81] A new constitution is in force, a new party is in power, but the continuities with

---

76 *Ibid.*, pp. 78–123.

77 Kenneth Good, "Debt and the One-Party State in Zambia", *The Journal of Modern African Studies*, vol. 27, no. 2, 1989, pp. 297–313, at 309.

78 Michael Bratton, "Zambia Starts Over", *Journal of Democracy*, vol. 3, no. 2, April 1992, pp. 81–94, at 85.

79 Gatian F. Lungu, "The Church, Labour and the Press in Zambia: The Role of Critical Observers in a One-Party State", *African Affairs*, vol. 85, no. 340, 1986, pp. 385–410; Burdette, *Zambia—Between Two Worlds*, pp. 127–131; Bratton, "Zambia Starts Over", pp. 84–86.

80 B.C. Chikulo, "End of an Era: An Analysis of the 1991 Zambian Presidential and Parliamentary Elections", *Politikon*, vol. 20, no. 1, June 1993, pp. 87–104, at 93, 94.

81 *Ibid.*, p. 99.

the previous regime are seen as being more significant. Chiluba's style of governing mirrors that of Kaunda: Presidential dominance in appointments, shuffling and reshuffling of appointees, the maintenance of security measures, including declaring states of emergency, political patronage, and ethnic balancing of the cabinet. Even the change in personnel was limited, as many of the MMD incumbents had defected from UNIP![82] The essential political culture of the old leadership has therefore endured in the ranks of the new leaders. The 1996 election appears to confirm this conclusion. Kaunda was banned from contesting the election, through a new constitutional rule, which led the UNIP to boycott the election. Amid accusations of practices by the state-run media which unfairly favoured Chiluba's MMD, turnout was a low 40 per cent of those registered, which in turn was below 60 per cent of eligible voters. The MMD won by a landslide margin, capturing 131 of the 150 seats.

The reasons for this continuity in government are found in the continuity with the problems faced by the old rulers.[83] The economy is still bound by the constraints imposed by the IMF; the accusations of ethnic bias (this time said to favour the Bemba) persist; the problems of state (in)solvency remains, and inequalities persist. Chiluba, like Kaunda, is resorting to measures to limit contestation so as to hold onto his unstable winning coalition, amidst, yet again, renewed ethnic splintering.[84] The prospect of MMD being able to consolidate a liberal democratic regime appears to be remote.

Malawi

Like in Botswana, the British colonization of Malawi was a reluctant affair, and unlike Zimbabwe, the process of decolonization was not through a prolonged violent civil war, nor were there deep divisions inside the liberation ranks.[85] The result was that independence was achieved relatively peacefully in 1964, under the leadership of Kamuzu Banda's Malawi Congress Party (MCP), which was an effective broad inclusive coalition.

---

82 Carolyn Baylies and Morris Szeftel, "The Fall and Rise of Multi-Party Politics in Zambia", *Review of African Political Economy*, no. 54, 1992, pp. 75–91; Chisepo J.J. Mphaisha, "Retreat from Democracy in Post One-Party State Zambia", *Journal of Commonwealth & Comparative Politics*, vol. 34, no. 2, July 1996, pp. 65–84; Keith Panther-Brick, "Prospects for Democracy in Zambia", *Government and Opposition*, vol. 29, no. 2, 1994, pp. 231–247.

83 Jan Kees van Donge, "Kaunda and Chiluba: Two instruments of God's Will or enduring patterns of Political Culture in Zambia", mimeo, n.d.

84 Gatian F. Lungu, "Zambia: Civil Society in the Aftermath of Democratic Transition", paper presented at the Conference on "Consolidating Democracy—What Role for Civil Society", August 14–15 1996, Cape Town, South Africa; *Africa Institute Bulletin*, vol. 35, no. 4, 1995.

85 T. David Williams, *Malawi—The Politics of Despair* (Ithaca: Cornell University Press, 1978), pp. 21–56.

The disparate forces in the coalition comprised a three-way regional/ethnic division, expressed largely in linguistic terms. Pre-colonial settlement patterns resulted in a very diverse cultural mix. (The 1966 census still recorded 13 different languages.) Administrative policies by the British colonial power dramatically affected the fortunes of different linguistic communities. The country was subdivided into three administrative regions, Northern, Central and Southern, and in each different policy measures evolved. The overall result was that in the North the Chitumbuka language achieved dominance, eventually reaching the status of a national language in 1947, along with Chinyanja (later to be renamed Chichewa by Banda). Thus the Tumbuka group achieved a comparative advantage over other groups, becoming the ascendant group in the region. In the Southern region the Yao were the beneficiaries of colonial preferential policies, and they, and their language, Chiyao, achieved regional dominance within the African cultures. In the central province the Chewa culture was dominant throughout, from pre-colonial times. Because of the divergent political economy of the three regions, each came to the independence campaign under the banner with different grievances, and contrasting demands. Each dominant group also sought different benefits from independence.[86]

It was this set of priorities which the MCP had to accommodate after independence. It failed from the outset. In the so-called Cabinet Crisis of September 1964 Banda, a Chewa, was faced with the collapse of the MCP through a challenge from young educated Northerners and Southerners. He met this by establishing a one-party state in July 1966 when the MCP was recognized as the only legal party.[87] Thereafter the dominance of Northerners and Southerners in the public service was eliminated.

In 1968 Chichewa was made the sole national language, compulsory in all government schools, and along with English the official language of the state. The new policy detrimentally affected the minority languages, as well as handicapping those from the south and the north, and two decades later is still a source of resentment.[88] Banda further consolidated his power base in ways similar to those used by Kaunda: an extensive patronage network, exil-

---

86 Leroy Vail and Landeg White, "Tribalism in the Political History of Malawi", in Leroy Vail, *The Creation of Tribalism in Southern Africa* (London: James Currey, 1989), pp. 151–192.

87 Williams, *Malawi—The Politics of Despair*, pp. 230–233.

88 Edrinne Kayambazinthu, "Patterns of Language-Use in Malawi: A Socio-Linguistic Investigation in the Domasi and Malindi Areas of Southern Malawi", *Journal of Contemporary African Studies*, vol. 8/9, no. 1/2, 1989/90, pp. 109–131; Pascal Kishindo, "The Impact of National Language on Minority Languages: The Case of Malawi", *Journal of Contemporary African Studies*, vol. 12, no. 2, 1994, pp. 127–150.

ing and/or imprisoning opponents, banning formal opposition, and seeking general public endorsement as a symbol of national unity.

The impact of Banda's rule on Malawian society has been varied. Overall poverty remains pervasive, and in 1989 the country was still ranked as the 7th poorest in the world, with a GNP per capita at US$ 180,[89] and overall dependence of the economy on global markets remains high. Through state capitalism a large parastatal sector was established, and the manufacturing sector expanded gradually (reaching 13.6 per cent of GDP in 1994). Most significant of this process, however, is the slice which Banda accrued for himself through his privately owned Press Holdings, a conglomerate said to control 40 per cent of the country's economy.[90]

Most importantly, after 1964 MCP proceeded to function as a regional party only, unable to maintain a maximum inclusive coalition, relying primarily on a narrow Chewa support base. Opposition mounted steadily, coming from the ranks of the churches, labour, students, and probably decisively, from the international donor community.[91] Banda conceded to the holding of a referendum on the issue of multi-party politics (in 1993), which went in favour of redemocratization. The process of liberalization was largely under the control of the government, but all the emerging political forces made efforts to ensure that the transition remained within the boundaries of legality, and proceeded through consensus.

The major contenders to emerge were the Alliance for the Restoration of Democracy (AFORD), led by Chakufwa Chihana, and the United Democratic Front (UDF), led by Bakili Muluzi. The MCP continued under the leadership of Banda. The 1994 elections strongly reaffirmed the ethnic/regional split in Malawi. AFORD won 33 of the 36 seats in the Northern region, the MCP held onto 51 of the 56 seats in the Central region, and the UDF took 71 of the 85 seats in the Southern region. Muluzi of the UDF won the Presidential contest with 47 per cent of the vote, against the 33 per cent for Banda and the 19.5 per cent for Chihana. The turnout was estimated at 84 per cent.[92] The UDF started off without a parliamentary majority, but succeeded in persuading AFORD to join them in a coalition, after the latter had briefly aligned themselves with the MCP.

---

89 World Bank: *World Development Report 1991* (New York: Oxford University Press, 1991), p. 204.

90 Williams, *Malawi*, p. 383, *Africa Institute Bulletin*, vol. 35, no. 6, 1995, p. 9.

91 Jonathan Newell, "'A Moment of Truth'? The Church and Political Change in Malawi, 1992", *The Journal of Modern African Studies*, vol. 33, no. 2, 1995, pp. 243–262.

92 Clement Ng'ong'ola, "Managing the Transition to Political Pluralism in Malawi: Legal and Constitutional Arrangements", *Journal of Commonwealth & Comparative Politics*, vol. 34, no. 2, July 1996, pp. 85–110, at 104.

The overall assessment of the transition at this stage is that neither the structure of society nor the character of politics has changed. The basis of political stability remains to be found in the elusive formula of constructing a stable inclusive coalition, able to transcend the ethnic/regional divides. This has still to be achieved. The political culture of the current power holders has also not changed from the Banda era: "…one partyism has persisted, but on a regional basis".[93] This continuity implies that future elections may become subject to the kind of constraints which can precipitate a slide towards electoralism, or even towards pseudodemocracy.

COMPARATIVE PERSPECTIVES: BRIDGE OR BRIDGEHEAD?

The major variables under consideration are those of party strength, party system strength, ideology, leadership, changes in the international system, and new crises of mobilization. Each will be considered in turn.

Party strength refers to the ability of parties to outlive their founding leader, to capture the support, to subordinate key interest groups and to harness the energy of ambitious individuals to the goals of the party. Only Botswana's BDP has thus far succeeded on all of these tests. The BDP has prospered after the death of Sir Seretse Khama, has successfully drawn in and held onto a wide range of interest group support (chiefs, bureaucrats, commercial farmers, tribal communities), and has not been taken on tow by any individual political entrepreneur. SWAPO is still tied to the career of Sam Nujoma, as is ZANU-PF to that of Robert Mugabe. And the future of both UNIP and MMD remains closely linked to the fortunes of Chiluba and Kaunda, respectively. Little can be said at the time of writing about the strength of the UDF and AFORD in Malawi.

Party system strength is revealed in the ability of competing parties to draw citizens into electoral politics within constitutional rules, instead of avenues of extra-parliamentary politics, and is reflected in the turnout at elections. Botswana again remains the only party system which commands high turnout by voters on a sustained basis. Turnout is falling in Zimbabwe as well as in Zambia. Namibia has run only two national elections, and although turnout in the second still remained high, it is too early to discern a clear trend. Malawi had a more promising start than Zambia, but no trend has emerged yet.

---

93 Jan Kees van Donge, "Kamuzu's Legacy: The Democratization of Malawi", *African Affairs*, vol. 94, pp. 227–257, at 256.

The ideologies which drive election campaigns, and eventually inform ruling policies, also shape party prospects of dominance. Parties with compelling ideologies are likely to secure long-term incumbency with which to try to restructure state and society, and to secure hegemony. None of the ruling parties have found such a formula. The BDP secured the longest rule, but with an uninspiring vision of technocratic priorities, fiscal discipline, limited welfare distribution, and cautious domestic and international growth policies. African Humanism in Zambia and Marxist socialism in Zimbabwe both foundered spectacularly on policies which failed to come to terms with global economic forces, and brought economic ruin instead. The Malawian parties' campaigns were virtually devoid of ideological content. None of these parties have brought an ethnic ingredient to their ideology. This is due, in part, either to the fact that the ruling party can rely on the assured support of an ethnic majority (Zimbabwe and Namibia), or that the ruling party has to build a multi-ethnic support base (Botswana and Zambia). Ethnic issues therefore tend to be avoided through the strategy of "purposeful ambiguity".[94] In Namibia, for example, SWAPO campaigned during the last election under the banner of "better opportunities for all Namibians", and in Zambia Chiluba brought in the even more vacuous slogan of "the hour has come".

Leadership, or more broadly, elite political culture, appears to be crucial in shaping dominant parties' role as bridge-builders to a system of multi-party politics or as bridgeheads to single party hegemony. Again Botswana shows a distinctively different leadership ethos to that of the other cases. Sir Seretse Khama and his "new men" who set up the BDP were guided by a perception that all major stakeholders in Botswana were in effect "mutual hostages" of one another—each dependent for its own well-being on the others, and each able to inflict great damage on the others.[95] This formative experience guided subsequent policy making, enabling the BDP not only to assemble a winning coalition based on an inclusive, cautious, conservative, technocratic worldview, but to consolidate it and to rule and prosper for more than three decades. The Zimbabwean leadership ethos, by contrast, shaped by intense competition between ZAPU and ZANU, as well as the civil war, has from the outset had an adversarial, combative and exclusive character. This accounts for the undemocratic domestic policies of ZANU-PF, and for their assertive

---

94 Alvin Rabushka and Kenneth A. Shepsle, *Politics in Plural Societies—A Theory of Democratic Instability* (Columbus, Ohio: Charles E. Merrill, 1972), pp. 76–80.

95 John Stephen Morrison, *Developmental Optimism and State Failure in Africa: How to understand Botswana's relative success?*, Ph.D., University of Wisconsin-Madison, 1987.

(and failed) attempt to confront international economic forces and to prevail over them.[96]

The Zambian leadership of both Kaunda and Chiluba shares this defensive and aggressive ethos of state action against domestic opponents and hostile international economic forces. Domestic opposition was met with moves to close avenues of constitutional opposition politics, and global economic forces were confronted with (again, failed) attempts at shutting out these actors through policies of nationalization. In the case of Namibia the emergent leadership ethos appears to be evolving in a direction similar to that of Zimbabwe. Leys and Saul find in the evolution of SWAPO in exile the "…pathology of liberation politics" which centres on the paradox of "…the possibility, even likelihood, that the very process of struggling for liberation, especially by resort to force of arms, may generate political practices that prefigure undemocratic outcomes in the wake of revolutionary success."[97] How this paradox will play out within SWAPO and within Namibian politics remains to be seen. The new ruling elite in Malawi has yet to show its colours, but early indications are that Banda's style may be perpetuated.

The changing international system is providing a dramatically new context within which ruling parties have to cope. The end of the Cold War, the Third Wave of democratization, and the accelerating process of neo-liberal globalization is generating new crises of mobilization for the ruling parties in every country. In every country reviewed above, the problems of unemployment are huge, socio-economic inequalities persist, and even increase, the prospects of growth which creates jobs amidst more open international and regional competition are daunting, and in every case opportunities for alleviating the hardship of those at the bottom of the economic ladder are slim. Not surprisingly, labour unions are at odds with the rulers in every country. In Namibia confrontation with SWAPO is becoming overt, as is the case in Zimbabwe.[98] In Zambia the MMD has already toppled UNIP with the help of union support, leaving Chiluba in power, but unable to escape the constraints of IMF conditionality, and with virtually no means of improving the conditions of the losers in the capitalist economy. And even in Botswana, with the region's most prosperous economy, the BNF is drawing support from the urbanized and unionized workers at the expense of the ruling BDP.

---

96 Du Toit, *State Building and Democracy in Southern Africa*, pp. 140–148.

97 Colin Leys and John S. Saul, "Liberation without Democracy? The SWAPO Crisis of 1976", *Journal of Southern African Studies*, vol. 20, no. 1, March 1994, pp. 123–147, at 146.

98 *Africa Confidential*, vol. 35, no. 14, 15 July, 1994, p. 5; Herbert Jauch, "Tension Grows—labour relations in Namibia", *SA Labour Bulletin*, vol. 20, no. 4, August 1996, pp. 90–93.

Under such conditions of rising relative and even absolute scarcity, politics is likely to take on a zero-sum distributive character, easily susceptible to ethnic demand generation, thus far so successfully avoided by the BDP.

CONCLUSION

Botswana therefore appears to be the only case where the dominant party in the party system may serve to bridge the gap towards a viable liberal democratic system. The strong dominant party, the strong party system, the technocratic ideology, and the prevailing leadership ethos are favourable factors. It must be noted that an erosion of the leadership ethos and discipline, in the form of rising corruption and political intolerance, serves as an inhibiting factor.[99] In all the other cases, weaker ruling parties in weaker party systems are likely to invite extra-parliamentary opposition politics, and the leadership ethos of the powerholders are unlikely to be conducive to a democratic political culture and practice.

The emerging crisis of mobilization being generated by the changing international system is, however, likely to be the greatest challenge to democratic politics throughout Southern Africa. Whichever party commands power in any of these states is likely to find that a peripheral economy in a peripheral continent is unable to remotely meet voter expectations. Voters in the states are likely to find this condition immune to election returns—the constraining forces of the global economy apply to whoever rules. These voters may end up having to learn that they "...can vote but not choose".[100] Under such conditions voters could prefer to exit from electoral politics, and dominant parties may prefer to construct bridgeheads towards securing dominance behind the facade of electoralism and pseudodemocracy.

---

99   Kenneth Good, "Corruption and Mismanagement in Botswana: a Best-Case Example?", *The Journal of Modern African Studies*, vol. 32, no. 3, 1994, pp. 499–521.

100   Adam Przeworski, "The Neo-Liberal Fallacy", *Journal of Democracy*, vol. 3, no. 3, July 1992.

Chapter 8

THE TRANSFORMATION OF LABOR-BASED ONE-PARTYISM AT THE END OF THE 20TH CENTURY: THE CASE OF MEXICO

RUTH BERINS COLLIER

The general, comparative issue addressed in this volume concerns the democratization of one-party regimes—how, and the conditions under which, one-party regimes (or dominant or predominant party regimes) become more competitive. The issue I take up here is a little more specific: to problematize the democratization of a particular type of dominant-party regime, one in which the dominant party is a labor-based party (LBP), that is, a party with a core support base in the labor movement. I explore this issue by examining the case of Mexico.

Mexico is a lens for viewing a larger category of regimes in which LBPs embraced a constituency that consistently afforded them an electoral majority (or sometimes plurality) on the basis of which they stayed in power over a long period, sometimes, as in Mexico, more or less continually during much of this century. This chapter suggests that these majoritarian-LBP regimes face serious challenges at the end of the twentieth century, challenges which exert pressures on both of their two central features: the dominance of a single party and the support base of the party and indeed of the state in the labor movement. The present time, then, is not propitious for labor-based one-partyism, and in the case of Mexico, the regime is unlikely to survive, at least in its historical form.

The analysis of regime change must rely on both a structural story about the common challenges or crises confronting governing LBPs and an actor-based story about political strategies and political struggle. The structural factors are the transformations in the world economy that change the preferences of key groups and actors. However these are insufficient. Structures constrain, enable, or facilitate; but the outcome is also a product of political struggle. Put another way, regime change is an outcome of 1) a changing set of preferences affected by the new opportunities and constraints of the new economic conditions, 2) existing political institutions that afford certain kinds of capacities and possibilities, 3) conjunctural factors, including external shocks, and 4) the strategic calculations of the main actors.

The structural argument is straightforward and probably well known. In many countries throughout the world, LBPs were formed with the emergence of the new class structure that arose with an urban, commercial and industrial economy, most obviously with the formation of a proletarianized working class and the organization of labor unions. These LBPs were able to achieve majoritarian or (pre)dominant status in the context of a world economy in which the dynamism and the major economic models were based on the creation of national industrial capacity and national markets (models which variously took the form of Keynesianism, ISI, or central planning). These economic models were consistent with class settlements or class compromises, which could simultaneously address the problem of sustained production and protect workers from an untrammeled labor market. They thus could potentially provide the material base for majoritarian political coalitions that included the labor movement as a core constituency. The political success, and even dominance of different LBPs, then, was due to their ability to oversee different sorts of class settlements.

The economic conditions that facilitated a proliferation of governing LBPs began to change in the 1970s, with a fundamental reordering of the world economy that took place on several levels—the global division of labor, the location of production, and the internationalization of markets and production, as well as firm restructuring involving new patterns of subcontracting, production technologies, and labor processes. If the old pattern of national industrialization was based on fixed, dependable patterns of production, the new model oriented toward internationally competitive production saw flexibilization of, rather than rigidities in, the labor market as compatible with increasing production. The policy basis for class settlements was severely challenged, if not eliminated, and the material base for governing LBPs was substantially reduced. These changed conditions have produced various political challenges to the governing LBP. Many LBPs have, in one way or another, been forced into opposition for the first time after decades in which they held power—as seen most dramatically in the Communist bloc, but also, to a lesser extent, for example, in Scandinavia.

The new structural conditions have produced dilemmas and strategic questions for both LBPs and labor movements. Governing LBPs are often torn between economic restructuring policies and their labor constituencies, which oppose those policies. Similarly, party-affiliated labor movements face the dilemma of deciding whether to remain loyal to the party and retain access to power or to risk political opposition and marginalization. Both parties and union movements have tended to be internally divided in confronting the new situation. In some cases the labor movement has factionalized as it has struggled to devise a strategic response to the new economic orientation, where one has been adopted. Demand-side economic models, like ISI and Keynesianism, homogenized labor and provided the logic for national and centralized labor confederations as a relatively unitary political actor and coalition partner. Supply-side and more market-based economic models fragment and heterogenize labor according to market power, undermining the logic of national and centralized labor organizations.[1] Thus, part of the story about the national labor movement is, to different degrees, its disarticulation as a unitary actor.

THE MEXICAN DOMINANT-LBP REGIME

In Mexico, the dominant party virtually monopolized political office for six decades after its founding in 1929. Though non-democratic practices were hardly unknown, an electoral majority was largely sustained by consent, achieved through continual negotiation, exchanges, distribution, and co-optation, as well as an ideological appeal based on the Mexican Revolution. The core labor constituency was cemented during the presidency of Lázaro Cárdenas (1936–40), who mobilized labor support through a radical appeal that included collective land-holding in the countryside and, under some conditions, worker ownership and management, as well as support for unions as organizations and for workers in terms of their wage demands and conflict with capital. The party was organized by "sectors" based on collective membership through unions: the labor sector—unions of primarily blue-collar workers; the popular sector—unions of primarily public service workers as well as various professional and occupational groups; and the peasant sector—unions of peasants. Union leaders held positions in the party and often ran as Institutional Revolutionary Party (PRI) candidates.

A conservative reaction to the radical populism of Cárdenas followed, leading to a reordering of the alliance on terms less favorable to labor, but nevertheless maintaining union support and effecting a kind of class compromise. The party (now called the Institutional Revolutionary Party (PRI)) conservatized and expanded the class base of its support to achieve something approaching a coalition-of-the-whole, including most sectors of capital. This

---

1 Harry C. Katz, "The Decentralization of Collective Bargaining: A Literature Review and Comparative Analysis," in *Industrial and Labor Relations Review*, vol. 47, no. 1, Oct. 1993; and Kathleen Thelen, "Beyond Corporatism: Toward a New Framework for the Study of Labor in Advanced Capitalism," in *Comparative Politics*, vol. 27, no. 1, Oct. 1994.

multi-class coalition, which continued to include most of the labor movement as a core constituency, formed the basis for a well-institutionalized, dominant-party regime. On this basis, the government had the political resources to defeat both dissident union movements and any electoral opposition.[2]

In addition to these political and organizational resources, the inclusionary, multi-class coalition of the whole was underwritten by the import-substitution industrialization model of economic growth. ISI relied on the domestic market as the outlet for nationally produced industrial goods. As the wage level is a central factor in determining the size of a domestic market, this model provided the conditions for a class compromise between labor and management: profits and production were enhanced by union and government activity which would solve the collective action problem of competing workers and competing firms, allowing both to forgo a competitive compression of wages and instead to achieve rising real wages (and hence an expanding market) in line with productivity gains. Indeed, after a plunge in real wages that occurred with the conservative reaction to radical populism in the immediate post-Cárdenas years, real wages rose steadily from the beginning of the 1950s to the mid-1970s, during which time a relatively sustained and robust pattern of growth led many analysts to refer to the "Mexican miracle".

In emphasizing these points, I do not want to make short shrift of the degree to which the dominant-LBP regime in Mexico was a mechanism of control over the working class. The populist LBP in Mexico institutionalized an alliance that largely deprived the labor movement of autonomous action but retained it as a support group, providing legitimacy for a one-party regime. Furthermore, coercion was employed to maintain control when corporatist resources were insufficient. From the point of view of labor, the PRI was an ambiguous or double-edged alliance. It meant both that organized labor was "cut in" with respect to the governing coalition and that it was a subordinated coalition partner that had lost its autonomy of action. Both of these are important factors in the preferences of factions within both the PRI and the labor movement to retain or oppose the dominant-LBP regime in Mexico.

In the 1980s, Mexico dramatically reoriented its economic policy. For a number of reasons—including its large debt (Mexico's insolvency initiated the world debt crisis in 1982), the asymmetrical balance of power between capital and labor, and the unusual political capacity afforded the state by the

---

2   Ruth Berins Collier and David Collier, *Shaping the Political Arena* (Princeton: Princeton University Press, 1991), Chs 6 and 7.

dominant-LBP regime itself—the PRI government turned abruptly from a highly protectionist, interventionist ISI model to a liberal economic model based on market rather than state coordination, free trade, and international competitiveness. Starting in response to the 1982 crisis as a short-term stabilization program under IMF conditionality, by 1985 the model became a long-term commitment to fundamental economic restructuring.

The new set of economic policies, first undertaken during the De la Madrid presidency (1982–88), clashed with labor interests along lines now quite familiar. Wages were held down both as a stabilization measure and as a way to cut costs and boost international competitiveness. After decades of nearly constant growth, the six years of the De la Madrid presidency saw average real manufacturing wages reduced by almost 40 per cent.[3] The working class also felt the employment effects of the worst recession since at least the Great Depression and the brunt of fiscal austerity, which directly affected social spending. Finally, the government reduced subsidies on the prices of many wage goods that were important components of workers' consumption basket, and it embarked on an extensive privatization campaign, restructuring and downsizing important industrial sectors and annulling labor contracts.

The new economic context undermined the dominant-LBP regime, from both within and without. From without it produced opposition to the right and the left. On the right, the marketizers sought a more competitive regime as a way to institutionalize political access and ensure a more consistent neo-liberal economic policy without reversions to "populist excesses". The left similarly sought to mobilize influence through more democratic political channels in order to exert pressure on economic policy but in the opposite direction: to slow down and moderate liberalization. From within, the new economic context led to tensions and contradictions within the LBP, which tried to reformulate or restructure its constituency relations—to look for new bases of popular support and to refashion its relationship with its old labor constituency. It also led to pressures on the labor constituency to defect from the PRI.

We can analyse the process of regime change in terms of a game of strategic interactions of four main actors across three rounds, each round roughly corresponding to a presidential term but more importantly, each initiated by a crisis that affected strategic calculations of key actors. The actors consist of

---

3 James G. Samstad and Ruth Berins Collier, "Mexican Labor and Structural Reform Under Salinas: New Unionism or Old Stalemate?", in *The Challenge of Institutional Reform in Mexico*, Riordan Roett, ed. (Boulder and London: Lynne Rienner Publishers, 1995), p. 15.

three party/electoral actors (LBP, right, and left) and the labor movement. Though the former are riven by factions and divided over strategies, one can treat them as unitary actors in terms of a party position actually adopted. The labor movement, which cannot be seen as a faction within the PRI since some unions have remained autonomous from the party, cannot be treated similarly as a unitary actor. Indeed one of the points of this analysis will be to demonstrate the increasing factionalization of the labor movement as it has struggled to devise a response to the changing regime and new economic orientation.

The different rounds of the regime-change game reflect the changing strengths of actors brought about by "external" crises as well as by the way the regime change game was played and the particular successes of or contradictions in the strategies. The first round is characterized by the emergence of three projects for regime change. Multiple lines of cleavage and cooperation make the game a complex one. Two of these projects were adopted by economic liberalizers and one by resisters. In a very different cut, one was adopted by the "ins" (or the governing party) and the others by the "outs" (or opposition forces). The result is a fluid and multi-faceted pattern of similar and opposing interests describing alternative cleavage and alliance patterns and heightened by the divisions over strategy within all four actors.

ROUND ONE: THREE NEW PROJECTS

The first round was ushered in by the debt crisis of 1982 and the dramatic bank nationalization of the same year. In the reverberations, three projects for regime change were launched. Two of these projects were adopted by advocates of the change to neoliberal economic policies: private-sector groups in alliance with and working through the Partido Accion Nacional (PAN), and the dominant faction within the PRI allied with the president. The third, adopted after 1982 by defectors from the PRI and the left opposition parties, was part of a reaction against the neoliberal policies.

The Right   The first project for political liberalization was adopted by the PAN, the major opposition party in Mexico, and a newly politicized private sector. Though its oppositional weight had been minimal, for four decades the PAN represented an alternative on the political right of the PRI, opposing the PRI's "collectivist", corporatist, and populist orientation and appealing to a middle-class constituency under a banner of liberalism—both economic and political. It was thus an obvious political vehicle for private-sector opposition when state–business relations began to fray in the 1970s. During that decade, the state sector grew enormously at the same time that, in line with the emerging new global economy, the export-processing sector on the US border was also becoming a center of economic dynamism, along with a new group of northern industrialists oriented toward free markets and international integration. While these businessmen were particularly irked by the populist rhetoric and policies of the 1970s, the *coup de grâce* came with the 1982 bank nationalization, which in their eyes finally delegitimated a government based on a populist coalition.

With the influx of businessmen as new party militants (called *neopanistas*), the PAN was transformed from a loyal and compliant to an assertive opposition party. The PAN and its business supporters criticized the government as beholden to labor and mobilized to bring about a regime that would afford greater access to and influence over policy-making by the private sector. Such a regime had two requirements: first, the dissolution of the state–labor coalition; and second, a more competitive regime with room for a party that would represent business interests and had a possibility of winning elections. The PAN began to achieve some electoral success, particularly in the north, in the 1980s.

The LBP   The second project for regime change was adopted by the government itself after 1985. Like the businessmen in the PAN, the government recognized that a marketizing economic project was inconsistent with the labor support base of the state. The government no longer wanted to win or reproduce workers' and peasants' support with concessions that would protect them from the market. Rather, it wanted to impose market discipline on these sectors. Further, in the context of unpopular economic policies, the dominant-LBP regime was declining in its ability to perform its main function: providing legitimacy. The economic shock treatment had induced a deep recession, which generated substantial discontent and political opposition. And even though the PRI was still the majority party, the PAN's electoral inroads seemed to undermine its legitimacy.

The solution was to change the legitimacy claim of the regime. The old claim had been to revolutionary legitimacy. The dominant-party system had been based on a broad inclusionary coalition of the "revolutionary classes" and its most powerful ideological symbols had continued to make reference to the Mexican Revolution. In the 1980s, however, these symbols were no longer readily available to the government and the "revolutionary classes" were no longer a convenient base of support. The new claim to legitimacy would be a democratic claim.

The project for regime change involved two different shifts. First, a democratic claim to legitimacy necessitated a shift from a dominant-party regime to a more competitive regime. What was envisioned was not that the PRI would actually lose power, but that it would win it through more competitive elections and share it somewhat more. The new government project was for an unequal 2-plus (or 1.5-plus) party system based on a majoritarian PRI, a challenging PAN, which had never won as much as 20 per cent of the national vote and which basically shared the PRI's economic orientation, and a number of small, leftist parties that had long been a manageable feature of Mexican political life. This project envisioned that for the first time the PAN could actually win—and be allowed to win—some local, state, and congressional elections. It was reflected in the electoral law of 1986, which not only increased the representation of opposition parties, guaranteeing them a minimum of 30 per cent of the seats in the House of Deputies, but no longer discriminated against the emergence of a second strong party as had previous reforms. It did, however, include a "governability clause," which guaranteed a bare congressional majority to the largest party.[4]

The second shift was in the constituency of the PRI. Corresponding to the new direction of economic policy was a need to establish greater state autonomy from those sectors the state had been protecting through populist policies. The PRI's project envisioned that the terms of the state–labor alliance would be substantially restructured and the party would be more centrally based in the growing urban middle classes. This shift in the core constituency of the PRI was premised on the party's ability to retain the support of the popular sectors as a captive voting block: with no viable alternative, the popular sectors would continue to vote PRI.

Needless to say, not everyone in the party fell in line behind the new project. In particular, three groups opposed the new direction. The first of these were the traditional party bosses, whose power was not based on popular electoral support but was embedded in the web of clientelistic relationships which had constituted the conciliating, negotiating basis of the coalition-of-the-whole. They also resisted aspects of economic reform insofar as these might undercut the material base of these clientelistic relationships. The traditional sectors of the PRI, particularly the Labor Sector, also opposed the economic and political projects (see below). While these first two groups stayed within the party, the third ended up leaving the party, reflecting the way in which economic liberalization splintered coalitions and produced the basis for multi-party politics. These dissidents were a central part of the third project for political reform.

---

4   For a more detailed discussion, see Ruth Berins Collier, *The Contradictory Alliance* (Berkeley: University of California, Berkeley International and Area Studies, 1992), p. 100.

The Left   The third project for regime change emerged later, just before the 1988 elections. It was pursued by those opposed to the new economic policies—particularly to the adverse social consequences of their relatively rapid implementation. The main groups behind this project were a combination of the traditional left and a new group of dissenters who split from the PRI. The latter was led by Cuauhtémoc Cárdenas, who ran as an opposition candidate in 1988.

Sharing with the PAN an oppositionist stance, the new splinter group joined minority parties primarily on the left in opposing one-partyism and became champions of free and fair electoral competition. The Cárdenas forces also sought to loosen the state–labor alliance effected through the PRI. More than the PAN, they saw workers as a potential support base and competed with the PRI for this constituency, arguing that a party opposed to the government's economic policies would better serve workers' interests than loyalty to a party that had abandoned them with its new economic direction. The political project was thus similar to that of the PAN, but the economic connection was different: they favored regime change to increase the political access of market resisters rather than of marketeers.

At the last minute, the Cárdenas campaign had surprising success in the 1988 elections, outpolling the inveterate PAN, coming in a strong second in official returns, and claiming fraud and outright victory.

The Labor Movement   How did the labor movement position itself with respect to these projects for regime change? The labor movement confronted its own dilemma. A victim of neoliberalism, the union movement generally opposed the new economic policies but was hesitant to break with the PRI politically. Since no opposition party had ever won, opting for political opposition ran a high risk of political marginalization and even retaliation. Under the leadership of its venerable leader Fidel Velázquez, the dominant faction in the labor movement rejected all of the projects, opposing both a more competitive regime and an alteration of the state–labor alliance. Instead it fought a rear-guard action to preserve the old regime.

This position was the mirror image of the PRI project as most of the labor movement opposed regime change for the same reason that the "modernizers" within the PRI found it attractive: the party-affiliated labor movement derived its position through negotiation within the PRI; political competition and reform could weaken its position. In explaining this opposition, one must take due account of the Michelsian role of a leadership oligarchy, of corruption and co-optation, and of state control both through corporatist political resources and through overt coercion, in short, of what has come to be known in Mexico as *charrismo*. However, one must also recognize that the alternative to negotiation was not simply greater labor autonomy from state control, but also the concomitant lack of existing levels of state protection. With weak market power and relatively weak electoral power due both to the size of the organized working class and to the difficulty of effective oppositional politics, particularly the weaker sectors of the labor movement had relied on their ability—albeit limited—to negotiate from a position of being formally cut in on the governing coalition.

The *fidelista* position of fighting to preserve the state–labor coalition was the dominant, but not the only position within the labor movement. A small number of unions had a history of political independence and even opposition, and some, including the powerful and newly defecting petroleum workers, supported Cárdenas. Thus, divisions within the labor movement were beginning to widen, but the *fidelistas* were the largest faction and retained dominance within the movement and the leadership of the CTM, the largest union confederation, and of the CT, the national labor central.

In sum, all three projects for regime change had two central concerns. First, all wanted to move away from the traditional dominant-party regime, though the PRI's enthusiasm was bounded by its continued capacity to retain an electoral majority. Each project also envisioned altering or abandoning the state–labor coalition, the PAN and the PRI in order to eliminate populist exchanges and flexibilize the labor market, the PRD in order to remove a mechanism of control over, institutionalized PRI ties to, and cooptation of the labor movement. Again, the PRI showed ambivalence and internal divisions, given both the labor sector's electoral importance and the government's reliance on the labor movement for what had become annual tripartite pacts on economic policy. To the degree the opposition parties, and particularly the PRD, remained weak, the labor movement had a collective action problem regarding the option of going into overt opposition to the government, given the risk of political marginalization and perhaps retaliation. This dilemma helps explain the dominant faction's opposition to regime change and continued commitment to the old pattern of LBP dominance.

The reorienting event that ushered in the second round and triggered a change in strategic calculations was the 1988 national elections and the unanticipated strength of the left. According to official returns, the PRI, accustomed to winning at least three-quarters of the popular vote, claimed only the barest of majorities: 50.4 per cent. The PAN got 17 per cent, up only slightly from its previous 16 per cent in 1982, prior to the real onset of the economic crisis or the change in policy. An astounding 31 per cent was officially recognized as the vote for the Cárdenas forces. Blatant fraud left no question that the PRI actually failed to win a majority of votes and left at least credible the claim that Cárdenas actually won a plurality. This strong showing by the parties in the electoral front that had backed Cárdenas created an impetus for founding a new opposition party on the left, the PRD.

The 1988 elections, then, seemed to mark the emergence of a viable electoral force to the left of the PRI. Furthermore, despite the formal endorsement of most unions, the election results revealed a significant erosion of support among the PRI's traditional working-class base. This development had important strategic implications for both the PRI and the PAN. Before the elections neither had figured on a left opposition party moving successfully into a more competitive electoral arena, but each in different ways had seen itself as the beneficiary. These calculations were clearly called into question. In the new context, a competing line of cleavage was presented as an alternative to the axis of opposition versus government that was salient before the elections: an axis on which the PRI and PAN might cooperate not only on economic policy but also on limited political reform to stop the PRD, whose victory would be the worst alternative for either the PRI or the PAN.

The Left   With its unexpected success, the PRD faced fewer strategic contradictions than the other forces, yet was singularly unable to forge ahead as a united opposition. After 1988, the left was encouraged in its oppositional stance. The PRD became a strong voice for a regime-change project, as it now seemed that voters would in fact be willing to defect from their habitual voting patterns and victory seemed within reach. It took a hard line against cooperating with the PRI, instead pushing hard for electoral reform to ensure free and fair elections, from which it expected to be the major beneficiary. With a presence in the lower chamber, the PRD, along with a more divided PAN, became a substantial force in the politics around a new reform law. At issue was the elimination of electoral fraud in all its many forms, from initial registration procedures, final counts and electoral oversight to the campaign advantages that accrued to the PRI as the incumbent and "official" party: privileged access to and control over the media, access to financial resources, including state funds, and so forth. The attack on the PRI became more fundamental: a competitive regime could not be realized short of an opposition victory; and this was sometimes seen as requiring the elimination of a basically unreformable PRI.

The position opposing the state–labor alliance was also further elaborated. Like the PAN, the PRD saw an unfair electoral advantage given to the PRI by its relationship with labor in terms of the interpenetration of party and union leadership and the collective form of party membership by which workers belonging to most unions were automatically members of the PRI by virtue of the union's membership in the party. Unlike the PAN, the PRD also opposed the state–labor alliance as a mechanism of control, which deprived organized workers of political autonomy through which they could pursue their own interests effectively and take independent policy positions.

All in all, the PRD did not come out of this round in good shape. Despite its 1988 successes, it fared poorly in elections held during the next presidential term. In part this outcome reflected government harassment (see below). In part it reflected its own inability to forge a coherently organized party out of the electoral front that had supported the Cárdenas candidacy. Not all the parties joined the PRD, and among those that did, divisions remained. Beyond that, it proved difficult to establish links with a mass base and institutionalize a capacity for electoral mobilization. By the end of the next presidential term, this formidable challenger had been reduced to a distant third electoral force, unable to capture power at the level of a single state.

The Right   The PAN's strategic situation was more complicated. The 1988 election seemed to indicate that contrary to what it had anticipated, it was not the PAN that would be the main beneficiary of a more competitive regime, but the PRD, a party whose economic policies the PAN regarded as much more objectionable than those of the newly neoliberal PRI. The outcome of the 1988 election thus seemed to pose a contradiction between a more competitive regime on the one hand and both PAN electoral success and neoliberalism on the other. The strategic choice, therefore, was whether to cooperate with the PRI as neoliberal partners in perhaps limited political opening and reform, or to cooperate with the PRD as opposition partners in pushing for more radical regime change. During the course of the second round, despite splits within the party over this issue, the PAN opted for cooperation with the PRI on issues like electoral reform and negotiated outcomes of disputed elections, often settled to the advantage of the PAN.

The PAN fared considerably better than the PRD during the second round, both in its organizational activities and in the corresponding electoral results. In several states where it had traditional strength, the PAN's victories effectively eliminated the dominant-party regime and effectuated a two-party system on this sub-national level.

The LBP   For the PRI, the unexpected rise of the PRD exposed the contradictions of its project of pursuing neoliberalism via greater party competition. The PRD challenged both the new policy direction and the PRI's electoral support base. It seemed that the PRI could no longer rely on a captive mass support base in the labor movement now that a surprisingly viable, potentially victorious alternative existed which could attract workers in a way the PAN could not. In fact, there had been substantial defection of workers in the 1988 elections.

Despite resulting pressure to moderate the hard-line approach to the economy, particularly from sizable and powerful party factions that favored such a move, the dominant PRI faction ensured that the policy orientation remained unchanged. What, then, was the response of the PRI with respect to the twin issues of party competitiveness and the state–labor alliance?

With respect to the former, the PRI did four things in the first years of the new Salinas government. First, it tried to recreate the strategic environment in which the old project made sense through a series of moves to ensure that the PAN and not the PRD would be the main opposition faced by the PRI. These included manipulation of electoral machinery to recognize PAN electoral victories but reject PRD victories, and harassment of the PRD, the scope of which is suggested by the large number of unsolved murders of PRD activists.

Second, from a position of still substantial strength, the PRI negotiated yet another electoral law. Its logic revealed that the PRI was continuing its strategy toward a more competitive regime while simultaneously maximizing the possibilities of its continued control of the government. This time, however, the electoral framework would have to respond to the new form of electoral challenge. If the 1986 law supported a change in the status of the PRI from a dominant to a majoritarian party, the new law protected the PRI's governing position by attempting to accommodate its possible decline to only a plurality party.[5]

Third, as it had in the past, the PRI undertook yet another attempt at internal party reform to renovate the party, to make it more competitive and advance the shift in its support base. On the one hand, the reforms actually implemented fell far short of the rhetoric of democratizing the party, and the labor sector was once again successful in defeating any attempt to decorporatize the party by moving from sectoral organization and collective membership to territorial organization and individual membership. On the other hand, the renewal process had some results, with the selection of more attractive candidates and a set of surprising electoral turn-arounds in off-term elections during the Salinas term.

Fourth, the PRI government attempted to increase its appeal to the unorganized lower classes, often in the informal sector, whose interests were

---

5 The analysis of this law can be found in ibid, pp. 142–4.

not in conflict with economic restructuring in the same way as those of unionized workers and peasants. To this end, the government launched National Solidarity Program (PRONASOL), a major community develop-ment program which counteracted some of the effects of neoliberalism on poor communities and which was often targeted at communities where the PRI wanted to increase its electoral support.

Strategy toward the state–labor alliance had to navigate carefully between the new economic policy and the newly heightened concern with retaining labor support. Despite initial speculation that as a weak president lacking legitimacy Salinas would actively court the traditional PRI constituencies, barely a month after occupying the presidency Salinas began a series of dramatic moves against traditional labor bosses—including one of the most powerful of them, the long-time head of the petroleum workers' union—when they ran afoul of government plans for industrial restructur-ing or privatization. The old constituency in its traditional form would not be preserved; yet political support was of central importance for the PRI.

Out of this concern came an attempt to redefine a new relationship between the party and its labor base that was called the New Unionism. The goal of the New Unionism was to replace the old corporatist basis of labor support with a new framework for preserving or renewing that support while simultaneously reducing the influence of organized labor in national politics and advancing economic restructuring. Unions were to be more internally representative and, as such, better interlocutors for generating working-class support than the traditional, often oligarchic unions. A com-panion component was the idea of the "participatory firm" that would emphasize cooperative labor relations and worker input to improve produc-tivity. The model was a "new union" that was oriented toward firm-level issues of production and away from national-level negotiations over state concessions and protection.[6]

The strategy of the PRI during this round was partially successful. First, aided by the end of the economic crisis, Salinas became an enormously pop-ular president, and by 1991 the PRI seemed to have recovered from the 1988 debacle, winning a landslide victory in mid-term elections. Second, with the decline in the popularity of the PRD, the PRI's project for a 1.5-plus or 2-plus party regime, in which the PRI faced an electoral challenge primarily from the PAN (a party with which it had basic economic agreement), seemed

---

6 Samstad and Collier, pp. 18–21.

back on track. On the other hand, internal party reform had been limited, and the New Unionism was fraught with contradictions that would render it unable to constitute an appropriate framework for a reconfigured labor constituency: union democracy had the obvious potential of producing a more militant unionism that might challenge firm restructuring, confront the state's neoliberal policies, and politically oppose the PRI.

The Labor Movement   The labor movement was deeply divided by the differential effect of market logic on workers in different economic sectors. The majority and minority factions of the first round were reinforced in round two, and a third faction got outlined more distinctively. This last, constituted by a small number of unions, fell in behind the New Unions, which in many ways grew out of the model already in place in one of these unions—the Telephone Workers' Union (STRM) under Francisco Hernández Juárez. These workers were in an unusual position in Mexico. They were not fundamentally threatened by industrial restructuring but able to adapt to it and even benefit from any resulting revitalization of the sector. Furthermore, the union was already internally democratic and had already opted out of the corporatist ties to the party, though the leadership individually supported the government and demonstrated a capacity to perform the desired interlocutory function with the rank and file. Few unions, however, were in this position, and Hernández Juárez was unable to extend his leadership over the larger union movement on the basis of this new model.[7]

Another group of unions confronted their firms and the government over economic restructuring and ended up (or remained) in political opposition to the PRI government. Both democratic unions and bureaucratized, oligarchic boss-led unions were in this confrontational category. Several of these unions were attacked by the state, quite literally when the military invaded the personal compound of the leader of the petroleum workers' union. Together, the actions of the government, firms, and traditional labor leaders severely limited the space available for confrontation.

The third response was retrenchment: a continuation of the strategy to preserve the state–labor alliance and the political position of organized labor within the PRI. This position was most associated with the traditional leaders of the national confederations which integrated the smaller, weaker unions in less dynamic or modern sectors. These labor centrals had most depended on the political connections of the old alliance, and these leaders had most benefited from that alliance through their personal position within the PRI.

---

7   Samstad and Collier, pp. 21–4.

Attempting to demonstrate their political indispensability to the PRI government by acceding to the main outlines of economic policy, supporting the government on firm restructuring, and even entering into a series of annual tripartite pacts which helped to stabilize the economy, the dominant PRI-affiliated faction managed to force something of a compromise to the extent it blocked plans to abolish the "sectoral" organization of the party or reform the labor law.

In sum, at the end of the Salinas presidency, with the partial success of its project, the PRI looked poised to do well in the upcoming elections, especially as it had overseen something of an economic recovery and had chosen an attractive presidential candidate. The vulnerability of the project was that, despite its apparent renewed popularity, the party had hardly been successful in consolidating a middle-class or an informal-sector constituency and it had failed to reconfigure a new basis for attracting labor support; indeed for the important, annually negotiated tripartite economic pacts the government continued to rely on cooperation with traditional labor bosses—those who most directly embodied the old pattern of labor support and exchange that the new project sought to supersede.

ROUND THREE: MULTIPLE CRISES AND NEW LEFT CHALLENGES

Round Three began with a multiplicity of crises in quick succession at the beginning of the Zedillo presidency. These can be grouped as three sorts of crises that affected the strategies of the major players. The first was the economic crisis and collapse following the December 1994 currency devaluation, which simultaneously got Zedillo's presidency off to a devastating start, as it was virtually his first policy move, and discredited Salinas, whose economic policies were directly implicated. In 1995, according to a government report, the gross domestic product declined by nearly 7 per cent, purchasing power dropped 15 to 20 per cent, unemployment more than doubled, and 5 million more Mexicans joined those classified as living in extreme poverty, bringing the figure to nearly a quarter of the population.[8] The second was the legitimacy crisis of the PRI regime, which not only had failed economically but had to endure nearly daily revelations of major scandals, including unsolved political murders (the most notable of which were the PRI's presidential candidate and secretary general), high-level corruption that included Salinas' brother, and

---

8   Latin American Data Base, *SourceMex*, 7, no. 14, April 3, 1996, p. 7.

the encroaching power and influence within state agencies of drug traffickers.

Third, left-wing opposition social movements emerged in reaction to the consequences of the new economic model. Most important was the rise of two novel movements: the Zapatistas, a peasant-based armed guerrilla movement (EZLN), and a largely middle-class debtors movement (El Barzón)—as well as the subsequent appearance of another, more radical guerrilla group. The Zapatistas' goals of full democracy in Mexico, an end to the government's neoliberal economic policies, and land and freedom for the indigenous peoples, combined with their skillful use of the Internet, and the personal appeal of Subcomandante Marcos, initially generated an enormous amount of sympathy both domestically and internationally. El Barzón, founded by farmers in 1993, rapidly spread to urban small producers and consumer credit card debtors. This organization of small debtors unable to repay their loans because of the high interest rates sustained by Mexican economic policy currently claims over a million members in all of Mexico's states.

Like Round Two, then, this round started out with the appearance of a new and unexpected player on the left and a crisis of legitimacy for the ruling party. Unlike the prior round, this one is characterized by economic crisis rather than by some degree of economic recovery. How did these crises affect the strategies of the major players?

The Right   The PAN started this round much stronger than it did the previous round, having moved from a disappointing third place outcome in the 1988 election to a significant second place showing in 1994. In the course of this round, the PAN has emerged as a viable challenger to the PRI. Compared to the PRD it has benefited not only from better treatment by the PRI but also from the greater "political mobility" of the constituencies it is wooing from the PRI. Unlike the popular sectors to whom the PRD looks, the middle classes, which are the PAN's natural constituency, are precisely the groups that the PRI never integrated into the party organizationally.

The party's strategy from the earlier round—fighting hard to contest elections while simultaneously negotiating with the PRI in order to hold local office—paid off, and party divisions seem to have become less intense. The PAN's electoral success has continued. Of the five gubernatorial races in 1995, the party won by large margins in three states and lost narrowly in the other two. In municipal elections the PAN has also performed well, winning several state capitals and thirteen of Mexico's twenty largest cities. Areas of the country are now seen as essentially having local two-party regimes, and the PAN claims to rule a third of the Mexican population at the local level.

The Left   The PRD has become an established force, but it started this round in a weak position by performing poorly in the 1994 election. In Round Two, while it had maintained a position of intransigent political opposition, the strategic temptation had been to be moderate programmatically: its emergence in 1988 as a potential national winner was an incentive to attract the center in order to put together a majority, while maintaining a harder, more principled line on political reform. By Round Three, however, much had changed. The PRD's electoral support had substantially declined, and it was being outflanked on the left by the eruption of new social movements, presenting a more dramatic and nonelectoral opposition. The PRD remains the primary electoral player on the left but has been divided over the strategy of appealing toward the center or radicalizing and allying with these new forces, building a core constituency, and capitalizing on the discontent.

Some cooperation has begun between the PRD and the left social movements, though most instances have taken place at the initiative of the EZLN, rather than the PRD. Following a national and international "consultation", which took place both conventionally and electronically (over the Internet), in January 1996 the EZLN called for the formation of two civic political organizations: the FZLN and the FAC-MLN. In July, the EZLN held a conference on state reform which gathered delegates from the PRD, Coordinadora Intersindical (see below), El Barzón, and other organizations. Following the conference, the EZLN announced the establishment of "formal ties" for some type of cooperation with the PRD in the 1997 mid-term elections to prevent the electoral domination of the right. The PRD has also stepped up its cooperative efforts. Cárdenas, for example, initially took a leading role in the FAC-MLN. The PRD has also undertaken new initiatives toward the labor movement by creating a new secretariat for union affairs in its executive committee and by participating in the dissident unions' demonstrations.

The Labor Movement   In Round Three the tripartite division of the labor movement has increasingly institutionalized, but at the same time labor opposition has become more marked. Under the leadership of Hernández Juárez, the "New Unions" were transformed and reorganized as the Foro. The Foro, representing more than two million workers from both CT-affiliated and independent unions, has moved from cooperation to substantial opposition to the government, seeking the democratization of the labor movement, autonomy from the PRI, and a new economic policy which defends jobs and salaries. It has engaged in several large-scale acts of defiance against the PRI and "official" unionism, including: a massive protest against a bill to reform the social security system, a reform which had the support of the CT, the CTM, and the PRI's labor-sector deputies; an independent May Day march despite threats of expulsion from the CT when Velázquez cancelled the traditional parade for the second year in a row; and abstention from the CT's internal elections.

The historically more independent and confrontational unions (and democratic currents within official unions) have also found a new organizational form in the Coordinadora Intersindical, which was created to organize the first independent May Day rally. The Coordinadora and Foro unions largely share the same goals, though the Coordinadora has taken a more aggressive stance against the government and has shown more willingness to ally with forces on the left.

On the other hand, the "official" unions have retained their strategy of cooperating with the government and affiliating with the PRI. At the same time, this faction of the labor movement has continued to exert pressure from the inside to preserve the old political relationships as much as possible. These unions played an important role in resisting a change in the labor law which would allow the flexibilization that business leaders propose, and they impeded the complete privatization of social security. However, they have failed to influence the overall direction of economic policy.

The LBP   The PRI has still not resolved the set of dilemmas it has faced all along. The party began this round severely weakened. Far from winning the anticipated landslide in the 1994 elections, the PRI managed only to repeat its officially declared 1988 performance, winning about half the votes. This time, the election results were not highly contested, but the party faced a serious legitimacy crisis as it began to sink ever deeper in a web of scandal and drug associations. Given a constrained situation at the beginning of this round, Zedillo has been deepening the PRI strategy of attempting to offset a firm commitment to neoliberal economic policy by identifying, beyond Salinas, with the project of furthering political reform and multi-party democracy. However, he has often faced intransigence from within the PRI and his own democratic conduct has proven inconsistent. With cross-pressures and the party deeply divided, political reform has seen advances and stalls.

He has pursued reform at three levels: in the party; in the relationship between the party, the state, and the presidency; and in the electoral arena. Within the party, Zedillo vowed to end the *dedazo*, indicating he will not choose party candidates for political office, including his successor, and his administration has taken steps to correct abuses by some of the reform-resistant local parties. He has also stated a commitment to alter the balance of power between the president and legislature, proposing congressional approval of major judicial appointments and congressional oversight of government spending through a new auditing agency.[9] Finally, Zedillo has taken credit for the electoral reform which the parties finally agreed upon in August, 1996, including some important measures—a directly elected mayor for Mexico City, better electoral oversight, and acts to distribute financial and media resources somewhat more equitably among the parties. The latter measures were later reversed to some degree by the PRI's congressional majority.

The PRI embrace of reform continues to be marked by ambivalence, both because of divisions within the party and because of the conflicting incentives derived from the party's strategic situation. Particularly at state and local levels, the PRI has continued to commit campaign and electoral fraud and to sanction police repression of opposition movements. In Zedillo's first year, over sixty PRD members were murdered.[10] After poor PRI showings in a string of elections in 1995, Zedillo seemed to be eager to regain the support of the hard-line factions within the party. This orientation was evident in the defense of the governor of Tabasco (who was accused of wild violation of campaign spending limits), in the premature closing down of the investigation of the "tortilla king" scandal (which implicated Zedillo in allowing huge subsidies to the PRI-supporting owner of Maseca), and in the setbacks in the new electoral law, which were demanded by groups within the party whose opposition erupted in the move to open the party to broader participation.

The key to the party's dilemma remains its constituency relationships in the face of neoliberal policies. Once again the government has been trying to reconfigure the relationship with its labor base, but a new formula remains elusive. The new attempt—dubbed the "New Labor Culture"—seems even more vague than the New Unionism, and many unions have rejected it. At the same time, the government has made some approach to the more *traditional* labor sectors and continues rhetorically to claim a commitment to the historic state–labor alliance, though it has not displayed any willingness to come forward with substantial corresponding economic concessions. Nevertheless, the growth of pressure from the union movement combined with the PRI's 1995 electoral losses has created some degree of instability within the party leadership, reflecting the changing influence of different factions.

All in all, the PRI has not fared well in this round. Far from winning back the support of dissident unions, which are centered in the more modern

---

9 Wayne Cornelius, *Mexican Politics in Transition* (San Diego: University of California, San Diego Center for U.S.–Mexican Studies, 1996), p. 36.

10 *Latin American Weekly Report*, 95, no. 38, 10/5/95, p. 445.

sectors of the economy, union opposition has continued to grow. The PRI remains politically dependent—both for electoral support and the annual renewal of the tripartite economic pacts—on the most traditional labor sector, which has opposed Zedillo's political reforms. The inability to respond to the multiple crises that began this round can be seen in opinion polls which predict a rather stunning electoral defeat for the PRI in the 1997 off-term congressional elections and in the first direct election of the mayor of the Federal District.

CONCLUSION

The current era is a difficult one for governing labor-based parties, and especially for labor-based party-dominant regimes. Changes in the world economy—and, in countries like Mexico, pressures deriving from the debt crisis—altered the interests and preferences of many state and social actors and thereby produced incentives to change the economic model, one that had been compatible with a form of compromise or settlement between capital and labor. These changes may have two major consequences for dominant-LBP regimes. First, they may challenge the regimes' base of support in the labor movement, which was consistent with the old economic model, but finds little scope in the new neoliberal model. Indeed, economic liberalization and the flexibilization of labor markets has contributed to the fragmentation of the labor movement, complicating its mobilization from above and from below as a popular electoral constituency. Second, by removing the material base for class compromise, the economic pressures may reduce the space for consensus and give rise to political opposition, thereby undermining one-partyism and producing more open political contestation. Thus, structural factors have challenged both the labor base of the state and party dominance.

Over the last decade, both of these effects have been playing out in Mexico, where the dominant-LBP regime is being undermined from within as well as without. From without, economic pressures have given rise to opposition from both the right and the left. From within, they have led to tensions and contradictions within the LBP, which has tried to reformulate or restructure its constituency—to look for new bases of electoral support and to refashion its relationship with its labor base. Thus structural changes have led to a process of regime change, an alteration in both the pattern of contestation and the support base of the state and of the regime, but the process and outcome of regime change must be seen in terms of the strategic interaction of the major actors, as they respond to the new economic conditions and engage in political struggle over both economic policy and political reform.

The above discussion analysed this political struggle as a "regime-change game" that was played by four key actors which took positions on these salient economic and political issues as each sought to change or retain the status quo with respect to economic policy (to radicalize or resist marketization) and the nature of the regime (LBP dominance, encompassing the twin issues of 1) the labor movement's political position—its coalitional and party affiliation and its status as a support base for the state, and 2) party competition and the degree of political contestation). Simplifying and dichotomizing the two dimensions produces four distinct combinations occupied by the different players while at the same time showing the possibility of different alliances, lines of cooperation, or coinciding strategies with the changing salience of the two issues. The actors and their positions on economic and political change are summarized in Fig. 8.1.

Economic

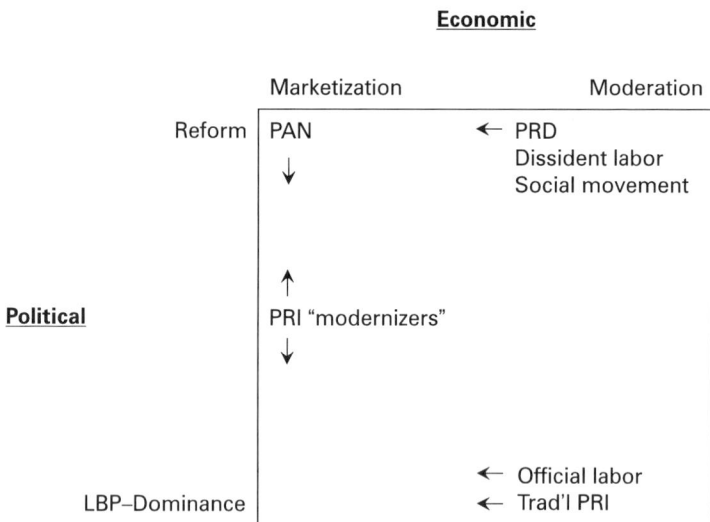

Figure: 8.1: Actors' Positions on Reform

Each of the three rounds of play began with a crisis—an exogenously or endogenously derived shock—that altered the resources and strategic calculations of the actors. As a result, fluctuating cleavages and patterns of cooperation emerged across the rounds. In Round One there was some tendency toward a horizontal line of cleavage over political reform, pitting the outs versus the ins, along political differences, a cleavage that emphasized the newly emerging opposition of both the PAN and what would become the PRD, while the governing PRI, internally split on political reform and also divided on economic policy, was only beginning to move, hesitantly and with enormous ambivalence, toward a position of political reform. In Round Two, the alternate line of cleavage along economic policy lines became more prominent in light of the PRD "threat" commonly felt by both the PRI and PAN, which therefore moved toward cooperation on political reform. Having started this round as a strong electoral challenger, the PRD remained firm and contentious on political reform but tended toward economic moderation to maximize what had appeared to be its promising electoral base. Patterns of cleavage and cooperation changed again in Round Three, with the prominence of new social movements spawned by the adverse consequences of the changed economic policy. These social movements have radicalized and potentially strengthened the position previously occupied primarily by the PRD and a minority, dissident current within the labor movement. They have produced a dynamic for the growth and revitalization of that pole, especially to the degree that its "occupants" can move toward cooperative or concerted action. At the same time, all three parties have cooperated in furthering political reform, though a newly assertive posture by the traditional forces within the PRI has recently been obstructive.

Over the rounds of the regime-change game, then, different patterns of cooperation and conflict emerged with some movement in certain directions in response to changes in the strategic environment as well as internal divisions: 1) PAN: vertical movement down somewhat, to the extent the party backs away from political reform to prevent a PRD victory; 2) PRI: vertical movement alternately toward and away from political reform, in response to a legitimacy crisis, impending electoral adversity, and the party's internal distribution of power; 3) PRD: horizontal movement on the axis of economic reform as the party is presented with the possibilities of appealing to a larger electoral constituency in the center *versus* capitalizing on the vigor of social movements on the left; 4) official labor: horizontal movement right, in the trade-off between retaining the state–labor alliance and accepting—indeed trying to appear indispensable in implementing—market reforms; in addition, there has been increasing vertical movement upward as cooperating unions defect to a more oppositionist stance.

The course of regime change, then, has been characterized by uncertainty and strategic fluctuations as actors respond to crises that initiate each new round and alter their calculations. At the same time, a secular trend of regime change has been evident across the rounds. With respect to economic policy, of course, the resisters have been unable to deflect what has generally been a dramatic, steady, and unidirectional move toward marketization. Similarly, and partly in response to this economic path, one can observe rather gradual but steady movement toward regime change. First, during the course of the decade-and-a-half analysed here, party competition and political contestation has increased. It is unlikely that dominant-partyism will last in Mexico. Second, the traditional state–labor alliance and the labor base of the state is being altered if not superseded. Step-by-step the long-standing LBP regime in Mexico is drawing to an end.

POSTSCRIPT

In the summer of 1997, after the above was written, a new round of play was inaugurated. Once again, elections changed the balance of power among the key actors and constituted a major step in our story of the demise of the labor-based one-partyism.

The July elections—for the Chamber of Deputies, one-quarter of the Senate, seven governors, and assemblies and municipal governments in one-third of the thirty-two states—dealt the PRI its most decisive defeat. It won just 39 per cent of the vote for the federal lower house (compared to about 26 per cent each for the PAN and the PRD), failing to retain a majority of the seats (though, due to the distortions written into the electoral law, being overrepresented with 48 per cent). Furthermore, it won only 38 per cent of the Senate seats contested and was rejected decisively by the voters of the Federal District, where newly introduced municipal elections gave an overwhelming victory to Cuauhtémoc Cárdenas as the new mayor and to his PRD in the new municipal assembly.

This dramatic defeat for the world's longest-standing dominant party represents a continuation of the trend toward greater electoral competitiveness and multi-partyism; but beyond incrementalism, it represents a qualitative change in the Mexican regime. First, of course, it means that for the first time the PRI does not hold a majority in the lower house, which will thus no longer function as a reliable handmaiden for the president: an important step has been taken toward a real separation of powers along with effective multi-partyism. Second, the elections represent an important victory for the PRD, which not only won a landslide in the Federal District, but edged out the PAN in the distribution of seats in the Chamber of Deputies. The PRD comeback thereby constitutes a major setback, or even defeat, for the project the PRI pursued in the intervening decade since the Cárdenas challenge originally emerged: a project to steer the regime toward a 2-plus party system based on the PRI and the PAN.

This new balance of forces will affect coalitional incentives and patterns of cooperation and conflict, but the outcome remains very much in flux. On the one hand, a PRI minority in the Chamber of Deputies is an incentive to the opposition to cooperate in order to democratize the regime and make the legislature an effective actor in policy-making. The area of "political" policy seems the most auspicious for such cooperation. The opposition set a new precedent in presenting a response to the president's state of the union address, has mounted a concerted effort to distribute committee seats in a way that diminishes PRI influence, and may find an opportunity to cooperate on the issue of government corruption.

Yet in many areas the opposition remains programmatically divided. The still emerging tax reform is an example: the opposition parties initially pledged concerted action to reduce the VAT to 10 per cent, even constituting a formal pact to that end; but in short order divisions over tax policy emerged and one cannot predict what the ultimate alignment on this or other substantive issues will be. On many issues the PRI will likely remain the focal point of coalition formation, forming ad hoc alliances with either of the major opposition parties depending on the issue because in some ways it programmatically occupies a "middle" position.

Important changes in the political affiliation of the labor movement may also be under way. The strategic dilemma of the labor movement has centered around the disadvantages of supporting a party that offers fewer and fewer concessions and the risks of political marginalization in supporting an opposition party. With the changing balance of power between the PRI and the PRD, these calculations begin to look quite different. In June, Fidel Velázquez died, opening up room for a more thorough-going leadership change and a shift in partisan linkages of the CTM and CT. Even before June, calls came from within the CTM for loosening ties to the PRI; and while the CTM closed ranks behind the PRI for the elections themselves, the electoral outcome has given greater impetus to the dissident faction. Furthermore, Hernández Juárez has continued to organize the Foro Sindical Unitario (FSU) as a rival to the CT and CTM structure. Thus, challenges to the corporatist ties between the labor movement and the PRI continue to mount both from changes within the PRI-affiliated labor organizations and from the growth and activism of those that are more autonomous.

The regime-change game, then, continues. Labor-LBP ties are loosening; multi-partyism is increasingly becoming effective. In a certain sense, Mexico is now characterized by several party systems: a PRI–PAN two-party system primarily in the north; a PRI–PRD two-party system primarily in the south; a three-party system at the national level and in the Federal District. The contours of the emerging balance of forces and patterns of alignment are fluid, heightened by factionalism and dissension within the PRI, including party defections. Patterns of coalition formation may remain very much in flux, shifting on an ad hoc basis. The certainty is the more stable trend in evidence since the debt crisis of 1982—another step has been taken in the playing out of a regime-change game from labor-based one-partyism towards a regime in which the PRI is neither the dominant party nor a labor-based party, at least in the same way or to the same degree.

Acknowledgement
I would like to acknowledge the research and editorial assistance of Benjamin Goldfrank.

Chapter 9

THE MEXICAN PARADOX: NEOLIBERALISM AND LABOR ENTRENCHMENT IN MEXICO'S RULING PARTY[1]

MARIA LORENA COOK

INTRODUCTION

Worldwide trends toward trade liberalization and economic competitiveness in the global economy would seem to pose a fundamental challenge to dominant labor-based political parties. Most of these parties established their links with the labor movement under very different conditions from those that predominate today. Labor support was sought by political parties during a period when the industrial working class was an important force in society and when national economies were more oriented toward import-substitution industrialization than toward export-promotion as a basis for national economic growth and development. Today's pressures to reduce the role of the state in the economy, deregulate labor markets, flexibilize working conditions, and reduce labor costs in production undermine the basic terms of the pact established between state/parties and the labor movement. In this sense, it is important to ask how is the new global economic environment affecting the ability of dominant labor-based parties to retain power? The answer is significant not only for labor's role in national political systems, but also for the nature of democracy and the prospects for economic growth and development in dominant labor-party systems.

The Mexican case is an important one to examine in this regard due to both the longevity of its labor-based dominant party regime and the extent of its economic liberalization and restructuring over the last decade. While Mexico has undergone a rapid opening of its economy and sought integration with the United States and Canada via the North American Free Trade Agreement (NAFTA), the Institutional Revolutionary Party (PRI), which has been in power since 1929, continues to dominate the federal legislature and the executive. Moreover, the PRI has retained the corporatist sectoral structure of the party in which labor continues to play an important role, in spite of recent efforts to curtail its influence. Given the tremendous changes that Mexico is currently undergoing in both the political and economic arenas, it

---

1 This chapter was written in February 1997, and therefore analyses developments in Mexico only up to that point.

THE AWKWARD EMBRACE   245

may be too early to declare definitively what the fate of the PRI and its relationship with the labor movement will be. Nonetheless, this chapter will attempt to answer the general question of whether labor-based parties must shed their labor base in order to remain dominant, by examining the recent evolution of labor's role in the Mexican PRI and the reasons for and implications of this "Mexican paradox"—the entrenchment of labor interests in the ruling party despite the country's continuing commitment to neoliberal economic reform.

MEXICO'S ECONOMIC AND POLITICAL REFORMS: THE IMPACT ON ORGANIZED LABOR AND CORPORATISM

Labor has been an important part of the Mexican political system since the early 1920s, when President Calles forged an alliance with the Mexican Regional Labor Confederation (*Confederación Regional Obrera Mexicana*, CROM) and made its leader, Luis Morones, his labor minister. The labor–state–party relationship was further institutionalized in 1936 under President Lázaro Cárdenas, who created the precursor to the Institutional Revolutionary Party (*Partido Revolucionario Institucional*, PRI) with the formation of the Party of the Mexican Revolution (*Partido de la Revolución Mexicana*). Cárdenas gave this party the sectoral composition (labor, peasant, and middle class sectors) that largely continues to define the PRI today. Since that time labor organizations have maintained a close and dependent relationship with the state and the ruling party, in spite of periodic tensions.[2] This "official" labor sector has played an important role in supporting the Mexican government and in turning out its members to vote for the PRI in electoral contests.[3] In return it has received material subsidies and support from the state against challengers from within the labor movement, and its members have been able to establish a presence in the political system through appointments to governorships and government administrative agencies as

---

2 It is this formal incorporation of the labor sector in the ruling party to which I apply the term "corporatist" throughout this chapter. The representation of labor, business, and government interests in periodic national accords on economic and wage policy also merit this label, but this is a more recent phenomenon, dating from 1987.

3 The "official" labor sector refers to those labor organizations affiliated with the PRI and which are represented in congress and party positions. Among the most important of these organizations in numerical and political terms is the CTM, but this category also includes smaller confederations and national industrial unions such as the oil, railroad, textile, and sugar workers, among others, and the federation of government employee unions. These organizations are all grouped within the umbrella Labor Congress (*Congreso del Trabajo*, CT), which also includes some independent unions.

well as through PRI electoral candidacies at municipal, state, and federal levels. Indeed, many analysts have attributed Mexico's remarkable political stability to the state's early incorporation of the labor movement into the PRI.

In recent years this close relationship between the government, the party, and the labor movement has been challenged. Since this relationship was based in large part on the state's ability to distribute material and symbolic rewards to its supporters, the debt-based economic crisis of the 1980s and the opening of the economy in the late 1980s and 1990s greatly constrained the state's ability to continue to play this role. The 1980s in particular were marked by dramatic real wage decline, privatization, widespread industrial restructuring that led to layoffs and the forced flexibilization of labor relations, the decline of the heavily-unionized manufacturing work force, the weakening of union control over wages, benefits, and working conditions, and the undermining of the strike as an instrument to defend worker interests. The clear inability of trade unions to secure wage increases and to defend the interests of their members during this period further undermined support within the union movement for the labor leadership. This development would further weaken the labor sector as it fought to retain its privileged relationship with the state, especially in the aftermath of the 1988 presidential and congressional elections, in which much of the PRI's labor constituency voted for the opposition for the first time. Mexico's basic shift in economic development strategy—from import-substitution to export-oriented industrialization—during the 1980s and 1990s also altered the balance of power among social forces in the country. The business sector, which in Mexico had always been somewhat estranged from the government and largely subordinate, was now involved in a "new alliance" with the state.[4] Whereas in the past the Mexican government had played the role of mediator between the interests of capital and labor, it was now clearly operating in defense of capital and acting in ways that undermined labor interests.

Political developments in this period were also undermining the close relationship between the state and labor. The number of protests over electoral fraud were increasing during the mid-1980s, especially among supporters of the conservative opposition National Action Party in the north of the country. The largest left challenge to the PRI occurred in 1988, when Carlos Salinas de Gortari declared victory after a highly controversial

---

4   María de los Angeles Pozas, *Industrial Restructuring in Mexico: Corporate Adaptation, Technological Innovation, and Changing Patterns of Industrial Relations in Monterrey* (La Jolla, Calif.: Center for U.S.–Mexican Studies, 1993).

contest against Cuauhtémoc Cárdenas in which electoral fraud was alleged. These external challenges to the PRI's hegemony led to internal questioning regarding the failure of the party's sectors to deliver votes and the need to "modernize" the party, which implied restructuring the party without sectoral representation. The peak of this threat to labor's role within the PRI and the greatest tension between the government and the labor movement occurred under the Salinas administration (1988–94). Under Salinas, the party's leaders attempted to restructure the PRI in a way that would grant representation to individual, territorially-based interests over the collective interests of the sectors. This was viewed as a way to capture the support of the large number of Mexicans who did not belong to any of the sectoral organizations affiliated with the party. It was also recognition that these organizations were largely bureaucratic institutions that had failed to sustain active support among their members. The restructuring of the party was seen, therefore, as an essential component of the party's modernization and preparation for future electoral competitions. In this light, the entrenched role of labor in the party and its overall influence in politics were viewed as obstacles to both political and economic reform.

President Salinas carried out a number of actions that made clear his intent to weaken the official labor sector. In the lower house of the federal congress the proportion of PRI nominations the labor sector received for congressional seats fell after the 1988 elections from 21.5 per cent to 15 per cent in 1991.[5] As mentioned, Salinas also tried to weaken labor's role within the party by pushing for the restructuring of the PRI in a way that would reduce the relative weight of the sectors in favor of new territorial organizations through reform proposals in 1990 and 1993. In addition, the traditional political influence of union bosses was directly attacked by Salinas on at least three occasions: the military capture of the oil workers' union head, "La Quina"; the arrest of the leader of the Matamoros Confederation of Mexican Workers (*Confederación de Trabajadores de México*, CTM), Agapito González; and the unseating of Carlos Jonguitud Barrios, leader of the large and important teachers' union. These depositions went a long way toward warning off other union leaders against criticism of the government. The president also lent his support to a rival union federation in an effort to further discipline the PRI's labor support base, in particular the CTM. Finally, he continued to promote wage restraint (through the tripartite

---

5   Juan Reyes del Campillo, "El movimiento obrero en la Cámara de Diputados, 1979–1988," *Revista Mexicana de Sociología*, 1990, vol. 52, no. 3, pp. 139–60.

"*pactos*")[6] as he pursued neoliberal economic policies and secured the passage of NAFTA.

There is no question that labor's political influence and economic bargaining power have weakened throughout this period. Nonetheless, the Salinas government was unsuccessful in securing all of the changes it intended. Evidence of the labor sector's continued political influence could be seen in the Salinas government's decision to postpone labor law reform and in its inability to completely alter the structure of the PRI.[7] And while Salinas began his administration with an attack on the official labor leaders, he did not in the end grant more room for maneuver to the more independent and militant sectors of the labor movement. The official labor sector maintained discipline and control over its members' demands in spite of limited benefits accruing to workers and in spite of government attacks. It came out in support of NAFTA and remained loyal to the PRI during electoral contests. It maintained labor peace and proffered political support during the presidential succession process, which was marred by the assassination of the PRI candidate in March 1994 and by the emergence of an armed guerrilla insurgency in January 1994. The labor sector proved itself to be the most consolidated and stable ally of a regime wracked by political crises. Moreover, Salinas had spent much of his administration dismantling traditional political institutions without yet consolidating an alternative. This context of crisis and flux led to a rapprochement between the administration and the official labor movement toward the end of the Salinas government.

Why did the official labor movement remain loyal to the PRI and the government in spite of the government's treatment of labor and the distinct shift in economic climate, which threatened to undermine labor's interests in the future? Many observers attribute labor's stance to its leaders' lack of vision and to bureaucratic inertia. They claim that labor's position is unintelligible

---

6   The "*pactos*" or pacts are national accords among government, business representatives, and representatives of labor and rural sectors on an array of economic and social policies such as trade liberalization, fiscal and monetary policy, investment targets, wage increases, price increases, subsidies, and so forth. Implemented since 1987, they have been credited with helping to lower inflation in Mexico. Although labor and rural groups are included in these pacts, they are not believed to have had much influence over the substance of the agreements. For more on labor's role in these pacts, see Laurence Whitehead, "Mexico's Economic Prospects: Implications for State–Labor Relations", in Kevin J. Middlebrook, ed., *Unions, Workers, and the State in Mexico* (La Jolla, Calif.: Center for U.S.–Mexican Studies, 1991).

7   Although new groups were recognized and some of the old sectoral organizations were reorganized, labor managed to maintain its presence and the PRI remained organized around a combination of territorial and sectoral bodies. See Kevin J. Middlebrook, *The Paradox of Revolution: Labor, the State, and Authoritarianism in Mexico* (Baltimore: Johns Hopkins University Press, 1995), p. 298.

given that it no longer receives any gain from its relationship with the PRI and the state, and that its unwillingness to lead strikes is evidence of its inability to respond strategically to the challenges of the new economic and political environment. Another perspective stresses the labor sector's ongoing commitment to a "political bargaining" relationship with the state, in which labor negotiates political representation and support during economic hard times in order to secure the opportunity to influence developments in the future. According to this view, what labor exchanges is political support and labor peace for continued labor representation in the party and for modification of some public policies that affect labor. This view accepts that labor, although weakened and still dependent on the government, is still capable of negotiating the terms of its relationship with the regime, and that it still has something to give which cannot yet be granted by anyone else. Judging from the relative strengthening of labor's position (in political terms) during the first part of the Zedillo administration, it appears that the official labor sector's strategy under the Salinas government may have paid off.

LABOR ENTRENCHMENT UNDER THE ZEDILLO GOVERNMENT

Despite the fact that Ernesto Zedillo was elected president in what were perhaps the cleanest elections in Mexican history, his administration immediately faltered with the devaluation of the peso in December 1994. The devaluation provoked Mexico's worst economic crisis since the Depression, putting one million Mexicans out of work and sending wages plummeting again after they had experienced a moderate recovery in some sectors in the early 1990s. Thousands of small and medium domestic businesses were forced to close under the weight of their debt burdens, produced in part by skyrocketing interest rates. The incidence of random violence increased dramatically in Mexican cities, and personal security became a paramount concern for many individuals for the first time. In spite of the legitimacy of the Zedillo government (in contrast with that of Salinas), he was widely viewed as a weak president who lacked leadership and vision and was allowing Mexico to drift, playing into the hands of the more authoritarian forces in Mexican politics. Political and economic conditions as well as presidential style under the Zedillo government contrasted sharply with the first five years of the Salinas administration.

It is in this context that one has to view the revitalization of labor's role within the ruling party and the administration. During the last year of the Salinas administration the labor movement had begun to strengthen its position vis-à-vis the regime. This was due, as explained above, to the importance of labor's role in supporting the regime during the presidential succession process and the political crises of 1994. Labor had also granted its support to Salinas's second choice for president, Zedillo, at a time when his candidacy was greatly weakened in the wake of the Colosio assassination. As Zedillo entered office, then, labor was again a political force to contend with.

Several early developments under the Zedillo administration point to the relatively stronger role for labor within the party and the administration.[8] First, the change in administration also signaled a change in the labor ministry that proved more favorable to labor. Zedillo's new labor minister, Santiago Oñate Laborde, represented a substantial shift from Arsenio Farell Cubillas, the labor secretary throughout the 1980s who oversaw labor's most dramatic decline. Oñate was much more open to dialogue and conciliation with the labor movement than Farell had been. Later, when Oñate was appointed president of the PRI in 1995, Juan Millán of the CTM was named to the position of party secretary general, signaling a greater degree of labor influence at the highest levels of the PRI than had been seen in a long time.

Another area where labor interests appeared fortified was labor law reform. Long an issue tabled by governments due to labor's strong resistance, hints that labor reform might be taken up under Zedillo began early in his administration. Nonetheless, the official labor sector led by the CTM managed to forestall the reform once again. In a move that broke with past practice, however, the CTM also entered into dialogue with one of the major employer groups, the Mexican Employers' Confederation (*Confederación Patronal de la República Mexicana*, COPARMEX), over what was termed "the new culture of employment relations." Touted as the beginning of a dialogue between business and labor on the need for a "new ethics" of the workplace rather than as a discussion of legal reform, some analysts viewed these discussions as the beginning of a conciliation over what changes might be acceptable in a future reform. Significantly, the COPARMEX scrapped its earlier proposals for labor reform in favor of what would come out of the "new culture" talks, and both labor and business were able to rescue the debate from the hands of the political parties in congress, where one of the parties had commissioned a reform proposal that threatened both groups' interests. By accepting to enter into a dialogue with employers, the

---

8   Under Zedillo, the labor sector in 1996 had three governors, 14 senators, 56 deputies in the lower house of Congress, and over 100 mayors at the local level, according to José Ramírez Gamero, political action secretary of the CTM (*Mexico and NAFTA Report*, 26 Sept. 1996, p. 3).

CTM was not only breaking with tradition, it was also grabbing center stage on the reform issue at a time when new challengers were emerging within the labor movement itself to usurp the dominant position of the CTM.

A third important area where labor appeared fortified was in the political arena. In spite of ongoing pressures to curtail labor's influence in politics and in the PRI, the official labor sector emerged revitalized out of an historic party congress in September 1996. It managed to recapture important political spaces it had lost under the Salinas administration, and succeeded in skirting around a couple of tricky reforms that should have undermined its power. In particular, an agreement negotiated in 1995–96 between the PRI and opposition parties called for a political reform that would include individual, not collective, affiliation to parties.[9] This issue was accepted as part of a package of constitutional reforms passed by the PRI-led congress in 1996. In addition, the PRI internal reform proposed for discussion at the 17th National Assembly of the PRI in September 1996 maintained the exclusion of sectoral representation in the national executive committee and proposed other measures that would limit sectoral influence, although it did not propose doing away with sectors in the party altogether.[10] Both the nature of labor representation within the party and the character of labor's political relationship with the membership and the party were key issues of concern to the union leadership. These were ultimately addressed by important compromises in the PRI assembly.

Overall, the 17th National Assembly of the PRI was significant for the revolt against the "technocrats" carried out by rank-and-file militants of the party.[11] Labor was clearly part of this revolt and favored many of the reforms

---

9 While this aspect of the reform does not seem to concern leaders of the official labor sector, others have argued that this change effectively ends the corporatist system by undermining labor unions' ability to assert that they represent blocs of guaranteed PRI votes. Labor leaders insist that rank-and-file members have had a free choice in voting for years.

10 "17 Asamblea Nacional del Partido Revolucionario Institucional," *La República*, 1996. The CTM voiced opposition to these changes; see CTM, "Propuestas de la Confederación de Trabajadores de México en Relación al Documento Base para la XVII Asamblea Nacional del Partido Revolucionario Institucional", 1996.

11 Although some observers initially lauded Zedillo's distance from the party's decisions and his claims to respect them, later measures he took raised questions about his willingness to stand apart from the party in the future. Immediately after the PRI assembly, Zedillo placed a close ally in the important Technical Secretary position of the National Council of the PRI. This was interpreted by some as the president's way of keeping tabs on the party leadership and of eventually unseating Oñate (confidential interview in the PRI, Mexico City, October 29, 1996; see also Julia Preston, "Mexican Leader Shifts Into More Political Gear", *New York Times*, January 19, 1997, p. 10, International Section).

approved by the assembly. Among the most significant outcomes from the point of view of labor were the following:

First, both party president Santiago Oñate and secretary general Juan Millán were ratified by the assembly to continue in their posts as leaders of the national executive committee of the PRI, a move that ensured a labor voice at the highest levels of the PRI.[12] Second, labor and the other sectors managed to reinstate sectoral representation within the national executive committee of the party after a lapse following the 14th National Assembly in 1990: The three sectors would be represented alongside several new regional secretariats.[13] Since this provision was not in the working documents circulated prior to the assembly, it reflects the successful pressure by sectoral interests to incorporate this change in the party's statutes. Third, the rejection of "social liberalism" (a Salinas term) and the return to revolutionary nationalism and sovereignty as dominating principles of the party also favored labor, even though the victory may be qualified because the party did not go so far as to call for a reorientation of economic policy.[14] Fourth, the principle that party candidates for president and governor must have ten years of party membership and have previously held a leadership position and elected office represented a rejection of the technocrats that had come to dominate the government in previous years and favored those who have been active within

---

12 In December 1996 Oñate was asked to resign from the party leadership. Viewed as a move by Zedillo to gain greater control over the PRI, Oñate was replaced by Humberto Roque Villanueva, the former majority leader in Congress and a man considered loyal to the President. See Andrew Downie, "Mexico's Ruling Party Names Hard-Line Leader to Top Post", *Houston Chronicle*, December 17, 1996, p. 15A.

13 The new national executive committee of the PRI would be smaller, composed of four secretariats with five Regional Coordination secretariats, and it would retain the presence of the three sectors of the party. See Roberto Noriega, "Los nuevos candidatos priístas deberán tener 10 años de militancia", *El Sol*, 22 Sept. 1996, p. 20-A. Also see Comité Ejecutivo Nacional, PRI, "Documentos Básicos", 1996.

14 See Salvador M. Pavón, "Aprueban Priístas por unanimidad la declaración de principios", *El Sol*, 22 Sept. 1996, p. 19-A: "...the farewell to social liberalism and the return of revolutionary nationalism will not imply a change in the party's position with regard to current economic policy and the strategy of privatization" (author's translation). Indeed, the PRI assembly was full of contradictory messages: delegates rejected social liberalism, but not its architect (a proposal to expel Salinas from the party was rejected); they appropriated revolutionary nationalism, but did not challenge the basic outlines of the government's economic strategy; they accepted individual affiliation as determined during the national political reform negotiations, but in a bow to traditionalism, gave the party's sectors control over registering party militants. The changes made during the party assembly reflect a moderation of the trajectory of economic and political reform, perhaps, but not their reversal. However, a proposal to reject full privatization of the secondary petrochemical industry was approved in the assembly, and although party leaders later tried to downplay the implications of this stance, President Zedillo bowed to popular pressure when he announced that the government would maintain 51 per cent ownership over the industry in opening it up to private investors.

the sectoral organizations of the party.[15] While the labor sector did not originally favor so stringent a set of requirements for candidacy, it did support the general thrust of the measure, which was to force candidates to high office to have some party experience. Finally, although the political reform passed by congress included the stipulation that party affiliation must be individual, not collective, the implementation of this clause in the PRI statutes remained favorable to entrenched labor groups. Sectoral organizations would oversee the individual affiliation of their members, while citizens who did not belong to one of the sector groups would be able to affiliate in their district or municipality.[16] This provision was also a change with respect to the original draft reform documents, and therefore also reflected successful lobbying on the part of the labor sector. Some analysts insist that this arrangement is in fundamental conflict with the constitutional reform stipulating individual affiliation, but until it is challenged by workers it is unlikely that much will change in the way that unions deal with their members at election time.

All of these reforms reveal the extent to which the labor sector and other traditional interests continue to exert substantial influence in the party. While it was previously held that the democratization of the PRI and of the political system as a whole would mean diluting labor's (and the so-called dinosaurs') influence within the party, increasing competitive pressures on the party have coincided with an entrenchment of labor's position.

LABOR ENTRENCHMENT UNDER MEXICAN NEOLIBERALISM: REASONS AND PROSPECTS

Despite an intensification of economic liberalization policies and of the integration process in North America and despite growing pressures for democratization, official labor sector interests have gained a new hold within the ruling party under the Zedillo administration. This is the party that has overseen Mexico's economic transition while retaining its corporative relationship with the majority of the organized labor movement. What is it

---

15 In preliminary documents the CTM questioned the wisdom of a requirement of a minimum number of years of party membership in order to run for office, given that this could "limit the registration of new militants" into the party. See CTM, "Propuestas de la Confederación de Trabajadores de Mexico en relación al documento base para la XVII Asamblea Nacional del Partido Revolucionario Institucional", 1996. The change approved by the assembly is even more restrictive than the original proposal, which was that gubernatorial and presidential candidates have *five* years of party militancy and have held *either* an elected post or leadership position in the party.

16 See Noriega, *op cit*. With regard to affiliation, relegating this activity to sectoral organizations means to a large extent a continuation of current practices and abuses, whereby unions and other organizations may pressure their members to affiliate with the ruling party.

about the Mexican case that accounts for this paradoxical situation? I believe an explanation can be found in three key areas: 1) the change in government and the process of state reform; 2) the economic crisis; and 3) changes within the labor movement.

Given the importance of presidentialism in the Mexican political system, the executive's personal style of ruling has an inordinate impact on politics and society. Whereas Salinas's style appeared hyper-controlling, Zedillo seems less concerned with (or less capable of) micro-managing the government's relations with social actors. This has had important implications for the degree of autonomy actors such as labor unions enjoy. Also important in this regard has been Zedillo's professed support for a greater degree of independence among the branches of government, a reform urged by the opposition for some time. While Mexico is far from arriving at some form of democratic pluralism and progress on reforms has been uneven, there have been important advances. To the extent that the party achieves greater independence from the executive, there may be more room for the expression of interests within it such as those of the labor sector. The PRI assembly in 1996 reflected this greater degree of independence to some extent, as has the recent behavior of the Mexican supreme court, which was appointed anew under the Zedillo administration. Although the increasing independence of party decisions may be a consequence of a greater degree of democracy in the Mexican system, there is no guarantee that the party's actions will produce outcomes that further perpetuate democratic reform in the political system as a whole.[17] Nonetheless, the ability of labor and other traditional interests (democratic or not) to recapture positions within the PRI seems due in part to the fact that their actions have been relatively unchecked by the executive power.

Paradoxically, the economic crisis generated by the 1994 peso devaluation may also have played a role in strengthening labor's hand in the political arena. Even as the crisis was devastating in economic terms, it helped to produce a convergence of disparate forces within the country that have begun to call for a moderation of economic policies and for more government attention to the problems of employment and poverty.[18] Significantly, this convergence

---

17 A classic recent example can be seen in the PRI congressional majority's decision not to approve the political reform negotiated by the PRI leaders and opposition parties over the course of 15 months. Instead they approved a much watered-down version that strongly favored the PRI over the opposition parties in the areas of media access and campaign financing and spending, in effect nullifying the earlier negotiations. See Julia Preston, "Ending Dialogue, Ruling Mexican Party Dilutes Reforms", *New York Times*, November 16, 1996, p. 3, International Section.
18 See "The Revolutionary Nationalists Are Back", *Mexico and NAFTA Report* (RM-95-10), October 12, 1995, p. 5. A backlash to neoliberal reforms has also been noted throughout the region; see "The Backlash in Latin America", *The Economist*, November 30, 1996, pp. 19–21.

includes both labor and employer groups, as well as a portion of the PRI and members from opposition parties. This "nationalist backlash" to the reforms perpetuated by Salinas tends to favor some labor positions. Moreover, the crisis further allows labor to play a key role as keeper of social peace at a time of dramatic real wage decline, high unemployment, and general social and political instability, thereby strengthening its utility to the regime. These concerns raised by the crisis were behind employer groups' search for dialogue with labor over the new employment culture.

Third, divisions within the umbrella Labor Congress helped to activate the CTM into maintaining and even reinforcing its interlocutor role vis-à-vis employers, the party, and the government. New formations of labor unions emerging in 1995 and 1996 challenged the CTM's dominance over the Labor Congress as well as the relative complacency of the Congress with respect to the economic crisis and certain policy reforms, such as that of social security.[19] The conflict within the labor movement is far from resolved and its outcome rendered more unclear given the uncertain future status of the CTM. Nonetheless, in the past the CTM has frequently responded to challengers by appropriating some of the demands and activist thrust of its opponents and by seeking to bolster its presence in the party and within the Labor Congress. By its recent actions in the PRI and its spearheading of the talks over labor reform with employers, it appears to have done the same here.

How likely is this entrenchment of labor under the Zedillo administration to persist? Are we witnessing the last gasp of a dying dinosaur, or an accommodation of traditional interests to a new economic and political environment? The answer may depend on future developments impossible to foresee here. One way to approach this question, however, is to analyse the bases of labor power in order to determine whether labor influence is likely to increase or decline in coming years.

A glance at the conventional measures of labor power would indicate it to be quite weak. In the economic arena, organized labor has been losing in areas of membership, jobs, and real wages for well over a decade. The large and growing informal sector acts to further undermine organized labor's market clout. The latest economic recession following the 1994 devaluation has worsened an already dire employment situation. Even if economic circumstances improved, labor's ability to mobilize its membership remains weak,

---

19 These new formations include the "Foro" (see note below) and the May 1 Inter-Union Coordinating Committee. The latter is a grouping of more left-leaning labor and community groups that joined together on the occasion of the May 1 march in Mexico City in 1995, from which the official labor sector had withdrawn.

given the heterogeneous nature of CTM unions and the tradition of top-down controls over the rank and file that serve to discourage mobilization. Those unions with a more independent profile, greater mobilizational capacity, and a higher degree of internal democracy have also been hit hard by the recession, restructuring, and labor repression of the 1980s and early 1990s. Compared to these unions the CTM has expanded or at least retained its control over strategic sectors of the economy such as autos, oil, and much of the maquiladora sector, and it has come out of the 1980s in better shape, giving it some bargaining power in the economic arena. More important, official labor's advantage is that it, and not a more independent and militant labor grouping, still exercises control over these key industries.

In the political arena, labor's bargaining strength vis-à-vis the government also rests with the CTM's ability to maintain discipline among its ranks and control of the Labor Congress. It is this unity and discipline which has compensated in the political arena for the loss of power in the economic sphere. But this is also the weakness of organized labor, since such unity and discipline are possible because of the figure of the 96-year-old patriarch of the CTM, Fidel Velázquez.[20] When he passes from the scene most observers agree that the result will be a more fragmented and nationally weak CTM, leaving behind regional federations vying for control of the organization. Such changes in the CTM will affect the balance of power within the Labor Congress, too, especially given the presence of unions now threatening to leave the umbrella organization. Under those circumstances future governments may face—and may well be content to deal with—a decentralized and nationally weak labor movement, one further weakened by market conditions at the regional or enterprise level, even if this means a greater degree of unpredictability and sporadic militancy at the local level in some sectors.

Does this necessarily mean the end of corporatism in Mexico? As we have seen, the fractioning of the main labor organization, the CTM, could usher in corporatism's demise by removing a unified, disciplined interlocutor that has been able to exercise significant control over the labor movement despite a growth in recent years of internal dissent. A major electoral loss by the PRI, such as in the upcoming congressional elections in July 1997 or presidential elections in 2000, may also undermine the bases of union support for the party. If the PRI were to split as a party under the pressure of electoral defeat, as some have predicted, then the labor sector (or different labor groups) would have to choose sides or else choose to remain independent. At the same time, if

---

20   Fidel Velázquez died June 21, 1997.

the PRI no longer exercised control over the state, the reasons for allying with that party would be weakened. In that case labor organizations may find that they are better off forging flexible and pragmatic alliances with parties in power, whichever these may be.[21] These hypothetical developments would not exclude another possibility: that a new party in power could fashion a corporatist arrangement with a new grouping of labor organizations. The most recent efforts on the part of a group of unions critical of the CTM to form an alternative labor confederation indicate that this possibility is not that farfetched.[22] Any of these developments would signal the end of the corporatist arrangements that have become a defining feature of the Mexican political system.

Given the rapid and often unpredictable changes affecting contemporary Mexico, assertions of corporatism's demise in that country are as reasonable today as predictions of its continuation. In both cases, though, what will determine the persistence or dismantling of Mexican corporatism is not primarily Mexico's economic situation, but rather the re-configuration of political forces as these are shaped by increasing electoral competition and by changes within the labor movement.

CONCLUSION

Do labor-based parties need to shed their labor base in order to continue dominating in today's economic environment? Upon first glance at Mexico, the answer is apparently "no". As I have argued here, Mexico has pursued market economic reforms and trade liberalization and is in the fourth year of a free-trade agreement with the United States and Canada. At the same time, the PRI has maintained control of both the presidency and both houses of congress. The official labor movement, spearheaded by the CTM, has maintained its allegiance to the party throughout this period despite conflict with the government over its wage policy and other economic reforms. Labor survived President Salinas's efforts to undermine labor influence and representation within the party, and re-emerged strengthened as a political force within the PRI under President Zedillo, despite the country's worst economic crisis

---

21   There are some early indications that the CTM is adapting successfully in states where the opposition PAN is in power.

22   Leaders from some 25 unions have been meeting over the course of 1996 and 1997 to discuss the future of unionism in Mexico. Recently they have begun to indicate that they would vote in July 1997 on whether to form a new labor central that would compete directly with the government-sanctioned Labor Congress. While the new grouping (called the "Foro") has been critical of government economic policy and of government controls over unions, some of the Foro's most prominent union leaders remain active in the PRI.

since the Depression. Even with a stronger voice within the PRI, however, labor has not lobbied to change Mexico's basic economic strategy. Instead, organized labor appears more interested in conserving and expanding its representation within the party and in grafting a more "populist" face onto the party in the belief that this will address the PRI's electoral weakness. How the party responds to the growing strength of populist forces while those who rule in its name deepen market economic reforms remains a fundamental question.

Is the PRI's growing electoral weakness due to its labor base? At one time the party's resistance to democratic and economic reforms was attributed to the "dinosaurs" of the party, into which category the labor sector fell. Limiting the labor influence in the party, then, was also a way of removing a key obstacle to political and economic reform. While official labor has resisted some reforms, both the extent of labor's influence in the party and the degree to which labor's role hurts the electoral competitiveness of the PRI have been overstated. The PRI has lost electoral ground for many reasons, not the least of which have been the corruption of government leaders, the unresolved political assassinations, the scandals surrounding former President Salinas and his brother and other members of the former cabinet, the peso devaluation and subsequent recession, the growing income inequality, and the unwillingness of the country's technocratic rulers to fully support political reform. In this context, labor cannot be seen as the actor that is primarily responsible for the declining electoral fortunes of the PRI.

Instead, the resurgence of popular sector interests in the party may be viewed as a response to the technocratic vision that has dominated the party in recent years and as a way to steer the party back toward representation of more nationalist, populist, and social justice concerns, if not toward the procedural transparency that the democratic opposition would prefer. The PRI cannot occupy the center-left of the political spectrum, its historic position and the only one that would enable it to retain dominance in an electorally competitive environment, without the support of the popular sectors that it has traditionally represented.[23] In order to retain its dominance, the party must not only *not* shed its labor base, it needs to fashion a new relationship with a broader labor sector and adopt a new responsiveness to labor interests. This may be done through some form of corporatism or in a context of liberal democracy. Forging a new responsiveness to labor will most certainly mean

---

23 A prominent former official in the Salinas government, Manuel Camacho, stated recently that he would form a new political party, the Party of the Democratic Center, that would compete in the 2000 presidential elections. This party would probably try to occupy the center-left space on the political spectrum between the PRD and the PRI.

some modification of economic policies, but this does not seem that far-fetched since such moderation has already begun and has been promoted by other forces in addition to labor. Moreover, thus far most parties appear to be satisfied with a slower pace of reform and have not insisted on a radical shift in the national strategy for economic development. What does seem clear is that an effective corporatist arrangement in lieu of full democratization is no longer possible in Mexico. Instead, corporatism must be seen as a complementary institutional arrangement to political democracy. Pushing further and faster on democratic reform is the only way to defuse the tensions that threaten to destroy the country's fragile balance as ongoing political and economic changes produce further social exclusion and raise the possibility of social explosion.

Today the differences between Mexico and South Africa could not be greater. While Mexican corporatism can be seen as still consisting of a primarily authoritarian, state-dominated arrangement with an aging and backward-looking labor bureaucracy, South Africa's corporatist experiment as reflected in NEDLAC is the product of a duly-elected democratic government that has ensured a voice for a highly-mobilized and autonomous trade union movement. In contrast, the long tenure of the PRI as a dominant party in Mexico's political system is not the product of elections that "express [...] the true will of the people" or that are "procedurally unflawed and free of corruption" (Adam, this volume). The Mexican challenge is to shift from authoritarian state corporatism to something approaching South Africa's democratic societal corporatism, at the very least, or else to a form of democratic pluralism, in which the social actors are autonomous and free of party and state control. Both the historic experience of Mexican corporatism and the newer South African case recall the advantages of ensuring labor representation and mediating among competing interests while undergoing a difficult economic transition.[24] Nonetheless, for corporatism to remain effective and useful in Mexico will require both that country's full transition to democracy and the increased autonomy of the labor movement vis-à-vis the state and political parties. It will also require that the labor partner in any corporatist arrangement be composed of representative trade unions. This means that along with changes in national politics must come changes in the internal practices of unions and in the numerous legal and practical restrictions on union formation and activities that currently inhibit the establishment of independent and democratic labor unions in Mexico.

---

24   On corporatism in the South Africa case, see Heribert Adam, this volume.

Chapter 10

CORPORATISM AS MINORITY VETO UNDER ANC HEGEMONY IN SOUTH AFRICA

HERIBERT ADAM

GLOBALIZATION AND CORPORATISM

One-party dominance without the prospect of a government rotation in the foreseeable future is said to constitute only a truncated, sham democracy. When a permanent majority holds sway due to ethnic voting, a futile and weak opposition cannot check majority arbitrariness effectively. Without the threat of replacement, powerholders presumably are tempted by corruption, arrogant mismanagement and self-serving policies. Majority despotism eschews the wisdom of consensus and ignores the advantages of a politics of inclusion.

This dismal prophecy of ANC hegemony in post-apartheid South Africa, however, needs to be questioned. While the warnings about the danger to liberal democracy sound justified, they overlook new constraints on any government's freedom of action at the turn of the millennium. These limits are imposed by the incorporation of the South African economy into the global market. Globalization has not only undermined the power of national governments in Western industrialized economies, but particularly affected the autonomy of semi-developed states to shape their political economy as they please. South Africa has already shifted from a demand economy in a protected domestic market to a supply-side economy, stimulated by export-driven growth. The need to be internationally competitive and to attract foreign investment forces a fundamental restructuring at home. The scope, pace and context of this shift, particularly the reduction of traditional public activity towards privatized services under profit imperatives, is of course highly contested.

In order to manage such conflicts more rationally, corporatism provides a more effective form of decision-making than adversarialism. Corporatism represents the national institutionalization of global imperatives, articulated by business organizations and state bureaucrats. Regulated bargaining between labour, business and the state replaces adversarial relations. Ideally, the force of arguments substitutes for the argument of force. In labour relations, trials of strength through strikes and lockouts are avoided in favour of mediation and compulsory arbitration. Since corporatism relies on consensus rather than the triumph of the stronger party, it provides, at least theoretic-ally, another veto against unilateral decision-making. Politically motivated restructuring by the state is dependent on reciprocal consent by labour and business; industrial action by unions is heavily prescribed and regulated; like-wise managerial autonomy is circumscribed by expanded and legislated union rights. All three actors are supposed to engage in trade-offs so that all conflicting interests are accommodated in rational compromises through bargaining.

A vast general literature on corporatism exists, dominated perhaps by three prolific writers: Philippe Schmitter, Gerhard Lehmbruch and, more recently, Markus Crepaz.[1] To which extent are the lessons and insights from thirty years of post-war corporatist reconstruction in some parts of Europe and Japan relevant for contemporary South Africa? Three issues in the liter-ature stand out that directly relate to the quite different history and unique conditions of South Africa with its current attempts of parallel corporatist decision-making: (1) the problem of minority influence in a majoritarian democracy; (2) the question of the effectiveness of corporatism to achieve higher growth rates, lower unemployment and fewer industrial disputes than in countries with laissez-faire pluralism of interest representation; and (3) the relative political power and ideological outlook of state, capital and labour. On all three counts, South Africa represents unique conditions.

1   The Swedish analyst Leif Lewin[2] has stated: "Corporatism is a method to pacify intense minorities by giving them another opportunity to influence politics when they have no chance in parliament". Where the will of the majority decides and in Stein Rokkans dictum, "votes are counted, not weighted", democracy is faced with a so-called intensity problem. Perman-ently excluded minorities with intense preferences opt out of the system or sabotage it. Corporatism fosters social integration by providing additional channels of influence. Interest organizations are formally given a voice, or even veto elsewhere, be it in board-rooms through co-determination or through representation in state agencies and committees that formulate pol-icies. This way, the state harnesses extra-parliamentary expertise, clears potential conflicts and smoothes the passage of legislation. Kenneth McRae has pointed out that corporatism and consociationalism both rely on "a dis-position among élites towards collaborative or co-operative rather than

---

1   The most comprehensive overview is still Gerhard Lehmbruch and Philippe C. Schmitter, eds., *Patterns of Corporatist Policy Making* (London: Sage, 1982).

2   Leif Lewin, "The Rise and Decline of Corporatism: The Case of Sweden", *European Journal of Political Research*, 26, 1994, 59–79.

authoritative or majoritarian modes of decision-making".[3] Lijphart and Crepaz explore the degree of corporatism and "consensus democracy" for 18 Western countries empirically.[4] They found that "corporatism can be thought of as a more broadly defined concept of consensus democracy"[5] with some of the smaller European countries (Netherlands, Switzerland, Finland, Denmark) leading the consensual states while the English-speaking Commonwealth countries and the United States are found among the most majoritarian democracies. Jenny Stewart[6] investigated how corporatist and pluralist polities process information and generate support. From her systems approach, she diagnosed "a greater learning capacity" of corporatist states, demonstrated by the post-war success of Germany and Japan on the basis of "rational" interest mediation.

2   Most European corporatist states, such as Austria, Norway, Sweden or Germany, constitute highly developed social welfare states with still relatively high employment rates. In those states, corporatism is in decline because postmaterial interests (ecology, feminism, participatory democracy) assert themselves in new political parties and a renewed role of parliament.[7] Ralf Dahrendorf, with Germany in mind, concludes: "The appearance of stability which it (corporatism) provided, soon turned into stagnation. In Europe, at any rate, corporatism did not lead to concerted action but to quarrelsome paralysis".[8] Indeed, corporatism appeals to the materialist logic of growth, as Crepaz has emphasized. It was designed for this purpose and fulfilled its function very successfully during three decades of post-war reconstruction in Europe. It may well have outlived its purpose in those societies.

However, Europe does not any longer command the resources to solve its problems with welfare state measures and South Africa was never in

---

3   Kenneth D. McRae, "Comment: Federation, Consociation, Corporatism", *Canadian Journal of Political Science*, 12, 1979, 520.

4   Arend Lijphart and Markus M.L. Crepaz, "Corporatism and Consensus Democracy in Eighteen Countries: Conceptual and Empirical Linkages", *British Journal of Political Science*, 21, 2, 1991, 235–256.

5   Ibid; 245.

6   "Corporatism, Pluralism and Political Learning", *Journal of Public Policy*, 12, 3 1992, 243–255.

7   For Austria, see Markus Crepaz, "From Semisovereignty to Sovereignty. The Decline of Corporatism and Rise of Parliament in Austria", *Comparative Politics*, 27, 1, October 1994, 45–65. See also his general overview, "Corporatism in Decline?" *Comparative Political Studies*, 25, 2, July 1992, 139–168. For Sweden, see Leif Lewin, "The Rise and Decline of Corporatism: The Case of Sweden", *European Journal of Political Research*, 26, 1994, 59–79. For Japan, see Dennis McNamara, "Corporatism and Cooperation among Japanese Labor", *Comparative Politics*, 28, 4, July 1996, 379–397. For Switzerland, see Gerhard Lehmbruch, "Consociational Democracy and Corporatism in Switzerland", *Publius. The Journal of Federalism*, 23, Spring 1993, 43–61.

8   Ralf Dahrendorf, "Terium non-datur", *Government and Opposition*, 24, 1989, 131–141.

a position to do so. Improving the life chances of its poorer half can only come through employment creation, massive efforts towards productivity performance, as well as regulated labour relations, orchestrated by what Schmitter, following Germany Chancellor Erhhard, called "concertation". While unlimited growth is the evil for environmentalists and post-industrialists in the welfare states of the West, growth as a desired goal unites the antagonists in less industrialized states, such as South Africa. Short of divisive and destabilizing redistribution, only with economic growth can the enormous inequalities be diminished. Leaving the material cleavages to laissez-faire pluralism, particularly when they overlap with ethnoracial divisions, provides a sure recipe for destructive class warfare that destroys all prospects for growth. Therefore, a country such as South Africa has no other option but to pursue corporatist social harmony.

3   In South Africa, the degree of union organization (30 per cent) straddles the lower end between Sweden (80 per cent) and the US (15 per cent). However, unionized labour is highly politicized, due to its having had to step into the vacuum left by banned anti-apartheid parties. Industrial democracy preceded political enfranchisement. Unlike other corporatist states, such as Germany and Japan, the broad political left is formally represented in the post-apartheid government, albeit with a declining influence. This left representation has facilitated corporatist arrangements in South Africa. Leading South African Communist Party (SACP) members pioneered the new Labour Relations Act which must rank among the most sophisticated balancing acts for conflict resolution in the world. Unlike the union-bashing of Thatcherites and the open class warfare in Britain, "promoting working-class interests within the framework of capitalism is an essential ingredient for the success of corporatism because it facilitates trade union involvement in a cooperative manner", as Peter J. Williamson has pointed out in a general synopsis on corporatist theory.[9] To which extent social democratic governments with union ties restrain or encourage labour militancy is debated inconclusively in the literature. In South Africa, a union-friendly ANC has clearly dampened industrial action of its alliance partner who did not wish to jeopardize ANC growth strategies. How long this restraint will last remains to be seen and is examined in more detail later. However, all empirical evidence points to a far lower strike rate in corporatist than pluralist states.

---

9   Peter J. Williamson, *Corporatism in Perspective: An Introductory Guide to Corporatist Theory* (London: Sage, 1989), 151.

CONTESTED VISIONS OF CORPORATISM: CO-OPTATION OR SOCIAL ADVANCE?

Consociationalism has as bad a name among radical democrats as corporatism is tainted among the left. Both arrangements for political power-sharing and joint economic decision-making are considered élitist, secretive, exclusive and undemocratic. Some union activists denounce the institutionalized bargaining between business, labour and the state as co-optation into the rules of capital by depriving the labour movement of its capacity for independent action. Others fear the development of a centralized unaccountable union bureaucracy, alienated from the grassroots.[10]

Business representatives, on the other hand, resent the institutionalized union power, particularly when the unions are part of the ruling party as in South Africa. Rather than being pressured to reach agreement with a class adversary, organized capital prefers to lobby state officials directly. South African capital also favours decentralized bargaining at plant level while corporatism implies national agreements to be implemented regardless of local conditions. Moreover, many small businesses which are not members of large chambers or federations feel left out of corporatist deals as are the unemployed, the rural poor and many weaker and less organized interests. In as far as these outsiders are deliberately excluded from corporatist institutions, the vested interests of the big players are strengthened. Collusion rather than consensual, inclusive interest mediation looms as a danger.[11]

Despite these misgivings, post-apartheid South Africa has begun to adopt corporatism while it implemented a modified form of consociationalism in the temporary power-sharing between political parties in a Government of National Unity. While the parties, labour unions and business organizations of the pacting are not explicit ethnic entities, their constituencies are dominated by distinct ethnic groups, which adds a consociational dimension to economic accommodation.

The role of the state bureaucracy is neither confined to be a passive bystander nor a neutral arbitrator when business and labour interests clash. Instead, the government actively participates not only in setting the legislative framework for corporate consociationalism but also in taking sides

---

10 For an overview of the debate among SA unions by a union organizer in favour of corporatism, see J. Baskin, "Corporatism: Some Obstacles Facing the South African Labour Movement", Johannesburg: Centre for Policy Studies, 1993, Research Report No. 30. For a comprehensive analytical review of corporatism, see: Louwrens Pretorius, "Relations between State, Capital and Labour in South Africa: Towards Corporatism?", *Journal of Theoretical Politics*, 8, 2, 255–281, 1996.

11 Arend Lijphart, "Prospects for Power-Sharing in the New South Africa", in Andrew Reynolds, ed., *Election '94 South Africa* (New York: St. Martins, 1994), 222.

according to its factional parts. The parties are not allies in an élite-cartel united by a common interest, except perhaps ensuring economic growth on which their survival depends. In this respect, the Reconstruction and Development Programme (RDP) has served as their common mantra. All parties can pay lip service to the RDP's noble goals because the all-embracing statement of intent avoids hard choices by not prioritizing its many contradictory visions. When the RDP was concretized in the government's neo-liberal Growth Employment and Restructuring (GEAR) strategy, the debates about macro-economic policy options become much harsher.

Corporatism diffuses and suspends class warfare. By implying a potential class harmony, it denies the fundamental tenets of socialist conceptualizations. Socialists insist that class antagonisms are irreconcilable. For Marxists, the conflicting interests of antagonistic forces cannot be overcome; they constitute the motor of history. At the most, business and labour may set aside their mutually exclusive interests temporarily for limited co-operation on specific issues. However, from a socialist perspective, corporatism or social partnerships do not provide solutions because they ignore the terms of co-operation in a capitalist setting. From this point of view, corporatism amounts to sophisticated union co-optation, because the more powerful business sector can dictate the terms of co-operation to weaker and dependent unions which are sapped of their militancy through false partnership models. This deeply entrenched world view underlies the opposition and suspicion towards corporatism on the left everywhere. For these left critics, South African unions are hoodwinked. Their foreign advisors wonder aloud why class partnership together with racial reconciliation is so widely embraced. Canadian Leo Panitch writes: "The term corporatism is used more positively on the South African left than anywhere else I have ever known in my many years of studying tripartite structures".[12] Other critics assert: "The rule of capital is being re-imposed on labour in the guise of what is called 'corporatism' and 'the adoption of corporatism' as a strategy by the mainstream of the labour movement is parasitic on the state and ill equips it to confront this new situation."[13]

The accusation leaves unanswered why labour allows the rule of capital to be re-imposed on itself at the very moment when COSATU assumes part of state power and consequently would be, for the first time, in a position to

---

12 Leo Panitch, "Cosatu and Corporatism", *Southern African Report*, April 1996, 6.
13 Robert Fine and Graham Van Wyk, "South Africa: State, Labour, and the Politics of Reconstruction", *Capital and Class*, Spring 1996, 19–31.

resist the logic of capital or replace it with its own strategy. The ultra-left critique seldom mentions the trade-offs that unions yield and gain by participating in tripartite relations. By juxtaposing the crossroads of "tripartite corporatism or democratic socialism"[14] the socialist critics postulate an ideal world, as if South Africa could realize socialism in global isolation at the very time when the South African economy is incorporated into global markets and pressures as never before. Nor should the ideology of social partnership obscure continuing conflicting class interests. Corporatism only promises more rational and less costly forms of interest representation, or in the suggestion of the much maligned World Bank advice for unions: trading "less industrial unrest for vigorous social action".[15]

While left critics fear the integration of independent unions into state structures and union subordination under wider than mere class goals, conservatives deplore the undue power of unions in tripartite arrangements. Neo-liberal observers lament "that South African unions will keep exercising influence over government not dissimilar to that of British unions in the pre-Thatcher era".[16] This assessment vastly overrates the clout of union leaders with government. It also underrates the alienation between members and leaders and overlooks that many union leaders are themselves engaged in embourgeoisement. When union leaders become partners in profit-making business enterprises, the nature of old-style class antagonism changes fundamentally.[17]

Social-democratic advocates of tripartitism, on the other hand, point to the innovative features of the relationship. Indeed, it differs from the Soviet model where unions acted as transmission belts for the ruling party. Conversely, it would diminish the strategic wisdom of seasoned COSATU leaders to view them as willing dupes of neo-liberal manipulation. Eddie Webster, a union-friendly supporter of corporatism, on the other hand, underestimates the absorbing power of business and overestimates the union clout when he writes: "Importantly, these tripartite arrangements are not part of

---

14 So the title of an article by Adrien Bird and Geoff Schreiner in *South African Labour Bulletin*, 16, 6, 1992.

15 World Bank, *Workers in an Integrated World*, Washington, DC: World Development Report, 1995.

16 John Kane-Berman, *Fast Facts*, February 1996, 5.

17 While the ascendancy of African women in the public realm has been dramatic since the ANC took over the government, the historical legacies persist in the private sector. McGregor's 1996 Directory of Directorships, for example, shows that of 8401 directorships, 7920 are in the hands of white men. White women hold 92 such positions, while black women only occupy 32 board chairs, although both categories are now highly sought after as appointees for a favourable affirmative action image.

neo-liberalism—instead, they are a creative challenge to the global agenda of neo-liberalism".[18]

Corporatism has undoubtedly expanded the space and influence of union activity in South Africa. In the final analysis, however, tripartism remains a sensible compromise which amounts to the important equivalent of the political pact on the labour front. It constitutes neither a victory nor a defeat of either opponent but brings both together in more rational arrangements of conflict resolution. However, there remain other dangers of corporatism for democratization. Not only are weaker, unorganized groups not represented where important decisions are made, the bargaining forum itself could undermine parliament.

NEDLAC AS BARGAINING FORUM

The state, labour and business have agreed that all legislation with important social and economic consequences should be discussed in the tripartite body, called National Economic Development and Labour Council (NEDLAC) prior to being tabled in Parliament. The National Economic, Development and Labour Council Act (No. 35 of 1994, Section 5.1) charges the body to "consider all significant changes to social and economic policy before it is implemented or introduced in Parliament". This is supposed to be done by way of seeking to "reach consensus and conclude agreements on matters pertaining to social and economic policy". As Pretorius rightly points out, this wide range of competence of NEDLAC does not aim at merely giving policy advice or representing sectoral interests to government. "Concluding agreements" to which government has been a party, implies "authoritative policy decisions" for which the participants take joint responsibility of implementation.

A framework agreement between business and labour is not meant to be a pact or accord. Instead, the national forum is regarded as a third tier of bargaining— "setting options at national level for improving sectoral and workplace level negotiations".[19] The corporatist model assumes that each constituency in NEDLAC supports the broad goals of creating jobs, economic growth, equity and participation by civil society in the political and economic reconstruction process. With this long-term vision, co-operation is envisaged on the basis of shorter term trade-offs.

---

18 Eddie Webster, "Cosatu: Old Alliances, New Strategies", *South African Report*, April 1996, 4.

19 *The Industrial Democracy Review*, Oct/Nov 1995, 40.

The four chambers of NEDLAC (labour market, trade and industry, public finance and monetary policy and development) have an ambitious programme of preparing legislation.

According to the institution's Executive Director, it covers "a new package of support measures for industry; the budget framework and a revised taxation system, a new Employment Act and urban–rural development".[20] During its first years the Trade and Industry Chamber mainly discussed industrial restructuring, resulting from supply-side measures through which firms are encouraged to invest in products that are internationally competitive. A "Social Plan Act" argues for informed worker participation and legal provisions to negotiate and manage industrial restructuring. A social-plan reserve fund, to be established, aims at ameliorating hardships of the process. At the insistence of labour, a social clause was negotiated for inclusion in all bilateral and multilateral trade agreements to which South Africa is a contracting party. A government draft bill on competition is being considered by the Chamber and a National Investment Promotion Agency was established. Sectoral issues, such as the liquid-fuels industry, also occupied the group as did initiatives for productivity workshops. The Public Finance and Monetary Policy Chamber focused on the next budget, the tax system, exchange-control and civil pension arrangements. The Development Chamber considered urban and rural development strategies, housing policy, job creation through a National Public Works Programme and a redefinition of the Masakhane campaign. The Labour Market Chamber worked on outstanding details of the Labour Relations Act, demarcation of industrial sectors and statutory councils, the appointment of judges to the Labour Court, codes of picketing and the establishment of the crucial "Commission for Conciliation, Mediation and Arbitration" (CCMA) under the Act. CCMA will ultimately employ 200 trained arbitrators who settle disputes quickly at the site rather than making the parties wait for a lengthy time for a costly hearing before the Labour Court.

With these vital and potentially divisive issues settled through "careful consensus-building, agreement-making and joint implementation" (J. Naidoo), the unelected star chamber undermines the elected parliament.

Parliament merely ratifies what has been decided elsewhere. Parliament is increasingly left with the symbolic issues that excite the public while the really important policies have long been settled in private bargaining. The arrangement is justified with avoiding costly conflicts.

---

20 Jayendra Naidoo, *Business Day*, 29 January, 1996.

Even if parliament retains the final say over corporatist-initiated legislation, parliamentarians are pressured not to undo a "careful equilibrium". To all intents and purposes, parliament could be reduced to rubber-stamping the outcome of acrimonious bargaining elsewhere. Alternatively, it would repeat the process which makes the elected chamber look redundant. Since most parliamentarians do not possess the expertise of corporatist negotiators, they are not only handicapped professionally but are also inclined to go along with pre-determined legislation psychologically. Particularly if the respective minister, as the party to the corporatist deal, presents it as "in the national interest", it requires independent and strong parliamentarians of the ruling party to upset the passage of a bill through critical scrutiny. Autonomous parliamentarians who rebel against a pre-set government agenda are unlikely to emerge in substantial numbers, given the severe sanctions and leadership control they face in the new South Africa.[21]

With government's greater confidence to implement macro-economic legislation without lengthy consultation, the role of NEDLAC is being diminished. At the same time, the resolve of union leaders to battle a more determined government has also waned as increasingly more union activists joined the civil service or vied for political careers. As a general trend, the independence of civil society institutions is increasingly undermined when its office-bearers depend on government favours for their personal careers or their organisations. Thus the once fiercely independent South African National Civic Organisation (SANCO) rescinded a prohibition that its official could not hold government appointments because the widespread exodus from the poorly paid civics had endangered its existence. Yet the spreading tentacles of government patronage drawing in its likely critics does not bode well for democracy.

OBSTACLES TO CORPORATISM IN SOUTH AFRICA

While the concept of negotiated compromises is theoretically embraced by all interest groups, it has not yet been established that the negotiating parties carry their own constituencies both for the process as well as for implementing controversial decisions. While Business SA, for example, successfully negotiated the innovative 1995 Labour Relations Act (LRA), soon afterwards the revived SA Foundation published its "Growth for All" document. This proposal by big business (the so-called Brenthust Group) was not negotiated through Nedlac. Yet it proposed to establish a two-tier wage system

---

21 Steven Friedman, "Big Business must accept our future rests on negotiation", *Business Day*, 30 March, 1996.

which directly affects the interests of organized labour and ignores the provisions of the LRA. The strategy adopted by the SA Foundation obviously relies on bringing business pressure directly on government with the hope that the ANC would bring recalcitrant unions into line to go along with the non-negotiated business blueprint. Not only does this strategy of circumventing NEDLAC undermine union confidence in business commitment to a negotiated compromise, it also led to a predictable rejection by the State.

Doubts exist on the union side as well about the leadership capacity to induce a suspicious constituency to stick to a compromise. If corporate consociationalism is to work in South Africa, it presupposes strong union leadership that can effectively discipline segments who disagree with controversial agreements. Business attempts to weaken union power therefore run counter to the concept of corporatism. In fact, sophisticated business needs to assist a negotiating union leadership to become an equal partner. Unfortunately, much of the strategic thinking on both sides still rests on steamrolling or manipulating the opponent into agreement. Ironically, at present, willingness to negotiate is based on the self-confidence of power and success in outmanoeuvering the other side rather than the readiness to adhere to genuine compromises.

The brain drain of experienced union officials to government and the private sector has caused a weakening of union clout. At the same time, the presence of less experienced union representatives has led to a marked increase in strike actions since the end of 1995. Grievances, as opposed to wage disputes, account for the majority of strikes now. With company restructuring and technology replacing jobs, retrenchment-related strikes are also likely to increase.

Ironically, the implementation of corporatist deal-making is undermined by the very process by which agreements are being reached. On the union side, corporatism leads to organizational élitism. It requires a centralized professional union bureaucracy. Leadership becomes alienated from the grassroots. The former editor of the *SA Labour Bulletin* has diagnosed the surge of militancy on the ground as a result of the gap between distant leaders: "The involvement of union and federation leaders in increasingly complex interactions and negotiations in industry forums, NEDLAC and other institutions has widened this gap and produced a sense of disempowerment at the base. Grassroot activists are keen to assert their militancy and their demands".[22] Particularly, public service unions are increasingly militant

---

22   K. von Holdt, "LRA Negotiations", *SA Labour Bulletin*, 19, 1995, 3.

towards the state as their employer. When senior state officials are perceived as looking after their own interest first through high salaries compared with underpaid nurses, teachers, or police personnel, it is doubtful how effectively appeals to the national interest can sustain labour peace.

The danger of too close a government–union association was amply demonstrated by the nurses' strike during October and November of 1995. A closer analysis of this event yields insights into the limits of SA corporatism.

Thousands of well-organized health care workers drew attention to their poor salaries and dismal working conditions by striking against their own union representatives as well as the state as their employer. While the government insisted that wage talks could only take place with recognized unions in a National Central Bargaining Chamber (CBC), the majority of angry nurses turned away representatives from the National Education, Health and Allied Workers' Union (NEHAWU) and the Hospital Personnel Association of South Africa (HOSPERSA). In the end, the nurses formed their own union, the South African Democratic Nurses Union (SADNU) which refused to seek affiliation with either of the country's two major union federations, COSATU or NACTU.

The undertones of the strike revealed not only a mood of disillusionment with the newly legitimated state by the most important sector of African professional women. It also signalled the inability of emerging corporatist arrangements to cope with a situation bordering on anarchy. In the illegal strike that amounted to a breach of contract, both sides issued ultimatums and ignored deadlines. The Director-General of Health warned that nurses could face criminal charges if patients died as a result of the strikes. The nurses demanded an apology from Mandela for his similar statement on the strike and suggested that the Minister of Health, Dr Nkosazana Zuma, should have been at Baragwanath instead of "staying in comfortable hotels in Beijing" for the UN Women's Conference. Other spokespersons declared: "We are qualified women, not just menial labour. We know our skills are needed to save lives. We refuse to subsidize the Government and their fancy cars. Viva RDP. We want some gravy".[23] While all the established institutions called for constructive negotiations towards resolving problems, "in the labour ward, women were delivering their own babies, sometimes with the aid of patients who were themselves in labour. Post-operative patients were being given over-the-counter pain killers instead of morphine. While doctors, matrons, workers and paramedics helped patients and strove to restore a semblance of

---

23   Cited in Trevor Bernhardt, "The Nurses' Strike: A Well-Organized Plea for Recognition", *Industrial Democracy Review*, 4, 5, Dec. 95–Jan. 96, 11–20.

order to the chaos…, the nurses toyi-toyied outside".[24] Doctors' reports spoke of life-support systems in a maternity ward deliberately being turned off and HIV-infected material being thrown around.

Potential failures of corporatism are revealed in the nurses' confrontation for three reasons: First, most victims of the strikers' ire were fellow Africans. Little empathy was extended to patients compared with the goals of a special interest group. If nurses, indoctrinated with ideologies of service to the community, can act with such callous blackmail, other unions are even more unlikely to accept compromises when the opponent is perceived as a greedy employer of a different race. Second, there are clear limits to government's appeals to take national interests or scarce resources into account. ANC loyalty is overshadowed by material needs that take priority, regardless of threats or pleas, even by a widely respected figure like Mandela. Government's moral authority is undermined by the different lifestyle and perceived self-enrichment of its representatives. The extraordinarily wide gap between the remuneration of politicians and the poverty of constituents has triggered expectations that sharing in the spoils of office is the right of all state employees. Third, in the confrontation between civil servants and the state, traditional union officials are simply sidelined. They cannot control a militant constituency because they are perceived as colluding with the government in the tripartite alliance. In the nurses' case, the gender difference between strikers and the predominantly male union leadership has fostered an additional element of alienation.

Similar alienation from established unions was evident at a bitter strike at Anglo American's Rustenburg Platinum Mines, where the National Union of Mineworkers (NUM) has a membership of about 30 per cent. After a change of ownership, workers demanded the repayment of their pension money, death benefits, long service and bonus amounts as well as income tax deducted. Since the union refused to negotiate with the employer about the uninformed demands, particularly the repayment of pension money (which had previously been paid to other miners from a dissolved Bantustan pension fund), allegiance shifted to a Workers' Committee of "five madoda" (men). Management, with the intention to restart production, then bypassed the union and negotiated with the Worker's Committee, thus further enhancing the union's rival credibility. Shop stewards were threatened by angry workers. In their view: "The NUM's leadership is no longer interested in worker's issues, all they are involved with now is the establishment of an investment

---

24 Bernhardt, op. cit, 13.

company and the buying of shares with our pension fund in the Johannesburg Stock Exchange. We do not want to see NUM's leadership here".[25]

As a general rule, it can be concluded that corporatist pacts and leadership trade-offs are not worth the paper they are written on, unless the signers, particularly on the union side, exercise influence over their constituency beyond being their remote spokespersons. Such influence is jeopardized by the very corporatist deals that put its participants outside the interest perceptions of constituents. With internal democracy further fading, without a clearly perceived mandate and without the public transparency and the political education to translate necessary trade-offs into ordinary understandings of benefits and cost for members, the social partnership of corporatism remains a delusion in the minds of its originators. Their increasingly technical and legalistic compromises of complex issues further add to the dichotomy, the goodwill and noble intention of all corporatist parties notwithstanding. Only a Gandhian revolution "to walk the talk" imaginatively and patiently would seem to be able to transform a nominal social democracy into a real one. Its test lies in how many actively identify with corporatist trade-offs rather than ignorantly live with its results.

Corporatist agreements have yet to be tested against a reality of increased class stratification within the black majority. As the ANC shifts towards more conservative policies with its firmer hold over the state, business may tend to seek corporatist agreements more than in the past, but union leaders will find themselves increasingly isolated from both their own disillusioned following and their former government allies. How far government can act as an honest broker between conflicting class interests will decide the fate of South African style corporate consociationalism.

THE SPECTRE OF ONE-PARTY DOMINANCE

In a one-party dominant system—as exists in many African states, Mexico or Malaysia—elections merely reconfirm the ruling party. State and party become indistinguishable. Even if elections are free and fair, a party that needs not doubt its renewal in office exists only in a "nominal democracy".

---

25 A representative of the Worker's Committee, quoted in *SA Labour Bulletin*, 20, 5, October 1996, 48. The same anonymous observer also reports that a witchdoctor moved in with the dismissed miners in the hills. The spirits and the medicines the workers were anointed with would not only protect their bodies from bullets, but also ensure that they would succeed in their demands. The Minister of Labour, who negotiated in vain with the Committee over this wide gap between modernity and superstition, blamed the apartheid system for not "empowering the workers". This leaves, of course, the reasons for the worker's alienation from union representation, unaddressed.

Yet it can also be argued, with equal validity, that the repeated reaffirmation of a party in power does not negate democracy, provided the election expresses the true will of the people, provided the majority party does not repress or exclude minorities from legitimate influence and, above all, provided the election is procedurally unflawed and free of corruption. It is an empirical question, yet to be answered, whether these provisions will prevail in a South Africa under ANC hegemony. Above all, several constraints on potential one-party dominance exist in South African that are absent in Mexico or Malaysia.

The fact that two important provinces (Western Cape/KwaZulu-Natal) voted for rival parties and the ANC barely managed to rule a third (North-West) mitigates against one-party dominance. Although the ANC may well win Natal in a future free campaign with access to the rural areas of Zulu-land, there remains entrenched pockets of ANC rejection that cannot be eliminated by fiat of a dominant center. Unlike ZANU in Zimbabwe, which first squashed and subsequently co-opted its opposition in Matebeleland, real power bases of opposition in South Africa prevail, in both local and provincial administrations as well as outside government institutions.

Vincent Maphai has rightly pointed out that besides consociationalism, other forms of power-sharing are practised in divided societies just as in liberal democracies.[26] Federalism, corporatism and the division of power between executive, parliament and an independent judiciary can all be considered widely accepted constraints on one-party dominance in South Africa. Consociationalism as explicit power-sharing between ethnic groups had been wisely diluted in the transitional period of the interim constitution to power-sharing among political parties as implicit representatives of ethnic groups. This resulted, as Maphai perceptively points out, "in a weaker and more fluid correspondence between party and ethnicity than consociationalism envisaged". All three non-African minorities, as well as Zulu-speakers, dispersed their vote among several parties and the ANC took great care not to present itself as an ethnic party but as a broad-based inclusive movement.

In its self-definition, the ANC does not wish to deprive minorities of an effective say in government. It only wants to limit the influence of minority parties to "a say proportionate to their electoral strength".[27] The ANC views a minority veto power beyond proportional representation as preventing majority rule. However, in as much as power-sharing during a transition

---

26 Vincent Maphai, "A Season for Power-Sharing", *Journal of Democracy*, January 1996, 67–81.

27 Blade Nzimande, "ANC cannot pander to privileged minorities", *Business Day*, 13 February, 1996.

period was necessary for jointly drafting the rules of the political game, so a disproportionate influence of minorities may be a requirement for future stability. Overrepresentation of minorities as a device for confidence-building is practised in many democratic constitutions, the most prominent of which is the equal representation of less populous US states in the US senate. The equal vote of all member states in the UN General Assembly, regardless of population size and financial contribution, also affirms the principle of over-representation, balanced by the veto power of each of the five permanent members of the Security Council.

Unlike Mexico, vote rigging and corruption by an institutionalized revolutionary party would also be exposed and opposed by a strong and watchful civil society in South Africa. While there are attempts to curtail civil society—for example the defeated bill to regulate NGOs and divert their foreign funding to the state—the political culture of the anti-apartheid struggle has greatly strengthened civil society. To be sure, liberal components have much to answer for their betrayal of principles and acquiescence in the often illiberal behaviour of liberation activists, as Jill Wentzel has demonstrated in her distressing account, *The Liberal Slideaway*.[28] Nonetheless, R.W. Johnson's warning about the possibility "that the liberal tradition will be snuffed out altogether under the new nationalist hegemony"[29] overstates the threat. Even if the new rulers were to try more forcefully to stifle dissent à la Zimbabwe, they would not succeed in South Africa because of the objective strength of countervailing forces. Such an optimistic conclusion does not rest on the incorruptible staying power of individuals or institutions that can be sidelined, silenced or taken in by the new hegemony, as Jill Wentzel has shown. The noble intentions of liberal democrats notwithstanding, their opposition alone cannot block a determined illiberal government. It is the objective economic forces that South African liberalism articulates, that constrains any government in Pretoria.

The withdrawal of the NP from the GNU in June 1996 has been widely interpreted as giving the ANC a free hand to pursue its own economic policy without the watchdog function and pressure of an inbuilt opposition. Overseas investors, in particular, are concerned about a populist-inclined African majority party now going it alone. However, far from strengthening the freedom of the ANC, the NP exit from formal power-sharing has weakened the government. Not only has the ANC to bear responsibility for failure of delivery alone, it now has to reinforce the impression that it pursues "responsible" policies.

---

28 Jill Wentzel, *The Liberal Slideaway* (Johannesburg: SA Institute of Race Relations, 1995).
29 R.W. Johnson, "Fear in the Miracle Nation", *London Review of Books*, 2 November, 1995.

Faced with a generalized distrust by a sceptical global audience, the ANC with exclusive power has to be doubly cautious to stay within approved parameters. While no longer settled with the burden of a conservative coalition-partner, the government has been burdened to appear conservative on its own.

The irony of additional constraints on a freer government does not mean that the self-appointed opposition NP has been strengthened by its turn. Not only had the NP become redundant in the GNU, as Maphai points out,[30] the party's internally controversial departure produced new rifts and disillusionment. Cut off from state patronage, it could no longer reward followers. As it also lost much of its role as power-broker, lobbyist for business and other special interest groups, the more ANC officials became directly accessible and responsive to new constituencies. When white-dominated business can negotiate all its essential interests in corporatist institutions or through direct contacts with officials, it marginalizes political parties as interlocutors and representatives of established class concerns. This "identity crisis" has not only affected the National Party but the DP as well. The loss of historical roles—to look after a well-defined constituency in the public realm and manage the legitimacy crisis of a racially limited democracy—has forced the two historically white parties to broaden their image for attracting non-white voters at the expense of their traditional ideological appeal and symbolic messages. Ironically, the NP has managed this transition far more effectively than the liberal Democratic Party. Fifty-one per cent of the NP vote in 1994 came from non-white voters, mainly coloureds and Indians, who eschewed the soft African-friendly stockbroker liberalism associated with the DP. NP inroads into non-white constituencies, however, undermine its traditional ethnic appeal. For Afrikaner representation of educational and cultural concerns, the moderately right-wing Freedom Front had long established itself as a more authentic force. Even Mandela and ANC officials treat the right-wing with greater respect than de Klerk.

Regardless of the dominant party behaviour, any South African government is dependent on many other diverse forces, particularly white-dominated business. It could ignore their interests only at its own peril. In as much as the private sector cherishes sympathetic government policies, so government needs the investment, growth and know-how that only business can deliver. Without this symbiotic relationship, both sides would falter. With massive capital flight and white emigration, South Africa would join many other African states that did not enjoy the dubious benefits of settler capitalism that brought about the negotiated revolution and democratization in the first place.

---

30 Maphai, "A Season for Power-Sharing", 67–81.

A mutually paralyzing stalemate, also guarantees the adherence to the new rules in the future.

CONCLUSION

The wailing about ANC majoritarianism assumes ethnic minorities as its main victim. This thinking still relies on racial antagonisms as the overriding cleavage in South Africa. In reality, however, the ANC's historical role is both to represent and control the poor majority. Political stability and economic relationships are not threatened by whites but by impoverished black masses whose lot is unlikely to improve dramatically. Ethnic minorities do not undermine the state or ANC hegemony, even if they vote in their majority for opposition parties. Dissatisfied blacks, on the other hand, pose a mortal danger not only to ANC dominance but to minority interests in particular. Therefore, only a credible ANC can manage the challenge—very much like union-friendly social-democratic administrations can handle sensitive wage restraints more efficiently than union-bashing conservatives. As Stanley Uys has aptly commented: "ANC majoritarianism is concerned less with suppressing minority ethnic groups than it is with placating and managing the majority black population...",[31] although foreign investors judge the country by its black–white relations. This does not mean that the ANC is leading an "Induna-state, keeping workers in line on behalf of capital".[32] Nor does the ANC government "merely manage the affairs of the bourgeoisie", as another SACP analyst questioned. The state is an agent neither of capital nor labour but attempts to reconcile and arbitrate their conflicting interests according to the shifting pressures of the day.

This unique objective constellation makes South Africa a pragmatically united rather than a deeply divided society. The projection of deep ethno-racial divisions on the basis of racial demographics overrates appearance at the expense of underlying forces. Hence, even knowledgeable observers are constantly surprised when their predictions of doom turn out to be overtaken by reluctant co-operation and pragmatic reconciliation. All they can offer is to abandon explanation and relegate the inexplicable to the unquestioned realm of a "miracle". In short, when South Africans and informed outside analysts talk openly about the collapse of public administration; when the net emigration of skills from the public to the private sector as well as to other countries reaches worrying heights; when a soaring crime rate, unemployment and a

---

31 Stanley Uys, "Pressing the ANC to take power," *The World Today*, May 1996.
32 *The African Communist*, III, 1995, 2.

declining currency engender collective despair, a broad-based stable one-party-dominant democracy may indeed be preferable to a rotating state administration which would add to the uncertainty and discontinuity.

The real test for the future South African democracy is whether it is based on an *inclusive* majoritarianism or on *ethnic* majoritarianism. It could well be argued that South Africa is developing into a state that has been called "ethnic democracies", à la Israel.[33] South Africa is likely to display a similar pattern of de facto African political dominance with the important difference that non-African minorities can join the nonracial ANC and exercise influence that Arab Israelis are denied by the very definition of an ethnic state.[34]

In South Africa, ethnoracial communalism is fortunately not constitutionally entrenched. Unlike Sri Lanka or Northern Ireland with their deadly ethnic majoritarianism, South African politics is unlikely to be transformed into a hotbed of competing communal identities whose ideological consolidation relies on targeting the "other" as the enemy. In fact, separate identities are hardly contested. Unlike Sri Lanka where English as the state language of communication was abolished in order to favour the Sinhalese majority over the Western-educated Tamil minority, post-apartheid nation-building is conducted in the idiom and values of the English-speaking minority. Anxieties about Africanization on the part of white and brown Afrikaners spring from concern about the abolition of previous racial privileges (Coloured Labor Preference in the Western Cape and Afrikaner control of the state) and poor state services but hardly about the loss of cultural or religious identity through the imposition of an alternative official ethnocultural definition of the state. Post-apartheid South Africa is officially a multi-ethnic and multi-cultural state. Its negotiated constitutional preamble, underwritten by majority and minority representatives, from communists to Afrikaner nationalists of the Freedom Front, says that the country "belongs to all who live in it, united in our diversity". While this noble idealism awaits its translation into practice, it enshrines the opposite of ethnic chauvinism. The vision of the new constitution is inclusive.

Corporatism in the decisive economic realm guarantees the consensual type of democracy that simple majoritarianism lacks in the political sphere.

---

33 See Sammy Smooha and Theo Hanf, "Minority Status in an Ethnic Democracy: The Status of the Arab Minority in Israel", *Ethnic and Racial Studies*, vol. 13, no. 3, 1990, 389–489.

34 Arab Israelis may hold the balance of power if Labor and Likud are tied and if they can be mobilized to vote in sufficient numbers. The suggestions by right-wing politicians that only Jewish voters should have a right to determine who their government leader should be, shows the fragility and second-class citizenship of the minority in an ethnic state despite formal equality.

Moreover, given the volatile and fragile state of South African society and its new political institutions, corporatism constitutes an effective and necessary substitute for interest mediation that would be difficult to achieve with electoral politics alone. David Welsh has rightly questioned whether a polity like South Africa can sustain competitive, confrontational and adversarial politics in which alternating government is "normal".[35] In short, with power-sharing abolished in the political realm since the unravelling of GNU, joint decision-making and bargaining elsewhere assumes added significance. Single-party dominance in the foreseeable future is balanced by corporatist veto powers. To which extent ANC hegemony is also rendered irrelevant as long as corporatist consensus politics checks basic legislation, remains to be seen.

Acknowledgement

The author thanks Hermann Giliomee and Kogila Moodley for stimulating disagreements and new perspectives.

---

35 David Welsh, "Majority Rules, OK?", *Indicator SA*, 13, 3, Winter 1996, 6–8.

Chapter 11

DEMOCRACY OR DEMOCRATIC HEGEMONY: THE FUTURE OF POLITICAL PLURALISM IN SOUTH AFRICA

LAWRENCE SCHLEMMER

INTRODUCTORY COMMENTS

One of the most distinguished writers on democracy, Robert Dahl postulated two basic dimensions of effective governance and democratisation, namely "general participation" and what he termed "contestation". The latter is an essential complement to the former since even where the formal participation of the citizenry is protected, any entrenched dominance of a single political party or movement and a lack of countervailing influences in the political process will render the participation of those positioned outside the sphere of dominance relatively meaningless.[1]

Dahl's two dimensions perhaps have to be complemented by a third dimension, relevant mainly in culturally less homogeneous societies or societies with consolidated regional divisions akin to "sub-societies". In such situations the two dimensions referred to above may not be sufficient to secure the balance of countervailing forces which would protect the integrity or survival of one or more of the components of the system. Dahl himself referred to this additional dimension as an "internal system of security for all major political interests".[2] Later, Terry Lynn Karl and Philippe Schmitter described this requirement in the context of emerging democracies as a "...foundational pact...explicit agreements between contending elites (providing) mutual guarantees for the vital interests of those involved".[3]

South Africa's negotiated transition, in its *initial* conceptualisation, appeared to conform to all three requirements. The acceptance of universal franchise, proportional representation to facilitate a multi-party system and the establishment of a Government of National Unity incorporating the three largest parties, each representing major racial and

---

1 Robert Dahl, *Polyarchy: Participation and Opposition* (New Haven: Yale University Press, 1971), Chapter 1.
2 Dahl, *Polyarchy*, Chapter 3.
3 Terry Lynn Karl, "Modes of Transition in South and Central America, Southern Europe and Central Europe", Center for Latin American Studies, Stanford University, 1990, mimeo.

ethnic segments of the electorate, appeared to comprise the necessary package.

In the actual situation of current South Africa, however, both the texture of the political dynamics and the fine print of the constitution are considerably less reassuring about the *quality of democracy*. The Government of National Unity suffered a premature collapse because, in a low trust situation, it veered towards a power play based on voting strength rather than convergence and the seeking of consensus. The outcome of the first general election and the subsequent local government elections have shown that, for whatever reasons, the political parties are primarily characterised by the racial identity of their support. The majority party, the ANC, is dominantly supported by blacks with less than 5 per cent of whites supporting it. Similarly, less than 5 per cent of blacks support parties which, collectively, most whites support.

Political minorities, therefore, can perhaps be forgiven for the perception that the balance of power from now on will be determined more by racial demography than by political outcomes based on any performance-related inter-party contestation. Hence, although formal constitutional provisions and formalities appear to guarantee a multi-party system, the racial polarisation of the electorate decrees South Africa to be, *potentially*, a one-party "dominant" state for the foreseeable future. The ANC considers itself entitled to call the system a "normal democracy", which it is in formal terms, but the very formal correctness of a numerically-based democracy leaves the political minorities with an intensified feeling that their political exclusion is constitutionally entrenched.

Hence, the period since the first open elections has been one in which a kind of unwritten distinction between "new" and "old" South African politics and political parties has been established. Despite good intentions and hopes to the contrary, the effect of this has been to perpetuate the polarisations created by apartheid and the liberation struggle. The political field has, as it were, been *cordoned off* into two major *symbolic camps*—a significant defeat for open pluralism.

This tendency has its parallels in civil society—among some government spokespeople there has been an inclination to use the term "civil society" in talking about the progressive, formerly liberation-linked non-government lobby but to use the term "vested interests" when referring to older voluntary associations.

In most ways this potential for one-party dominance depends utterly on the political responses of the "demographic" majority, the African voters. While one can argue with justification that whites themselves set a bad example by in effect forming a consolidated "opposition" bloc, their smaller numbers make them incapable of imposing electoral hegemony any more. Since African voters are numerically able to exercise electoral hegemony with ease, the only way out of the trap of one-party dominance would be if political pluralism were to take root in the African electorate. It is to this possibility that the analysis must turn.

POPULAR ATTITUDES IN THE ELECTORATE

The section which follows is based very largely on opinion survey data. There are obviously very great difficulties in linking opinion to actual behaviour and therefore the data are often more suggestive than conclusive. Most other types of evidence, however, are equally uncertain in their implications for electoral behaviour in the future, and opinion survey evidence fully deserves to be judged with the rest.

Pluralist democracy does not necessarily depend on good intentions or democratic consciousness among voters or their party leaders. It depends more directly on the constraints upon unilateral initiatives which the balance of power might impose. One must assume that all politicians tend to enjoy the rewards of power and that extended periods of office, which can deteriorate into hegemony, are a temptation even in fully-consolidated democracies. Therefore, this analysis will not cover the conventional questions about democratic tolerance, but rather those aspects of political attitudes which seem to relate to the potential extent of electoral differentiation and to the strength of opposition in the future.

As already signalled, the selection of evidence has to place a major (but not exclusive) emphasis on the African electorate. This is not because of any hypothesised failings of democratic consciousness among Africans but simply because of the demographic realities already mentioned. The prospects of a power balance emerging through strengthened opposition in South Africa depends largely on the future choices made by African voters. In certain cases, findings for whites and in a few cases for coloured and Indian voters are merely quoted by way of comparison.

The Diversity of Political Attitudes and Orientations

Obviously a very basic requirement for the emergence of political pluralism is the relative absence of any strong majority convictions which would lock voters into inevitable support for one political faction on an enduring basis. At a level below partisan choice, there is abundant evidence of *variation* in the political views of African voters. Only one example of this will be given, drawn from a nation-wide study made in 1992, reported in 1994.[4]

Briefly, the political and policy choices of the African electorate as a whole showed considerable internal variation. A summary is extracted from this publication in Table 11.1.

Table 11.1: Selected examples of the co-incidence of "radical" and "conservative" views on policy issues among a sample of African voters (N 1660, Nation-wide personal interviews, 1991/2, Market and Opinion Surveys)

Radical/progressive views: 55% or more endorse:

- free occupation of vacant land
- quota-based affirmative action
- theft seen to be justified by past discrimination
- maximum state welfare for the poor
- enforced land redistribution
- greater influence for trade unions
- wage increases irrespective of productivity

Conservative/moderate views: 55% or more endorse:

- power-sharing between ANC and NP
- approval of concessions to minority interests for the sake of reconciliation
- individual rights and protection from punitive redistribution for all races
- protection of language and cultural minorities
- beneficial role of private companies
- strict law and order and preservation of conventional social values
- checks and balances in the constitution
- acceptance of international economic realities
- protection of former homeland elites

Very broadly, the results shown in the table and many others from similar surveys, suggest that there is far from a consolidation of values and attitudes around progressive goals of redistribution and welfare policy. There would appear to be ample scope in the African electorate for appeals by parties both to the "right" and to the "left" of the ANC.

Furthermore, in the same analysis, data from a July 1993 nation-wide survey (N 1100 Africans) suggested that an *average* of over 50 per cent of African voters and as many as 45 per cent of ANC supporters had reservations about the future competence and effectiveness of black-dominated government,

---

4 Lawrence Schlemmer and Ian Hirschfeld, *Founding Democracy and the New South African Voter* (Pretoria: HSRC, 1994), Chapter 4.

suggesting that in terms of issues of governance, there would not necessarily be an exclusion of non-African parties from their range of choices.[5]

The only issue which appeared to elicit an overwhelming consensus or consolidated response among African voters was that of *black dignity and status* (over 80 per cent endorsement). The most serious injury that apartheid was perceived to have wrought was its denial of self-worth for people of colour. This concern was fairly evenly distributed across supporters of different parties and was highest among IFP supporters (98 per cent). The intensity of this sentiment would link up with the "symbolic segregation" of the party-political field into white and black referred to earlier, in the sense of making it very difficult for Africans to vote for "old South Africa" parties which are inevitably associated with the denial of dignity.

Support for the Principle of Opposition

While one cannot expect the leaders of political parties to feel enthusiastic about opposition, the attitudes of the voters are crucial, particularly the extent to which they concede the positive effects of political competition and critical vigilance. In the 1991/92 nation-wide survey and subsequent nation-wide surveys conducted on this author's behalf by MarkData (stratified probability samples covering all adult South Africans), various items were put to respondents which give relevant insights. In a synoptic form, these items and the responses are given in Table 11.2. Additional evidence is available in the study *Launching Democracy*.[6]

Table 11.2: Levels of endorsement of propositions relating to opposition and the balance of power in society

	African voters		Whites
	All	High School	
Survey 1991/2, N 2600 Market and Opinion Surveys			
* Security forces controlled by largest party — "good"	32%	41%	12%
* Legal constraint on criticism of new black government — "good"	42%	40%	7%

5 Schlemmer and Hirschfeld, *Founding Democracy*, p. 59.
6 Johnson and Schlemmer, *Launching Democracy*, p. 255.

Table 11.2 (*contd.*)

	African voters		Whites
	All	High School	
* Freedom of majority party to rule without influence by opposition parties — "good"	55%	54%	37%
* Blacks should preferably support a single party/whites should stand together politically — "good"	64%	58%	83%
* Strongest political party should rule on its own (vs. rule by coalition of large parties)	45%	44%	32%
* Strong political party should govern without fear of losing elections (vs. strong competition for support)	74%	77%	39%
* A President who listens to all views and tries to satisfy as many as possible (vs. strong views, power and charisma)	75%	80%	62%
June 1996 Survey, N 1893, MarkData * An extremely dominant ANC governing alone: "very good/good" (ANC supporters: All: 53% (n 1080) Whites: 78% (n 10) Asians: 42% (n 55) Coloured: 49% (n 56)	45%	57%	na

Note In the MarkData survey, the "high-school plus" category denoted post-school qualifications whereas in the first set of results it is high-school graduate and above.

In a special survey in South Africa's major economic heartland. Gauteng, which has the most sophisticated voters, the patterns among Africans and whites in response to a question on the *relative influence which opposition parties should enjoy* are shown in Table 11.3.

Table 11.3: Results on opposition from a special survey of Gauteng, N 2400, Feb. 1994, MarkData

Desirable opposition	Africans	Coloureds	Asians	Whites
"Weak"	46%	16%	14%	9%
"Strong enough to influence government"	27%	54%	24%	27%
"Collectively strong enough to force government to concede issues"	14%	10%	25%	54%

The full range of results given in Tables 11.1–11.3 suggest that many voters prefer a "consensus" democracy to a "competitive" system, certainly under South Africa's current circumstances of immediate post-transition. Some further evidence on this is available (Table 11.4).

Table 11.4: Views of voters on systems of government

	Africans	Whites
November 1993 survey (N 2966, Market and Opinion Surveys):		
Various non-democratic options (partition/ethnic group domination/single party systems)	26%	26%
Competitive democracy, rule by winner	31%	14%
Consensus democracy, power-sharing	42%	57%
February 1994, Gauteng survey:[7]		
"One party strong enough to govern on own":	28%	12%
"Winning party includes others in government":	52%	32%
"Largest party not strong enough to govern alone — coalition":	14%	48%
December 1994 survey (N 1871, MarkData):		
In the GNU, should there be:		
– more co-operation?	75%	61%
– more opposition?	6%	31%

There is nothing surprising in the support by whites of strong opposition and consensus government; their political minority status inevitably makes these options very attractive. The Africans are the more interesting group, and while it is generally clear that they want their favoured party to be strong, there is very substantial support for the sharing of power and the reconciliation of opposing views.

More broadly, the results suggest that some 40–45 per cent of African voters are consistently rather hegemonically oriented, with little sympathy for democratic opposition or for competitive politics. On the other hand, at least some African voters, roughly one-quarter but clearly well short of a majority, appear to have a firm commitment to strong opposition and constraints on majority power. It is perhaps worth noting that the high-school graduates among Africans tended generally to be *less* tolerant of opposition influence than the rank-and-file voters—an indication that the

---

7 R.W. Johnson and Lawrence Schlemmer, *Launching Democracy in South Africa: The First Open Election* (New Haven: Yale University Press, 1996) p. 255.

emergence of a new middle class will not strengthen democracy for some time to come.

The distribution of all these attitudes is obviously conditioned by the strong position of the favourite African political choice, the ANC, and hence they are probably not principled or absolute choices. Whites are more committed to strong opposition, precisely because it would counter their fears of powerlessness. Nevertheless, it is within the reality of a strong ANC majority that democracy will be tested at the present time.

The Bases of Party Choice

A factor which is somewhat less conditioned by present assessments by voters of their strength or vulnerability is the considerations which voters bring to bear in making partisan choices. This factor is significant for the theme of this chapter because if voter choices are essentially concerned with the policies and performance of a government, one may expect a rather more fluid and competitive political system to emerge than would be the case if choices are determined by symbolic or identity concerns.

The survey in Gauteng for the *Launching Democracy* project probed the major reasons for supporting a particular political party. The summarised and paraphrased results are shown in Table 11.5. The responses in this survey were undoubtedly influenced by the impending 1994 open election in which people were voting on a very special occasion with very specific objectives and sentiments. In the 1992 Market and Opinion Surveys study, referred to earlier, a similar question was posed, but no election was in the offing, and the response alternatives differed somewhat. The results, also summarised and paraphrased, are shown in Tables 11.6 and 11.7.

Table 11.5: Reasons for party choice, Feb. 1994, Gauteng

	African	White
Ethnic/racial motivations	21%	43%
Charisma, strength and conviction	32%	13%
Religious/moral considerations	12%	22%
Law and order	21%	13%
Service delivery and socio-economic goals	4%	2%
Other/uncertain/DK	9%	7%

Table 11.6: Reasons for party choice nation-wide, 1992 (1st and 2nd answers summed, hence they exceed 100%)

	African	White
Strength and popularity	21%	4%
Will bring national prestige	28%	7%
Charisma and inspiration	21%	6%
Ethnic/racial motivations	16%	32%
Attention to socio-economic needs	50%	50%
Economic growth/investment	53%	67%

Table 11.7: Reasons for supporting a particular leader, 1992 (open question, answers categorised). (1st and 2nd answers summed as above)

	African	White
Charisma and symbolic status	40%	22%
Ability to bring peace	19%	16%
Ethnic/racial identity	13%	18%
Ability, intelligence, character	53%	67%
Socio-economic policy	68%	36%

The second and third sets of results (Tables 11.6 and 11.7) appear to represent the kind of motivations which would support a competitive democracy, with economic factors and socio-economic and welfare policy, or ability and policy commitments in a leader, as the prominent motivations. As one would expect, whites are more concerned with ethnic or minority group status than Africans in all sets. The items are sufficiently different to make comparisons hazardous, but the enormous difference in the selection of socio-economic factors between the 1992 and the 1994 responses cannot be explained entirely on the basis of the different items or response alternatives. There is a possibility, therefore, that the immediacy of the election in the first survey reported was associated with a *narrowing* of consciousness, with the focus shifting sharply to "security-based" or primordial concerns. It is possible that this "narrowing" of political consciousness will occur in the run-up to future elections as well.

One also has to bear in mind that the "socio-economic" issues which feature prominantly as a basis of party choice generally do not bridge black and white interests. Because of the mass of poverty in the African communities, most important socio-economic issues tend to reinforce the perceptions of fundamental divisions between the races.

From a slightly different perspective, respondents in the 1992 survey were asked what kind of person would be best able to articulate their interests in the political arena. Among Africans, 38 per cent mentioned racial identity and among whites the proportion was slightly higher at 42 per cent. There is therefore a quite considerable but not overwhelming imposition of the racial factor in political expression. Here again this would resonate with the symbolically segregated party-political field discussed earlier.

On balance, the responses reviewed immediately above, from the vantage point of the voter orientations which would support a competitive democracy, reflect a reasonably mixed situation. While whites are clearly historically conditioned and impelled by their present political minority status to be very concerned about ethnic interests, which would impart an inflexibility to their choices in politics, Africans seem to approach politics substantially from a concern with their circumstances, and with symbolic commitments less prominent. This set of findings, therefore, could be seen as reassuring for pluralism, with one very important aspect of uncertainty. This is the possibility that under conditions of mobilisation for an election, issues of policy might be displaced by the symbolism of the divided party-political field.

Popular Expectations: Consolidating Support or an Overload?
Giliomee, following T.J. Pempel and Di Palma, identifies one possible element in the consolidation of one-party dominant states as the establishment by the party winning the first democratic elections of a "national project": a high-visibility programme which, by convincing the mass electorate that the government will transform their lives, secures an intense identification between the party and a majority in the electorate. This is more than an issue of good governance—usually such projects are in the realm of the politics of "redemption".[8]

The ANC established just such a project in the Reconstruction and Development Programme (RDP): a co-ordinated, centrally planned and interlocking approach to the national upliftment of the formerly disadvantaged. Being based on central planning and co-ordination, it was a semi-socialist project which, in the light of international experience of "five-year plans" of various types, was a very high-risk venture, driven by all the pent-up idealism of progressive intellectuals who had been ignored or rejected by the previous government.

---

8 Hermann Giliomee, "Implications of the RDP for Consolidated Democracy", unpublished paper of which an abridged version appeared in *Frontiers of Freedom*, 6, 1995.

The risk did not pay off, and the RDP as a centrally controlled programme was suspended in 1996 after it had earned the government sustained bad press for falling behind delivery targets. Nevertheless, one must ask the question of whether it might not have achieved the aim of securing the *sympathy* of many in the electorate through the very good intentions which it signalled for nearly two years.

In a MarkData national survey in May/June, 1995, this author put the following statement to the African respondents: "Since coming into power, the new government has done its best for people like myself". Some 59 per cent of African voters agreed, and ANC supporters, at 61 per cent agreement, were most positive—supporters of other parties were some 10 per cent to 15 per cent lower than the ANC in levels of agreement. Significantly, however, people with no political affiliation were almost as positive as ANC supporters. About one-third of the African voters, and the same proportion among ANC supporters, disagreed. One can say, on this basis, that the government was substantially successful in convincing the electorate of its good intentions, but the one-third level of dissenting opinion is politically significant nonetheless.

Another item in the survey was: "Political leaders all make false promises and should not be completely trusted". In response, more than the dissenting one-third above, namely 48 per cent, agreed, and among ANC supporters 44 per cent agreed. It would seem, therefore, that the South African electorate may be a little too sophisticated for any one great mobilising project to have the full effect intended. As other results to be quoted in due course will show, the binding-in of the electorate in a party-linked development programme has only been semi-successful.

There is also an opposite outcome of ambitious national projects and the mobilisation of expectations. One of the major sources of instability in new political systems is the expectations that popular participation can create and the danger that no party could conceivably rise to the challenge of the intensely-felt needs and wants. This situation is commonly assumed to be the precursor to increasingly restrictive government and creeping authoritarianism.

At the present time, there is sufficient evidence of protest in the society to leave many observers with the impression that this problem may be a major future threat to democratic stability. There have been protests and demonstrations by nurses, teachers, policemen, shack-dwellers, pupils, university students, migrant workers and many other categories of interests, there is an ongoing failure among a majority of township residents in major towns and cities and particularly in Gauteng to pay rents and service charges, there are violent taxi wars, protests against traffic laws, illegal occupation of land and a host of other occurrences.

Yet, at the same time, one has to realise that the present time is one of much reallocation of expenditure and revisions to state funding formulae. Many of these sudden adjustments can be questioned for their wisdom, but given the fluidity of governance, it is perhaps surprising that there have not been more manifestations of protest. The protests and civil action which have occurred have most often been "opportunity-oriented" or reactive rather than displaying any more enduring commitment to social dissent. There has been little mass-protest in which a generalised *groundswell* of discontent has been evident, except in regard to the issue of crime.

The overall picture, on the basis of actual occurrences of protest, is therefore somewhat ambiguous—it does not necessarily show a future democracy to be under threat. Therefore, evidence from opinion surveys can be helpful in indicating the depth or otherwise of popular discontent, its potential to disrupt public life and the prospects for creeping authoritarianism in the governing party. The opinion surveys are not completely up to date but are recent enough to reflect emerging trends.

In December 1994, some six months after the Reconstruction and Development Programme (RDP), referred to earlier, had been in progress, this author, in conjunction with MarkData, ran a survey on expectations and their satisfaction or otherwise, based on a nation-wide sample which included 1463 Africans. Some 44 per cent of the African voters could already name the RDP and many more knew about the programme. When asked how soon they expected to feel the benefits, nearly 70 per cent said that they expected results within six months, a proportion more than three times higher than any previous findings by MarkData on the issue of time horizons of expectations. Expectations, therefore, had well and truly been raised.

Some 45 per cent felt that the programme was not working as well as they had expected, and this only dropped very slightly to 43 per cent among ANC supporters. On the other hand, less than 50 per cent indicated that they were actually disappointed or angry about the lack of results. When questioned about their understanding of the causes of slow delivery, a majority of the African voters took very sensible positions, blaming fiscal and financial constraints, too many expectations, high population growth, and the like. Some 14 per cent "blamed" the civil service, and only 8 per cent "blamed" their political leaders.

However, nearly one-third did not believe that the government was short of money and expected improvements to result from better administration and organisation, which may or may not occur. Those who did believe that the government was short of money tended, overwhelmingly, to emphasise the need for more economic growth and foreign investment. Fewer than

5 per cent spontaneously suggested increasing taxes on the wealthy and not a single respondent suggested forced redistribution from white to black.

In overall terms, therefore, although expectations had been raised, the "analysis" that the average African voter was making was much more sensible than most observers would have expected. The only danger sign for the ANC in government was the fact that some 16 per cent of African respondents, and roughly the same proportion of ANC respondents, offered the *spontaneous* criticism that the government was helping political "insiders" and the educated elite more than the masses—an early indication of an emerging perception of patronage and a "gravy train".

Some seven months later, in a follow-up survey, the balance of perceptions had not really shifted (MarkData, May/June Omnibus, N 1407 Africans). Over 60 per cent felt that their lives were improving and only slightly over one-third indicated that they felt that their circumstances were deteriorating. About 40 per cent declared themselves to be dissatisfied with the performance of the government, and the proportion was almost as high among ANC supporters.

In a more recent 1996 study in KwaZulu-Natal, Valerie Moller has also found that more people blame objective conditions for the failure of rapid reform than blame government performance. There was, however, a more negative than positive perception of the RDP Committees, through which the government had hoped to bind itself to grass-roots communities.[9] Given the preponderance of non-ANC supporters in KwaZulu-Natal, Moller's results were predictably more negative than those reported on above and the general impression from the Moller survey is that nation-wide perceptions would probably be very similar to those reported on the basis of the earlier surveys.

From these results, taken together, one can conclude that the government is not facing a typical "revolution of rising expectations" which is likely to lead to more civil disobedience or instability than already exists, with the possible exception of protests over crime. At the same time, at least one-third of ANC supporters are clearly disillusioned. A brief consideration of the likely effect of such disillusionment on political support patterns is necessary, therefore.

Table 11.8 presents estimates of the strength of political parties over time. In the table, the results presented for each survey *exclude* the voters who make no choice, which gives a rough estimate of what an election outcome

---

9 Valerie Moller, *Perceptions of Development in KwaZulu-Natal* (Durban: University of Natal, 1996).

would be. The results of the 1994 election and the 1995/96 local government elections are included as reference points, although local government
elections do not predict the outcomes of a general election, if for no other
reason than that the turnout is usually significantly below that typical of a
general election.

Table 11.8: Voter support patterns over time: election results and
MarkData surveys

	Feb. 1994	Election April 94	Feb-Sept 1995	Local Govt. Elec. 95	1996 June	Oct
ANC	69%	63%	64%	58%	62%	64%
PAC/AZAPO	1	1	2	1	2	4
NP	17	20	20	18	18	15
RATEPAY/IND	na	na	na	4	na	na
IFP	7	11	7	9	11	11
DP	1	2	2	3	1	2
RIGHT W.	1	2	4	3	3	3
OTHER	1	1	2	1	2	2
(N)	(2250)	–	(11000)	–	(4500)	(4500)

(Note   the local government election results are provisional)

The survey results are based on very large samples and hence are fairly
reliable. The level of support for the ANC over the period is best judged from
the survey data, because the elections are influenced by the fact that the supporters of the minority parties are more likely to be motivated to cast a vote
than the supporters of the majority party, which is expected by its supporters
to win.

Generally speaking, the results suggest a considerable stability in support
patterns after the pre- to post-election drop in ANC support. One must
expect that the first "liberation" election would have maximised ANC support up to a level which could not be sustained, even in the election itself.
Since then, however, ANC support has been stable. The only possible exceptions to this stability might be a slight increase in support for the PAC and a
slight decrease in support for the NP.

The stability of the levels of support for the ANC exists in contra-distinction
to the evidence of dissatisfaction encountered in the results already discussed, and it would suggest a fairly resilient "bonding" which has occurred
between the ANC and the mass of the black electorate.

It is perhaps worth bearing in mind that the trends which have been reflected so far have occurred in a fairly buoyant economic climate, which has been characterised by an expansion of consumer expenditure and credit growth. This favourable economic mood will not last: the first signs of a cyclical downturn in the economy are present and the government's new economic commitments are going to force it to curtail the growth of real state expenditure from now on. Hence, it is perhaps unlikely that the ANC will retain quite the level of dominance which it currently enjoys.

Dissent within the ANC must also be increased by the expulsion from the party of one of its most popular leaders, General Bantubonke Holomisa, and by the dissatisfaction of particularly the Eastern Cape traditional leaders, formerly staunch supporters of the ANC, over the lack of long-term protection of their powers in the new constitution.

At the same time, however, the stability of the findings in Table 11.8 would suggest that the party will retain a very powerful position despite some reduction of support. This general impression is strengthened by the responses of voters themselves in survey data. In a June 1994 MarkData survey (including a national sub-sample of 1400 Africans), respondents were asked whether or not they would consider voting for an alternative party to the one they had voted for. Among all African voters, only some 24 per cent indicated that they would consider an alternative party. Among ANC supporters, the percentage was much the same at 23 per cent—divided as follows: 12 per cent for the PAC, 9 per cent for the NP and no more than 2–3 per cent for other parties. Generally there was greater party loyalty evident among ANC supporters than among supporters of other parties among Africans.

On the whole these results suggest that it is unlikely that dissatisfied ANC supporters will swing to an alternative party in substantial numbers (they are more likely to simply not vote). While it certainly appears to be very possible that support for the ANC will drop closer to the 50 per cent level in the years leading up to the next election, the existing indications are that a clear African voter-based majority will be maintained. At the same time, however, if the opposition parties can maintain or raise the level of electoral motivation of their supporters, the constitutional threshold of a two-thirds majority required for constitutional changes could very well be unattainable for the ANC in the foreseeable future.

This possibility is somewhat constrained by the tendency for opposition parties faced with the type of demographic imbalance discussed to become demoralised. The signs in Table 11.8 of a fall in support for the National Party could well be an indication of this.

Freedom of Voter Choice

The anticipation of a slight fall in ANC support and the possibility of some increase in opposition support also presuppose un-coerced voting. The results of survey research conducted just before the 1994 elections provided very disturbing evidence of pressure on particularly African voters to vote in solidarity with the major liberation party or at least not to openly oppose it. In these pre-election surveys, some 28 per cent of Africans indicated that "groups controlling the area would make sure that one voted in a particular way", some 24 per cent agreed that "neighbours are hard on a person who disagrees politically", and 20 per cent claimed that there was "pressure on them to vote for a party they did not support".[10]

In a June 1994 nationwide MarkData survey (±1500 African voters), 23 per cent indicated that it was "dangerous" to talk about party-political choice in their communities. More recently, in special research undertaken just before the local government elections in KwaZulu-Natal, there was still evidence of anxiety and lack of confidence to venture out to vote among non-ANC supporters in ANC-dominated townships, and a similar discouragement of ANC supporters was evident in IFP-controlled rural areas. Whether the fears were justified or not is difficult to say, but the outcome of those local elections appeared to this author to be quite significantly influenced by the perceptions mentioned.

It is, of course, up to opposition parties to take the political offensive and challenge any constraints on freedom through counter-mobilisation—opposition parties enjoy the fullest formal protection under the constitution to do that. It is very hard work, however, and canvassing in the townships is a far cry from the congenial encounters in the leafy suburbs of their core constituencies.

It is possible, of course, that the agents of the pressures which were brought to bear on voters in 1994 will no longer be at full strength in 1999. Firstly, many of the activists who "called" people to vote and exerted pressure on dissenters have subsequently assumed political office or have obtained work in the public services. They now have issues to concern them other than political mobilisation, and in any event no longer have the time to organise "street committees". Furthermore, some of the youthful activists have become somewhat alienated from the ANC, if not by dissent in the ANC, then by their own behaviour. Since the 1994 election, there has had to be official action against self-perpetuating ANC-linked "Self-defence Units" and semi-political gangs that some of the less-successful activists have

---

10 Johnson and Schlemmer, *Launching Democracy*, pp. 96–97.

become involved in. (In KwaMashu, an ANC stronghold in Durban, for example, youthful criminal gangs have absorbed many of the non-employable activists from the period of mobilisation before the 1994 elections, and at one point forced the closure of schools and clinics and virtually caused a temporary informal state of emergency to be declared in the area.)

While it is not predicted that the problem of voter coercion will go away, it has become attenuated, and the 1999 elections are likely to be somewhat more free than the 1994 elections. That they will not be completely free is suggested by findings very recently adduced by R.W. Johnson. On the basis of October 1996 nation-wide survey data in which questions on political constraint were asked which were identical to those which we asked earlier, he concludes that no less than 46 per cent of South African voters feel that it is difficult to live in their neighbourhoods if their political views differ from those around them, and the proportion is substantially higher among African voters. Johnson talks of "…a clear and quasi-coercive push towards a particular version of political correctness".[11]

HEGEMONY IN BALANCE: BRIEF CONCLUSIONS

At the time of drafting this chapter, the Institute for a Democratic Alternative (IDASA) had published a nation-wide poll suggesting that only 41 per cent of South African voters are satisfied with the functioning of democracy. Among Africans the proportion was 47 per cent, with 52 per cent expressing dissatisfaction.[12] These results lend some additional weight to the strong possibility, identified in this analysis, that the high percentage polls and intense commitment which characterised the 1994 election will not be repeated. More broadly, readers of contemporary commentary in South Africa are becoming quite bored by the phrase "the honeymoon is over". Almost equally frequently one encounters predictions that the ANC is bound to split because of the wide differences in ideology and sentiment within its ranks. Hence it is not difficult to envisage a future in which a larger number of parties compete for power. This scenario, however, has to compete with the equally persuasive impression that the ANC, through its new appointees to public administration and its sponsorship of the surge of black empowerment taking place in the society, is firmly consolidating an unassailable electoral position.

---

11   R.W. Johnson, "The South African electorate at mid-term", *Focus Letter of the Helen Suzman Foundation*, 6, 1997, p. 2.
12   Bob Mattes *et al.*, *Opinion Poll*, IDASA, 2, 1, 1996.

The evidence bearing upon the prospects for a one-party dominant state which have been reviewed in this chapter are rather more mixed and complex, however. One the one hand, the opinion poll data show that majorities of the African voters, especially among the better-educated emerging middle class, tend to favour a hegemonic position for the most popular party. Furthermore, there is the suggestion in the data that when an election is at hand, issues of governance and policy might be displaced by simpler loyalties based on a symbolic division following almost neo-colonial lines. This has been referred to as the "segregation" of the political field into the "new" and "old" South Africa political parties; the latter, with the exception of the small Democratic Party, continuing to be stigmatised in the minds of African voters by a daily diet of disclosures of murderous apartheid excesses. This division in the political field is supported by an almost equally defined difference in political culture between newer and more established voluntary associations. Perceived (and possibly real) community pressure to conform to modal political sympathies will possibly cement these loyalties.

On the other hand, it would be surprising indeed if the extent of disappointment at the performance of government in living up to its election promises were not to depress enthusiasm for voting among its supporters. Furthermore, significant *minorities* of African voters appear to value the role of opposition and have developed a healthy cynicism with regard to political leadership.

While there is very little prospect that there will be a large increase in support by Africans for the formerly white parties or that the ANC will lose its status as the largest party, there is every chance that an energetic performance by the opposition parties, both to the left and the right of the ANC, coupled with a decline in ANC voter enthusiasm, could somewhat reduce the present super-dominance of a single party. For this to happen, however, the major opposition parties will have to counter the fall in morale of their supporters which seems to be occurring because of the overriding demographic imbalance in the electorate.

Even if there is a decline in support for the ANC and some revitalisation of non-African opposition parties, however, it will not necessarily mean that a system of alternating majorities—one condition on which majority rule preserves political equality and inclusiveness—will become acceptable and established in time. The symbolic division of the party-political field into parties of the "new" and the "old" order makes it extremely unlikely that, say, an alliance of parties from the "pre-liberation" period will be able to form an effective government. This would simply re-stimulate the already active perceptions of apartheid divisions, and reintroduce the dynamics of the struggle against "minority rule", possibly threatening the rather brittle stability in the country. This could occur despite the fact that somewhat more Africans than at present might be supporting the hypothetical minority alliance. The division of civil society into progressive and establishment camps would facilitate the rebirth of the culture of "struggle".

Any hypothetical opposition-based ruling formation therefore, might be forced would have to include the ANC. In fact, perhaps the most that political minorities can hope for is the re-establishment, on more defensive and electorally legitimate grounds, of the early Government of National Unity. As the results quoted in this analysis show, this would be in perfect alignment with the very strong endorsement of "consensus" government among South African Voters. Despite decades of emphatic ANC rejection of the principle of "consociational" government as a response to a divided polity, the notion is alive and well in the consciousness of both black and white voters.

Put differently, it is almost as if South Africans will be fated to choose between either a one-party dominant system or a *consociation* which includes the strongest "African" party. Such an outcome will not be a formally-defined *ethnic* coalition, as one might find in, say, Belgium or the Lebanon, but rather a coalition with mixed elements of class, race and ethnicity as its essential features, defined in their relationship to one another by the divisions of the past.

The suggestion arising from this review, therefore, is that a one-party dominant system is the most likely outcome for the foreseeable future. It will not be quite the dead hand of majoritarianism that has developed elsewhere in parts of Africa, because there are substantial minorities of voters who are committed to "contestation" as Dahl has termed it. This will at least keep active political debate alive. At the same time, however, it will persistently undermine the electoral motivations and morale of the sections of the electorate whose social identities exclude them from the political majority.

A remotely feasible alternative to this segmental hegemony is not likely to be the open pluralist democracy with political parties alternating in executive authority. Rather, it will be a consociation of racial majority and racial minority-based parties. Such an outcome would not be the first prize of multi-party pluralism but, by countering the political alienation of minorities, it would be infinitely superior to a one-party dominant system.

It must be emphasised, however, that it is a very much less-probable future scenario, because the minority parties would not be taken very seriously unless collectively they achieve 50 per cent of voter support or more; a very large challenge. Furthermore, the ANC always has the option of a coalition between itself, the IFP and/or the PAC if the minority-based parties appear to threaten its hegemony, thus effectively retaining power in the hands of Africans. Recently there has been a relaxation of the tensions which exist between the ANC and the IFP in Natal and closer cooperation between these parties appears to be becoming more and more likely. President Mandela has in a sense symbolised this possibility by appointing Chief Buthelezi, the leader of the IFP, acting President for a brief while. He has also had discussions with the PAC about the possibility of that party joining the cabinet, in a government of unity with the ANC and the IFP.

On the balance of probabilities, therefore, a one-party dominant system or at least an "Africanist" party-dominant system is the likely future of electoral democracy in South Africa. The alternative of some form of cross-racial coalition is an outside possibility, but it will require almost superhuman electoral efforts on the part of minority-based parties, in the course of which they will have to counter the demoralisation of their own supporters. Minority groups in South Africa would therefore be well advised to develop strategies for political participation which do not assume electoral growth and leverage. Mobilisation for a more effective voice in civil society and in the lobbying process seems to be the obvious strategy to follow.

Chapter 12

GRASSROOTS ELECTORAL ORGANIZATION AND POLITICAL REFORM IN THE ROC ON TAIWAN AND MEXICO

SHELLEY RIGGER

In Mexico and in the Republic of China on Taiwan, elections have proven to be both a boon and a threat to dominant parties. Elections can be an effective tool for reinforcing a dominant party's power and legitimacy, and for gaining international support for a regime whose autocratic features otherwise discomfit potential supporters overseas. But elections can be dangerous too. If they are too clean and open, they will enjoy a high degree of support and legitimacy, but the dominant party will have to expend vast resources to face down challenges from its opponents. If elections are obviously staged or fraudulent, the very institution that was designed to boost the dominant party's legitimacy may end up undermining it. A dominant party which hopes to use elections to achieve domestic and international legitimacy must develop an electoral system capable of providing political benefits at a cost the dominant party can afford to pay. I shall call on political strategy that combines vigorous citizen participation with strict dominant party control over political and policy outcomes "mobilizational authoritarianism". This strategy characterizes the approach to grassroots electoral politics in Mexico and in the ROC on Taiwan.

Beginning in the 1970s, the governments of Mexico and Taiwan faced increasingly urgent demands from domestic and international forces to implement political reforms, demands which had become irresistible by the late 1980s. Reform, in turn, intensified the pressure on the dominant parties, Mexico's PRI and Taiwan's KMT. To a great extent, this pressure manifested itself through the electoral system. In Mexico, electoral reform continues to be relatively modest, and the PRI still maintains substantial control over electoral outcomes. In Taiwan, however, electoral liberalization was more far-reaching, and still more reforms are planned. As a result, the KMT's dominant position in ROC politics faces severe challenges, not only from opposition parties, but from dissident groups and individuals within the KMT itself.

The leaders of the dominant parties in Mexico (the Party of Institutional Revolution, or PRI) and Taiwan (the Kuomintang, or KMT) appreciate both the benefits and the risks of elections. To escape this dilemma, the two parties developed electoral systems based on controlled participation to help consolidate their dominant party states. In Mexico the process occurred just after the Revolution; in Taiwan it took place in the early 1950s after the KMT was forced to take up residence in Taiwan. Mexican elections encompassed all levels of government, including the presidency. In Taiwan, electoral competition was limited to local offices until the 1970s at which point a small number of seats in national legislative bodies were opened to election. Using carefully constructed mobilizational networks, the dominant parties were able to win elections by large margins, resorting only rarely to excessive fraud or coercion. As a result, citizens and, indeed, many outside observers, accepted the legitimacy of elections in general, even if they occasionally questioned the procedures and outcomes in particular contests. This is not to suggest that fraud and corruption are unknown in Taiwan and Mexico, but, at least until recently, the dominant parties' mobilization systems worked smoothly enough to ensure wide margins of victory in most races even without strong-arm tactics.

In both Taiwan and Mexico, a two-pronged strategy allowed the dominant party to add consistent popular support in elections to its other political resources. The first prong was a corporatist interest group structure; the second, a patronage-based system of electoral mobilization. Prior to the introduction of reforms, one or the other of these channels captured nearly every voter in Taiwan and Mexico. This chapter will focus on patronage-based electoral mobilization and its gradual weakening over the course of the liberalization process. It is important to keep in mind that for many voters, corporatist organizational ties—including affiliations with state-sponsored labor unions, public employees' organizations, farmers associations, women's and youth associations and business groups—are a more important link to the dominant party than are the patronage-based networks. Political liberalization in Taiwan and major economic and political reforms in Mexico helped to undermine the effectiveness of both the patronage-based and the corporatist components of the two countries' electoral mobilization systems.

GRASSROOTS ELECTORAL ORGANIZATION IN TAIWAN

Electoral mobilization in Taiwan follows a classic clientelistic, machine politics model. At the village or neighborhood level, vote brokers known as *tiau-a-ka* (*zhuangjiao* in Mandarin) solicit votes on behalf of candidates with whom they enjoy long-standing patron–client relationships. *Tiau-a-ka* rely on three main sources of influence to secure votes for their patrons. First, many *tiau-a-ka* are community opinion leaders whose judgment in political matters is respected. Clan heads, successful businessmen and physicians, religious leaders and others whose knowledge of politics is admired can sway many voters through ordinary persuasion.

Second, many *tiau-a-ka* occupy low-level political offices that enable them to claim credit for community benefits, which indeed are often made possible by the largess of a *tiau-a-ka*'s patron. In these cases, a neighborhood head (an appointed official responsible to an elected ward leader) might organize votes on behalf of the ward, village or township head in exchange for improved public services in the neighborhood. Likewise, a higher official (a county council member or municipal executive) might use connections in the provincial and central governments to arrange large-scale construction to benefit his or her constituents. *Tiau-a-ka* point to these projects in their conversations with voters, offering them both as proof of the politician's effectiveness and as benefits that would disappear were the patron not re-elected.

Third, *tiau-a-ka* offer selective benefits to individual voters in exchange for their support. Often, these benefits fall into the category of constituent service. As is common in democracies, politicians use local representatives to assist voters with bureaucratic transactions and other minor matters in order to secure their confidence and support. In other cases, selective benefits take a more sinister form, known as *huixuan* (electoral corruption) or *maipiao xingwei* (vote buying behavior). This widespread practice began as an exchange of low-value gifts (soap, cigarettes) for votes, but has metastasized into a major social problem, with large sums of money changing hands in each electoral season. From the politicians' perspective, vote buying is dangerous (because illegal), costly, and necessary, as long as opponents are doing it. From the *tiau-a-ka*'s perspective, vote-buying is profitable (vote brokers routinely skim a "commission" from the vote buying funds provided by candidates), and useful in ensuring compliance with the *tiau-a-ka*'s advice. Still, vote buying is an unreliable tool of mobilization: campaign activists interviewed in 1991 estimated that only about twenty per cent of the voters accepting a bribe from a campaign actually cast their ballots for the candidate offering the money.

In the 1980s, political reform increased the competitiveness of Taiwanese elections, driving up the price of votes. At the same time, public and private campaigns to persuade Taiwanese that vote buying is unethical succeeded to the point where most voters (especially in urban areas) feel little moral commitment to *tiau-a-ka* who offer bribes. Many voters accept money from several campaigns for the same office, and they increasingly reject the notion that they are obligated to vote for candidates from whom they accept a gift.

Vote buying has had a number of regrettable effects on Taiwanese elections. Above all, it has created strong incentives for elected officials to abuse their power as office-holders in the hope of recovering the enormous costs of electoral campaigns, leading to the widely-lamented phenomenon of "money politics". In addition, the enormous sums of money involved in today's highly competitive market for votes contribute to the rising involvement of organized crime groups in politics, resulting in both corruption and violence. Importantly, however, electoral violence in Taiwan is limited to competing candidates, their campaign assistants and their *tiau-a-ka*; it is rare for vote brokers to abuse or threaten voters in this seller's market for votes. What is significant about these developments is that despite the enormous advantages that would accrue both to politicians and the public were vote buying to be abandoned, the practice is so deeply embedded in Taiwan's electoral mobilization system that it has so far proven impossible to eradicate.

Tiau-a-ka use personal charisma, community benefits and individual benefits to mobilize votes for their patrons. In exchange, politicians reward their clients with other sorts of selective benefits. Often, a politician boosts the reputation and status of a *tiau-a-ka* by singling him out for recognition. It is common to see large inscribed placards in the homes and offices of local opinion leaders, conveying the good wishes of an important political figure. In addition, politicians offer money, often in the form of the commission on vote buying, and they support their vote brokers' own political ambitions. The chains of patronage that begin at the grassroots level extend upward through many layers of elected officials. The village head who uses clan leaders and neighborhood bosses as *tiau-a-ka* in turn serves as a vote broker for the township head, who for his part solicits votes for county council candidates, and so on, up to the level of the Taiwan provincial assembly and the Legislative Yuan, Taiwan's national law-making body.

In its bare outlines, Taiwan's patronage system is little different from many other political machines. And like other political machines, it is dominated by a single political party. Even after two decades of political reform, opposition parties have captured the mobilization system in only a handful of localities. Whatever their conflicts at the local level, and whatever their private opinions of the central leadership, those who wish to take part in the patronage system have little choice but to do so through the Kuomintang. The reason is simple: As the dominant party, the KMT controls access to the selective benefits *tiau-a-ka* use to win votes: civil service employment, public construction funds and bureaucratic resources. In short, in an electoral mobilization system based on material rewards, the dominant party controls the resources, and so controls the system.

Even before the reform era began, Taiwan's patronage system had a number of unique characteristics. Most importantly, its political machine embraces internal competition. Beginning at the village or neighborhood level, Taiwan's municipalities are riven by conflicts between local factions (*difang paixi*). Each of Taiwan's 23 municipalities is the home of two or three county- or city-wide factions, most of which have existed for decades. Because Taiwan's electoral districts follow municipal boundaries, it is possible to win election to all but the two highest offices in the land (Taiwan provincial governor and ROC president, which became elective in 1995 and 1996, respectively) without expanding local factions beyond the municipal level. Competition among these local factions is ferocious.[1]

On the surface, local factionalism would seem to threaten the stability of a dominant party system, but in practice, Taiwan's factionalism actually reinforced the KMT's power in the pre-reform era. In fact, the dominant party encouraged local factions to grow and compete as part of its strategy for electoral mobilization. With a handful of important exceptions, all local factions in Taiwan are affiliated with the KMT. The candidates they support run for office as nominees of the dominant party, and they coordinate their nominations and campaign strategies through local KMT party headquarters. Local factions were willing to cooperate with the dominant party for a number of reasons. Most importantly, until 1986, opposition parties were outlawed in Taiwan. A local faction that refused to join the KMT would have had to operate entirely on its own, against a vastly better-funded and more powerful opponent. Eventually, some local factions did break with the KMT, but they were few, and scattered.

Local factions cooperated with the dominant party also because it held the purse strings—even at the local level. Even today, municipalities rely on the central and provincial governments for most of their revenue; as long as the KMT holds a majority of votes in the provincial assembly and Legislative Yuan, any county or city that refuses to cooperate with the party could find itself cut off from necessary funds and services. Finally, the KMT's electoral resources were so overwhelming as to virtually guarantee success for any candidate running as a party nominee. Even as late as 1989, three years after the ban on new parties was lifted, 82 per cent of KMT nominees for national and provincial offices were elected, compared to 37 per cent for nominees of other parties (independent candidates' chances were

---

1 For a detailed study of the factional competition see Shelley Rigger, "The Risk of Reform: Factional Conflict in Taiwan's 1989 Local Elections", *American Journal of Chinese Studies*, 2, 2 (1994).

negligible.[2] Recognizing these realities, most local politicians were willing to be recruited into the ruling party early in their careers, and local factions made little effort to resist incorporation. In fact, local factions competed with one another for votes in part to impress the KMT. Each faction hoped to out-poll its competition, thereby proving itself worthy of nomination to such plum offices as municipal executive or national legislator.

Allowing local factions to exert themselves on the dominant party's behalf in exchange for political patronage was an extraordinarily successful strategy for promoting controlled participation. Above all, the local factions' vigorous competition kept voter turnout extremely high; factions mobilized millions of Taiwanese into regime-supportive political activity. Until the late 1970s, when the ROC government began easing restrictions on opposition candidates, even the most competitive local elections were contests between candidates affiliated with the KMT. These politicians fought fiercely for votes for the dominant party, then quietly acquiesced in its policy agenda. Since the basis of factional competition was providing selective benefits to voters, and not promoting ideological or policy positions, candidates felt little pressure to distinguish themselves from their opponents once in office. What is more, local factionalism had no effect on the central government, because factional conflicts were limited to the municipalities, insulating the central government from factional strife.

Local factionalism also benefitted the dominant party by identifying authentic grassroots leaders and integrating them (and their followers) into the party. In the process of competing for local offices and the spoils that came with them, capable and popular local figures emerged as candidates. In order to win elections, these local leaders allowed themselves to be coopted by the dominant party. This was especially valuable to the KMT, which, as an exile regime, depended upon winning over the Taiwanese people for its very survival. A third advantage of promoting competition was that the benefits of doing so clearly outweighed the costs. Not only did competitive local elections excite enthusiastic participation in KMT politics; what was more, competition facilitated a divide-and-rule strategy by which the KMT could use its control over centralized resources to ensure that no local faction ever challenged the party at the level of policy. Finally, local factional conflict absorbed political energies that might otherwise have gone into opposition activity. By allowing Taiwanese to fight their way up a prestigious electoral ladder, the KMT was able to suppress demands for liberalization for more

---

2 Rigger, "The Risk of Reform", p. 137.

than two decades. Finally, permitting competition to flourish at the local level did not endanger the KMT's control over the central state, because until the late 1980s, the KMT effectively walled off the central government from electoral competition.

In sum, the KMT's network of competitive local political machines proved to be an effective tool for mobilizing active support for Taiwan's dominant party. A number of institutional features of Taiwan's electoral process facilitated this strategy. Above all, Taiwan's unusual electoral system, the single, non-transferrable vote formula, made competitive clientelism possible. Voters in all non-executive races in Taiwan select a single candidate to represent them in multi-member districts. Candidates with the highest vote totals are elected, until all of a district's seats are filled (most districts have between two and eight seats, although some urban legislative districts elect a more than a dozen representatives). If it is to maximize its representation in elected bodies, the KMT must elect more than one candidate in each district. The dominant party turned this necessity into a virtue by encouraging local factions to support different candidates for the same office. The rivalries that resulted ensured high levels of participation and enthusiasm, since *tiau-a-ka* and voters saw the elections as highly competitive, but the make-up of the representative bodies that resulted from these elections overwhelmingly favored the KMT.

Besides the single, non-transferrable vote formula, other aspects of Taiwan's electoral system also contributed to the success of the KMT's electoral mobilization strategy. For example, the dominant party outlawed new opposition parties in 1947, as part of a martial law enacted in the last years of the Chinese civil war. In theory, two small alternative parties did exist, but the KMT thoroughly coopted them both, and they have never provided an organizational framework for opposition views. In the absence of opposition parties, politically ambitious Taiwanese were forced into the KMT. The dominant party welcomed Taiwanese participation at the local level, granting politicians access to valuable patronage and status benefits. In addition, the regime strictly regulated campaign activities, making it nearly impossible to appeal to voters except through clientelistic networks. All forms of mass communication were off-limits to political candidates, including broadcast and newspaper advertising, broad distribution of campaign posters, and privately sponsored gatherings of candidates and voters.

Finally, the dominant party balanced the need for the appearance of democracy with its desire to control policy-making by limiting elected offices to the provincial level and below. The justification for not holding elections for central government offices was that the ROC government represented all of China. As a result, it would be inappropriate and illegitimate to allow the people of Taiwan (only one province) to elect a government for the entire nation. Instead, the ROC government froze the legislators and National Assembly members elected in mainland China in 1947 in office until the early 1990s. The practical result of this policy was to ensure total party control over decision-making at the national level. By concentrating power over public spending at all levels of administration in central government hands, the dominant party guaranteed that its policies never faced serious challenges from elected representatives.

Taiwan's patronage machine mobilized voters through the entreaties of vote brokers (*tiau-a-ka*) linked to local factions sponsoring candidates for village, township, county and provincial offices. In exchange for their efforts, local politicians and vote brokers received selective benefits for themselves and for those whose votes they won. This system, combined with a corporatist interest group structure, succeeded in tying most Taiwanese voters to the KMT in the first three decades of ROC rule on Taiwan. However, the system inadvertently planted the seeds of its own destruction. As political liberalization accelerated in the 1980s, mobilizational authoritarianism came under threat from several directions. In particular, reforms eroded the institutional arrangements that protected the political machines, at the same time that increasing competition for local offices undermined the willingness of politicians and *tiau-a-ka* to cooperate with KMT strategies. In the 1990s, the KMT's survival as a dominant party is in doubt.

GRASSROOTS ELECTORAL ORGANIZATION IN MEXICO

Mexico's dominant party uses a strategy of controlled participation to achieve the political benefits of elections without losing its grip on policy outcomes. And like Taiwan's KMT, the PRI is finding this task increasingly difficult as it implements reforms. Nonetheless, there are significant differences between the Mexican and Taiwanese versions of mobilizational authoritarianism; likewise, their experiences with reform have differed. To an even greater extent than in Taiwan, Mexico's dominant party has used corporatist ties to mobilize support and participation. As a result, Mexico's clientelist networks of vote brokers, known as *caciques*, have operated mainly in rural communities and poor urban neighborhoods where corporatist organizations were not effective (in Taiwan, patronage networks were important in all communities). In addition, the *cacique's* powers were more extensive than those of his Taiwanese counterpart. According to Wayne Cornelius,

In both urban and rural contexts in Mexico, a *cacique* is recognized both by the residents of the community in which he operates and by the supralocal authorities of the government and the PRI as being the most powerful person in the local political arena. Public officials invariably deal with him in all matters affecting the community, to the exclusion of other potential leaders. The *cacique* also possesses the de facto authority to make decisions that are binding on the community under his control.[3]

Caciques' sources of influence and power were similar to those of Taiwan's *tiau-a-ka*, but more extensive. They included the *cacique's* personal charisma, economic resources, and coercive abilities; a retinue of supporters (*comitiva*) of low-level government and party officials who owed their posts to the *cacique's* patronage efforts; and power derived from contacts with higher officials. One of the major differences between the *cacique* and the *tiau-a-ka* was the use of coercion and negative sanctions by *cacique* to compel cooperation from ordinary Mexicans. In Taiwan, the *tiau-a-ka*'s function was persuasive; the existence of competing factions at the local level limited the degree to which a *tiau-a-ka* could force compliance (although threats are not unheard of, especially in small villages).

The *cacique* was not only a vote broker, but a full-scale community boss, with all sorts of coercive means at his disposal. According to Coppedge, the *caciques'* distinguishing characteristics were greed and brutality. In rural areas, *caciques* "enlarged their estates by tricking, intimidating, and murdering peasant farmers...made themselves partners in any profitable ventures in the region, and...gained monopolistic control over the local economy in order to extract the greatest possible profit...Indeed, it is hard to escape the impression that this was the whole point of being a *cacique*."[4] Urban *caciques'* power was more limited, but they nonetheless managed to enrich themselves and compel political support for the PRI within their individual bailiwicks.

Politically, *caciques* performed most of the functions of Taiwanese vote brokers. The *cacique* was responsible for seeing to it that his territory was quiescent and supportive of the PRI at election time. He was permitted to use whatever methods he deemed necessary, whether carrot or stick, to achieve those goals. At the same time, the *cacique* made sure that opposition activism did not arise on his turf, even to the point of violently suppressing it. He also was expected to mobilize his community in support of the dominant party

---

3   Wayne A. Cornelius, *Politics and the Migrant Poor in Mexico City* (Stanford: Stanford University Press, 1975), p. 141.
4   Michael Coppedge, "Party and Society in Mexico and Venezuela: Why competition matters", *Comparative Politics*, 1993, p. 264.

between elections, turning out crowds for "patriotic celebrations, official party meetings and rallies, the inauguration of public works, and peaceful demonstrations in support of the incumbent authorities."[5] Mexican officials rewarded *caciques* for their efforts in two ways: with opportunities for personal enrichment and with community-wide patronage and public works for which *caciques* claimed credit, whether deservedly or not.

As in Taiwan, Mexico's political machine belonged to the dominant party. Even *caciques* who rose to power in their communities without PRI help "once in power...invariably allied with a PRI governor, deputy, or senator to insure good connections with the government...Eventually, many of these *caciques* became PRI deputies, senators, or governors themselves."[6] In the event that an opposition party gained a foothold in a neighborhood or village, whether by winning over or challenging the *cacique*, the PRI used its resources to coopt or repress the dissident faction. As a result, Mexico's grassroots political scene was entirely lacking in competition, either between political parties or within the dominant party. As Cornelius put it, "The *cacique*...seeks to monopolize all links between the community under his control and the political and bureaucratic structures in the external environment. He will take pains to portray himself as the only officially recognized intermediary, and thus the only person in a position to work productively with the government for the betterment of the community."[7] PRI officials encouraged this monopoly, except when they were actively working to replace an incompetent or unco-operative *cacique*.

Caciques and *tiau-a-ka* share many basic functions and characteristics. Both provided a vital service within the mobilizational authoritarian strategy, linking dominant party politicians with voters. Without these vote brokers, the dominant parties would have been forced to invest far more heavily in programs and campaigns to attract support. As it was, they channeled state resources to individual vote brokers, who performed the leg work of mobilizing grassroots support. Despite these similarities, there are a number of important differences between the Mexican and Taiwanese versions of the mobilizational authoritarian strategy. As we have seen, *caciques* were far more powerful than *tiau-a-ka*, exercising nearly dictatorial power in small communities, and enriching themselves in the process. In addition, the exertions required of citizens were greater in Mexico, where the grassroots were required to take their support beyond the polling station, to meetings and rallies.

---

5   Cornelius, *Politics and the Migrant Poor*, p. 80.
6   Coppedge, "Parties and Society", p. 262.
7   Cornelius, *Politics and the Migrant Poor*, p. 159.

The most significant contrast between the Mexican and Taiwanese versions of mobilizational authoritarianism lies in the absence of competition in Mexican politics at the grassroots level. As Coppedge has convincingly argued (in a comparison of Mexican and Venezuelan *caciquismo*), in the absence of competition, *caciques'* power within local communities was virtually unchecked. As a result, *caciques* in Mexico indulged in avarice and violence, whereas their Taiwanese counterparts, operating in a competitive environment, were forced to rely on positive persuasion. As Coppedge put it, "*Caciques* who have to compete use more carrots than sticks, while a broker who is the only game in town can operate with impunity."[8]

The major differences in Mexican and Taiwanese grassroots political organization can be attributed to historical and structural factors. In Mexico, permitting local bosses to run their communities in the name of the PRI was less risky than it would have been in Taiwan, because the PRI did not have the same need to establish its legitimacy. The PRI was not an outsider regime; on the contrary, it was the heir to the ideologically-powerful Mexican Revolution. However, given its link to the democratic ideals of the revolution, the PRI regime's legitimacy and stability depended upon regular demonstrations of support at the ballot box. As a result, even though the real route to power for PRI officials is through the bureaucracy, it was extremely important that ambitious politicians be able to turn out grassroots supporters for PRI activities. The KMT, for its part, claimed legitimacy through its historical position in mainland China. Winning elections in Taiwan was not a central pillar of the KMT's claim to authority. Therefore, in the pre-reform era, electoral performance was not an important factor determining an individual's promotion within the KMT.

Structurally, Mexico's winner-take-all electoral system meant that, unlike the KMT, the PRI had no incentive to nominate multiple candidates for each office. This, in turn, eliminated the need for competitive local factions as a vote-getting strategy. At the same time, the PRI had a much stronger need to control electoral outcomes than did Taiwan. Because Mexican voters were entrusted with the selection of leaders at all levels, including the national legislature and the president, the PRI needed to win every election by a wide margin. In Taiwan, national policy makers were insulated from electoral competition; even if the KMT were to lose some local races, the effect on its control of policy outcomes was negligible.

---

8 Coppedge, "Parties and Society", p. 264.

POLITICAL REFORM AND GRASSROOTS MOBILIZATION
IN MEXICO AND TAIWAN

The grassroots mobilization efforts of the dominant parties in Mexico and Taiwan worked extraordinarily well into the 1970s and '80s. Both dominant parties consistently won elections by wide margins, with high levels of voter participation. Beginning in the 1970s, however, the two regimes recognized a growing need for electoral and political reform. In both cases, the experience of reform altered the effectiveness of the mobilization system; however, the causes, nature and results of the reforms differed widely. In Taiwan, the need for reform emerged from a number of converging historical and political processes. Perhaps most importantly, the KMT lost much of its international prestige and standing in the 1970s, when it was removed from the United Nations and lost its diplomatic ties with the US and other major countries. The crisis of confidence these international setbacks provoked deepened in the face of domestic financial and political scandals.

President Chiang Ching-kuo is widely credited with realizing the need for political reform in Taiwan and pressing for change within the KMT. In 1969, the central government held direct elections to replace a handful of Legislative Yuan members who had died in office, the first national elections held in Taiwan. At the same time, domestic political forces demanding reform began to challenge the KMT's dominant position. The opposition concentrated on two major demands, both of which quickly gained sympathy in Taiwan and internationally. First, the opposition demanded democratization, which it understood to mean the full implementation of the Republic of China's constitution. (In later years, the opposition would demand constitutional revisions; however, in the 1970s and '80s, the emphasis was on realizing the document's democratic promises.) Second, the opposition sought a larger role for the Taiwan-born population in the central government. From the time of Taiwan's retrocession to ROC control in 1945, its administration was dominated by officials from mainland China. After the ROC government moved to Taipei in 1949, the policy-making monopoly of the so-called Mainlanders was nearly absolute. The opposition asked that Taiwanese be given a policy-making role more nearly proportional to their share of the population, at that time about 85 per cent.

Opposition political activists fell into two categories. First, in urban areas, a cadre of independent professionals were building an activist movement centered on an ever-changing selection of political journals. Because the regime tightly censored opposition publications, the activists played a cat-and-mouse game, reopening banned publications under new names and publishing journals as books series (book censorship was looser than magazine censorship). In the late 1970s, some of these activists began to seek elected offices. They gradually combined their efforts, hiding proto-party activities behind publications and an island-wide network of "service centers". The second opposition force emerged from the KMT's own grassroots networks. These were local politicians who, for various reasons, had become disenchanted with the ruling party. Men like the Kaohsiung County political boss Yu Teng-fa had built large grassroots followings as leaders of local factions. When they defected to the opposition, most of their supporters defected with them. These grassroots figures joined forces with the urban intellectuals to pose a formidable challenge to the KMT.

Through the 1970s and early 1980s, the electoral performance of the opposition improved gradually, and the crescendo of demands for democratization and ethnic justice grew too loud to ignore. Throughout the 1980s, Taiwan's government implemented one reform after another, promoting ever-larger numbers of Taiwanese to government offices, scheduling direct elections for a growing number of legislative seats and removing restrictions on speech, publication and political activity. In 1986, the opposition defied the ban on new political parties to form the Democratic Progressive Party. Instead of suppressing the move, the regime lifted the ban the following year. At the same time, the regime lifted many restrictions on campaign activity. In 1991 and 1992, the last of the national legislators chosen in 1947 retired, and were replaced through direct elections. In 1994 and 1996, the two highest executive positions in the land, the governor of Taiwan Province and the ROC president, were popularly elected under election rules no more restrictive than in most other democracies.

All of these institutional reforms tended to have the same effect at the grassroots level: they improved opposition candidates' chances of winning. Lifting campaign restrictions meant unknown candidates could use mass communications to reach wide audiences, gain name recognition and appeal to voters. Opening more responsible offices to direct election increased the weight of campaigns in voters' eyes; in some cases, debates over issues and policy replaced patronage in the political foreground. Allowing new political parties gave opposition candidates organizational resources to compete on a more equal footing (although the KMT still enjoys huge advantages in terms of economic and political resources). As competitiveness increased, however, the KMT's ability to dominate local elections diminished. Local KMT headquarters no longer could promise local factions easy victories if they cooperated with party strategy. Opposition candidates acted as spoilers in these carefully orchestrated contests, setting KMT candidates at odds and driving factions into one another's territory to steal away *tiau-a-ka* and votes. Some *tiau-a-ka* affiliated with opposition candidates and parties, while others learned to bargain with various candidates and factions for a better deal.

Another critically important consequence of the rising competitiveness of ROC elections is the growing influence of local factions in the process. No longer are factions the tail, wagging obediently at the behest of KMT leaders. Increasingly, local factions are wagging the dog. Between 1950 and 1990, local factions gained a powerful emotional dimension; vote brokers and politicians felt a deeper loyalty to their factions than to the KMT itself. With the appearance of the Democratic Progressive Party, factions quickly learned to use the opposition to gain leverage over the dominant party. In some cases, local factions actually defected to the opposition to protest what they saw as the KMT's failure to reward them adequately. And even when the KMT wins elections, it cannot always control the elected candidates, some of whom recognize that the party needs their cooperation at least as much as they need its support.

As the ROC opened national-level offices to electoral competition, the KMT was forced to rely more than ever on local factions to retain its hold on the legislature. Increasingly, the KMT's efforts to maintain party discipline and control policy outcomes are complicated and even thwarted by the pressure to win local elections. One of the most unfortunate trends in Taiwanese politics is the growing influence of gangsters entering politics through local factions. In some municipalities, a majority of council members have gangland connections. Needless to say, this has led to corruption and politically motivated violence, including the brutal murder of a county executive and his assistants in 1996. In sum, competitiveness has undermined the KMT's dominance both at the level of elected bodies, where opposition victories have slashed the ruling party's majority, and at the grassroots level, where the KMT finds itself in the uncomfortable position of depending upon self-interested grassroots political forces to deliver the votes needed to maintain the dominant party's increasingly narrow majority.

Mexico's grassroots electoral mobilization strategy also came under pressure in the 1970s, pressure which intensified in the '80s. In the '70s, national party leaders began to worry that Mexico's authoritarian reputation, both at the national level and at the local level (as represented by the *cacique* phenomenon), was alienating Mexican voters. Falling voter turnout was undermining the party's claim to legitimacy based on broad popular support. In response, the regime implemented a series of electoral and administrative reforms in 1977. The electoral reforms were designed to promote voter participation by increasing the role of opposition parties. The new rules provided for a combination of winner-take-all and proportional representation in

Congress, and they reserved a bloc of seats for opposition parties. The hope was that new rules would increase voter participation, but that the new votes would be spread among many small leftist parties. This would allow the dominant party to claim credit for democratic reforms, while actually consolidating its hold on power. In practice, voter turnout did not increase as hoped, and the party that grew most quickly in the wake of the reforms was the right of center Party of National Action (PAN). And the existence of nationally represented opposition parties undercut the PRI's electoral monopoly in the 1980s, when a wave of economic problems drove voters to support alternative parties.

Administrative reforms at the municipal level regularized some aspects of local administration, replacing *caciques* with elected residents' associations and block chiefs. Although these reforms alleviated some of the worst abuses of the *cacique* system, the new structures continued to operate along a patronage model. Party and government officials at the local level were comfortable in their role as managers of a patronage-based system. The new local leaders found their influence limited by a lack of funding, regulations barring them from pressuring higher level officials, and Mexico's no-reelection rule, which made it impossible to build a lasting power base. In sum, the role of the new officials was to pass along policy from above, rather than serve as a channel for interest articulation from below. The reform package, writes Susan Eckstein, "… institutionalizes a new mechanism of communication and control while giving the 'masses' more say over who rules, or who serves as ombudsmen, within their community. The democratization does not effectively empower the poor."[9] Not surprisingly, this reform did little to improve the PRI's electoral performance.

Electoral and administrative reform gained momentum in the 1980s, as Mexico's economic situation deteriorated. Economic crisis increased the need for government assistance just as public resources fell short. Mexico's economic stabilization program damaged the regime's close ties to unions and labor confederations. At the same time, economic liberalization created new and competing centers of power within the society.[10] In 1988, opposition to economic austerity policies provoked a serious electoral backlash, nearly upsetting the PRI's decades-long monopoly over the presidency. Economic

---

9 Susan Eckstein, "Formal versus Substantive Democracy: Poor People's Politics in Mexico City", Jorge Dominguez ed., *Parties, Elections and Political Participation in Latin America* (New York: Garland Publishing, Inc., 1994), p. 354.

10 Luis Rubio, "Economic Change and Political Reform in Mexico", Riordan Roett ed., *Political and Economic Liberalization in Mexico: At a Critical Juncture?* (Boulder and London: Lynne Rienner Publishers, 1993), p. 48.

reforms also affected the grassroots electoral system. As the economy was delinked from the state, state and party officials lost control of many of the benefits they traditionally used to mobilize electoral support. Writes M. Delal Baer, "Depoliticizing the Mexican economy meant confronting the reality of inefficiency, uncompetitiveness, and vested interests. However, depoliticizing the economy also meant repoliticizing society. Economic reform undercuts the submissive, paternalistic, and petitionary political culture."[11]

To respond to the decline in grassroots support, President Salinas created a nationwide welfare program aimed at relieving economic need and winning the support of popular forces. This initiative, called the National Solidarity Program (PRONASOL), replaced some of the patronage functions of the *cacique* system. It appears to have helped the PRI electorally, but it has not ended the downward trends in voter turnout and PRI vote share. Even more recently, in the late '80s and early '90s, the PRI attempted to recreate itself yet again. Under party strategist Luis Donaldo Colosio, the PRI recruited an army of precinct captains and began building a network of party activists charged with regaining votes lost to apathy and opposition. Whether this modernization drive will succeed in supplanting *cacique* politics and regaining reliable grassroots support for the dominant party remains to be seen. If it fails, the PRI's dominance will be increasingly imperiled.

CONCLUSION

Taiwan's grassroots patronage system was extraordinarily strong as long as the KMT suppressed inter-party competition. Its strength was due in large part to its internal competitiveness; intra-party competition turns out to be an enormously effective device for encouraging participation and for helping voters identify with a dominant party. But liberalization revealed how thin that party support really was. Once the KMT was forced to compete with opposition parties, local factions seized the opportunity to operate independently and extract concessions from the ruling party. The PRI, for its part, never allowed competition in its patronage system. But monopolizing power at the grassroots level in party hands creates problems of its own. The *cacique* may have been hated more than he was loved, but he turns out to have been a more effective vote-getter than the party bureaucrat who has replaced him. In sum, dominant parties in Mexico and the Republic of China on Taiwan established similar strategies for grassroots electoral mobilization.

---

11 M. Delal Baer, "Mexico's Second Revolution: Pathways to Liberalization", Riordan Roett ed. *Political and Economic Liberalization in Mexico* (Boulder: Lynne Rienner, 1993), p. 56.

As economic and political circumstances eroded the legitimacy of those grassroots structures, both parties cast about for reform programs that would allow them to enjoy continued political domination, without these awkward and embarrassing patronage structures. As it turns out, neither party has found a strategy to replace the vote broker; *caciques* and *tiau-a-ka*, for all their faults, have proven themselves to be more effective vote-getting machines for dominant parties than any other mechanism yet invented in Taiwan or Mexico.

Chapter 13

DOES DEMOCRACY REQUIRE AN OPPOSITION PARTY? IMPLICATIONS OF SOME RECENT AFRICAN EXPERIENCE

DONAL B. CRUISE O'BRIEN

René Otayek in a French round-table discussion of 1994 noted that "discussion of democracy in Africa (by Africans) is usually in a foreign language, almost never in local languages,"[1] a fair point which he developed with reference to the Mossi of Burkina Faso. Fred Schaffer's study[2] of rural Wolof discussion of *demokaraasi* in Senegal is to be welcomed in this context. The Wolof example is an important one for the present study of possible democratic transitions in Africa: not only is Senegal the African state which has had the longest exposure to multi-party politics, with universal adult male suffrage in the coastal communes dating from 1848,[3] but the Wolof are the ethno-linguistic group which has come to dominate the state of Senegal. What the Wolof have made of *demokaraasi* is thus an important question for the political study of Africa.

What is *demokaraasi*? It is like its Western cousin in at least one respect, that it is generally taken to be good thing, but *demokaraasi* doesn't have much to do with accountability, with liberal values, even with multi-party competition. *Demokaraasi*, as understood by the rural Wolof, is above all about consensus, about patronage, about material security. Democracy is thus valued in some respects, on some conditions, in certain terms. Like the state itself, representative democracy is a Western import, and like the state it is becoming Africanised. The terms of Africanisation in the Wolof case, stressing consensus and patronage, make good sense in terms of Wolof historical experience.[4] Dr Schaffer's country informants do not have exaggerated expectations of their *demokaraasi*, the near-millenarian hopes identified

---

1   Forum, "La Démocratisation en Afrique Sub-Saharienne", *Revue Internationale de Politique Comparée*, vol. 1, no. 3, 1994, 489–504 (p. 489).

2   Frederic C. Schaffer, "Demokaraasi in Africa. What Wolof Political Concepts Teach Us about How to Study Democracy", Ph.D. (Political Science) (University of California at Berkeley, 1994).

3   Senegal is also a territory with a long record of study of the electoral process, from Pierre Mille, "The Black Vote in Senegal", *African Affairs*, vol I, 1901, pp. 64–79.

4   D. Cruise O'Brien, "Clans, Clienteles and Communities", in D. Cruise O'Brien, *Saints and Politicians* (Cambridge: Cambridge University Press, 1975).

in other African democratic transitions:[5] they look on the state with some suspicion, but also with hope of material reward. The Wolof have done well enough out of the state, better than any other ethnic group in Senegal, and they have learned how to sell their votes on a well-organised basis. Their desire is not for a textbook-style impartial government, but for a partial government, in their favour. That's *demokaraasi*.

The most important basis of political difference in Senegal is not however that between different ethnic groups, a difference which is present but is on the whole of low political salience. The boundaries of the Wolof group are notably blurred, regularly crossed in the towns by migrants adopting the Wolof language and culture as their own.[6] The social cleavage which matters most in electoral terms is between the voters who live in the countryside and those who live in the towns (especially those who live in the capital city, Dakar). In the towns not only does one find some support for the idea of multi-party politics, especially among the better educated, but also there has been extensive popular support for one party of opposition, the Senegalese Democratic Party.[7] In the countryside, however, partisan division is often feared: the Wolof agriculturalists of north-western Senegal value consensus in politics, and they have their own Sufi Muslim religious system, a way of life which does have its own concealed democratic aspects,[8] as an effective vehicle for that consensus.

Demokaraasi for Dr Schaffer's informants has a range of possible meanings, including the act of voting, but also and above all has the meanings of "consensus (the achievement of agreement)", of solidarity (being united), of neutrality or evenhandedness.[9] These are some of the principles around

---

5   Jan Kees van Donge thus reports "a widespread, almost eschatological expectation that multi-partyism would cure Zambia's economic ills. "Zambia. Kaunda and Chiluba: enduring patterns of political culture", in John Wiseman (ed), *Democracy and Political Change in Sub-Saharan Africa* (London and New York: Routledge, 1995), pp. 193–219, quotation p. 205.
    Denis Ventner on Malawi similarly writes of "a restive electorate that naively believes that the new-found democracy is a magic wand that can produce miracles" (p. 183). "Malawi. The Transition to Multi-party Politics", in John Wiseman (ed), *Democracy and Political Change in Sub-Saharan Africa* (London and New York: Routledge, 1995), pp. 152–92.
6   D. Cruise O'Brien, "The Shadow Politics of Wolofization", forthcoming in *Journal of Modern African Studies* (1998).
7   D. Cruise O'Brien, "Les Elections Sénégalaises du 27 Février 1983", in *Politique Africaine*, no. 11, Sept 1983, pp. 7–12.
    Leonardo A. Villalon, "The Senegalese Elections of 1993" in *African Affairs*, vol. 93, no. 371, April 1994.
8   D. Cruise O'Brien, "Wails and Whispers. The People's Voice in West African Muslim Politics", in Patrick Chabal (ed), *Political Domination in Africa* (Cambridge: Cambridge University Press, 1986), pp. 71–83.
9   Frederic C. Schaffer, "Demokaraasi in Africa…" *op. cit.*, p. 179.

which it has been possible to organise a viable existence in the difficult environment of the Sahelian fringe, principles not to be sacrificed for what might turn out to be a passing fashion coming from the big city. Party programmes and ideological differences are of secondary interest in this perspective, as "the quality of the agreement matters less than the fact itself of having achieved some kind of consensus, a consensus that has come to be synonymous with *demokaraasi*".[10] The Muslim informants spell this out with regard to local and religious brotherhood disputation over the sighting of the moon (especially important at the end of the fasting month of Ramadan): "if everyone looks for the moon and sees it at the same time, that is *demokaraasi*".[11]

A preference for peaceful agreement, for consensus, is understandable above all in terms of the feared results of disagreement: and the Wolof have another word for that. "*Demokaraasi* has its opposite. Mutual trust betrayed, reciprocal obligations snubbed, social bonds abused, and *demokaraasi* thwarted are in Wolof called *politig*."[12] There has been experience of *politig* stretching back to the period of rural enfranchisement after the Second World War, the wild promises then made to the peasant voters: "to *politig* is to abuse the confidence someone has placed in you. It refers to any act the purpose of which is duplicity and betrayal."[13] There was of course duplicity and betrayal in the countryside before the right to vote was extended (1945–57) but what then happened was remarkable enough to be recognised in that new word, *politig*. And country people have learned caution over the years, teaching the priority of agreement: in practical terms the priority is explained by a villager, Modou, concerning two candidates for office who came to his village. "Some chose the first candidate, others the second. When we saw the first candidate had more support, those who had initially chosen the second candidate immediately joined the majority, to make things run better."[14]

Things would run better for the villagers if they were united: even if their chosen candidate were to lose the election, they would have maintained the social ties upon which they might depend for survival, or at least prevented the weakening of those ties from the intrusion of electoral politics. Elementary rational choice theory stipulates the priority of survival: we are not dealing with any utopia of Merrie Africa.[15] Hope and fear are allied in the

---

10 F. Schaffer, *op. cit.*, p. 167.
11 F. Schaffer, *op. cit.*, p. 168 ff.
12 Ibid, p. 196.
13 Ibid, p. 201.
14 Ibid, p. 159.
15 This taunt to traditionalism in A.G. Hopkins, *An Economic History of West Africa* (London: Longman, 1973).

electoral choices of *demokaraasi*, the hope of winning access to some form of official patronage, the fear of the perils of division. Where the perils are concerned, the Wolof can look not only to the warning of post Second World War *politig*, but also to the more distant but still remembered example of their own nineteenth-century civil wars.

The Wolof have had their experience of the collapsed state, of anarchy and war, in a time vividly enough recalled in the folk memory.[16] They have worked hard since that time to build institutions which can express one form of consensus in the shared veneration of Muslim saintly figures. These Sufi brotherhoods are now cited as examples of *demokaraasi*; the Mouride brotherhood is seen as an "institution shot through with *demokaraasi* because it offers material security, whether from participation in its offshoot associations (*dahira*) or from reciprocal exchanges with religious clerics".[17] The five-yearly electoral instruction of the Mouride Khalifa-General, his *Ndiggal* to the disciples to vote for the governing party in the multi-party national elections of 1983 and 1988, was seen by some urban disciples as an infringement on their personal liberty. In the countryside, however, they see the matter differently. As one rural Mouride put it, "if the marabout does not give us a *Ndiggal*, each one of us would vote for the candidate of his choice, and that is not to our advantage".[18] The block vote of Mouride disciples has helped to keep the Socialist Party in power, and the governing Socialists in return have allocated development spending to Mouride areas for roads, for electricity, for water supplies. That's *demokaraasi*, that's "to our advantage".

Such Mouride appraisals are unashamedly sectional, and non-Mourides are thus pressed to put together their own *demokaraasi*. An important point to emerge from Dr Schaffer's study, however, is that rural Senegalese views of the subject also have a national range. Consensus and *demokaraasi* are preferred not only for the preservation of the institutions necessary to local survival, they are preferred at the summit of the state. Multi-party politics at the national level has seen the emergence of one principal opposition force (especially in the cities and among the young), the Senegalese Democratic Party led by Abdoulaye Wade. And Professor Wade has tried the patience of some of those young townspeople by his apparent hesitation between opposition, the call for "change" from what has long been a situation of single-party

---

16   D. Cruise O'Brien, "Warlord, Saint and Knight" in D. Cruise O'Brien, *Saints and Politicians…op. cit*. See also D. Cruise O'Brien, *The Mourides of Senegal* (Oxford: Clarendon Press, 1971), pp. 11–57, 141–52.

17   F. Schaffer, "Demokaraasi in Africa…" *op. cit.*, p. 298.

18   F. Schaffer, *op. cit.*, p. 268.

dominance, and "contribution", in accepting ministerial positions after the defeat of his party at the polls. Thus Wade was a Minister of State in a coalition with the Socialist Party until October 1992, then contested the elections in 1993, lost, and rejoined the government after the election. In the capital city, Dakar, and especially among the secondary school educated, these turnabouts have appeared to be a betrayal of the hopes of a real political change in Senegal.[19] But in the countryside, among those without secondary education, it makes very good sense for Abdoulaye Wade and Abdou Diouf to come together in government after taking opposite sides in the national election: "the vast majority of the non-Francophone population... wholeheartedly accepted the government coalition as the natural endpoint of *demokaraasi*".[20]

Rural Wolof appraisals of *demokaraasi*, with their emphasis on consensus and coalition, are to be compared with at least one other African language translation of democracy, as revealed in M. Karlström's research among the rural Baganda. Democracy is translated by the Baganda as *eddembe ly' obuntu: eddembe* has a meaning of freedom to act without constraint, *obuntu* a meaning of civility on the part of ruler and ruled (the abstract noun of *muntu/bantu*, person/people). Democracy, for Dr Karlström's informants, above all meant to be able to speak, "the speech of subjects directed towards their rulers",[21] as to a good Kabaka in bygone days.

Like *demokaraasi* and democracy, *eddembe ly' obuntu* is seen as a good thing, although these are not precisely the same good things. The Luganda concept refers to freedom from the destructive results of political disorder, a destruction for which Uganda's rival political parties are held responsible: political parties are thus still distrusted as vehicles of democracy. "Political parties make each man the enemy of his fellow man. They just kill each other."[22] Competing parties which are "partial totalities" are seen to have brought a winner-take-all attitude to political competition, disenfranchising the losers and thus creating permanent resentments and antagonisms. *Eddembe ly' obuntu* is a concept partly shaped by dread of Uganda's terror regimes of 1971–85, partly by nostalgia for Buganda's pre-independence monarchy. Now the National Resistance Movement in government is seen as upholding free speech and reconciliation, as leading figures from each of the

19 D. Cruise O'Brien, "Islamic Attitudes Towards the West: the Case of Senegal" (Washington: U.S.I.A., 1990) (unpublished report number R–3–90 (February 1990)).

20 F. Schaffer, *op. cit.*, p. 283. See also Babacar Kante, "Senegal's Empty Elections" in *Journal of Democracy*, vol 5, no 1, Jan 1994, reflecting the urban view of the absence of *alternance*.

21 Mikael Karlström, "Imagining Democracy: Political Culture and Democratization in Buganda", in *Africa*, vol 66, no 4, Jan. 1996, pp. 485–505.

22 An informant cited in M. Karlström, *op. cit.*

old parties have joined the government. The paternalistic and reassuring Yoweri Museveni, who has allowed a "cultural" restoration of Buganda's monarchy (1993), is "a leader who listens". And the Baganda in return apparently don't want that restoration to be more than cultural. Democracy as *eddembe ly' obuntu* begins to sound something like *noblesse oblige*.

The French anthropologist Claude Fay, studying the peasantry of Maasina in Mali after the overthrow of the military regime of Moussa Traore in 1991, makes no mention of Malian language translations of democracy. He does however present a dark rural outlook on the subject. The Malian peasantry saw the arrival of democracy with dismay, a weakening of the state which would lead to rampant segmentary conflict: "*Le pouvoir est parti en pâturage*" (the state has gone off to graze). "There is no more government (*pouvoir*) because there is nobody to frighten us."[23] The result has been that old feuds have reappeared all over Maasina, and that peasants have taken to arming themselves against the Tuareg. External force and domination alone had kept the peace between factions and peoples who were otherwise in permanent conflict. Now a pro-democratic government was trying to "encourage all of Mali to come to agreement like a single lineage", as "the citizens should settle their differences among themselves". These exhortations from above were heard by an elderly informant of Claude Fay as "the lies that they told us so that we would kill each other".[24] And another of Fay's informants, discussing the "white man's democracy", remarked that the "whites know how to conceal the force behind government", while "for blacks the force must be out in the open".[25] In the rural Malian perspective not only is multi-party democracy an invitation to chaos, but ideas of social consensus also are dangerous lies which amount to the same invitation.

The society of Maasina has a lengthy experience of government by autocracy, from pre-colonial times through French colonial rule to the Moussa Traoré military regime, no room for ideas such as surround the Wolof *demokaraasi*. A Malian pastoralist society of balanced opposites, akin to that of Somalia, is to be compared with a more elaborate social structure in agriculturalist Senegal. There are, to be sure, important similarities between Mali and Senegal, neighbouring states with some ecological problems in common, both states also having experienced French colonial rule. Post-colonial politics in the two states has an important clientelist component, patron–client

---

23 Claude Fay, "La Démocratie au Mali", in *Cahiers d'Etudes Africaines*, vol. XXXV-I, no. 137, 1995, pp. 47–8.
24 C. Fay, *op. cit.*, p. 46.
25 C. Fay, *op. cit.*, p. 48.

clusters (factions or clans) which are uneasily incorporated within political parties or bureaucracy. But in Senegal not only has there been a much lengthier exposure to the formalities of electoral politics (going back to 1848 as against 1945 for Mali, then French Soudan), the social structure of Sufi brotherhoods has provided a peculiarly effective counterpoise to the power of the colonial or post-colonial state. It is from that brotherhood environment that the Wolof understandings of *demokaraasi* appear to have emerged, with their emphasis on consensus and mutuality. The Wolof have built their own political order in the Sufi brotherhoods, in an ongoing dialogue with the state,[26] and they have valued the politics of consensus for more than a century past—in part as a way of containing the sort of rampant factionalism recently experienced in Mali, and which had been experienced in Senegal in the nineteenth century.

Dr Schaffer's research here has contributed to an understanding of Senegal's relative political stability since independence. A French army detachment in the capital city, and the financial assistance of many international donors, have also helped to underpin that stability, but the country's governance since before independence has been by a series of incorporations of opposition parties, factions and personalities. The main parties involved were the pre-independence branch of the Section Française de l'Internationale Ouvrière (SFIO) led by Lamine Guèye, joining with Leopold Senghor's Bloc Démocratique Sénégalais to form the Bloc Populaire Sénégalais in 1958; the Parti du Regroupement Africain of Abdoulaye Ly and Amadou Moctar Mbow which joined the governing B.P.S. in 1966 to create a new party, the Union Progressiste Sénégalaise. These amalgamations were above all the work of Leopold Senghor, whose style of coalition building prevailed during his twenty-year presidency of Senegal (1960–1980).[27]

The same coalition-building procedures have been maintained under President Abdou Diouf, working notably to the partial incorporation of the Senegalese Democratic Party. Thus there has been a series of "governments of national unity" in 1991, 1993 and 1995; in part it seems a response to some international pressure (from France and the USA).[28] The result in any case is that there has been regular renewal within a single-party dominant situation,

26 Leonardo A. Villalon, *Islamic Society and State Power in Senegal* (Cambridge: Cambridge University Press, 1995).

27 Donal B. Cruise O'Brien, "Senegal", in J. Dunn (ed), *West African States. Failure and Promise* (Cambridge: Cambridge University Press, 1978), pp. 173–88.
    See also Janet Vaillant, *Black, French and African. A Biography of Leopold Sedar Senghor* (Cambridge, Mass.: Harvard University Press, 1990).

28 *Africa Confidential*, April 17, 1992.

in a style which enjoys enough of mass approval to provide tacit but substantial support to the governing regime. All those incorporations (of individuals, factions and parties) to the government might appear (in the city, among the educated, among those left out) as so many acts of betrayal, so many sell-outs, so much proof of the corrupting appeal of money and power. These bitter feelings are however to be balanced against the feeling in the countryside that the building of coalition and consensus is an eminently worthy end. Leopold Senghor built his political career on an understanding of rural politics, combined with his French language intellectual and poetic vocation, and his sense of the politically possible in Senegal revolved around the principle of coalition—the substance of democracy as practiced in Senegal since 1960.[29]

In their study on the first multi-racial elections in the Republic of South Africa, R.W. Johnson and Lawrence Schlemmer point to the emergence of what they see as a "corporatist" preference on the part of the electorate: "the broad pattern emerging among South Africa's new voters, the Africans, was that they favoured accommodation between political parties...rather more strongly than liberal democracy."[30] Attitudes to the principle of opposition in a democracy were "very much divided".[31] In their contribution on "Public Opinion in Kwa Zulu Natal", R.W. Johnson and Paulus Zulu are concerned about "the restriction on democratic choice apparent in a situation where 43 per cent of urban Africans (and 41 per cent of rural Africans) said it was difficult or impossible to live next to a neighbour with political views different from their own";[32] 29 per cent of Africans in the Western Cape stated the same difficulty in living next to the politically different.[33] Political differences in these cases are not reducible to different preferences in newspaper reading, or to ideological tastes, but are to be seen at least in part as the expressions of ethnic or racial allegiance, allegiances not felt to be negotiable. And in such situations, as for example in Northern Ireland, fear is an important part of the average voter's motivation. In their sombre concluding assessment,

---

29 Donal B. Cruise O'Brien, "Senegal", in J. Dunn (ed), *West African States...op. cit.*, notably pp. 187–8. See also Christian Coulon and Donal B. Cruise O'Brien, "Senegal", in Donal B. Cruise O'Brien, John Dunn and Richard Rathbone (eds), *Contemporary West African States* (Cambridge: Cambridge University Press, 1989), pp. 145–64.

30 R.W. Johnson and Lawrence Schlemmer, "Political Attitudes in South Africa's Economic Heartland", in R.W. Johnson and L. Schlemmer (eds), *Launching Democracy in South Africa. The First Open Election, April 1994* (New Haven and London: Yale University Press, 1996), p. 265.

31 R.W. Johnson and L. Schlemmer, "Political Attitudes in South Africa's Economic Heartland..." *op. cit.*, p. 273.

32 R.W. Johnson and Paulus Zulu, "Public Opinion in Kwa Zulu Natal", in R.W. Johnson and L. Schlemmer, *Launching Democracy in South Africa...op. cit.*, p. 199.

33 Idem.

Johnson and Schlemmer turn to the question of the political participation to be expected from the expanded electorate: "the long, bitter and violent political struggle in South Africa has been a trauma which has left people of all groups nervously conscious of the risks of political participation. They would far, far rather leave tricky issues to their leaders than stick out their own necks. There has been a certain amount of rhetoric about participatory democracy in the new South Africa but everything suggests that the electorate is currently quite particularly unsuited to it."[34] So let's leave it to the party leaders to work out the terms of a viable consensus?

The South African example is to be compared with political experiences elsewhere in Africa, notably over the past seven years of possible transitions in the direction of multi-party democracy (eleven years in the exceptional case of Senegal, from the presidential reintroduction of an ideologically defined multi-party system in 1976).[35] Two cases in particular, those of Ghana and Uganda, may first be considered as cases of governmentally directed attempts to develop a consensual democracy in the states concerned, attempts which have tended to reveal both a substantial popular support in the short term for such initiatives and some emerging difficulties for the longer term. These are two cases of militarily directed reform of previously semi-collapsed states, Ghana under Jerry Rawlings and the People's National Defence Council from 1979, Uganda under Yoweri Museveni and the National Resistance Movement from 1986, in each case with a structural adjustment programme applied with some rigour and economic success. In relative terms these have been the success stories of the international donor institutions; the states have been rescued from their condition of semi-collapse with the help of some large-scale lending. Most importantly, the loans have been used to revive the agricultural and commercial economies, building a base of popular support for the reforming regimes in the rural areas of the states concerned. The two leaders, Rawlings and Museveni, have each sought to use that rural goodwill as a defence against international and domestic demands for the return to multi-party democracy. Such demands have been distrusted by the populist Rawlings as likely to lead to corruption and to "the self-serving behaviour of politicians",[36] by Museveni as likely to

---

34 R.W. Johnson and L. Schlemmer, "Into the Brave New World: Post-Election South Africa" in R.W. Johnson and L. Schlemmer, *Launching Democracy...op. cit.*, pp. 361–2.

35 On that reintroduction see D. Cruise O'Brien, "Senegal", in J. Dunn (ed), *West African States...op. cit.*, notably pp. 173–81.

36 Quoted in Jeffrey Haynes, "Ghana: from personalist to democratic rule", in John Wiseman (ed), *Democracy and Political Change in Sub-Saharan Africa* (London and New York: Routledge, 1995), p. 101.

lead to a renewed ethnic–regional factionalism which would once again tear Uganda apart.

How then to get a popular mandate against pluralist democracy? That was the question facing these two leaders in the 1990s, two leaders with records of notable if contested political and economic achievement. The Ghanaian political scientist Maxwell Owusu suggests one possible answer, with reference to the establishment of non-partisan district assemblies in Ghana (1988–90). These assemblies had transformed centre–periphery relations, redefining the role of the state in the countryside, giving local people a real control in the matter of service provision. In his "View from the Village" Owusu declares that "it is in the countryside, not the towns and cities where the new institutions of democracy should take root and radiate to regional and national political centres".[37] Country values can in this view nurture the politics of consensus and reconciliation which Ghana must develop if it is to escape from its political feuds. In Ghana the idea of a no-party democracy was considered in 1990 in PNDC circles, drawing on "an idealised version of Ghana's pre-colonial past as a model".[38]

The problem with such ideas in Africa is that they too have a past, in the rhetoric of some discredited previous rulers: as Jeffrey Haynes notes, "Rawlings' support of the no-party option was to many Ghanaians unfortunately reminiscent of the attempt in 1978 to legitimise the breathtakingly corrupt regime of General Acheampong."[39] Rawlings as head of state had his friends and associates, virtually a political party, and the PNDC its network of associated organisations, making the no-party notion look all the more like an invitation to return to the single-party past. Similar considerations are relevant to the situation in Uganda as the National Resistance Movement maintains its ban on party competition: opposition parties may exist, but must not engage in an electoral campaign. In elections for a Constituent Assembly in March 1994 it "became clear that 'no-party democracy' supporters outnumbered proponents of an early resumption of 'multi-party politics' in Uganda by roughly two to one".[40] A clear enough mandate, it might appear, but this while the National Resistance Movement "seems set on turning itself into a political

---

37 M. Owusu, "Democracy in Africa—A View from the Village", in *Journal of Modern African Studies*, vol. 30, no. 3, Sept 1992, p. 376.

38 J. Haynes, "Ghana: from personalist to democratic rule…" *op. cit.*, p. 97.

39 Idem. See also R.D. Jeffries, "Ghana", in D. Cruise O'Brien *et. al.* (eds), *Contemporary West African States* (Cambridge: Cambridge University Press, 1989), pp. 75–98.

40 H.B. Hansen and Michael Twaddle, "Uganda: the advent of no-party democracy", in J. Wiseman, *Democracy and Political Change…op. cit.*, p. 149.

party".[41] Museveni too has his friends and associates, a leadership group hardened by a shared experience of insurrectionary war, and the National Resistance Movement under present conditions already amounts to a political party.[42] To condemn political parties as responsible for the war and factionalism of Uganda's past, and ban their activity while developing your own party, looks unlikely to be a sustainable position. A renewal of multi-party competition may be preferred to a slide towards war.

Yet Rawlings and Museveni have in the immediate past both won fairly impressive electoral victories (1992, 1994), votes of thanks especially in rural areas where structural adjustment has brought some visible rewards. Their regimes now have their democratic credentials, their aspiration to express a popular consensus translated into majority electoral support. But the question of opposition does remain in either case, two cases of what have become *de facto* single-party situations, or at least situations of single-party dominance. Jerry Rawlings may have had good reason to suspect that his programme of structural adjustment could not be fully implemented once his regime was exposed to multi-party competition, that corruption under those circumstances would return to Ghana. Democracy thus has its costs, attested in the Ghanaian case by independent observers since the 1992 elections: corruption has indeed returned, as the PNDC and the President defended their position in some of the old clientelist style in advance of the next elections (November 1996). Such costs of multi-party democracy are real (as for example in the case of Nigeria's second republic, 1979–82, an interlude of multi-party politics and a time of some fairly spectacular corruption), but what of the costs of not having multi-party elections? In the Ghanaian case, opposition to the Rawlings regime has come most obviously from urban "middle class" sources, but that opposition also has an ethnic/regional dimension. Had there not been multi-party elections in 1992, Ashanti grievances would have continued to accumulate. The fact that many of the leaders of the New Patriotic Party had Ashanti loyalties, including its presidential candidate, Professor Adu Boahen, provided some outlet for ethnic–regional feeling—however loudly the NPP's supporters protested their electoral defeat of 1992—"The Stolen Verdict".[43] Even a flawed multi-party democracy under such conditions is helping to shore up the state.

---

41 H.B. Hansen and M. Twaddle, *op. cit.*, p. 150.

42 Richard Banegas, "Ouganda: un pays en mutation au coeur d'une zone de fractures" (Paris: Les Etudes du C.E.R.I. no. 4, Sept 1995) (roneo) p. 31.

43 Mike Ocquaye, "The Ghanaian Election of 1992: a dissenting view", in *African Affairs*, vol 94, no 375, April 1995.

Single-party regimes in a certain number of African situations have in their time also worked to sustain the state, the more durable of them by a process of coalition building, which has provided representation for a range of regional and other interests. Coalition under such circumstances may be an alternative to consensus, with the same practical effect, where representatives are selected for each of the main ethnic, regional or religious communities in the state. What does it matter, as J.F. Bayart[44] dismissively asks, whether those representatives are elected by the people or chosen by a state leader? As under the Parti Démocratique de Côte d'Ivoire in Ivory Coast since 1960, the presidential ruler, Felix Houphouët-Boigny, controlled a distributive system with a very careful eye to ethnic and regional balance in appointments—the distributive politics of the "verandah", following the model of the anthropologist Emmanuel Terray, clientelist counterpart to the bureaucratic politics of the "air-conditioner".[45]

The building of a maximum coalition in Zambia, whether under Kenneth Kaunda or Frederic Chiluba, has been by similar procedures of cooptation. The Christian background of these leaders may have predisposed them to coalition politics (as much might be said of the Roman Catholic Leopold Senghor in Senegal). This is a costly political style: Kenneth Kaunda's downfall in 1991 came when he had run out of resources to distribute, when the means of corruption had been exhausted.[46] And now, as the Movement for Multi-party Democracy works to become a governing single party, again building its maximum coalition, it too may have its problems when faced with the bill. The Senegalese political leadership seems always to have found some obliging foreigners, whether from the International Monetary Fund, the World Bank, or other overseas donors, when that ugly moment comes around. The formal appearances (and some of the substance) of multi-party politics in Senegal since 1976 have greatly helped in raising these overseas resources. And the subtle politicians of Senegal can make their basic point discreetly, that the cost of state collapse for the international community would be much greater, perhaps just by deploring recent events in Somalia. The democracy of international appearance in this context very definitely does require an opposition party, even if local reality is dominated by what

44 J.F. Bayart, *The State in Africa. The Politics of the Belly* (London: Longman, 1993). See also on this point Arend Lijphart, *Democracy in Plural Societies* (New Haven and London: Yale University Press, 1977) with reference to the idea of a "consociational" democracy.
45 E. Terray, "Le Climatiseur et la Véranda" in Collectif, *Afrique Plurielle, Afrique Actuelle*. Hommages à Georges Balandier. Paris, 1986.
46 Jan Kees Van Donge, "Zambia. Kaunda and Chiluba. Enduring patterns of political culture", in J. Wiseman (ed), *Democracy and Political Change...op. cit.*, p. 198.

Senegalese social scientists term the "single-party culture" of the Socialist Party regime.[47]

Within that single-party culture, under the enduring hegemony of the Socialist Party, there is room for what in African terms has been a remarkable freedom of expression and indeed of organisation. In Senegal you are allowed to say or write nearly what you like, to set up your own political party almost as you will. What you do not seem to be allowed to do, however, is to win an election, not since 1952. Dr Schaffer's research among the Wolof identifies a French word, *la démocratie*, as covering this area of liberty of expression, a liberty which is valued especially by the urban and the educated, a liberty which these Senegalese see as putting them ahead of the citizens of other African states. With that liberty, with a free press and an active associational life, with many legally recognised political parties, there is a future problem for maintaining the consensus of folk *demokaraasi*.

Consensual understandings of democracy appear to have more of an audience in rural Africa, as measured by recent election results in Ghana or Uganda or by political science research in Senegal.[48] The country people are less schooled, certainly, less easily reached by opposition party propaganda, although perhaps they are more sharply conscious of some of the perils of division, if one is to look to anthropological research in Mali, or to political science research in Senegal.[49] The Senegalese government in its Wolof language broadcasting associates democracy with the liberty of political parties to organise freely, and the Socialist Party develops this theme of freedom in terms of a "mosque metaphor": the leaders of the different political parties are *muezzins*, their programmes are calls to prayer, the voters are the faithful. "The mosque metaphor is…attractive to (President) Diouf because it pushes the issue of *alternance* (electoral turnover) to the background."[50] When one inserts an Imam into this mosque metaphor, one recognises that there can only be one Imam: "Muezzins, who are often casted (of low social status), do not in practice become Imams."[51] Thanks to this mosque metaphor,

---

47   Momar Coumba Diop (ed), *Senegal. Essays in Statecraft* (Dakar: Codesria, 1993).
48   Frederic Schaffer, *Demokaraasi in Africa…op. cit.*
     Leonardo Villalon, *Islamic Society and State Power in Senegal* (Cambridge: Cambridge University Press, 1995).
     Senegal has been fortunate in its American political scientist visitors.
49   C. Fay, "La Démocratie au Mali", in *Cahiers d'Etudes Africaines*, vol. XXXV-I, no. 137.
     F. Schaffer, *op. cit.*
50   F. Schaffer, *op. cit.*, p. 125.
51   *op. cit.*, p. 132.

then, one may come to terms with a situation where Abdou Diouf may remain President into an indefinite future.

The town is where such expressions of the single-party culture are most sharply questioned, and it is in the town that the voters are most insistent on making their own electoral choices—without, or in disregard of, the guidance of spiritual or other superiors. In the town, too, you find the youthful tearaways, student-vandals in Mali or unemployed *casseurs* in Senegal,[52] an important part of whose political expression is in the periodic riot. The post-electoral riot of 1988 in Dakar, on behalf of the defeated Senegalese Democratic Party, was a direct challenge to the hegemony of the ruling Socialist Party, with a scale of destruction not seen since the late 1960s. The student rioters of Bamako were the heroes of democracy in 1991, since which time they have turned to predation, a source of continuing disquiet to their elders.[53]

It is in the town, too, that one finds some of the social elements for what could become a sub-structure for multi-party democracy, a network of associations, newspapers, professionals, entrepreneurs, the social basis for political debate, a possible civil society. The towns are where the better educated tend to cluster, those educated to secondary level or beyond, and this is where one finds the greatest reluctance to accept propositions of a consensual democracy. Political opposition, whether to the Diouf regime in Senegal, the Rawlings regime in Ghana, or more broadly in sub-Saharan Africa, tends to be most active, and to have the largest constituency, in the large towns. And these towns are growing absolutely and proportionately, so that the demand for political voice is unlikely to subside. In the most favourable circumstances that demand for voice can be translated into multi-party electoral competition, into what Johnson and Schlemmer call a liberal democracy, although few observers of contemporary African politics are optimistic as to those circumstances. If not a liberal democracy, then, what other terms of democracy are applicable in Africa now?

Here one returns to the continuing relevance of notions of political consensus. Dankwart Rustow in a very broad comparative sweep remarked on the general importance of an underlying social consensus at the base of a viable multi-party democracy.[54] Just as there must be social division and political

---

52 D. Cruise O'Brien, "A Lost Generation? Youth Identity and State Decay in Africa" in R. Werbner and T. Ranger (eds), *Postcolonialism in Africa* (London and New Jersey: Zed Books, 1996), pp. 55–74.

53 Sophie Wigram, "Elites, Vanguards and Vandals. The Political Role of Students in Senegal and Mali, 1968–1993", M.Sc. dissertation (politics), School of Oriental and African Studies, 1994.

54 Dankwart Rustow, "Transitions to Democracy. Toward a Dynamic Model", in *Comparative Politics*, April 1970, pp. 337–63.

disagreement to translate into electoral partisanship, so also there must be enough underlying agreement to prevent those political divisions from sliding into armed confrontation, if one is to see the emergence of a viable multiparty democracy: "the basis of democracy is not maximum consensus. It is the tenuous middle ground between imposed conformity…and implacable hostility."[55] And the approach to that tenuous middle ground for Rustow requires that there be "a sense of national unity" in the electorate, at the same time as it is recognised that "a people who were not in conflict about some rather fundamental matters would have little need to devise democracy's elaborate rules for conflict resolution".[56] Where Africa is concerned, that requirement of a sense of national unity has looked a daunting one, in a context of ethnic or religious loyalties which are often strong, although there has also in many cases been a consolidation of loyalties at the level of the (nation) state. A partial sense of nationality, perhaps, and certainly not one which excludes other loyalties—ethnic, regional or religious—but a great deal is at stake in its emergence. We are here in the shadow of state collapse, a situation in which some form of democracy seems to be a vital necessity to the survival of the state. As Christopher Clapham and John Wiseman remark, in consideration of the record of Africa's authoritarianisms over the past three decades, the authoritarian proposition for the future risks the further alienation of the citizenry and further political disintegration; here again we are on a tenuous middle ground, as "the middle way between states which achieve at least some form of democracy on the one hand, and the traumatic experience of state collapse on the other, becomes frighteningly narrow".[57]

A partial sense of nationality, as for example in Ghana, in Senegal, in Zambia or in Côte d'Ivoire, four states in which ethnic issues have on the whole had a low political salience; a partial democracy, with periodic elections enjoying fairly widespread popular credibility, even if the results and the electoral process are regularly denounced by the losing parties; these are, to be sure, still contested situations, although it is well to remember that no nationhood and few fully functioning democracies in the world have been arrived at without a great deal of historical difficulty. Virtually all African states have their distinct ethnic and linguistic components, their rival religious allegiances, and René Lemarchand has remarked of Africa's democratic

---

55 D. Rustow, *op. cit.*, p. 363.

56 *op. cit.*, pp. 361–2.

57 C. Clapham and J. Wiseman, "Conclusion: Assessing the Prospects for the Consolidation of Democracy in Africa", in J. Wiseman (ed), *Democracy and Political Change in Sub-Saharan Africa…op. cit.*, p. 232.

transitions that "in case after case, from South Africa to Burundi, from the Congo to Rwanda and Kenya, the evidence shows that democracy is generally perceived as a zero-sum game with definite winners and losers among competing ethno-regional groupings".[58] That sort of popular perception could be counted as a fact of political life in Africa, even if the perception is sharper in some of the states of central Africa. The absence of electoral opportunity under military regimes, however, has risked that "zero-sum game" turning to armed conflict, to the collapse of the state.

The politics of ethnic confrontation is a possibility in all African states, an element even in the relatively viable semi-nations: the problem of the African foreigners in Côte d'Ivoire, the secessionist drive among the Diola in Casamance, Senegal since 1981,[59] the opposition strength in Ashanti, Ghana. But African politics is not reducible to the politics of tribalism: in most of the case studies of democratic transition collected by Clapham and Wiseman, the ethnic component of political partisanship is established, but not treated as dominant. Ethnic confrontation may be deliberately stimulated and provoked by state leaders, as by Daniel Arap Moi in Kenya, by Hastings Banda in Malawi, by President Mobutu in Zaire, the autocrat creating the conditions for a demonstration of his own indispensability (the Mobutu or chaos model). Electoral democracy without such guidance does not necessarily aggravate ethnic confrontation, if only because electoral victory within existing state boundaries usually depends on the building of some sort of multi-ethnic coalition.

The cases when African statehood has been kept at some distance from collapse are those where such a ruling coalition is maintained, with some democratic basis. Democracy, however, is in itself no guarantee, and any form of representation includes the possibility of a more or less permanent exclusion of particular ethnic/regional/religious minorities. Those who are thus excluded may then work towards secession, helping towards the collapse of existing states. Again, these are facts of political life in Africa, commonplaces, and one must insist that the sentiment of exclusion on the part of particular communities is more complete, less redeemable, under conditions of military autocracy with a tribally recruited army. The search for some form of workable democratic consensus, flawed through it usually is, thus in

---

58 R. Lemarchand, "Africa's Troubled Transitions", in *Journal of Democracy*, vol. 3, no. 4, October 1992, p. 104.

59 Peter Geschiere and Jos Van Der Klei, "Popular Protest Among the Diola of South Senegal", in Philip Quarles van Ufford and Matthew Schoffeleers (eds), *Religion and Development. Towards an Integrated Approach* (Amsterdam: Free Press, 1988), pp. 209–27.

practical terms often amounts to no less than a matter of the survival of the state.

Whether such an element of democracy requires an opposition party remains to be seen: the preference for consensus, in no-party or single-party form, has been given some recent electoral approval, as in Uganda. There is a rural vote to be reached in favour of consensus at the top, as in Senegal or Mali: and rural votes have been decisive in winning the 1992 and 1996 elections in Ghana for Rawlings and the PNDC. The country people who put their priority on state survival have some good Hobbesian reasons for their recent electoral choices. *Demokaraasi* in the Wolof style is unimpressed by differences of party programme or ideology (such differences as are discernible to any observer), frightened by the possible consequences of partisan division. Consensus comes first. That preference for consensus can provide a short-term electoral validation for particular rulers, or in the medium term for particular regimes, although in the longer term the claims of political difference are unlikely to be denied. In the longer term, with what J.F. Bayart terms the descent of politics to the masses, other bases of political confrontation will emerge. Insofar as these future confrontations are to be reconciled by democratic mechanisms, popular ideas of consensus and coalition will continue to be a possible resource for state leaders, implicitly votes for the survival of the state. So we may continue to learn from *demokaraasi*: whether democracy requires an opposition party or not, it certainly requires a significant element of consensus. That last lesson at present seems to be something to be learned from country people.

The partial experience of multi-party democracy in Africa over the past decade tends to suggest the enduring relevance of the model of single-party dominance: thus the Movement for Multiparty Democracy in Zambia becomes a ruling party, intolerant of opposition. Even in the cases counted as ones of a relatively successful multi-party democracy, such as Senegal, with open elections, a relatively viable civil society and some historical record of political pluralism, the single-party culture still rules at the centre of the regime. But it is unhelpful to contrast Africa's recent experience with an idealised version of Western multi-party democracy. The elements of democracy within African single-party dominant situations continue to give durability to the state: thus the toleration even of a formal opposition allows a possible channel of recruitment to the excluded, who may hope for a future incorporation to the ruling coalition; the allowance of a freedom of the press and of associational life similarly limits the sense of exclusion among the educated. The partial democracy of the single-party dominant situation allows for a range of hopes, a range of possible political futures: decisively better than political despair and the solution of despair, state collapse. Beyond that, the single-party culture allows for all kinds of a long learning experience.

One may return in conclusion to that Wolof word, *demokaraasi*, and to some of the political implications of its consensual meaning. The itinerary of this concept began of course with *démocratie*, specifically with the discourse of the Francophone elite in Senegal at the time of the government-impelled reintroduction of multi-party politics, 1974–76. The next step on the journey was the Wolof language reaction, insisting on consensus and material security as attributes of the desirable *demokaraasi*. The most recent step, with the series of multi-party governments of national unity from 1991 to 1995, appears to be one where the Wolof folk priorities are becoming part of the language of Senegal's power elite. The opposition parties continue to measure their political options within this culture of consensus, a culture which gives the government a reservoir of popular support. The majority of the Senegalese people remain to be convinced by the opposition; they haven't been convinced since 1952. But if that's the majority view, that's still democracy.

Chapter 14

CONCLUSION

HERMANN GILIOMEE AND CHARLES SIMKINS

"I'll vote for the opposition when they are in power"
—Anonymous Serb peasant[1]

CONSOLIDATION OF DEMOCRACY OR DOMINANCE?

In all societies considered in this volume a basic tension exists between dominant-party rule and democracy. Democracy in the final analysis rests on countervailing power able to check tendencies toward authoritarian domination. The best counter is undoubtedly the presence of a strong opposition party that can guard against the erosion of the autonomy of democratic institutions and can replace a governing party that has outstayed its welcome. The development of opposition to authoritarian rule has traditionally been associated with the rise of a middle class; by contrast, the transitions literature covering the new democracies of the past two decades emphasised the role of trade unions. Generally unions have assisted in hastening the departure of authoritarian regimes, but have been less successful in helping to sustain a competitive democracy.

Taiwan bears out the structural or environmental approach, which emphasises broad-based socio-economic development as a prerequisite for the maintenance of democracy. The country's steady progress away from a quasi-Leninist party-state through a dominant-party system to the approximation of a competitive, liberal democracy occurred within a context where a strong, independent middle class has become assertive and where economic inequalities by the early 1980s had narrowed to the lowest in the semi-industrialised world. However, as Malaysia and Singapore demonstrate, socio-economic development does not generate an inexorable movement towards democracy. While the middle class in Malaysia during the 1970s and 1980s increased by half, the democratic system deteriorated to a point where authoritarian rule rather than democracy is being consolidated. The main reasons are the state-dependent nature of the Malay middle class and the lack of international incentives rewarding democracy. Such incentives have spurred the Taiwanese

---

1 Cited by Timothy Garton Ash, "In the Serbian Soup", *NY Review of Books*, 24 April 1997, p. 26.

in their quest for diplomatic recognition. In Singapore the one-party state is maintained despite the absence of a fundamental need for it on the part of any fraction of the bourgeoisie or middle class.[2] The government's criticism of "Western-style" democracy shows the importance of the leadership variable in the process which leads to consolidation of a democracy or the lack of it.

In the last decade the literature has been dominated by another approach, the genetic or process-driven one. This has a strong focus on pacts between leading class actors in the transition to a democracy. In a recent formulation, with special reference to Latin America, Karl has suggested that the mode of transition to a large extent shapes the type of democracy that is subsequently established.[3] Taiwan illustrates the point that the prospects for a competitive system are best when a democracy is the result of transition through government-led transformation. South Africa, however, can be considered as a potentially contrary case. The mode of transition was what Huntington called a transplacement, resting on the co-operative efforts of the ANC and NP representing the white and black groups respectively. The Government of National Unity, which flowed from the political pact that was concluded, fell apart sooner than most observers expected. The present system is neither corporatist nor consociational.

Our argument is that it is not so much the mode of transition but the re-alignment of forces after a new democratic government has established itself in office that determines the type of domination, the existence (or absence) of countervailing forces and the kind of democracy a society will have. Pacts which made the transition possible are not necessarily the same that sustain a new government. As Lipset has remarked in a recent restatement of his thesis, pacts are merely the means towards institutionalising a democracy. Whether they emerge or hold depends largely on whether socio-economic conditions are such that a fragile democracy can take root and grow. Formulated in this way it is not necessary to present the theory of democratic requisites and the emphasis on pact-building as stark alternatives but rather as complementary. Those stressing socio-economic requisites have firm ground for arguing that countries at the lowest socio-economic level will struggle to consolidate anything resembling a liberal democracy. Du Toit's chapter on the countries on the South African northern border vividly demonstrates that

---

2 Garry Rodan, "Preserving the one-party state in contemporary Singapore", K. Hewison ed., *Southeast Asia in the 1990s* (London: Allen and Unwin, 1994), pp. 77–108.
3 Terry Lynn Karl, "Dilemmas of Democratization in Latin America", *Comparative Politics*, 23 (1990), p. 15.

without vigorous economic growth producing rising per capita incomes it is unlikely that democratic structures will be effective.[4]

South Africa is a case which has to be treated with circumspection when applying these perspectives. Just before the transition started in 1990 it had a per capita GNP of US$ 2,290, which groups it with the upper-middle-income Latin American countries and an Eastern European country like Hungary. At a superficial glance it looks well within the per capita zone where transitions to democracy could be expected. However, if one focuses on the previously disenfranchised, namely the African population, one found a per capita income of only US$ 670. White and black South Africa form two quite different groups with a sharp contrast between their respective per capita incomes.[5]

In these unpropitious conditions there are two pacts to consider in order to understand the political process in South Africa during the first half of the 1990s. The first pact was between the white and black political elites, based on a white and a black dominant party respectively, to make possible the founding of a democracy. After the elections this was replaced by a second pact, that between an African elite and the poor African masses. It has two projects: to establish an African middle class mainly through the occupancy of senior positions in the civil service and state contracts to African suppliers, and to entrench a black labour aristocracy. The pre-April 1994 pact and the post-April 1994 pact are quite different and it was not possible to predict purely on the basis of the first pact what type of democracy was to be expected. What was predictable was that big business would quickly switch from the erstwhile dominant party to meet the demands of the new one. It has sponsored the enrichment of a small African elite, accepted labour legislation that only the bigger companies can afford and has not spoken up against affirmative action.

In a context of the mass demand for redress and empowerment there is little that can prompt black voters to vote for opposition parties, a sentiment which the dominant party of course encourages. Writing about the dominant party in India, Morris-Jones puts it well: People see the competition "not as between parties to become government but between government and others". Even if a dominant party supporter is displeased with what

---

4 Seymour Martin Lipset *et al.*, "A Comparative Analysis of the Social Requisites of Democracy", *International Social Science Journal*, 136 (1993), pp. 155–75. See also Adam Przeworski and Fernanado Limongi, "Modernization", *World Politics*, 49 (1997), pp. 155–83.

5 Hermann Giliomee, Democratization in South Africa", *Political Science Quarterly*, 110, 1 (1995), pp. 98–99.

government has done he still asks: "Who else but government is in a position to do things for him?"[6]

Thus the vital elements of democracy, namely genuine competition and uncertainty in electoral outcomes, are removed in a process that is self-sustaining. The factors that underpin the process of entrenching dominance (and the relative absence of competition) are the following: first, the steady elimination of the dividing line between the ruling party and the state with the result that the ruling party comes to be seen as the state rather than the temporary government. This in turn steadily erodes the capacity of any class (for instance business or labour) or ethnic group to retain a sufficient degree of autonomy to provide the basis of a party that forms part of a competitive party system. Finally the dominant party's sheer preponderance of political power increasingly leads to unilateral, and even arbitrary decision-making that undermines the integrity of democratic institutions, particularly that of the legislature and its ability to check the executive. The ruling party abuses the advantages of incumbency and the state media to get re-elected time and again.

Dominant parties in advanced industrialised societies like those that ruled in Sweden, Japan and Italy occasionally and with varying degrees of impropriety also made use of the advantages of incumbency to get re-elected, but they were careful about setting precedents which their adversaries could turn against them once they lost power. They, too, occasionally went to improper lengths in trying to force the legislature into the mould they desired. However, in the cases described in *Uncommon Democracies* arbitrariness by government was much more likely to be punished by the electorate than in any of the cases described in this volume. In the cases of *Uncommon Democracies* the dominant party needed compromises with opposition parties to rule effectively and smooth the process of legislating. Accordingly the dominant parties were much more likely to limit the abuse of power—maybe not as much as their opponents would have liked, but certainly more than in the cases described in this book.[7]

The key is that in less advanced and highly unequal societies—this a description that fits all the societies in the volume at one time or another—a capitalist state has great difficulty establishing any real autonomy from the capitalist interests on which it is dependent for investment decisions. Forced to maintain friendly relations with the business sector which it long considered

---

6 W.H. Morris-Jones, *The Government and Politics of India* (London: Hutchinson, 1964), p. 151.

7 T.J. Pempel ed., *Uncommon Democracies; The One-party Dominant Regimes* (Ithaca: Cornell University Press, 1990), and personal communication.

an enemy, the dominant party is compelled to shed its radical populism at an early stage. To be able to "afford" this fateful compromise the party establishes a mass base which encapsulates and captures all the popular sectors. They do offer concessions, particularly to organised labour, but the price for labour is its political emasculation. This attracts big business to the ruling party for as long as the integrative coalition provides stability. In societies with deep ethnic divisions, like South Africa and Malaysia, this popular base is at the same time a racial or ethnic base which becomes the real basis of the party. While ethnic or racial solidarity provides no clear basis for political action in a capitalist system premised on competitiveness, the party is increasingly forced to rely on ethnic or racial appeals, particularly when both growth and redistribution are modest. Given the superiority of ethnic to class appeals, an alternation in government is much more unlikely in South Africa and Malaysia than in Mexico or Taiwan.[8]

We shall look briefly at our four main cases to explore the dynamic tendencies of the different regimes. In Mexico the party was based on a number of subordinate classes which, in a state committed to capitalist development, were unable to challenge effectively the economic power of the middle class. A prolonged stalemate in the class struggle was carried into the dominant party hierarchy. It managed to appease both the dominant and subordinate classes but only as long as there was steady growth based on import-substitution. Once this was overtaken by the increasing globalisation of production and markets limiting state patronage and control, the door was opened to a competitive form of democracy. As Collier remarks in her postscript commenting on the elections of mid-1997, the PRI suffered its most decisive defeat ever. It won less than 40 per cent of the seats for the Chamber of Deputies and was comprehensively rejected in the municipal election for the Federal District. As a result multi-partyism has become more effective while the corporatist ties between the party and its labour allies have come under serious strain. It seems as if the future of the PRI both as a labour-based party and as a dominant party is in balance.

In Taiwan initial developments pointed to a state beholden to mainlander interests. Mainlanders were vastly over-represented in the central

---

8 Jannie Gagiano and Pierre du Toit, "Consolidating democracy in South Africa: the role of civil society" Hennie Kotze ed., *Consolidating Democracy: What role for civil society in South Africa?* (Stellenbosch: Centre for International and Comparative Politics, 1996), pp. 47–74; Ruth Berins Collier and David Collier, *Shaping the Political Arena: critical junctures, the labour movement and regime dynamics in Latin America* (Princeton: Princeton University Press, 1991); Nora Hamilton, *The Limits of State Autonomy: Post Revolutionary Mexico* (Princeton: Princeton University Press, 1982).

government, the managerial ranks of state-owned businesses, academia and cultural life. But the state bureaucracy, although acting in the interests of a new emerging business class of mainlanders and Taiwanese, was not subservient to them. As an analyst commented, "[It] retained its hegemonic position and acted in the bourgeoisie's interests without allowing itself to become its instrument".[9] Using local factions in its "mobilisational authoritarianism", the KMT succeeded in building up a support base that cuts across class and ethnic cleavages. As Chu's writings make clear, the Taiwanese state and dominant party are still not sufficiently separated for the system to be called a liberal democracy. The military, the national security agencies, the judicial branch and the civil service have still to embrace true neutrality. The KMT is also very reluctant to relinquish its grip on the island's three television networks or the massive financial empire the party has built up.[10]

Nevertheless, should Beijing stop threatening Taipei, it is possible to imagine the KMT losing power in the not too distant future with a further substantial shift towards a liberal democracy taking place. The prospects for a liberal democracy are promising due to the following factors: the broad-based economic development in Taiwan, the rise of a large middle class based primarily on a decentralised private sector, the virtual elimination of poverty, and the remarkable capacity of the dominant party to attract votes from all sectors of society.

In Malaysia democracy was in a better shape in the 1960s when *laissez-faire* economic policies held sway, with Chinese business and multi-national corporations dominating the economy and forming a counter weight to Malay political domination. The high growth rate of the past twenty-five years and the doubling of the Malay middle class have not served to broaden democracy. Indeed Malaysia demonstrates the fact that semi-democracies and even dictatorships can be stable at a certain level of socio-economic development. The key is the adaptive capacity of the dominant party and in particular its ability to shift its support base to the dynamic sectors of the economy. Once single-mindedly concerned with Malay advancement, UMNO is now presenting itself as indispensable for broadly based economic growth and an enhanced national status in the international community. Apart from a brief spell in the late 1980s it now stands stronger than ever. In

---

9   Thomas Gold cited in Shelley Rigger, "Mobilisational authoritarianism and political opposition in Taiwan", Gary Rodan, ed., *Political Opposition in Industrialising Asia* (London: Routledge, 1996), p. 308.

10 See particularly Yun-han Chu, "Taiwan's unique challenges, *Journal of Democracy*, July 1996, pp. 74–76.

the case of Malays, as in that of the Afrikaners, one can understand that a state-sponsored middle class is unlikely to turn away from the party that had made its rise possible. But even Chinese businessmen whose fortunes have improved consider good relations with the dominant party with a view to future business opportunities more important than strengthening civil society and opposition parties. Similarly the softening of the ethnic divisions as a result of economic growth has not weakened UMNO which earlier had thrived on them. Holding up a future in which the different ethnic communities can see an acceptable political destiny for themselves, the ruling alliance has in the most recent election attracted large support from Chinese classes who earlier had rejected it. As long as growth remains high and corruption within bounds the Malaysian people seem willing to accept their semi-democracy presided over by the dominant party.

DOMINANT PARTY AND DEMOCRACY IN CONTEMPORARY SOUTH AFRICA

We can now review South Africa in the light of developments in our other three main cases. It has a dual base: like the PRI in Mexico it is supported by the subordinate classes, like UMNO it rests on the indigenous population with a profound sense of grievance and victimhood. For quite some time the ANC will have to live with the economic domination of whites and of the corporate world by a few large companies controlled by whites. As a result of sanctions the share of multi-nationals in the economy has been disproportionally reduced, which means that there cannot be the Malaysian pattern of redistribution between 1971 and 1990 when the Malay share of equity increased to 20 per cent while the foreign share of equity dropped from 62 to 25 per cent. The liberal macro-economics of the 1990s put severe limits on government intervention in the private sector or on using state corporations to expand the share of African equity holding.

Compared to the KMT, PRI and UMNO, the ANC's success in establishing itself as a coalition that transcends both ethnic groups and classes has been much more modest. Based on the support of 94 per cent of blacks, it also won the support of most of the better educated coloured and Indians in 1994. Against this, however, stands the fact that it captured the votes of only two to three per cent of whites, who dominate the economy. Its project of building a "rainbow nation" in which everyone can find a place for itself remains vague and riddled with contradictions. Severe budget constraints and an inefficient civil service make it unlikely that its support among whites will improve. While the ANC has done well to keep populist tendencies in check, its leadership is showing growing irritation with what it terms reactionary elements of the old regime. It is directed at the press and white-led opposition parties as "counter-revolutionary" for their lack of support for "nation-building" and constant criticism. Where UMNO deals with sections of Malaysian society specifically on an ethnic basis, the ANC refuses to do so except in the case of the fringe Afrikaner party desiring a separate state. Its preferred method is corporatist or pseudo-corporatist, like meetings behind closed doors with delegations from teacher bodies or organised agriculture. The problem is that deals struck here tend to be sabotaged by ANC-aligned civil servants or rejected by the ANC caucus. This again fuels opposition discontent.

As a result the ANC has increasingly abandoned its 1994 election appeal of non-racialism for an explicit call to African solidarity. While mocking the "Mickey Mouse white parties", Mandela calls on all predominantly black parties to unite.[11] The superior pressure of the black middle class and labour aristocracy in this racial alliance ensures that their interests take precedence at the expense of the non-unionised and unemployed blacks. This is taking place particularly in two areas. The unionised work force enjoys a degree of statutory protection in certain areas of labour legislation approaching that of Scandinavian countries. (In areas like unemployment benefits it is considerably worse off.)

Such policies make it very difficult for the large army of unemployed to get into the labour market. Furthermore, with very little job creation in the economy the competition for employment between whites and blacks will increasingly take on a zero-sum quality. This stands in sharp contrast to Malaysia, where despite preferential policies favouring Malays, labour force growth in the manufacturing sector has been high enough also to absorb Chinese as well as Malay entrants. Finally the South African economy is remarkably open with exports and imports accounting for two-thirds of GDP. Any policy that interferes too much with the competitiveness of firms will negatively impact on the balance of payments.

The ANC will be forced to straddle seemingly impossible contradictions in its attempts to reconcile the majority and minorities. Apart from the "broad church" and populist character of the party there are two other reasons. The ANC's dominance of the political system is heavily qualified by forces outside the area of formal politics which it does not control, like organised business, the international financial community, the courts whose benches are still staffed by whites, and the military which is still white-led. Although

---

11 *Rapport*, 14 September 1997, p. 1.

weak, the minority parties have put up stiff fights in the areas of health and education policy. The result is compromises which increasingly strain the coherence of the party, but this does not really threaten to result in a split. As in the case of Malaysia, dominant-party rule of South Africa as a deeply divided society has given rise to a "syncretic state". This is a state with a remarkable ability to combine a mix of ideological approaches, allowing the leadership to blur the lines between state and society.[12] As a result South Africa has seen a bewildering mix of clashing commitments: colour-blind merit and affirmative action rules of ethnic preferment, non-racialism and Africanisation, free market acceptance and tight regulation of the labour market, state patronage for African contractors and near-monopolies for large white-controlled corporations, and so on.

Largely to contain the pressures which managing the syncretic state produces, the ANC leadership has tended to concentrate as much power as possible in its own hands both in its control of the party and on governmental level. The party hierarchy has tried to impose its choice on virtually every leadership vacancy or intra-party feud at the provincial level. At the same time central government has refused to share any power with the provinces by devolving a meaningful measure of discretion in the vital areas of policing, health care and education. While this route will, for the present, yield success at the polls it will come at the cost of the increasing organisational decay of the party and of racial polarisation. It could put South Africa on the same road as Zimbabwe where dominance and corruption have produced such cynicism and apathy that elections are a travesty of democracy.

Against this background three responses towards domination have emerged in the ranks of liberal democrats. The first is the expectation in classic liberal mould that race-based voting which ensures ANC dominance is a temporary phenomenon. Voters are expected to become policy and issue oriented as they pursue the different material aspirations and shed their racial or ethnic concerns. In a recent statement, the chairman of the largest conglomerate, Anglo American Corporation, expressed the view that too many critics are "pessimistic" about the democratic prospects of South Africa. He believes there to be sufficient democratic checks and balances, while the development of a market economy will bring about a political realignment with both the ruling party and opposition "more accurately reflecting values and interests".[13]

---

12 James Jesudason, "The syncretic state and the structuring of oppositional politics", *Political Oppositions in Industrialising Asia*, pp. 128–160.

13 AAC, Chairman's statement, June 1997.

This volume presents evidence that such an expectation is not realistic. As in the case of the Malays and the Afrikaners in pre-1994 South Africa, the state explicitly favours black South Africans. Ethnic patronage in the form of favouritism in bureaucratic appointments and state contracts awarded to businessmen produces a state-sponsored middle class whose commitment to the dominant party outweighs that to a neutral state or the need for opposition politics. South Africa's electoral system enables the black elite to mobilise the mass of blacks behind it, a task made easier by the known fact that wealth is still concentrated among whites and that the system does not offer rewards for racial moderation. While this is the case, election results are likely to continue to resemble a racial census with the democracy threatening to degenerate into mere electoralism.

The second interpretation, which is reflected in Friedman's chapter, is to put South Africa in the category of liberal democracies although it concedes that minority parties are quite possibly doomed to a permanent minority by racial cleavages. It works with a dichotomy: either dominance is achieved by partly or wholly undemocratic means like in Mexico and Singapore; or dominance is an expression of the will of the electorate and the success of the dominant party in appealing to it. Putting South Africa in the second category, it sees ANC dominance as a democratic achievement. But Friedman implicitly argues that South Africa's classification as a liberal democracy will only hold if the ANC maintains an "internal pluralism" that allows every faction in the party to win at least some battles, and if it keeps its hold over the greater part of civil society, a part that is proving fractious and difficult to control. At the same time South Africa must sustain an "external pluralism" embodied by opposition parties able (and tacitly encouraged) to represent significant constituencies.

The basis of Friedman's cautious optimism, then, is that political competition is the central issue, and that this happens in South Africa—as in liberal democracies. The trouble with this approach is firstly its dichotomy between democratic and authoritarian politics while there is in fact a continuum of possibilities. One cannot make sense of the Taiwanese experience without thinking of movement along a continuum in a liberal democratic direction over the past decade. Nor can one explore South African issues without taking into account that democratic practices are not yet well enough established to use the notion of competition without some qualifications. For instance, the white-led opposition parties were prevented from campaigning in black townships where the ANC swept the floor in the 1994 election. If this happens again the notion of competition will be severely compromised. A dichotomous approach also does not take into account that matters could get worse by degrees (as happened in South Africa after 1960) as well as better by degrees.

More importantly the chapter relies too much on the model of dominant parties in advanced industrialised societies like Sweden, Italy and Japan where the socio-economic conditions for democratic competition are much better realised and where there are no deep ethnic cleavages which correspond with socio-economic inequalities. Also, the dominant parties in these cases did not originate in a crisis that gripped the entire society but more mildly when the opportunity arose for fundamentally reshaping political alignments. They all seized the moment to cobble certain socio-economic blocs together in a durable dominant coalition. South Africa stands in very stark contrast to those societies.

The third interpretation is that presented in the chapter written by Adam for this volume and later elaborated in the study *Comrades in Business: Post-liberation politics in South Africa* co-authored with Kogila Moodley and Van Zyl Slabbert. The central thrust is to see South Africa as an increasingly homogeneous society while the ANC is depicted as an upper-middle-income country version of a social democratic party in government, but one quite severely compromised by its dependence on business.[14] It argues that the ANC is the only party that can guarantee democracy and stabilise the new order.

As editors we see this study as in rather sharp contrast with our interpretation and concerns. While recognising the stabilising capacity of a dominant party we see equal, if not greater, dangers in its rule. We believe that dominant parties may both reflect and cause suppression of political competition. On the one hand there is the behaviour of the electorate which returns the same party again and again to a position of dominance; on the other hand there is the ability of a dominant party to close out opposition in a number of possible ways: delegitimating the opposition, entrenching permanent minorities, eroding the conditions for competition by muzzling or intimidating the press, taking administrative action against opponents, allowing or encouraging no-go areas during election campaigns (as happened on a wide scale in 1994) and stealing elections. Closing out the opposition feeds back into electoral behaviour.

Comrades in Business is a cynical celebration of ANC political dominance and manipulative capacity. The study states: the ANC has (a) "taken over the state with the connivance, if not active support, of the more sophisticated

---

14 It was published in mid-1997 by Tafelberg Publishers in Cape Town.

sectors of the global and local neo-liberal establishment", (b) only the ANC can guarantee that the poorest of the poor, i.e. the majority, feels represented and part of the system, and (c) only the ANC can manage a "pragmatically united rather than a deeply divided South Africa". Nevertheless in the same passage the ANC is depicted as a "capitalist nomenclature, noble sentiments for the poor notwithstanding". *Comrades* is disparaging of those "wailing about ANC majoritarianism" and believes that their thinking "still relies on racial antagonism as the overriding cleavage in South Africa". Those concerned about the weakness of the opposition institutions are told to reflect on the real possibility of an ANC split after 1999, although the study immediately questions "whether a split is desirable for political stability and public order". Commentators worrying about the tyranny of the majority and about permanent winners and permanent losers are instructed to remember that "in a sociological sense a minority is defined in power, not in terms of numbers". Barely concealed is an irritation with white critics for not being grateful enough for the ANC. They should remember that only the ANC can protect the propertied classes from destabilisation through radical populism.[15]

But what has the government at its disposal in the battle against a polarising distribution of income? Not, alas, a rational, efficient state. *Comrades* decries the new government's "squandering of public money amidst a sea of poverty", the "venal self-justification of office-holders" and the "unauthorised expenditures, neglect of prescribed tender procedures and other irregularities". And yet it asserts that "leaving the material cleavages to laissez faire pluralism, particularly when they overlap with ethno-racial divisions, provides a sure recipe for destructive class warfare that destroys all prospects for growth".

The study latches onto corporatism as some kind of panacea, but as in so many other passages the authors' interpretation becomes a roller coaster of contradictory moods and perspectives. On one page it is observed that corporatism is in decline in Europe as it has become associated with economic stagnation and because Europe no longer has the resources to solve its problems with social welfare measures. But on the very next page it is stated that South Africa "has no other option but to pursue corporatist social harmony". On one page corporatism is defined as "representing the national institutionalisation of global imperatives, articulated by business organisations and state bureaucrats", but on the very next page it is described as "a method to

---

15 Adam *et al.*, *Comrades in Business*, pp. 157, 177, 198, 214–216.

pacify intense minorities by giving them another opportunity to influence politics when they have no chance in parliament". In fact, the National Economic Development and Labour Council (NEDLAC), the corporatist body in South Africa, does not discuss issues that vitally concern minorities, like language or cultural policy or displacement in the job market, but *Comrades* nevertheless manages to argue that, since business and labour organisations are dominated by distinct ethnic/racial groups, the proceedings of the corporatist body also entail a form of consociationalism.[16]

A calmer perspective on South Africa's future is needed, one that focuses on the prerequisites for higher economic growth and broader-based development as prerequisites for democratic consolidation. The very first point to recognise is continuity rather than stake everything on the high and hollow policies of the dominant party. In 1990, the executive director of the South African Institute of Race Relations, which every year published a survey that exhaustively documented life under apartheid, stated that in the preceding 15 to 20 years the country had undergone a "Silent Revolution". Urban blacks undramatically but purposefully not only broke down much of apartheid but also advanced their position through their own efforts of organisation. They did the latter despite the relative absence of government intervention on their behalf and even government curbs.[17] Unrealistic campaign promises by the dominant party have tended to stifle some of the remarkable efforts of the poor to take their fate in their own hands.

The second point to make is that nothing suggests that the potential South African growth rate is high. It will take time to eliminate the lag between the development of its human capital and its relatively sophisticated physical capital. Conflicts over claims to current output are high with a consequent adverse impact on savings and investment. The state's ability to support private enterprise without appropriate infrastructure is limited, and is not helped by the ANC's frequent opting for complicated, rather than the simplest possible, programmes and procedures. To question the ability of the ANC to manage both the state apparatus and intra-ethnic conflict is not to subscribe to the "racist assumption that blacks in charge will fail sooner or later", as *Comrades in Business* phrases it.[18] Rather it is to assert the limits of managerial expertise presently available in government and to make the point, following Migdal, that a certain type of "strong man politics", characteristic of developing countries, serves to vitiate, rather than build up,

---

16 Adam *et al.*, *Comrades*, pp. 140–142.
17 John Kane-Berman, *The Silent Revolution* (Johannesburg: SA Institute of Race Relations, 1990).
18 Adam *et al.*, *Comrades in Business*, p. 183.

developmental capacity.[19] On the positive side of the South African balance sheet is declining fertility and a slowing population growth rate which, with a given economic growth rate, means rising living standards. It will be through the steady efforts of millions of South Africans that economic growth and democracy will be slowly realised. In many areas it will be despite, rather than because of, the policies of the dominant party.

CONCLUSION

Party dominance as described in this volume emerges in different ways. In the case of Mexico and Taiwan the party, its leader, its apparatus, both inside and outside the legislative assembly, and its vote brokers at local level were the most visible features of the political landscape. In South Africa, Malaysia and Singapore, dominance is also palpable, but its manifestations are more cloaked by the British-style parliament based on the assumption of parties engaged in a contest to form the government. Nevertheless, in all the major cases in the study we have a similar pattern in the way in which dominant parties build up their position: loyalty to the party is equated with loyalty to the nation or with patriotism, and criticism of especially the partly leader is associated with disloyalty towards nation and state. What distinguishes the dominant party system from authoritarian regimes is the electoral endorsement the dominant party regularly receives to define and shape the nation and state.

To move in a liberal democratic direction it is important, firstly, that the government maintain a clear distinction between party and state, that ministers distinguish between acting in a state and a party capacity, and that civil servants remain neutral in the competition between the dominant party and the rest. Political pluralism in the state will not exist without internal democracy in the dominant party. A sure indicator of the latter is elections at all levels of the party and a leadership refraining from imposing its will. Finally, the definition of the nation and what constitutes loyalty to it cannot be the prerogative of the dominant party but has to be resolved by way of a compromise between the majority and the minority.

The case of the KMT in Taiwan illustrates that it is possible for a dominant party both to rejuvenate itself and to revitalise the democratic system. Both the PRI in Mexico and the ANC in South Africa now face this challenge. For a *liberal* democracy to come about in these countries, they must strengthen

---

19 Joel Migdal, *Strong Societies and Weak States: State–Society Relations and State Capabilities in the Third World* (Princeton: Princeton University Press, 1988).

democratic institutions against the might of the executive, maintain vigilance against corruption, curb state patronage, clean up the electoral process, and bring in the opposition in formulating the identity of the nation. None of these demands are easily met by any dominant political elite, because the result will almost certainly be loss of power and electoral support. A resourceful leadership could offset this loss by radically improvig the organisational structure of the party and making it more focused ideologically. Such attempts will entail commitment and risk-taking, but it is ultimately the only way in which to build a liberal democracy.

POSTSCRIPT (SEPTEMBER 1998)

The fate of the dominant parties described in this volume has suddenly become a pressing issue in view of the crises in the economies of Japan and the emerging markets in Southeast Asia, as well as the economic troubles of South America and even those of the developed nations. With respect to South Africa, the immediate question is whether the ANC, as the most recent addition in the list of dominant parties, will enjoy a much shorter spell of political hegemony than its counterparts analysed in this volume. This links up with another question: Will a drop in support for the ANC political fortunes in the second democratic election, scheduled for mid-1999, signal enhanced prospects for a liberal democracy and even the possibility of the ANC being forced to enter a coalition government after the election of 2004? Or will South Africa be condemned to enjoy none of the benefits of the liberty that a democracy is supposed to bring while suffering from all the worst features of an ineffective democracy—constant bickering among parties, the unwillingness to make tough decisions, a weakening judicial system, rampant crime and corruption, and a hesitant, hectoring government frantically trying to preserve its political dominance in a state that is collapsing?

In the final week of August 1998 two noteworthy opinion polls appeared, highlighting important trends in the South African political system. First a Markdata poll revealed that the likely outcome of the 1999 election would be for the ANC to receive 57 per cent of the vote, five percentage points below its 1994 election tally and 10 percentage points below at two-thirds majority, which is its declared objective. A second poll undertaken for the Helen Suzman Foundation, which was set up to promote liberal democracy, revealed important data about voter's view about the prospects of an ANC two-thirds majority. The potential two-thirds majority are set to become a key issue in the election of 1999 following a statement by the ANC Secretary-General that the party would consider using such a majority to change the constitution unilaterally and particularly for bringing independent bodies such as the Reserve Bank, the Auditor-General, the provincial Attorneys-General and judiciary under tighter political control.

These two polls provide grounds for cautious optimism about a significant strengthening of a liberal democracy. The Helen Suzman Foundation poll showed that 49 per cent of all voters thought that it would be good thing if the ANC won such a majority, against 45 per cent who thought it would be a bad thing. (The 45 per cent includes overwhelming support in the case of the non-African minorities, as well as 28 per cent of Africans.) Asked about their response to the prospect of the ANC changing the constitution unilaterally after having won a two-third majority, 60 per cent of the electorate, 53 per cent of Africans, and 39 per cent of ANC supporters, said it would be a bad thing. Among those who did not want the ANC to enjoy such great power 27 per cent (but 31 per cent of Africans) endorsed the statement that "a strong Opposition is vital". More than 85 per cent of Africans voted for the ANC in 1994, but only 60 per cent of African voters now say that they would be likely to vote ANC if there was a prospect of a two-thirds majority.[20] The new evidence in brief show that the ANC's call for a two-thirds majority had elicited a response, which, for the party, represents the worst of two worlds: it united the non-black minorities against them and divided its own supporters.

There are other signs pointing to a weakening of ANC dominance. In 1997 the total amount of money the party received from membership dues (R12 or US$ 2) was down two-thirds on the 1995 figure. This may be taken as evidence of a considerable measure of depoliticisation, which is important for democratic consolidation. On the other hand, it may also augur the kind of cynicism and voter apathy which, if not checked, could develop into the Zimbabwean situation where the low turn-out at the polls make a mockery of democraric elections.

A distinct weakening of the party machinery has forced the ANC to rely increasingly on the ANC-supporting trade unions for mobilising support for elections. For this support the ANC has been forced to pay the high price of union-friendly legislation passed in 1997 and 1998. This is bound to exacerbate an already very serious unemployment crisis and reduce South Africa's competitiveness further. Moreover, in a far too zealous effort to bestow patronage, the new government has deprived the civil service of some of its most competent non-African staff while allocating too high a proportion of its revenue to civil servant salaries. Dr. Mangosuthu Buthelezi, leader of

---

20 Helen Suzman Foundation, Press Statement, 27 August 1998.

Inkatha and Minister of Home Affairs, recently pointed out that almost 80 per cent of the money appropriated by the government is spent by government on government to run itself. For instance, in the public school system widespread dissatisfaction exists with the Department of Education which cannot supply pupils with textbooks because its salary bill is too high. This affects. African children severely since the parents of the great majority cannot afford to buy the books.

But while these developments restrict the ANC, it is likely to maintain its dominance and continue to preside over a regime that is decreasingly liberal. There are several reasons for such an assessment. The ANC will be able to continue to count on the vote of the large ethnic blocs—the Xhosa, the Sotho and the urban Zulu, who are reasonably satisfied with their representation through the ANC at the different levels of government. The greatest actual or potential support is from either the non-African minorities (whites, coloureds and Indians) and from the smaller African ethnic groups who feel marginalised. large sections of these minorities are either disaffected or so intimidated by the majority that they may stay away at the next election.

The big-business sector, which is capable of forming a democratic countervailing force is, with a few exceptions, guided almost completely by short-term calculations. As in the days of apartheid, it is quite comfortable with one-party domination and all too keen to accept the assurances of the dominant party's leadership. It has little interest in building a proper democracy, for instance through bolstering the generally pusillanimous English press, and resisting the blurring of the lines between the state and ruling party—even to the point of supporting the appointment of party activists in positions that are supposed to be politically neutral. Many of the conglomerates are more interested in currying favour with the dominant party in order to obtain state contracts or concessions than helping to build a stable, democratic and non-corrupt framework in which to do business.

Although unemployment is the Achilles heel of the country, big business has been quite prepared to accept labour legislation in a corporatist forum that is extremely detrimental to small and medium business. It also had little compunction about selling out the male work-seekers of the non-African minorities through supporting "Employment Equity" legislation at a time when the economy is shedding jobs. This law compels companies to meet Affirmative Action quotas in new appointments of its managerial and executive staff. It also imposes exorbitant fins on companies that fail to set or meet these quotas. Since the state does not have the capacity to police this law, the most likely development is that of companies paying bribes to get the state off its neck. It will make business even less willing to incur the displeasure of government. And it is almost certain to contribute to a further worsening of the already desperate unemployment crisis.

But while the prognosis is not good, globalisation through increased competition puts some pressure on corrupt or inefficient state–business links. This may help South Africa to avoid some of the worst experiences of Malaysia and Mexico. It will not be the first time that South Africa is favoured by external developments. Of all the countries dealt with in this book, South Africa is the only one that had the good fortune of experiencing the transition to a full democracy after Communism had collapsed, thus benefiting from a more pluralistic international political order. South Africa has a chance of rooting out a corrupt business–state relationship with its insidious effects on the economy and society before it becomes firmly rooted.

Index

Barisan Sosialis (BS) or Socialist
Front (Singapore)   135, 144
Barrios, Carlos Jonguitud
(Mexico)   248
Bechuanaland Protectorate,
see under Botswana
Beijing   27
against Taiwan independence
87–8
missile tests off Taiwan coast   87
Belgium   299
Ben-Gurion, David (Israel)   101–2
as charismatic figure   109
Bloc Démocratique Sénégalais
(Senegal)   325
Bloc Populaire Sénégalais   325
Boahen, Adu (Ghana)   329
Botswana   52, 100, 195–9,
215, 216
Bakwena people   199
Bamangwato people   199
Bangwaketse people   199
Barolong people   199
BDP, *see under* Botswana
Democratic Party
BNF, *see under* Botswana
National Front
BPP, *see under* Botswana
People's Party
colonial policies, influence
of   195–7
diamonds, revenue from   198
multi-ethnic support base   215
Tswana chieftaincies   196
Botswana Democratic Party
(BDP)   196, 199, 214,
215, 216
compared with SA National
Party   99
Botswana National Front (BNF)
197, 198, 216
Botswana People's Party (BPP)   197
Brazil   52, 53

Britain
under Conservative Party   99, 104
union-bashing of Thatcherites   264
Buthelezi, Mangosuthu (South
Africa)   107

Calles, President (Mexico)   246
Canada and Mexico   258
Cárdenas, Cuauhtémoc (Mexico)
178, 181, 227, 229, 230, 248
Cárdenas, Lázaro (Mexico)   181, 221,
246
Central Provident Fund (CPF)
(Singapore)   149–51
Chaim See Tong (Singapore)   160
Chee Soon Juan (Singapore)   164
Chen Ting-nan (Taiwan)   73
Chiang Ching-kuo (Taiwan)   45,
64, 70, 79, 312
Chihana, Chakufwa (Malawi)   213
Chile   52, 53
Chiluba, Frederick (Zambia)   210,
211, 214, 215, 216, 330
China, mainland   57, 308, 311, 312
one-China principle   66, 79, 81,
82, 88
Tiananmen crackdown   93
Chinese Development Assistance
Council (Singapore)   143
Christian Democrats (Italy)   100,
102, 113, 193
Colosio, Luis Donaldo (Mexico)
183–4, 316
communist bloc and labor-based
parties   220
Communist Party (South Africa)   60
Congress of South African Trade
Unions (COSATU) (South
Africa)   29, 60, 108, 117,
119, 120, 122, 123, 266,
267, 272
Congress of Traditional Leaders
(Contralesa) (South Africa)   117

Mohamad, Mahathir (Malaysia)
137, 155, 162, 169
Morones, Luis (Mexico) 246
Movement for Multi-Party
Democracy (MMD) (Zambia)
210, 214, 216, 330
Mugabe, Robert (Zimbabwe) 110,
205, 214
Muluzi, Bakili (Malawi) 213
Museveni, Yoweri (Uganda) 324,
327, 329

NAFTA, *see* North American Free
Trade Agreement
Namibia 52, 199–204, 216
apartheid from South
Africa 200
delegitimization of
opposition 203
Democratic Turnhalle
Alliance (DTA) 201
ethnic majority 215
Herero War (1904) 200
independence 202
Kavango people 200
Kwanyama people 204
Makololo people 200
Nama War (1905) 200
National Parliamentary and
Presidential elections 203
Odendaal Commission 200
Ovamboland People's
Organization (OPO) 200
Ovambo people 200
South West African People's
Organization (SWAPO)
200–5, 214, 215, 216
UN Security Council
Resolution 435 200–1
Walvis Bay 203
National Central Bargaining
Chamber (CBC) (South
Africa) 272

National Confederation of Trade
Unions (NACTU) 272
National Council of Provinces
(South Africa) 114
National Economic Development
and Labour Advisory Council
(NEDLAC) (South Africa)
29, 30, 31, 260, 268–70, 349
National Education, Health and
Allied Workers' Union
(NEHAWU) (South Africa) 272
National Investment Promotion
Agency (South Africa) 269
National Party (NP), South Africa
59–60, 99, 105, 118, 119,
276–7, 294, 338
Afrikaner Broederbond as part
of 117
apartheid under 34, 110
as "volksbeweging" (national
movement) 120
delegitimation of 33–4, 110
Government of National Unity,
departure from 113, 276–7
State Security Council 34
National Progress Party (NPP)
(Zambia) 208
National Public Works Programme
(South Africa) 269
National Resistance Movement
(Uganda) 323–4, 327, 328–9
National Solidarity Program
(PRONASOL) (Mexico) 181,
185, 232, 316
National Trades Union Congress
(NTUC) (Singapore) 144, 150
National Union of Mineworkers
(NUM) (South Africa) 273
National Wages Council
(Singapore) 150
Nehru, Jawaharlal (India) 102
as charismatic figure 109
Netherlands 263

PRI (Institutional Revolutionary
  Party) (Mexico)   11, 57,
  127, 128, 181, 184, 185,
  226, 227, 228, 231, 232–3,
  234, 235, 241, 242, 243,
  244, 245, 259, 260, 341,
  343, 350
  as labor-based party   219–44
  compared with ANC (SA)   32
  compared with KMT (TAIWAN)
    311
  congress (1996)   252
  corporatism   28–9, 31–2, 38–9,
    246–50
  economic policies, new   223
  election methods   19–20, 44,
    301–2, 308–11, 314–16
  electoral organization   308–11
  future role of   189–90
  mobilization of grassroots
    314–16
  organized labour   246–50
  peso devaluation   255
  rule of no re-election   9–10
  World debt crisis   222–3, 224
PRONOSOL (National Solidarity
  Program) (Mexico)   181,
  185, 232, 316

Ramaphosa, Cyril (South Africa)
  123
Ramathlodi, Ngoako (South Africa)
  108
Rawlings, Jerry (Ghana)   327,
  329, 335
Razaleigh, Tengku (Malaysia)
  148, 149
RDP, see Reconstruction and
  Development Programme
Reconstruction and Development
  Programme (RDP) (South
  Africa)   29, 120–1, 266,
  290–2

Republic of China (ROC)
  Constitution   66–7, 81
  see also under Taiwan
Republic of China on Taiwan
  88, 301–8, 312–14
Rhodesian Front (Zimbabwe)   110
ROC, see under Republic of China

Salinas de Gortari, Carlos
  (Mexico)   174, 179, 180,
  182, 184, 186, 187, 189,
  231, 232, 234, 247–50, 251,
  252, 255, 256, 258, 259, 316
Saudi Arabia   52
Scandinavia   220
Section Française de
  l'Internationale Ouvrière
  (SFIO) (Senegal)   325
Senegal   330, 333, 334, 335
  Bloc Démocratique Sénégalais
    325
  Bloc Populaire Sénégalais   325
  demokaraasi concept   319–25
  "mosque metaphor"   331
  Mouride brotherhood   322
  Parti du Regroupement
    Africain   325
  Section Française
    de l'Internationale
    Ouvrière (SFIO)   325
  Socialist Party   322, 331, 332
  Sufi Muslim religious system
    320, 322
  Union Progressiste
    Sénégalaise   325
  Wolof people   319–23, 331, 336
Senegalese Democratic Party
  320, 322, 325, 332
Senghor, Leopold (Senegal)
  325, 326, 330
Seychelles   51
Singapore   47, 51, 52, 53, 57,
  99, 337–8, 346, 350

INDEX